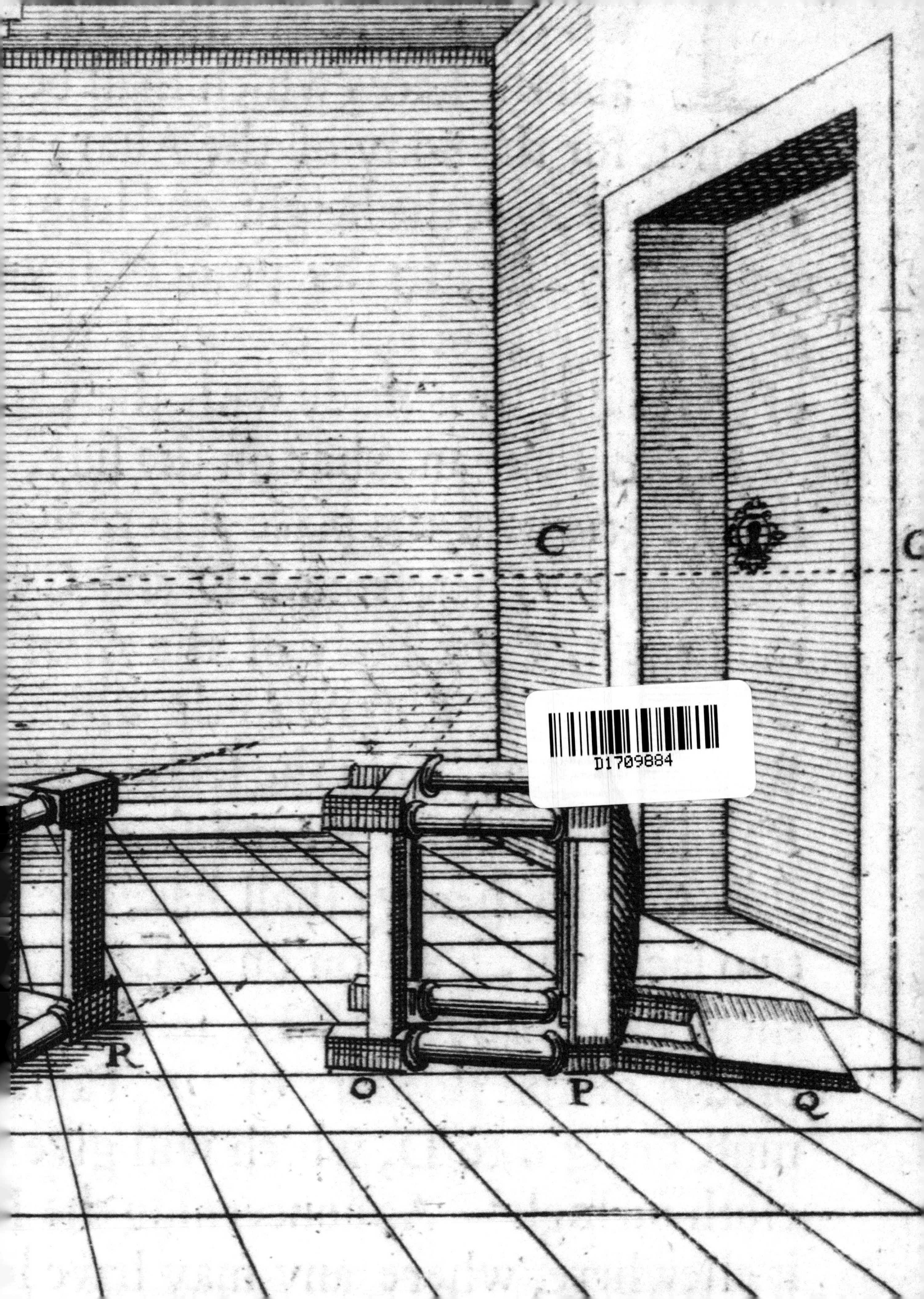
C
C
R
O
P
Q

American Furniture

AMERICAN FURNITURE 2005

Edited by Luke Beckerdite

Published by the CHIPSTONE FOUNDATION

Distributed by University Press of New England

Hanover and London

Cover Illustration: Detail of the back of a joined great chair attributed to Thomas Dennis, Ipswich, Massachusetts, ca. 1670. (Courtesy, Peabody Essex Museum; photo, Gavin Ashworth.)

Design: Wynne Patterson, Pittsfield, VT
Copyediting: Fronia Simpson, Bennington, VT
Typesetting: Aardvark Type, Hartford, CT
Printing: Meridian Printing, East Greenwich, RI

Published by the Chipstone Foundation, 7820 North Club Circle, Milwaukee, WI 53217
Distributed by University Press of New England, Hanover, NH 03755

Printed in the United States of America 5 4 3 2 1
ISSN 1069–4188
ISBN 0-9724353-6-0

Contents

Editorial Statement

American Furniture is an interdisciplinary journal dedicated to advancing knowledge of furniture made or used in the Americas from the seventeenth century to the present. Authors are encouraged to submit articles on any aspect of furniture history, essays on conservation and historic technology, reproductions or transcripts of documents, annotated photographs of new furniture discoveries, and book and exhibition reviews. References for compiling an annual bibliography also are welcome.

Manuscripts must be typed, double-spaced, illustrated with black-and-white prints or transparencies, and prepared in accordance with the *Chicago Manual of Style*. Computer disk copy is requested but not required. The Chipstone Foundation will offer significant honoraria for manuscripts accepted for publication and reimburse authors for all photography approved in writing by the editor. Low resolution digital images are not acceptable.

Luke Beckerdite

American Furniture

Figure 1 Gateleg table, Newport, Rhode Island, 1710–1740. Maple with white pine and chestnut. H. 28", W. 59⅛" (open), D. 48⅜". (Private collection; photo, Gavin Ashworth.)

Erik Kyle Gronning
and
Dennis Andrew Carr

Early Rhode Island Turning

▼ DRIVEN PRIMARILY BY the marketplace, the majority of twentieth-century Rhode Island furniture scholarship has focused on the late baroque and rococo styles. Although the admiration bestowed on these objects is justified, it has left a chasm in the study of that colony's early furniture. As noted by Robert Blair St. George and Robert Trent, this lapse is further exacerbated by the limited amount of seventeenth- and early eighteenth-century furniture that survives. A recent study by the authors has identified an important group of Rhode Island gateleg tables (see fig. 1) and shown how elements of their design were adapted to later furniture forms. This article elaborates on this research and examines the origin of the turning designs, the architectural prototypes, the breadth and diversity of objects made, and the probability of multiple makers.[1]

Irving W. Lyon was the first scholar to illustrate an example of what is now considered a classic Rhode Island turning in his seminal book *The Colonial Furniture of New England* (1891). A decade later, Frances Clary Morse published a gateleg table from that colony in *Furniture of the Olden Time*. Neither Lyon nor Morse, however, ascribed these objects to a particular area. It was not until 1950 that Albert Sack attributed this turning pattern to Rhode Island in *Fine Points of Furniture*.[2]

Rhode Island tables differ significantly from those made in the other New England colonies, which typically have legs with symmetrical turnings (figs. 2, 3). An antecedent for this symmetrical design is found on plate 94 in Augustin-Charles d'Aviler's (1653–1701) *Cours d'architecture qui comprend les ordres de Vignole* (1691) (fig. 4). Mirrored balusters were occasionally described as *double poire,* or "double pear." During the first half of the eighteenth century, craftsmen working along Narragansett Bay developed alternatives to this archetypal design. The origins of these patterns are unknown, but similar baluster shapes and arrangements occur in late seventeenth- and early eighteenth-century British furniture and interior architecture (fig. 5).[3]

Recent research has established links between Rhode Island furniture turnings and related architectural work. In an earlier volume of *American Furniture* Luke Beckerdite pointed out similarities between turned balusters from the Seventh Day Baptist Meeting House in Newport (fig. 6) and those on regional gateleg tables. Although the balusters from the meetinghouse and similar examples salvaged from the Governor Coddington House (fig. 7) are not exact cognates for the furniture turnings under discussion, they do have individual elements handled in much the same way.

Figure 2 Table, Boston, Massachusetts, 1700–1730. American walnut, European walnut, and fruitwood with white pine; slate. H. 27¼", W. 40", D. 25⅛". (Courtesy, American Antiquarian Society.) This table originally belonged to the Reverend Nehemiah Walter (1663–1751) of Roxbury, Massachusetts.

Figure 3 Tea table, Boston, Massachusetts, 1700–1730. Mahogany. H. 26½", W. 32½", D. 21¾". (Private collection; photo, Gavin Ashworth.)

Most notably, the upper sections of the architectural turnings have attenuated balusters of the same basic shape as those on the gates of several Rhode Island tables. The architectural turnings lack the intricate moldings that separate the balusters and lower spherical turnings on many tables, but that does not eliminate the possibility that some are products of the same shop or turning tradition. The architectural turnings from the Seventh Day Baptist Meeting House and Coddington House may be slightly later than some of the tables.[4]

Figure 4 Baluster design illustrated on pl. 94 in Augustin-Charles d'Aviler's *Cours d'architecture qui comprend les ordres de Vignole* (1691). (Courtesy, Beinecke Rare Book and Manuscript Library, Yale University.)

Figure 5 Detail of a staircase in Harvard House, Stratford-upon-Avon, Warwickshire, England, late seventeenth century. (Courtesy, Shakespeare Birthplace Trust.) Built in 1596, this house was the boyhood home of John Harvard (1607–1683), founder of Harvard University.

Figure 6 Detail of the balusters leading to the gallery of the Seventh Day Baptist Meeting House, Newport, Rhode Island, ca. 1730. (Courtesy, Newport Historical Society; photo, Gavin Ashworth.)

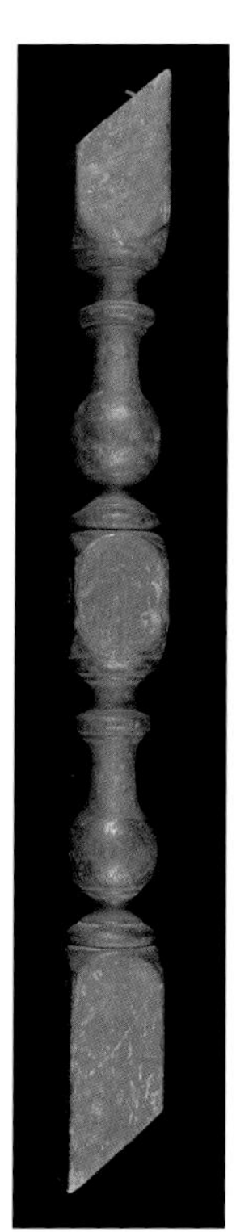

Figure 7 Baluster from the staircase in the Governor William Coddington House (demolished in 1835), Newport, Rhode Island, ca. 1641. (Courtesy, Newport Historical Society; photo, Gavin Ashworth.) This staircase baluster salvaged from the house likely dates to ca. 1730.

Figure 8 Wanton-Lyman-Hazard House, Newport, Rhode Island, ca. 1697. (Photo, Gavin Ashworth.) One of the few surviving Newport buildings with details rooted in baroque classicism, this house has undergone extensive renovations during its history.

Figure 9 Detail of the staircase in the Wanton-Lyman-Hazard House. (Photo, Gavin Ashworth.) This staircase was probably added during an eighteenth-century renovation.

Figure 10 Detail of a baluster from the staircase in the Wanton-Lyman-Hazard House. (Photo, Gavin Ashworth.) This oak baluster was part of what was likely the original attic staircase.

Figure 11 Table, Newport, Rhode Island, 1700–1730. Maple with white pine, H. 26¾", W. 54¾", D. 28⅝". (Courtesy, National Park Service, William Floyd Homestead.) This table was originally constructed as a draw-bar table. The drawer is a later addition, the top is a replacement, and the feet are missing.

The stair balusters in the Wanton-Lyman-Hazard House (figs. 8–10) are among the earliest architectural turnings from Newport. More important, they relate closely to the legs on a Newport table (fig. 11) that reputedly belonged to William Floyd (1734–1821) of Brookhaven, Long Island. Given the fact that the Floyd family had resided in Seatucket since the mid–seventeenth century, it is likely that the table arrived in Long Island soon after its construction. The repetitive nature of the eighteenth-century turner's trade lent itself to the production of standard forms that were easily adaptable to various architectural and furniture components. As the balusters in the Wanton-Lyman-Hazard House and those on the Floyd table reveal, turners often used the same basic designs for both furniture and architectural work.[5]

Rhode Island Gateleg Tables: The Development of a Regional School of Turning

Most of the known Rhode Island gateleg tables can be divided into three groups based on their turnings and construction (see fig. 12). Group one consists of eight examples with complex leg turnings. The balusters of the legs have spherical bases with abrupt transitions to tall slender necks, and seven of these tables have two different ring turnings at the top. Only two of these tables have relevant histories. One descended in the Easton family of Newport, and the other (fig. 13) in the Alden-Southworth-Cooke family of Little

Figure 12 Details of the legs of the gateleg tables illustrated (from left to right) in figs. 1, 19, 21. The leg on the left is from a table in group one, the leg in the center is from a table in group two, and the leg on the right is from a table in group three. (Photos, Gavin Ashworth.)

Figure 13 Gateleg table, Newport, Rhode Island, 1710–1740. Maple with white pine and oak. H. 27¾", W. 60" (open) 21¼", D. 48¼". (Private collection; photo, P. Richard Eells.)

Figure 14 Detail of the drawer knob of the gateleg table illustrated in fig. 13. (Photo, Gavin Ashworth.)

Figure 15 Detail of the drawer dovetail of the gateleg table illustrated in fig. 13. (Photo, Gavin Ashworth.)

Figure 16 Drawing representing how the stationary legs of the table illustrated in fig. 1 are laminated, (Artwork, Wynne Patterson.)

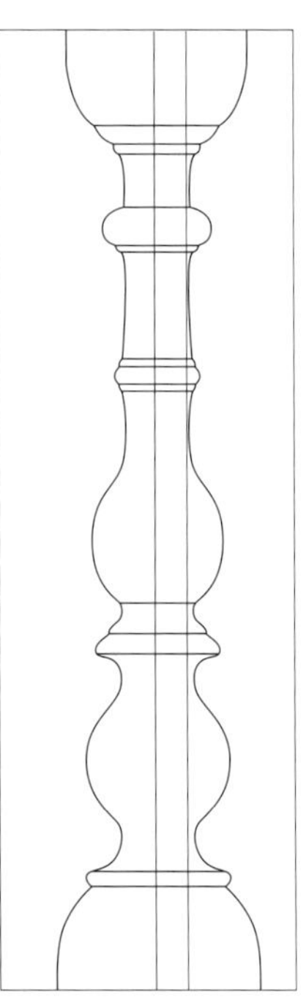

Compton and Newport. The latter table is strikingly similar to the one illustrated in figure 1; even the drawer knobs are virtually identical (fig. 14).[6]

The construction of tables in the first group is consistent but relatively generic. Drawers are supported on runners attached to the side rails, drawer fronts are secured at each side with a single large dovetail (fig. 15), top boards are pinned to the side rails, and gates pivot from the same end of the table. Tables from Britain and New York occasionally exhibit this gate arrangement.[7]

Of all the gateleg tables in the first group, the example illustrated in figure 1 is in the best condition. Its feet have minimal wear, and most of the original black paint survives on the base. The legs are made of laminated boards (fig. 16), a rare detail in colonial American furniture. Because the turner glued up the stock from boards of different sizes, the joints are not centered. Furniture makers often laminated stock to avoid removing excess waste or to compensate for lack of materials. Neither scenario is completely satisfactory in explaining the laminated legs of this table because the turning cross-sections are relatively uniform and there was an abundance of maple, the table's primary wood, in New England.[8]

Figure 17 Gateleg table, Newport, Rhode Island, 1710–1740. Maple with white pine. H. 28", W. 57¾" (open), D. 48⅜". (Courtesy, Metropolitan Museum of Art, gift of Mrs. Russell Sage.)

Figure 18 Detail of the stationary leg of the gateleg table illustrated in fig. 17. (Photo, Gavin Ashworth.)

The table illustrated in figure 17 is included in the first group, even though its stationary legs have balusters with a single, pronounced ring turning on the neck (fig. 18). The molding sequence below its balusters, however, is similar to that on other tables in the first group and its construction and gate arrangement are identical. Of all the tables in group one, the turnings on this example are the most exaggerated. The rings on the necks of the balusters are broad with sharp torus moldings, and the upper and lower necks of the spherical turnings below the balusters are unusually long. In both execution and conception they differ significantly from the more academic turnings on the tables shown in figures 1 and 13.

The second group of gateleg tables is composed of four examples (see fig. 19) with turnings that are simpler than those of group one (see fig. 12). The lower sections of the balusters are more compressed, there is a single ring on the neck, and the molding sequence separating the baluster from the spherical turning below consists of a distorted cavetto over a conventional

Figure 19 Gateleg table, Rhode Island, 1710–1740. Maple with unidentified secondary woods. H. 27", W. 53½" (open), D. 49½". (Courtesy, Nathan Liverant & Son, Inc.)

astragal. Structural differences include the use of a central drawer runner, a conventional gate arrangement, and pins driven through the top into the upper stiles of the stationary legs. Like the tables in the first group, those in group two have drawer fronts secured with a single large dovetail at each side and hinges that do not extend under the sides of the frame (fig. 20). This eliminated the need to notch the side rails as was done on many colonial gateleg tables.[9]

Figure 20 Underside of the gateleg table illustrated in fig. 13. The rectangular hinges are positioned outside the frame and the gates pivot at the same end.

Figure 21 Gateleg table, Rhode Island, 1710–1740. Maple with white pine. H. 27¼", W. 41" (open), D. 49⅝". (Private collection; photo, Gavin Ashworth.)

The stationary legs on tables in the third group have baluster turnings with a more conventional shape, displaying a gradual sweep from the base to the neck (fig. 21). These tables have gates that pivot at the same end and moldings below the balusters similar to those in group one, central drawer supports like tables in group two, and drawer dovetailing and hinge placement consistent with both groups.[10]

Two other gateleg tables can be considered part of this regional school, but neither can be associated with a known group. The turnings on the table

Figure 22 Gateleg table, Rhode Island, 1710–1740. Maple with white pine and cherry. H. 28½", W. 57" (open), D. 47¾". (Chipstone Foundation; photo, Gavin Ashworth.)

Figure 23 Detail of the stationary leg of the gateleg table illustrated in fig. 22. (Photo, Gavin Ashworth.)

illustrated in figure 22, in particular the shallow ring on the neck (fig. 23) and distinctive ball feet, are unlike those on other Rhode Island examples (see fig. 1). The leg turnings on the table, however, are nearly identical to the back post turnings of a bannister-back side chair attributed to Rhode Island (fig. 24). Both objects also have remarkably similar stretchers. The table has been altered significantly, and the drawer replaces what was originally a simple end rail with a molded lower edge.[11]

The other Rhode Island gateleg table made without a drawer (fig. 25) bears no relation to the altered one (fig. 22). The large torus on the upper leg squares and pronounced single ring on the column are idiosyncratic, as

Figure 24 Side chair, Rhode Island, 1710–1740. Ash. H. 49½", W. 20¼", D. 15". (Private collection; photo, Gavin Ashworth.) The crest, finials, and bottom row of stretchers are replacements.

are the form and placement of the hinges. The maker used crude wrought-iron straps (fig. 26) rather than the conventional rectangular or butterfly hinges found on other Rhode Island examples and attached them to the underside of the top inside the frame. This location helped compensate for the weakness of the thin straps. The maker may have been unable to obtain imported hardware or simply preferred the products of a local blacksmith.[12]

Related Furniture Forms

Several tables and stools have turning sequences that match those found on Rhode Island gateleg tables. The legs of the small stool illustrated in figure

Figure 25 Gateleg table, Rhode Island, 1710–1740. Maple. H. 27¾", W. 59" (open), D. 47¼". (Private collection; photo, Gavin Ashworth.) The feet are replacements.

Figure 26 Detail of a wrought-iron hinge on the gateleg table illustrated in fig. 25.

27 relate directly to those on tables in group one, but the maker eliminated the lower spherical element to compensate for the difference in height. Three other stools with similar turnings are known. Another related example has a spherical turning at the bottom (fig. 28). Turners often used similar designs for architectural components and the legs of tables and stools, adding or subtracting elements to accommodate the size, function, and context of the finished product.[13]

A number of rectangular tables (figs. 29, 30) can be linked with the examples constituting group two. Like the gateleg tables, the rectangular forms have balusters with ball-shaped bottoms and similar moldings separating them from the spherical turning below. Another trait common among the small tables is a V-shaped astragal on the neck of the baluster.[14]

Figure 27 Stool, Newport, Rhode Island, 1710–1740. Maple. H. 21¼", W. 22⅞", D. 13½". (Courtesy, Yale University Art Gallery, gift of C. Sanford Bull, B.A. 1893.) Although the lower ball turning is omitted, the rings and moldings of this stool are virtually identical to those on the gateleg tables in group one.

Figure 28 Stool, Newport, Rhode Island, 1710–1740. Maple. H. 22", W. 13¼", D. 23¼". (Courtesy, Winterthur Museum.)

The table illustrated in figure 31 is from group three, and, as with nearly all Rhode Island examples of this form, each of its legs splays outward, canting in only one direction. Only two tables and a stool with legs canted in two directions are known. The oval-top table illustrated in figure 32 has turnings that are reminiscent of those on the gateleg examples in group three, but the upper ring turning on its balusters is unusual and its dome feet have an added fillet. All of the double-canted forms have identical feet and similar transitions from the upper and lower turnings into the leg squares. These objects may constitute an entirely separate group.[15]

Figure 29 Table, Rhode Island, 1710–1740. Maple. H. 25⅞", W. 15½", D. 26". (Private collection; photo, Gavin Ashworth.)

Figure 30 Table, Rhode Island, 1710–1740. Maple with white pine. H. 29", W. 48", D. 29¾". (Courtesy, Sotheby's Inc.)

Variations from the Standard

The gateleg tables and related forms discussed above document the emergence and development of a Rhode Island school of turning; however,

Figure 31 Table, Rhode Island, 1710–1740. Maple frame. H. 22⅞", W. 15½", D. 23¾". (Private collection; photo, Gavin Ashworth.) The top is an incorrect replacement.

Figure 32 Table, Rhode Island, 1710–1740, Maple. H. 23½", W. 20", D. 28¾". (Private collection.)

regional styles were rarely monolithic. Several tables attributed to that colony differ significantly from those in or on the periphery of the standard subgroups. The table illustrated in figure 33 has stationary legs with symmetrical balusters separated by a thin V-shaped torus molding; thus the mass of the turning is located in the center of the design rather than at the bottom. It does, however, have balusters with a relatively sharp break at the neck and shares some construction features with the examples in the second group.[16]

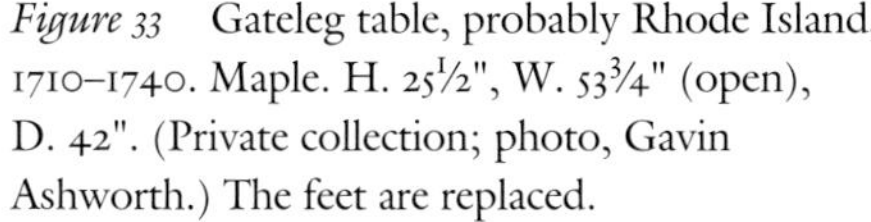

Figure 33 Gateleg table, probably Rhode Island, 1710–1740. Maple. H. 25½", W. 53¾" (open), D. 42". (Private collection; photo, Gavin Ashworth.) The feet are replaced.

Figure 34 Gateleg table frame, probably Rhode Island, 1710–1740. Maple. H. 25⅝", W. 15⅞", D. 31⅞". (Private collection; photo, Gavin Ashworth.)

Figure 35 Gateleg table, probably Rhode Island, 1710–1740. Maple. H. 27", W. 53" (open), D. 48". (Private collection; photo, Gavin Ashworth.)

Figure 36 Table, probably Rhode Island, 1710–1740. Maple with oak and white pine. H. 26", W. 24", D. 17". (Private collection; courtesy, Peter Eaton Inc.)

Two additional gateleg tables (figs. 34, 35), a trestle table (fig. 36), and a small group of candlestands (fig. 37) have related turnings. The V-shaped astragal molding separating the baluster turnings on the stand is identical to those in the same position on the legs of the gateleg table frame illustrated in figure 34. Cross-base candlestands and trestle tables are usually associated with Massachusetts and Connecticut; thus it is plausible that these objects were made in the border areas of Rhode Island.[17]

Figure 37 Candlestand, probably Rhode Island, 1710–1740. Maple. H. 23¾", W. 13½", D. 13¼". (Private collection; photo, Gavin Ashworth.)

Figure 38 Gateleg table, probably Rhode Island, 1710–1740. Maple. H. 27", W. 53¾" (open), D. 45¾". (Private collection; photo, Gavin Ashworth.)

Another variant of the opposing baluster design can be observed on the gateleg table illustrated in figure 38. With precise and delicate turnings, it is the most refined example of this genre. The turnings are reminiscent of those on the gateleg table illustrated in figure 33, but the elements are more in scale with the form. Aside from the two dovetails joining the drawer front and sides, the construction is similar to that of tables in group two. Although the table illustrated in figure 38 is somewhat idiosyncratic, it could easily be an urban product. A sophisticated candlestand that reputedly descended in a Rhode Island family has similar turnings (fig. 39). With its scroll legs, octagonal top, and pendant drop, this stand represents the pinnacle of the baroque design and fashion in Rhode Island furniture.[18]

Figure 39 Candlestand, probably Rhode Island, 1710–1740. Maple. H. 29⅛", W. 12¾", D. 12⅝". (Private collection; photo, Gavin Ashworth.)

The school of turning covered in this study reflects the work of a core group of furniture craftsmen and other regional artisans influenced by them. Surprisingly, few references to turners occur in early eighteenth-century Rhode Island records, and none are listed in Newport documents from this period. A few tradesmen described as "turners" were active in other areas of Rhode Island including King's County (present-day Washington County) in the colonial period. The 1727 inventory of Judah Wordin (d. 1727) of Westerly lists carpenters' and turners' tools, but like many rural artisans he probably performed a variety of woodworking activities, such as joinery, chair making, and turning, as well as doing seasonal farming. It is doubtful that many of the turned tables in the Rhode Island school were produced in rural areas, as nonurban craftsmen rarely achieved the production levels or had sufficient long-term patronage and stylistic sophistication to account for this large group of furniture. Rather, the artisans who produced these table, stool, stand, and architectural turnings were probably among the many joiners and house carpenters listed in the records of Newport and other Rhode Island towns. Period documents describe Reuben Peckham (1676–1736) of Newport and East Greenwich, Rhode Island, as a joiner, but he did turning as well. The 1736 inventory of his East Greenwich shop lists joiners' tools, two workbenches, unfinished case furniture, "1 Leath [lathe] and turning tools," "1 grindstone," and "Sundry Table Legs." His household goods included three oval tables, one described as "small." The executors of Peckham's estate sold the small table for £1.11 in May 1737. The oval tables were probably gateleg forms or simpler four-leg examples without folding leaves. Similarly, recent scholarship suggests that the renowned Newport furniture maker Christopher Townsend (1701–1787) made turned and joined tables, stair balusters and pendants, and architectural paneling as well as ambitious case furniture.[19]

Given the fact that it represents the work of several different hands, the Rhode Island school of turning is remarkably cohesive. It is likely that many factors contributed to the development and persistence of this regional style. As a group, the colony's inhabitants differed from their counterparts in other areas of New England. During the seventeenth century, Rhode Island became a destination for Quakers escaping persecution in England and Massachusetts. Religious strictures against marriage outside their faith and social pressures emphasizing the support of other Quakers facilitated the establishment of family businesses and patronage networks. Given the fact that many Quaker artisans were linked through marriage, apprenticeship, or business, it should come as no surprise that strong regional styles emerged in several areas of Rhode Island. A desire for commercial independence from Massachusetts may also have been an influence. In a 1739 letter to John Thomlinson of London, Newport merchant John Bannister wrote that the residents of his town desired "to make themselves independent of the Bay Government to whom they have a mortal aversion." The stylistic independence manifest in the Rhode Island school of turning foreshadowed what was to come. By the time Bannister wrote his letter, Newport furniture makers had developed innovative construction methods and established alliances with merchants and shippers that would enable them to compete with their counterparts in Boston and other northern ports.[20]

ACKNOWLEDGMENTS For kind assistance with this article, the authors thank Glenn Adamson, Alan Anderson, Mr. and Mrs. Brian Bartizek, Luke Beckerdite, John Benson, Richard Benson, Victor Chinnery, Edward S. Cooke Jr., Phillip DeDominicis, Mr. and Mrs. John Demos, Ann Donnelly, Peter Eaton, Mr. and Mrs. Dudley Godfrey, Mr. and Mrs. Norman Gronning, Morrison Heckscher, Patricia Kane, Kevin Keane, Kimberly Krauer, Brock Jobe, Rev. Ledlie Laughlin Jr., Dean Levy, Frank Levy, Bertram Lippincott, Mr. and Mrs. John Little, Arthur Liverant, Dr. and Mrs. Richard Mones, John Philbrick, Marie Plummer, Jonathan Prown, Frances Safford, Myron Stackiw, Mr. and Mrs. Stanley Tananbaum, Adams Taylor, Mr. and Mrs. Tonnesen, Robert Trent, Tony Trowles, Kevin Tulimieri, Mr. and Mrs. Fred Vogel, and Joan Youngken.

1. Robert Blair St. George, *The Wrought Covenant: Source Material for the Study of Craftsmen and Community in Southeastern New England, 1620–1700* (Brockton, Mass.: Brockton Art Center and Fuller Memorial, 1979); Robert F. Trent, "New Insights on Early Rhode Island Furniture," in *American Furniture,* edited by Luke Beckerdite (Hanover, N.H.: University Press of New England for the Chipstone Foundation, 1999), pp. 209–23; and Erik K. Gronning and Dennis Carr, "Rhode Island Gateleg Tables," *Antiques* 165, no. 5 (May 2004): 122–27.

2. Irving Whitall Lyon, *The Colonial Furniture of New England* (New York: E. P. Dutton, 1891), p. 202, fig. 102; Frances Clary Morse, *Furniture of the Olden Time* (New York: Macmillan Co., 1901), p. 224. Albert Sack, *Fine Points of Furniture: Early American* (New York: Crown Publishers, 1950), pp. 238, 240. Oswaldo Rodriguez Roque discussed two tables with a history of ownership in Rhode Island in *American Furniture at Chipstone* (Madison: University of Wisconsin Press, 1984), pp. 278–79.

3. Augustin-Charles d'Aviler, *Cours d'architecture qui comprend les ordres de Vignole.* 2 vols. (Paris: Chez Nicolas Langlois, 1691), 1: 319, pl. 94. This book was reissued several times during the first half of the eighteenth century. The authors thank Victor Chinnery for providing information about British antecedents for Newport turnings—particularly the staircase at Harvard House (Shakespeare Birthplace Trust)—and for sharing his knowledge of related English furniture turnings. For a staircase with similar details, see *Royal Commission on Historical Monuments (England): An Inventory of the Historical Monuments in London,* vol. 1, *Westminster Abbey* (London: His Majesty's Stationery Office, 1924), pl. 179. This stair was added to the Little Cloister of Westminster Abbey in the late seventeenth century. A similar staircase is illustrated in Walter H. Godfrey, *The English Staircase: An Historical Account of Its Characteristic Types to the End of the XVIIIth Century* (London: B. T. Batsford, 1911), pls. 40, 41.

4. Luke Beckerdite, "The Early Furniture of Christopher and Job Townsend," in *American Furniture,* edited by Luke Beckerdite (Hanover, N.H.: University Press of New England for the Chipstone Foundation, 2000), pp. 7–10. Myron O. Stackiw, *The Early Architecture and Landscapes of the Narragansett Basin,* vol. 1, *Newport* (Newport, R.I.: Vernacular Architecture Forum, 2001), pp. 107–9.

5. For more on the Wanton-Lyman-Hazard House, see Antoinette F. Dowling and Vincent J. Scully Jr., *The Architectural Heritage of Newport Rhode Island: 1640–1915,* 2nd ed. (New York: Bramhall House, 1967), pp. 435–37, pls. 29–37; Antoinette F. Dowling, *Early Homes of Rhode Island* (Richmond, Va.: Garrett & Massie, 1937), pp. 70–72. The date of this house is based on recent dendrochronology. The authors thank Myron Stackiw for providing this information and discussing his study of the house. Dean F. Failey, *Long Island Is My Nation: The Decorative Arts and Craftsmen, 1640–1830,* 2nd ed. (Cold Spring Harbor, N.Y.: Society for the Preservation of Long Island Antiquities, 1998), p. 28, fig. 26. St. George, *Wrought Covenant,* p. 44, fig. 34b. Roderick H. Blackburn et al., *Dutch Colonial Homes in America* (New York:

Rizzoli, 2002), p. 84. Originally constructed as a draw-bar table, the Floyd table is a unique New England example. All other known draw-bar tables originate in New York, and very few are known with related turnings.

6. For the eight known tables, see Northeast Auctions, *New Hampshire Auction*, Portsmouth, N.H., August 1–3, 2003, lot 778; Ruth Davidson, "Living with Antiques: The Connecticut Home of Mrs. C. McGregory Well Jr.," *Antiques* 81, no. 1 (January 1962): 101–3; Sotheby's, *Important Americana: The Collection of Dr. and Mrs. Henry P. Deyerle,* Charlottesville, Va., May 26–27, 1995, lot 372; Christie's, *Fine American Furniture, Silver, and Decorative Arts,* New York, September 19, 1981, lot 539 (Easton table); Gronning and Carr, "Rhode Island Gateleg Tables," pp. 122–23 (Bernard & S. Dean Levy, New York); Metropolitan Museum of Art; private collection, Milwaukee; and private collection, Connecticut. Trent, "New Insights on Early Rhode Island Furniture," pp. 220–21. The current owner of the Alden-Southworth-Cooke table provided its provenance based on a letter from Bertram Lippincott III, dated May 19, 1996. The table illustrated in figure 13 resided in the Maudsley-Garner-Watson-Pitman House in Newport during the twentieth century. The drawer pull on the table illustrated in figure 14 has moldings similar to those found on newel pendants in Trinity Church and the Colony House, both in Newport.

7. A New York table with gates pivoting at the same end is in a private collection in Milwaukee. For English examples with similar gate arrangements, see John T. Kirk, *American Furniture and the British Tradition to 1830* (New York: Alfred A. Knopf, 1982), p. 317.

8. The table illustrated in figure 1 is the only Rhode Island example with laminated legs known.

9. Two other tables not illustrated here are published in Morse, *Furniture of the Olden Time,* p. 224; and in an advertisement of Melvin Hubley, *Antiques* 44, no. 5 (November 1953): 408. A third table is in a private collection.

10. The two other tables are illustrated in Skinner's, *Fine Americana*, Bolton, Mass., May 30, 1986, lot 132; and Olga O. Ottoson, "Living with Antiques: The Ryerson House in New Jersey," *Antiques* 128, no. 4 (October 1985): 756, pl. 3.

11. For more on the table illustrated in figure 22, see Sack, *Fine Points of Furniture,* pp. 238, 240; Stanley Stone, "Rhode Island Furniture at Chipstone, Part I," *Antiques* 91, no. 2 (February 1967): 211; Roque, *American Furniture at Chipstone,* pp. 278–79; and Trent, "New Insights on Early Rhode Island Furniture," pp. 220–21.

12. With its conventional gate arrangement and top pinned to the legs, the construction of the table illustrated in figure 25 has parallels with those in group two. However, these features cannot be considered diagnostic since they occur on other colonial gateleg tables. The molding between the turned balls of a table at the Winterthur Museum is similar to the fat astragal on the necks of the balusters of the table illustrated in figure 25 (John A. H. Sweeney, *Winterthur Illustrated* [Winterthur, Del.: Winterthur Museum, 1963], p. 27).

13. A related stool is illustrated in Edgar G. Miller Jr., *American Antique Furniture: A Book for Amateurs,* 2 vols. (New York: Dover Publications, 1966), 2: 849, fig. 1695 (Metropolitan Museum of Art). Unpublished stools similar to the one shown in figure 27 are in the collections of Bernard & S. Dean Levy (formerly owned by Katherine Prentis Murphy) and the Winterthur Museum. For an object with turnings similar to those on the legs of the stool illustrated in figure 28, see Wallace Nutting, *Furniture of the Pilgrim Century: 1620–1720* (New York: Bonanza Books, 1921), p. 433 (second example).

14. For other examples, see Trent, "New Insights on Early Rhode Island Furniture," p. 220 (Winterthur); Lyon, *Colonial Furniture,* p. 202, fig. 102 (Metropolitan Museum of Art); Jonathan L. Fairbanks, "American Antiques in the Collection of Mr. and Mrs. Charles L. Bybee, Part 1," *Antiques* 92, no. 6 (December 1967): 834 (formerly owned by Henry A. Hoffman of Barrington, R.I., and subsequently destroyed in a fire); Alice Winchester, "Living with Antiques: Time Stone Farm in Marlboro, Massachusetts," *Antiques* 59, no. 6 (June 1951): 462; Sotheby Parke-Bernet, *Important Collection of 17th, 18th & 19th Century American Furniture & Decorations,* New York, June 23, 1972, lot 21; and Nutting, *Furniture of the Pilgrim Century,* p. 433 (first example). A related table has a long history of use in the John Stevens stonecutting shop in Newport. That business has been in continuous operation since 1705.

15. Another tavern table associated with group three is illustrated in Nutting, *Furniture of the Pilgrim Century,* p. 432. The other fixed-top table is illustrated in Skinner, *Fine Americana Including the Private Collection of Kenneth Hammitt of Woodbury, Conn.,* Boston, Mass., October 28–29, 2004, lot 114. Two gateleg tables have similar domed feet, but the transitions from the turnings to the square sections of the legs are different from the tables in

group three. See Sotheby's, *Important Americana,* New York, January 30, 1988, lot 1805; and Sotheby's, *The Collection of Mr. and Mrs. Walter Jeffords,* New York, October 28–29, 2004, lot 295.

16. The table has a drawer supported on a central runner, a conventional gate arrangement, a top pinned to the legs, and hinges attached outside the frame.

17. Currently three candlestands of this form are known. Two have circular tops and the third, illustrated here, has an octagonal top. One stand deaccessioned by the Art Institute of Chicago is currently in a private collection. See Nutting, *Furniture of the Pilgrim Century,* p. 467 (example on far right); and Skinner, *Fine Americana,* Boston, Mass., October 30–31, 1993, lot 336. Another stand in a private collection is illustrated in *American Antiques from Israel Sack Collection,* 10 vols. (Alexandria, Va.: Highland House Publishers, 1989), 6: 1572, fig. P4673.

18. Nina Fletcher Little, *Little by Little: Six Decades of Collecting American Decorative Arts* (Hanover, N.H.: University Press of New England for the Society for the Preservation of New England Antiquities, 1998), pp. 215, 218, fig. 286. The Little stand (fig. 39) was purchased through Roger Bacon from George Cousidine, who discovered it in a house in Providence. A nearly identical stand is at the Winterthur Museum (Sweeney, *Winterthur Illustrated,* p. 25).

19. David Sprague, a "turner," worked in Scituate, a small town near Providence, in 1732 (*Israel Arnold v. David Sprague,* June term, 1732, Providence County Court of Common Pleas Record Book, vol. 1, p. 38). Inventory of Judah Wordin of Westerly, October 10, 1727, with an addition made March 28, 1748, Westerly Town Council and Probate Records, vol. 3 (1719–1731), p. 151. Gateleg tables were typically called "oval" tables during the seventeenth and eighteenth centuries. Inventory of Reuben Peckham, joiner, East Greenwich, East Greenwich Probate Records, vol. 1, pp. 167–70. Sale of estate of Reuben Peckham, May 3, 1737, in *William Allen, yeoman, North Kingstown, v. John Peckham, laborer, Little Compton, and Sarah Peckham, widow, Newport,* Newport County Court of Common Pleas, May term 1741, decon 62. Beckerdite, "Christopher and Job Townsend," pp. 1–30.

20. As quoted in Leigh Keno, Joan Barzilay Freund, and Alan Miller, "The Very Pink of the Mode: Boston Georgian Chairs, Their Export, and Their Influence," in *American Furniture,* edited by Luke Beckerdite (Hanover, N.H.: University Press of New England for the Chipstone Foundation, 1996), p. 298.

Figure 1 Benno M. Forman, undated photo. (Courtesy, Winterthur Museum.)

Glenn Adamson

Mannerism in Early American Furniture: Connoisseurship, Intention, and Theatricality

▼ THE ATTENTIVE READER will find the groundbreaking writings of American furniture historian Benno Forman to be a sobering legacy (fig. 1). In his capacity as curator of furniture at the Winterthur Museum from 1968 until his death in 1982, Forman amassed a body of research that is daunting in its scope. His astonishingly broad, if often intuitive, observations about the relations between European and American furniture are intertwined with incisive analyses of individual shops. In these writings a grand art historical view is tempered by an almost obsessive patience for detail; in the distinctive construction of a single joint, Forman was able to discern the situation of a joiner in the transatlantic sweep of furniture production. Perhaps the most significant thing about his writings, though, is that they reveal an author frustrated by his own limitations. He was unable to bring his magnum opus on early American seating furniture to print, and thus his only book appeared posthumously, thanks to the efforts of two of his leading students, Robert F. Trent and Robert Blair St. George. Reams upon reams of his unfinished manuscripts, lively correspondence, and promising research leads languish in archival boxes at Winterthur.

Forman's decision to hold back much of his work from publication makes perfect sense in light of his declared principles of furniture history. "The intuition of the present-day commentator is not that of the craftsman who made the object or that of the people who used it and brings us no closer to historical truth after all," Forman wrote in his landmark text "Connoisseurship and Furniture History," an unapologetic defense of traditional methodology that was printed as the foreword to *Early American Seating Furniture, 1630–1730*. Elsewhere in that volume, Forman mused, "Every historian hopes to find Truth. My aim has been more modest. I have hoped merely to find some truths and uncover what insights I could into the life of the people who used this furniture, its meaning to them and, perhaps most important of all in the absence of verbal documents on the point, to synthesize or make a composite of the way in which the craftsman may have seen it and may have thought about it." In these lines Forman stakes out a position of hermeneutic humility, as if reminding himself of the poverty of our modern access to the mind of the craftsman: the paucity of means for reconstructing the period artisan's *mentalité*.[1]

Forman's example, that of a brilliant scholar who was nearly thwarted by his own realization of the difficulty of his task, ought to haunt furniture historians today. His work is now more than two decades old and his attachment to the term "connoisseurship," with the particular sort of rigor that word implies, is likely to strike academic readers as antiquated, and possibly even quaint. Yet Forman's understanding of the term has much to recommend it. He railed against the compartmentalized view of connoisseurship as an elaborate system of data collection, insisting instead that it entailed knowledge of the aesthetic quality of early furniture—not as a way of justifying its present-day value in the market, but as the crucial entry point into the conceptual configuration of the object. "The failure of aesthetic judgment to enlarge our understanding of furniture has caused us to draw the lines of battle too strongly in the matter of the qualities of simple versus complex, village versus urban, vernacular versus high-style furniture," Forman wrote in 1980. "What we have failed to see is that the merits of one of these artificially polarized states neither destroy nor compete in kind with the merits of the other." Forman was pointing to the bifurcation between traditional modes of connoisseurship and the new dispensation of material culture, which had by the time of his mature career started to rip the field of American furniture history into the two camps into which it is now divided. On one side, an academic wing was developing, forming itself on the model of vernacular architecture scholars, who tried to overthrow the furniture establishment's overemphasis on elite objects, and the attribution, verification, and tabulation thereof. On the other side, a market-driven wing was becoming entrenched, already rather set by the 1970s; progress on that side since has been characterized by a dramatic enlarging of the franchise of "valuable" furniture, but it has still been guided by the fine shadings of good, better, and best. (In 1993, when Albert Sack updated his landmark 1950 connoisseur's guide, *Fine Points of Furniture: Good, Better, Best,* he chose not to revoke his earlier framework of hierarchical quality but instead added the categories of "superior" and "masterpiece.") This is the predicament we find ourselves in today: the academic side of the discipline chary of conceptualizing furniture in aesthetic terms, and the market side divorced from many of the interpretative accomplishments of the past thirty years. Although numerous individual historians have navigated creatively between these two poles, it has been impossible to escape them entirely—to conceptualize a disciplinary practice that transcends the seeming opposition between social history and aesthetics. Forman saw this impasse coming. He realized that a pure art historical model, in which objects were treated as master texts to be decoded like paintings, could not work for American furniture; but he also realized that a pure material culture model, which treated objects as information rather than art, would result in histories that were not only flat and uncompelling, and insufficiently attuned to the attractions of old furniture in the first place, but also, perhaps most important, unable to cope with individual artisanal intent.[2]

Mannerism Revisited

Forman returns forcefully to the present because our understanding of the subject matter to which he devoted his career—American furniture of the late seventeenth and early eighteenth centuries—has recently been fundamentally doubted. Joseph Manca's article "A Question of Style," published

Figure 2 Cabinet attributed to the Symonds shops, Salem, Massachusetts, 1679. Red oak, black walnut, eastern red cedar, and soft maple with white pine. H. 17¾", W. 17¼", D. 9¾". (Courtesy, Metropolitan Museum of Art, gift of Mrs. Russell Sage; photo, Gavin Ashworth.) This cabinet has a history of ownership in the Herrick family.

in *Winterthur Portfolio,* challenges the notion that seventeenth-century American furniture should be seen as mannerist in style, as most scholars in the field have been accustomed to thinking. Instead, he argues, it should be seen as "a vernacular, yet creative, adaptation of the classical revival of the fifteenth through the seventeenth centuries." Manca is also a specialist in Italian Renaissance painting and interiors and is therefore qualified to speak to the normative use of the term "mannerism" in art historical discourse. There are two platforms to the negative aspect of his argument. The first is semantic in nature and has to do with the simple choice of "mannerism" as an accurate descriptor. Though acknowledging that the word is a modern invention and can be applied in varied and contradictory ways, Manca would prefer to limit its proper usage to courtly artistic practice in Italy carried out in response to Renaissance humanism. He might be willing to extend the term to close French and northern European cognates of Italian work, but no further. So, for example, Manca sees the valuables cabinets made by the Symonds shops in Salem as "remarkably simple and unaffected," like "little buildings in the classical tradition, with linear crispness and clear readability that are among the hallmarks of the Renaissance style" (fig. 2). Here he departs from the judgment of other scholars who have seen the ornament and particularly the carving on the sides of these objects as mannerist. Not so, Manca says; the cabinets are simple medieval forms with Renaissance architectural motifs grafted onto them. As Manca summarizes the matter,

"Anglo American craftsmen [worked] without sophisticated knowledge of classical canons of form." This is not to say, of course, that they had no knowledge of classical form whatsoever, just that we should not overestimate their conversance with that language, or their ability to manipulate it.[3]

The second part of Manca's thesis is at once more argumentative and less terminological. It is his contention that mannerism, by definition, entails irony, wit, or inversion—typically in relation to some proper classical precedent. In this view mannerism always involves an element of willful, intentional distortion. This understanding of mannerism is authorized by stray period comments about the new styles of the Italian *seicento,* such as the statement by antiquarian and diplomat Celio Calcagnini in 1541 that "there are certain things that are beautiful just because they are deformed, and thus please by giving displeasure," or the fact that mannerist architectural theorist and designer Sebastiano Serlio worried about *voluto rompere e guastare la bella forma*—intentionally breaking and destroying beautiful form. Modern art historians consider such views as typical of Italian and northern European painting and architecture of the sixteenth century. Erwin Panofsky, for example, wrote in 1924 that "the specifically 'Mannerist' art distorted and twisted the balanced and universally valid forms of the classic style in order to achieve a more intense expressivity . . . an internal dualism, an inner tension." Manca argues that such highly self-conscious gamesmanship—in his words, "delightful and witty divergence"—is intrinsic to mannerism, and he is unwilling to attribute this capacity to early American craftsmen.[4]

The original sponsor of the mannerist label as applied to early American furniture is Robert F. Trent, the scholar who has done the most to carry Forman's mantle into the twenty-first century. Trent first laid out the case for interpreting seventeenth-century American objects as mannerist in the 1982 catalogue for the seminal exhibition *New England Begins.* His brief but incisive discussion identified the style as dominant in seventeenth-century New England and enumerated various aspects of its importance in that context: an interest in grotesquerie; an emblematic sensibility; and a complex system of geometric ornament "derived, in general, from the proportional system of classical architecture." Trent acknowledged that it was surprising that a courtly, Catholic style would find root in provincial, Calvinist New England, but argued that the style had become so endemic to the English bourgeoisie by the early seventeenth century that it constituted a sort of lingua franca in the minds of early joiners and other craftsmen. Manca's critique of Trent's position is made clear in his discussion of an Essex County court cupboard in the collection of the Museum of Fine Arts, Boston (fig. 3). For Trent, it sports typically mannerist features: abstract ornamental forms reminiscent of urns are suspended in the middle of panels; the double arches on the side panels of the trapezoidal section lack a jamb or visual support in their center; and, most important perhaps, the linear ornamental elements are not properly architectural in character but are instead scratch-stock moldings of an "enriched ogee" profile (fig. 4). For Trent, these are all instances of the mannerist manipulation of form. For Manca, however, some of these features are not significantly divergent from classi-

Figure 3 Cupboard, northern Essex County, Massachusetts, 1685–1690. Oak and maple with oak and pine. H. 58¾", W. 48½", D. 19⅜". (Courtesy, Museum of Fine Arts, Boston, gift of Maurice Geeraerts in memory of Mr. and Mrs. William H. Robeson.)

Figure 4 Detail of the canted panel of the cupboard illustrated in fig. 3.

cal propriety and all are "unlikely to have been witty breaks with Palladian rules." Rather, they constitute "a sensible use of individual decorative motifs, in line with the taste for the ornate so widespread in the 16th and 17th centuries." "Without marking a rupture from the High Renaissance," Manca argues, "the appearance in America of a Renaissance manner apparently occurred without the kind of humor, sarcasm, strain, or rule consciousness often associated with Italian Mannerism." In a telling phrase, Manca describes the vertically elongated urns in the canted panel of the cupboard as "merely present and serving to divide the space." In short, he resists the intentionality that Trent imputes to the maker of the cupboard and hence its claim to the mantle of mannerism.[5]

The first reaction of the decorative art historian, on reading Manca's critique, may simply be to reject it on the grounds of historiographic precedent. While Trent occupied a vanguard position in applying the term to American material, his work came out of a long tradition of describing northern European and English work of the late sixteenth and early seventeenth century as mannerist. Trent refers particularly to the books of Sebastiano Serlio (1475–ca. 1554), Flemish designer Hans (or Jan) Vredeman de Vries (1527–1604), German fantasist Wendel Dietterlin (1550/51–1599),

Figure 5 Bedstead, probably Ware, England, 1590–1600. Oak and unidentified light and dark woods. H. 105 1/8", W. 128 3/8", D. 133". (Courtesy, Victoria & Albert Museum; purchased with the assistance of the National Art Collections Fund.)

and French architect Philibert de l'Orme (ca. 1512–1570) of the school of Fontainebleau, all of whom are routinely called mannerist by decorative art historians, as originating sources for the motifs that appear on numerous American objects. Nor is it difficult to establish the means by which such Continental influences may have come to New England by the mid-seventeenth century. As Timothy Mowl points out, English designers did not even need to consult printed works: "Historians tend to drop the names of Dietterlin and de Vries arbitrarily as the sources of English Mannerist design, but in fact there was a sizable colony of Flemings like [Nicaise] Roussel working at Southwark in monumental masonry and woodwork

Figure 6 Stephen Harrison, design for a triumphal arch, London, 1603. Engraving. (Courtesy, Victoria & Albert Museum.)

Figure 7 Stephen Harrison, design for a triumphal arch, London, 1603. Engraving. (Courtesy, Victoria & Albert Museum.)

from the mid-sixteenth century onwards and they are far more likely to have influenced the English design scene than foreign pattern books." While Trent may have exaggerated in writing that northern European mannerism underwent a "mass-marketing" in England, numerous monuments of architecture, metalwork, woodwork, and plasterwork attest to the importance of this Flemish influence under the Elizabethan and Stuart courts. Joinery was among the least significant media for such transmission, but even so, many surviving pieces of interior woodwork in the style survive from Elizabethan and Jacobean England, as well as such ambitious freestanding artifacts as the "Great Bed of Ware," probably made in the 1590s (fig. 5). Mentioned in Shakespeare's *As You Like It* when it was new, and famous ever since, this bed features on its headboard extraordinary marquetry panels taken directly from Hans Vredeman de Vries.[6]

A more suggestive, if less well-known, example of this "mannerist" northern European style in English woodworking of the Stuart era is the set of seven triumphal arches erected in London to celebrate the formal entry of James I into the city as king in 1604 (fig. 6). Based directly on similar urban stage sets made in the Netherlands during the late sixteenth century, these arches were designed and built by joiner Stephen Harrison, who had at least eighty woodworkers under his management on the project—a significant percentage of the joiners in the city. The entry of James I is unusually well documented in a book of engravings by artist William Kip and in an explanatory text by Harrison, but it was only one of many public civic pageants during this era, suggesting that this ceremonial apparatus was not an isolated occurrence but the apex of what may have been a common application of decorative woodwork. Harrison's arches were temporary, to be sure, but they were also huge (the first arch, located in Fenchurch Street, was about fifty feet tall and took about forty days to build) and likely seen by thousands of people. Most British architectural historians have dismissed this amazing prodigy of joinery as a muddle. Brian Earnshaw and Timothy Mowl, for example, damn Harrison as "reveal[ing] the total stylistic confusion of contemporary London with five chaotically detailed arches that greeted James I unpropitiously on his first entry into London," while John Peacock describes them as "teeming farragoes of infelicitous detail, their chaos emphasized by a busy, rebarbative Flemish mannerist style." Yet, as literary historian David M. Bergeron has argued, the arches represented a major advance in the conscious use of classical stylistic features. Harrison's text demonstrates familiarity with the orders—"*Tuscane, Doricke, Ionicke,* and *Cornithian* . . . the name of *Composita* or *Italica*"—as well as such architectural terms as "postern," "term," "corbel," "capital," "cant," "cornice," "frieze," "architrave," 'baluster," and "pilaster," all of which were recent imports into the English language. It is hard to dispute the notion that the arches were understood as a highly self-conscious statement of the primacy of classicism during the Stuart reign, given Harrison's choice of the word *Londinium* (the original Roman name for the city) (fig. 7) and the close involvement of the classically informed poet and playwright Ben Jonson in their design and accompanying theatrical script. They were also clearly framed as totems of internationalism, in that two of the arches were paid for by the Dutch and Italian merchants living in London, clearly associating the new style on display and the geographic sources of that mode. Harrison's arches serve as a reminder that joiners participated fully in the extraordinary ornamental style propagated through Continental print images seen in elaborate English chimneypieces, hall screens, tombs, and architectural "frontispieces" surrounding front entry doors that were built throughout England in the early seventeenth century (figs. 8, 9).[7]

Figure 8 Wendel Dietterlin, design for a chimneypiece, 1598. Etching. (Courtesy, Victoria & Albert Museum.)

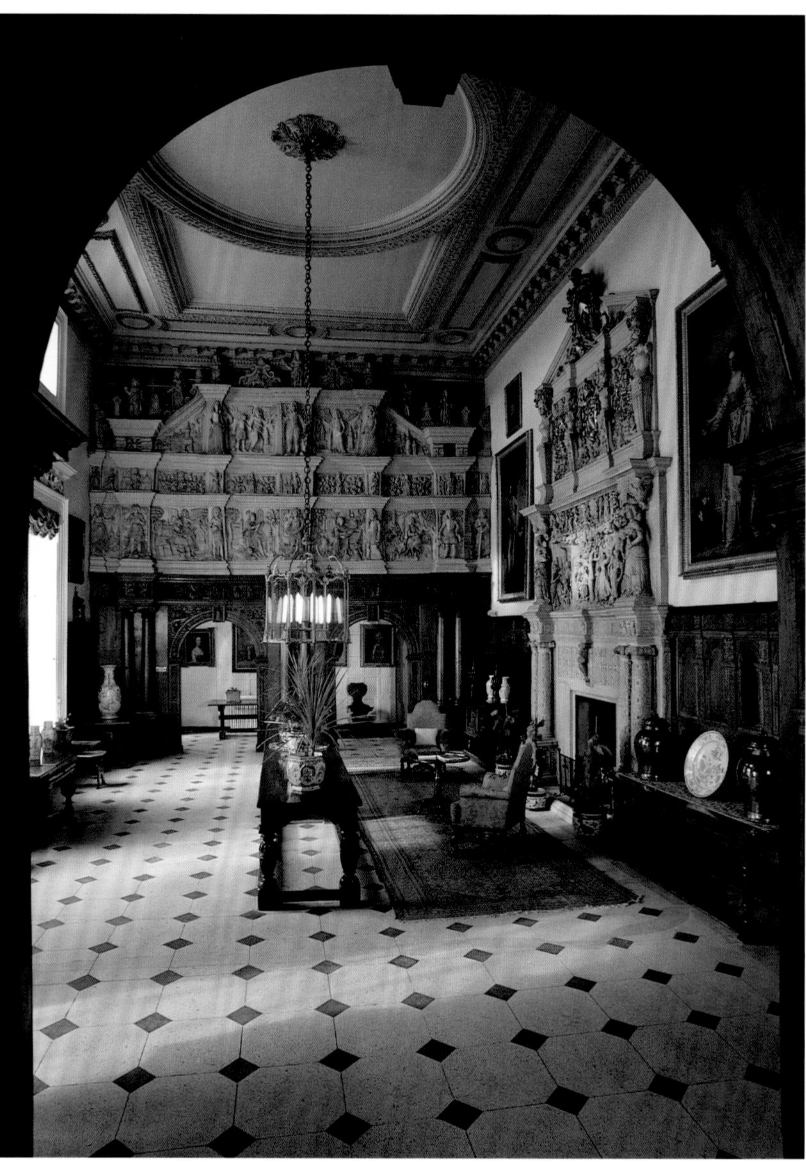

Figure 9 Hall screen, Burton Agnes Hall, Yorkshire, England, 1610. (Courtesy, Jarrold Publishing and Burton Agnes Hall.)

Though Manca does not specifically address such instances of the transmission of Continental "mannerist" design to English woodworking, he does object to reading English architecture of the same time and style as mannerist. Comparing a leading candidate for a British mannerist architect to a canonical Italian mannerist architect, Manca writes: "the 'Mannerism' of someone like a Robert Smythson is very different from the art of Giulio

Romano. Based not on a controverting of classical rules, it is an accretion of forms, with medieval elements and borrowings from Flemish design grafted onto a creative adaptation of the classicizing structural system" (fig. 10). Manca concludes, "the 'mannerism' of England would be better regarded as the equivalent not of a pun but of the efforts of a beginner in a second language who occasionally gets the new grammar wrong and who continues to spice his speech with elements of his native language. English masters themselves were not demonstrably aware of their departure from

Figure 10 Robert Smythson, Surveyor, Wollaton Hall, Nottinghamshire, England, 1580–1588. (Courtesy, Wollaton Hall.)

classical models." In staking out this position, which might be applied to a joiner like Harrison as easily as to an architect like Smythson, Manca is participating in a historiographical lineage that views the architecture of the English Renaissance, before the rise of the informed classicist Inigo Jones in the early seventeenth century, as a mess of ill-digested Italianate and Flemish influences. This skeptical tradition goes back to the 1920s, when architectural historians Horace Field and Michael Bunney wrote:

> In Elizabethan work the orders, as a rule, were always used in the crudest fashion: as compared with the building, they were almost always small in scale, never occupying more than one storey in height, and no attempt was made to impart the real spirit of Classic work to the mouldings and details. A good deal of taste and knowledge appears in their use on much of the work, more especially in small decorative items such as paneling etc., but as a whole the result is most unsatisfactory when we remember that the Renaissance decoration had filtered through German and other foreign mediums, and was carried out more in the manner of a schoolboy writing an essay than as the true expression of the feelings of the workers themselves.

The greatest of British architectural historians, John Summerson, adopted a sophisticated variation on this position when he described the majority of ambitious early seventeenth-century English buildings as "artisan mannerist," by which he meant that they were designed according to exuberant, craft-based intuition rather than an intellectual program. For Summerson,

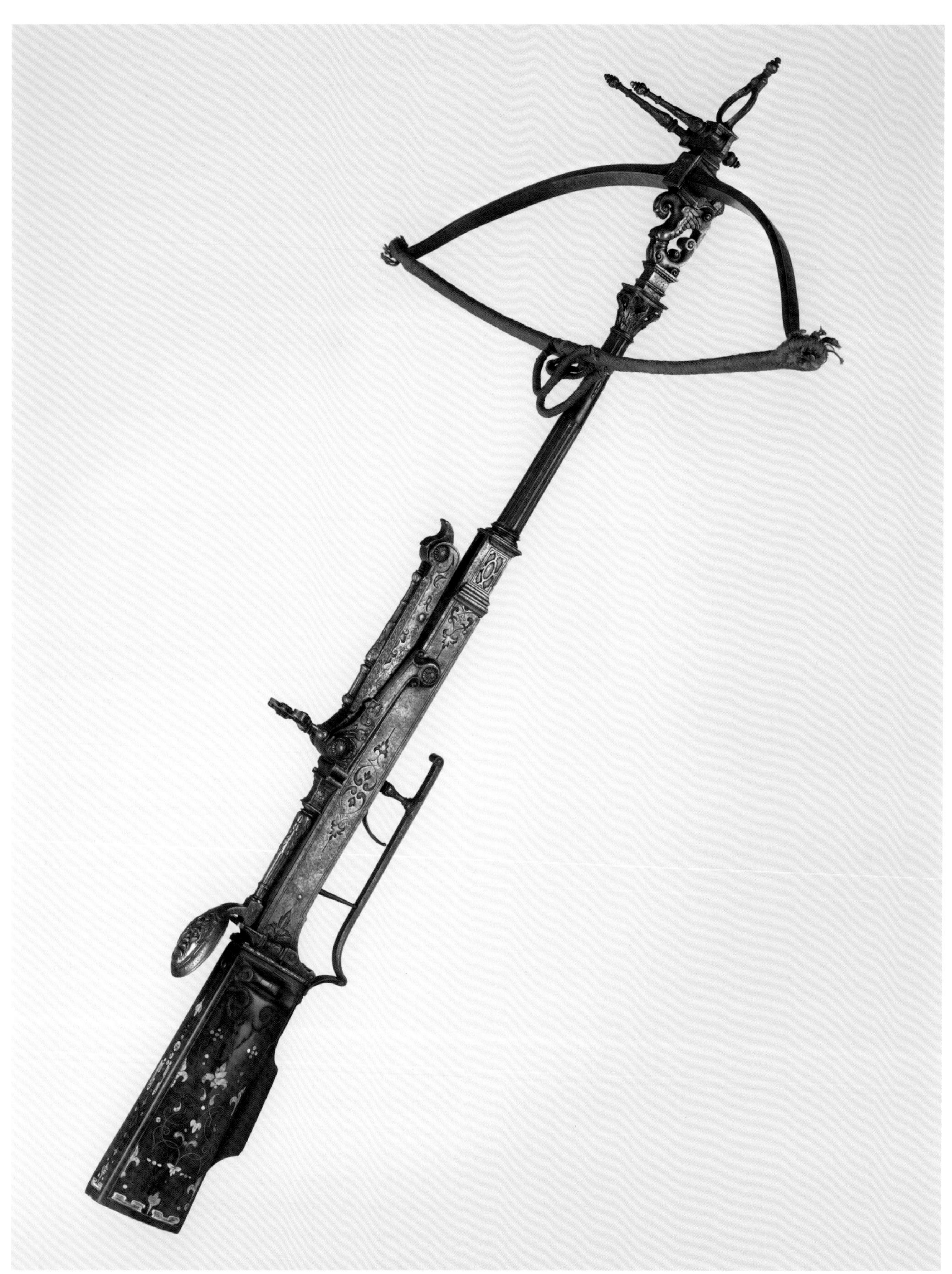

Figure 11 Stone bow, probably eastern France or Germany, early seventeenth century. Fruitwood, unidentified marquetry woods, steel, silver wire inlay, mother-of-pearl, gilding. L. 33". (Courtesy, Joe Kindig Antiques; photo, Gavin Ashworth.)

the mason or carpenter builder of the Jacobean period, despite his notable creativity, "exert[ed] himself in a field where discipline was of the essence but where discipline had not yet been imposed."[8]

By extension, one might stake out a conservative position on the question of mannerism that draws bright lines around Italian and French practice and that portrays other work of the period, even the sophisticated flights of fancy of Hans Vredeman de Vries and other Flemish artists, not as properly mannerist, but as one among many varieties of "Late Renaissance" design. Citing recent work by Henri Zerner and others, Manca argues that this position has become normative of late among scholars of Continental decorative art. Nonetheless, it seems that "mannerism" is still frequently used with reference to Flemish design in particular, and Flemish design was by far the most powerful Continental influence on Elizabethan and Jacobean work. Whatever the nomenclature of the moment, the danger for the American furniture historian is clear: if the term "mannerism" is used very strictly in reference to its place of origin, Italy, and with increasing permissiveness in reference to its successively more far-flung manifestations in northern Europe, England, and New England, then this is surely a matter for concern. Yet abandoning the term "mannerism" entirely as a descriptor of this international style, exemplified by some aspects of Serlio's work and brought to a fever pitch by Vredeman and Dietterlin, does face three immediate objections. The first is practical in nature. The style in question, whatever we may choose to call it, is so widespread and distinctive as to require its own name. If one chooses not to call these things "mannerist," that is of course defensible, since "mannerism" is a modern term and not a period one. But if one does not feel comfortable using that term for this style, with its easily identifiable combination of overlaid ornament, classical reference, twisting strapwork, and willfully idiosyncratic composition, then one will simply have to come up with another term. ("Late Renaissance," the phrase Manca proposes, strikes this author as both unclear and insufficiently descriptive.) Since mannerism is in such general use among British architectural and decorative art historians—who typically use it to mean, in the words of Alice Friedman, "a broad-based, international style rooted in Italian painting, sculpture and architecture, but ultimately flourishing in the ornamental and decorative motifs of the minor arts of northern Europe"—it seems unlikely to be dropped in that quarter, even if, like most stylistic terms, it is somewhat rough-and-ready in its application (see fig. 11).[9]

A second objection, less obvious but also important, is that Manca's argument rests on a misapprehension regarding the nature of stylistic transmission. To say that the application of a new design grammar is "wrong," and therefore disqualified from participation in a style, is to ignore the nature of all stylistic transmission, which is always partly "right" and partly "wrong." Such misinterpretation is the only possible mode of stylistic development, not only in the New World but in the rest of the world as well. As Forman wrote, style "is an idea in the mind, an abstraction." Even objects that may seem to be as easily described, stylistically, as anything in the American canon only participate in certain ways with the words we usually employ. It

Figure 12 Side chair, Philadelphia, Pennsylvania, 1740–1750. Walnut. H. 41⅝", W. 20¾", D. 21". (Chipstone Foundation; photo, Gavin Ashworth.)

is customary to say that the chair illustrated in figure 12, for example, is a fully developed representation of what we often call the "late baroque" style in Philadelphia. This is perfectly correct if we mean that it is curvaceous and stylistically unified. But is this chair conspicuously emotional, as baroque art is supposed to be? Does it display volumetric rhythm? Similarly, the suite of furniture represented by the chair shown in figure 13 has been described as " the most aggressively rococo . . . of all Philadelphia furniture." Again, this characterization is correct if one focuses on the object's carved decoration. But does this object exhibit an animistic or sexualized character or offer the observer a surprising or amusing experience? And does the "neoclassical" chair illustrated in figure 14 exhibit idealism of form? Does it offer a notion of perfection based on antique precedent? We might be able to say "yes" to some of these questions, all of which address baseline notions of the styles these chairs supposedly represent, but certainly not all of them.

Figure 13 Side chair attributed to the shop of Benjamin Randolph, Philadelphia, Pennsylvania, ca. 1769. Mahogany with white cedar. H. 36¾", W. 21¾", D. 17⅞" (seat). (Chipstone Foundation; photograph, Gavin Ashworth.)

Figure 14 Side chair, Boston, Massachusetts, ca. 1800. Maple, birch, and maple veneer. H. 35", W. 22½", D. 23⅛". (Chipstone Foundation; photo, Gavin Ashworth.)

In effect, if we want to say that these three chairs are baroque, rococo, and neoclassical respectively, we have to give them more credit, as it were, than Manca would extend to the valuables cabinet shown in figure 2 or the court cupboard illustrated in figure 3.[10]

Finally, we might recall that Forman had chastening words for those who become preoccupied with terminology in the first place: "Is 'what to call it' really what we want to learn about the furniture of the past? Ours must be a frivolous discipline, indeed, if our greatest concern is what cubbyhole of language an object ought to be fitted into." Stylistic description, he argued, was a matter of utility rather than historical truth. A term like "mannerist" is a tool, not an end in itself; it serves a purpose only insofar as it helps us to understand historical artifacts. "A work of art exists in a non-verbal context," Forman argued. "The words we use to categorize an object represent only our ideas about that object and not the object itself." By these lights, if the category of mannerism provides powerful interpretative insights—even if only by giving a widespread network of related artifacts a convenient label—then one should simply embrace it and get on to the business of interpretation.[11]

Yet these terminological objections, while they have a certain persuasive force, nonetheless miss the most provocative point of Manca's essay: that mannerism is unlike other, seemingly parallel, stylistic terms. While the words "baroque," "rococo," or "neoclassical" can be used merely descriptively, he argues that the word "mannerist" necessarily implies a dialectical frame of mind. In Panofsky's words, the style is premised on an "internal dualism" in which material form is made to indicate a transcendent plane beyond itself. Indeed, in the narrowest understanding of mannerism (which is not necessarily espoused by Manca), it is not so much a style as an esoteric theory of religious art that derives from form's inability to capture the divinity of its own subjects. Broadening that definition slightly, mannerism might be understood as a reaction against humanistic Renaissance naturalism that consists of a reversion to abstract ideas, an idealization of form that is motivated by an acute awareness of *maniera*—of style itself. In this understanding, mannerism was a shift in art theory that gave new priority to the inner life of the artist. This precept was best captured in the writings of Federico Zuccari (1542–1609), whose 1607 treatise *L'idea de' scultori, pittori e architetti* placed emphasis on internal design, *disegno interno,* which was the "example and shadow of the divine" and could only be translated into physical form through imagination. For Zuccari, a devotion to the rules of proper classical form typical of Renaissance academicism made such a translation impossible: "instead of increasing practical skill, spirit, and liveliness, this kind of thing would take them all away: the mind would debase itself, the judgment extinguish itself, and all grace, all spirit and savor, would be taken away from art." Insofar as the idea of mannerism is bound up with such introspection concerning artistic intention itself, it is not difficult to see why Manca would see use of the term "mannerist" to describe American furniture as too charitable by far: it bestows a richness of intention and intellectual context to the objects that is not justified by the objects' humble artisanal origins.[12]

At this point one reaches an apparent impasse with Manca's skeptical position. In the absence of written documents, the attribution of particular intentions to an anonymous historical craftsman does indeed seem a purely subjective exercise. Yet we know that style progresses everywhere and always (among Forman's notes at Winterthur is the boldly scrawled maxim "All is transition!") and that creativity, of a sort, must therefore be a constant presence. This insoluble conflict between the fundamentally transformative act of making a piece of furniture, on the one hand, and the comparative textual weakness of furniture as a medium, on the other, could be said to lie at the heart of interpretation for the field. Indeed, following this line of reasoning to its logical conclusion, it might be said that the casual use of all stylistic terms drawn from fine art in furniture history disguises a basic methodological uncertainty about the conceptual framework of the people who made the objects of our study. Because mannerism is, at its root, a matter of knowingness—what might be called metatextuality—it throws this

Figure 15 Side chair, Milford, Connecticut, ca. 1820. (Courtesy, New Haven Colony Historical Society; reproduced from an illustration in Robert F. Trent, *Hearts and Crowns: Folk Chairs of the Connecticut Coast, 1720–1840* [New Haven, Conn.: New Haven Colony Historical Society, 1977], p. 73.)

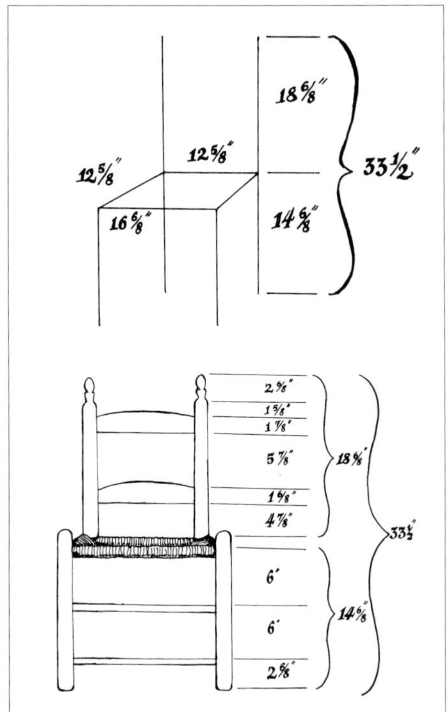

Figure 16 Dimensional diagram of the chair illustrated in fig. 15. (Courtesy, New Haven Colony Historical Society; reproduced from an illustration in Robert F. Trent, *Hearts and Crowns: Folk Chairs of the Connecticut Coast, 1720–1840* [New Haven, Conn.: New Haven Colony Historical Society, 1977], p. 73.)

predicament into high relief. Mannerism may be the ultimate test case for modern connoisseurship, because like connoisseurship itself (the discipline of knowing), it is recursive: as art historian John Shearman famously put it, it is the "stylish style."[13]

Trent himself has shown an acute sensitivity to this methodological problem of intentionality, and indeed, it motivated his seminal study on vernacular chairs from Connecticut, *Hearts and Crowns.* Most unusually for a work of American decorative art history, Trent's book began with a methodological preface centered on the classic text *The Life of Forms in Art* by medieval art historian Henri Focillon (1881–1943). Focusing directly on the question of stylistic transmission, Trent wrote, "Focillon posited a spontaneous interaction of and mutual interdependence between forms and materials. This interdependence suggests that a form worked in one material is not the same when worked in another; it is transformed. Knowledge of technique is one way of lending the art historian a sort of objectivity, since it allows him to reconstruct the artistic process." This search for "objectivity" led Trent to apply to seating furniture Henry Glassie's technique for examining vernacular architecture through mathematical models. Just as Glassie had mined the folk housing of Virginia and found unexpectedly rich systems of composition, Trent argued that rural Connecticut chairs were constructed using modular units of measure (figs. 15, 16). Of course, the presence of mathematical systems is no proof of properly artistic intention—it could merely indicate a turner's use of pattern sticks—but even so, it is not hard to see why the hidden structural logic of a chair appealed to Trent. "One has to respect the creative ability of the old-time turners," he wrote. "They were *thinking,* not merely reacting." This search for the active mind of the craftsman is what impelled Trent to use the term "mannerism" in his explication of seventeenth-century furniture. Just as Manca considers early American furniture to lack a high degree of self-consciousness, Trent is looking for its manifestations.[14]

To be sure, Trent has never argued that the craftsmen who made mannerist furniture intended their products to be "witty" per se. As he noted in *New England Begins,* "the joiners of New England almost without question worked on the basis of set formulas repeated by rote; the actual designing had taken place one or two generations previously in much more elevated circumstances." Initially, this concession seems to conflict with Trent's other statements about mannerism, as when he writes that the same joiners "were breaking the rules in a deliberate, not an inadvertent, way." This contradiction can be resolved, however, if we understand Trent as saying that the quality of mannerist self-consciousness is not literally a matter of a given maker's attitude. It is, rather, inscribed into the very bones of the style. These joiners were not chuckling ironically to themselves in their shops, but they were upholding period notions of good design, in which classical orders and ornament were seen as a system defined not by constancy, as we now think of it, but by and through constant variation. This is self-consciousness, perhaps, but self-consciousness of a very particular sort. It is the crucial subtlety that cannot be captured in Manca's persuasively commonsensical understanding of style, which sees in American furniture distillation, diffusion, simplicity, and even "naïve charm," but not "crisis, alienation, decadence, gross self-consciousness, or a clever rebellion against a norm." In taking the apparent simplicity of much American furniture at face value, Manca shuts out the interpretative possibilities that lie just beneath its surfaces.[15]

To make the case for mannerism in American furniture, we must adopt a broader methodological principle than simple categorization: style must be seen simultaneously as embodied physically within a single artifact and as an intangible cluster of ideas, which travel on many registers above and outside individual shop practice. Forman made this point with charming concision in his unpublished notes at Winterthur: "Each social group from the largest (Western civilization) to the smallest (you and your spouse) defines the rightness of what you perceive, especially in the matter of proportion and other ordered relationships spatial, temporal and harmonic." Understanding style in this telescopic fashion means responding to Forman's call for a modernized connoisseurship, in which period aesthetics are considered in all their abstract global complexity but also tested against every aspect of what a particular joiner's design sensibility could have been (and vice versa). Ultimately this is the best way of settling the debate about mannerism in American furniture: not by appealing to prevailing norms of nomenclature, nor by establishing a firmly bounded stylistic category, but instead by trying to understand mannerism, all at once, as a style and as a complete view of the world.[16]

All the World's a Stage: The Theatricality of Anglo-American Furniture

In any attempt to establish a useful understanding of New England's mid-seventeenth-century furniture, it makes sense to start in Old England in the Jacobean period, for it was in that place and time that the salient designs, and indeed many of the joiners themselves, originated. This is the half century circumscribed by Shakespeare's comedy *As You Like It* (ca. 1598–1600), which declared "All the world's a stage / and all the men and women merely players," and Thomas Hobbes's 1651 political treatise *Leviathan,* in which he penned the legalistic lines "a *Person,* is the same that an *Actor* is, both on the Stage and in common Conversation; and to *Personate,* is to *Act,* or *Represent,* himselfe, or an other; and he that acteth another, is said to beare his Person, or act in his name." As both Shakespeare's and Hobbes's words attest, the British worldview of the time was characterized by extreme self-consciousness. This was not, admittedly, the self-consciousness of Italian theorists such as Zuccari, which circulated around problems of representation and the divine. English artistic preoccupations were no less abstract, but in a different key: appropriately for a Protestant culture, they centered on the more secular problem of framing political power. More particularly, it might be said that the distinctively British version of mannerism took the form that was to concern Hobbes so greatly: a staging of power through the metaphor of theater. It is this developed but in some ways parochial structure of mannerist thought that informs Anglo-American furniture of the early seventeenth century.[17]

Let us begin at the end of the trail, with a table made in Boston during the third quarter of the seventeenth century, well after its basic design had been developed in London (fig. 17). It is an object of somewhat uncertain purpose. Its hinged-leaf top encourages the historian to see it as a mobile domestic form intended for serving food, an ancestor of eighteenth-century breakfast, card, and tea tables. Its British antecedents, also normally fitted with folding tops, have been called "credence tables" since at least the nineteenth century, suggesting that they were placed on the south side of a

Figure 17 Folding table, Boston, Massachusetts, 1650–1680. Black walnut, red oak, maple, and cedrela with oak and white pine. H. 28½", W. 28¾", D. 28¾" (open). (Chipstone Foundation; photo, Gavin Ashworth.)

church altar to hold sacramental equipment for the Mass. Victor Chinnery, however, has dismissed the term "credence table" as a nineteenth-century antiquarian fantasy. He convincingly argues that the form would have been called a "livery table" or "cubberd table" and used to dispense food and wine to the members of a household. Though it is not inconceivable that these forms may have seen some ecclesiastical use, the design was almost certainly intended for a domestic context.[18]

Sometimes these British tables are three-legged and have a triangular base, but the majority of them are, like the Boston example, structured around a trapezoidal core with a drawer in the front rail (figs. 18, 19). Though such tables may have been covered with cloth extending to the floor on ceremo-

Figure 18 Folding table, England, 1600–1650. Oak. Dimensions not recorded. (Private collectoin; photo, Peter Frahm.)

Figure 19 Folding table, England, 1600–1650. Oak. Dimensions not recorded. (Courtesy, William H. Stokes.)

nial occasions, it is obvious that they were sometimes left uncovered, for their ornament is often impressive. The Boston table features four notable and highly charged pieces of decoration: banding around the turned legs; maple bosses on the upper and lower stiles; glyphs made of imported cedrela at the angles of the rails; and, most strikingly, vestigial strapwork on the integral skirt brackets (figs. 20, 21). These features, particularly the first and last, place the table in a stylistic continuum with European design—the strapwork drawn from Flemish pattern books, furniture, metalwork, and architecture, and the banded legs an adaptation of de l'Orme's "French Order" (fig. 22). De l'Orme proposed this new classical order in his 1561 *Nouvelles inventions pour bien bastir et à petits frais* as a consciously nationalistic gesture in his departing from classicism as a way of showing France's importance;

the appearance of this feature approximately a century later in an English colonial context is an unusually powerful reminder of the interconnected nature of seventeenth-century European design. In short, if there is mannerist furniture from New England, then this table is surely it.[19]

Figure 21 Detail showing a carved bracket, bosses, and glyphs on the table illustrated in fig. 17. (Photo, Gavin Ashworth.)

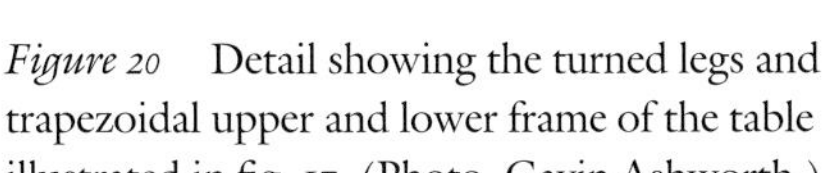

Figure 20 Detail showing the turned legs and trapezoidal upper and lower frame of the table illustrated in fig. 17. (Photo, Gavin Ashworth.)

Figure 22 Plate 120 verso in Philibert de l'Orme, *Le premier tome de l'architecture,* 1568. (Courtesy, Department of Printing and Graphic Arts, Houghton Library, Harvard College Library.)

Figure 23 Detail showing the pentagonal leg stiles of the table illustrated in fig. 17. (Photo, Gavin Ashworth.)

Figure 24 Cupboard, England, ca. 1540. Oak. Dimensions not recorded. (Private collection.) This remarkable early cupboard has a set-back upper section with "secret" sliding panels.

Yet, if we are to take up Manca's challenge and describe this table as mannerist in more than a semantic sense, such instances of stylistic quotation are hardly sufficient. For the concept of mannerism to prove its worth for the interpretation of a table like this one, the object must be shown to be part of a worldview that itself demands to be called mannerist. To make this case, we might redirect our attention from the table's ornament to its basic form: that of a two-tiered trapezoid. This structure, hardly an obvious choice for a circular folding table, necessitated the fashioning of pentagonal blocks integral with the turned legs, on either side of the central shaped skirt (fig. 23). Nor is the conceit confined to folding tables: similar trapezoidal projections, and corresponding angular complexities of construction, are echoed in much Elizabethan and Jacobean design: cabinets, court cupboards, and even the exterior window bays of buildings all feature the same projecting form, with sides canted between thirty and forty-five degrees to the frontal plane (figs. 24, 25). Why would joiners in

Figure 25 House front, London, ca. 1600. Oak and leaded glass. (Courtesy, Victoria & Albert Museum.)

London and Boston go to the trouble of creating this strange geometry? The effect of this leitmotif is fundamentally presentational, and it might even be seen as implicitly pictorial, in that it conveys a sense of spatial recession. One is struck, looking at the Boston folding table, that it was made exactly at the time that the British learned of perspective—that is, artificial space. During the Tudor and Stuart eras, perspective was understood as a feature of classical learning no less important than the architectural orders themselves; the Elizabethan magus John Dee described it in 1570 as "an Art Mathematicall, which demonstrateth the maner, and properties, of all Radiations Direct, Broken, and Reflected . . . it reacheth so farre, as the world is wyde."[20]

While it might seem fanciful to connect a New England table with abstract Italian geometric principles, the leap is not as far as it might at first appear. Many other pieces of seventeenth-century furniture, both Continental and

Figure 26 Chest, England, ca. 1680. Oak, bone, and mother-of-pearl inlay with unidentified secondary wood. H. 31", W. 67", D. 26¾". (Courtesy, Sotheby's Olympia, London.)

British, feature explicit instances of perspective images, sometimes simply incised and at other times carved or inlaid (fig. 26). In British church pulpits, the trapezoidal plan we have seen on other pieces of furniture is sometimes combined with a summary perspectival scene, suggesting a connection between literal and pictorial spatial recession (fig. 27). Furthermore, architectural and ornamental pattern books of the period, which were increasingly important sources for joiners and artisanal builders, often included lengthy treatises on the subject of perspective. The most important and influential of these was the second book of Serlio's *Tutte l'opere d'archittetura et prospetiva,* translated and printed in London in 1611. Other volumes that brought Continental decorative motifs to London were primarily treatises on perspective and served as pattern books only incidentally (fig. 28). We know, too, that Joseph Moxon's *Mechanick Exercises* (London,

Figure 27 Pulpit, Lincolnshire, England, 1646. Oak. (Courtesy, St. Margaret's Church, Bucknall, and Reverend Simon Witcombe.)

Figure 28 Plate 30 in Hans Vredeman de Vries, *La perspective* (1604–5; reprint, Amsterdam, 1629). (Courtesy, University of Madison–Wisconsin Library, Special Collections.)

1678) recommended treatises on proper perspective by Serlio, Vincenzo Scamozzi (1548–1616), and Samuel Marolois (1572–1627) for study by craftsmen. As might be expected in perspective treatises, which are filled with lines converging on vanishing points, these books feature one trapezoidal space after another. Most depict exterior architectural scenes, but occasionally they depict rooms populated with furniture—a notable example being Jean du Brueil's *La perspective pratique* (1642–1649, published in English in 1672), in which cupboards, chairs, and tables are pressed into the matrix of illusionary recession (fig. 29).[21]

As has been suggested, theater was a powerful underlying metaphor for early-seventeenth century British culture, and it is to the theater, and particularly to stage design, that one must look for the connective tissue

Figure 29 Jean du Brueil, *La perspective pratique,* London, ca. 1645. Engraving. (Reproduced by permission of the Huntington Library, San Marino, California.) This treatise was initially published between 1642 and 1649.

between the comparatively new science of perspective and the established trade of joinery. Like perspective, theatrical set design was an Italian invention that featured prominently in printed source books of the period. Writers who specifically addressed the subject included Italians Serlio, Scamozzi, Guido Ubaldi, and Nicola Sabbatini, as well as such northern European authorities as Dietterlin, Vredeman de Vries, and French engineer Salomon de Caus; all presented perspective, architecture, and scenography as interpenetrating and overlapping disciplines. The great interpreter of this body of thought in England was the architect Inigo Jones, whose early work consisted, not of the classically correct buildings for which he is so justly famous, but courtly masque designs in the mannerist style. Jones identified perspective as the single tool in the architect's intellectual arsenal that permitted him to invent successful new designs, noting in his copy of Daniello Barbaro's 1559 *La pratica della perspectiva:* "great creditte to the Architecte whe[n] beinge forced to goe fro[m] the simitri nothing is taken fro[m] the beauti of the aspecte. therfor prospective is nessesary." His work for the theater served as a kind of laboratory for experimentation with the new system, and not coincidentally the trapezoidal leitmotif also appears repeatedly in his masque designs (fig. 30).[22]

Figure 30 Inigo Jones, design for the House of Fame, from the *Masque of Queens,* performed in 1609. (Courtesy, Chatsworth House.)

Like Stephen Harrison's triumphal arches of 1604, Inigo Jones's contemporaneous masque designs would have been a major undertaking for the elite woodworkers of early seventeenth-century London. Though built elements from these ephemeral constructions do not survive, we know that they were made largely of wood and sometimes painted, much like the case furniture and interior joinery of the period. Serlio noted that the foreshortened architecture of a stage set should be "built by Carpenters or Masons, skilful in Perspective Worke," and such seems to have been the case in England. As early as 1573 Elizabethan artisans were described in a document recording the responsibilities of the office of revels:

> The connynge of the office resteth in skill of devise, in understandinge of hystories, in iugement of comedies, tragedyes and shewes, in sight of perspective and architecture, some smacke of geometrye and other thinges wherefore the best helpe is for the officers to make good choyce of cunynge artificers severally accordinge to their best qualitie, and for one man to allowe of an other mans invencion as it is worthie.

Whether this was learned wishful thinking, rather than an accurate description of the capabilities of the office's craftsmen, might be doubted, but by the time of the Stuart court there is ample proof that English artisans had mastered the construction of three-dimensional perspective scenes. So much is clear not only from the many drawings of the masque sets themselves (many of them covered with carpenter's grid lines to ensure accurate translation into three dimensions) but also from period eyewitnesses. For example, Venetian chaplain Orazio Busino, visiting London in 1618 in an ambassadorial company, commented on the decorations for the masque *Pleasure Reconciled to Virtue* (1618): "Whilst waiting for the King we amused ourselves admiring the decorations and beauty of the house, with its two orders of columns, one above the other, their distance from the wall equalling the breadth of the passage, that of the second row being upheld by Doric pillars, while above these rise Ionic columns supporting the roof. The whole is of wood, including even the shafts, which are carved and gilt with much skill."[23]

Finally, we have it on the authority of no less a figure than Ben Jonson, who frequently collaborated with Jones in the creation of the *Gesamtkunstwerk* that was the Stuart masque, that woodworkers were involved in the production of masque sets. Famously, the partnership between these two giants of English culture ended in an acrimonious feud, leading Jonson to pen his poisonous "Expostulation with Inigo Jones" in 1611:

> You are the spectacles of state, 'tis true,
> Court-hieroglyphics, and all arts afford
> In the mere perspective of an inch-board;
> You ask no more than certain politic eyes,
> Eyes that can pierce into the mysteries
> Of many colours, read them, and reveal
> Mythology, there painted on slit deal.
> Or to make boards to speak! there is a task
> Painting and carpentry are the soul of masque.

Jonson refers here to the flat recessional image that formed the backdrop of the masque set (an "inch-board" of "slit deal"). But in fact, as is suggested by his mention of "carpentry," the backdrop was only the simplest element in a masque stage. Unlike a modern theatrical presentation, a masque lacked a defined demarcation between the fictional space and the space of the audience. It was a transitional phenomenon in the history of theatrical design, lying between the open, ancient theater-in-the-round, in which the stage projects into the space of the audience, and the modern closed form in which a proscenium frames the action. The key zone in a masque was the "dancing place" in front of the stage. Here spectators became participants, as courtiers moved on to the stage itself to dance for the pleasure of the monarch. The wooden arch or "ornament" served simultaneously as a pictorial frame for the perspectival "stage picture" to the rear and a physical frame for this live spectacle of dance and playacting. One such frame, designed for Jones's 1632 production *Albion's Triumph,* was described in the published text of the masque:

> The first thing that presented itself to the eye, was the Ornament that went about the Scene: in the middest of which was placed a great Armes of the Kings, with Angels holding an Emperiall Crowne, from which hung a Drapery, of crimson Velvet, fringed with Gold, tact in severall knotts, that on each-side, with many folds, was wound about a Pillaster . . . and at the foot of the pilasters, on each side, stood two Women, the one young, in a watchet Robe looking upwards, and on her head, a paire of Compasses of gold, the poynts standing towards Heaven: the other more ancient, and of a venerable aspect, appareled in tawney, looking downewards; in the one hand a long ruler and in the other, a great paire of iron Compasses, one Poynt whereof, stood on the ground, and the other touched part of the ruler. Above their heads, were fixt, compartiments of a new composition, and in that over the first, was written Theorica, and over the second Practica, shewing that [in] these two, all works of Architecture, and Inginiring have their perfection.

Figure 31 Inigo Jones, set design for the masque *Albion's Triumph*, 1632. (Courtesy, Courtauld Institute of Art.)

Figure 32 Cupboard, Boston, Massachusetts, 1670–1680. Oak, maple, cedar, and walnut with oak and white pine. H. 55⅝", W. 49½", D. 21¾". (Chipstone Foundation; photo, Gavin Ashworth.)

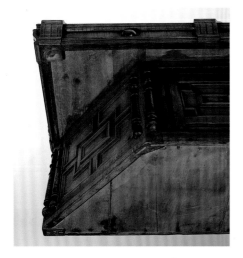

Figure 33 Detail showing the underside of the upper section of the cupboard illustrated in fig. 32. (Photo, Gavin Ashworth.)

The construction of such an elaborate allegorical affair would have necessitated the contribution not only of joiners but also of textile purveyors, painters, and carvers—an artisanal community that is itself represented by the symbolic statue of "venerable" Practica with her twin compasses, a device that was also a central feature in the coat of arms granted to the Worshipful Company of Joiners and Ceilers of London in 1571 (fig. 31).[24]

Returning to the folding table (fig. 17), we might make the observation that the overall shape of the design is not unlike that of a masque stage. It has framing columns, a decorated skirt suggesting the swags of fabric atop a proscenium arch, and, as we have seen, the sense of dramatic recession that, in an actual masque, would have been achieved using an architectural backdrop. This metaphorical reading of the table would take on additional persuasiveness were we to see it set with silver, ceramic, and textile accoutrements, as it might have originally been, for this would have created a massed decorative effect like that of a masque stage populated with costumed dancers. The same comparison might be made with even greater force with reference to the most impressive of mannerist furniture forms made in America, the domestic cupboard (fig. 32). Though numerous renditions of this form survive from elsewhere in Massachusetts (see fig. 3) and Connecticut, only one example survives from the Boston shop tradition that made the table. Like the table, the cupboard is based closely on London precedents (figs. 32, 34). Its upper "stage" is indeed like a miniature theatrical set, with columns at each side and the now-familiar recessional trapezoidal

Figure 34 Cupboard, Yorkshire, England, first half of the seventeenth century. Oak. H. 53", W. 52½", D. 22". (Courtesy, Huntington Antiques, Stow on the Wold, Gloucestershire, England.)

layout reminiscent of scenographic renderings in perspective. Like the folding table, such cupboards present something of a conundrum in terms of nomenclature. In period New England accounts they are described as "cant cupboards," which indicates that in their own time their backward-raking panels were thought to be their defining feature. Today they are most commonly called "court cupboards," which is also a period term (Shakespeare used it, among others), but which may have specifically designated open storage units of two or more shelves, not examples featuring an enclosed compartment. The term "court cupboard" implies diffusion from some palatial form, but it has also been seen as an English borrowing of a French term for a cupboard (or *buffet*) that was short *(court)* in comparison to earlier, more massive designs.[25]

Whether or not this etymology is accurate, it is possible that the precedents for such cupboards were indeed much larger—perhaps "stage cupboards" used at court in the sixteenth century. An entry in the Declared Accounts for the Royal Works in the year 1581/1582 records payments for construction in the new Whitehall Banqueting House that include "frayminge of hallpaces and two stage Cuburdes with railes." This Banqueting House, one of several precursors to Inigo Jones's famous building of 1622, was a curious temporary structure with painted canvas walls, a roof held up on large posts, and lavish interior woodwork including a full stage and danc-

Figure 35 Drawing of a stage cupboard, Flemish, 1549. (Courtesy, Warburg Institute and Cadland House, Fawley, Southampton.)

ing floor. It was used mainly for the entertainment of Queen Elizabeth, and masques were repeatedly staged inside the space. The stage cupboards themselves were large wooden constructions for the display of plate, like an oversize nineteenth-century étagère. The form was made yet more monumental by setting it on a "hallpace," from the French *haut pas,* a raised floor or dais. Like the arches made for civic pageants and the sets for masques themselves, the stage cupboard is a form that does not survive to the present day but suggests a lost connection between the worlds of architecture, courtly theater, and joinery. Also like architecture and theatrical set design, the stage cupboard was an import from the Continent. The best-known example dates from 1549, when the Spanish prince (who, six years later, would become King Philip II) visited the town of Binche in the Netherlands. There he was fêted at an entertainment featuring a stage cupboard three storeys high, fitted with a canopy supported by two large Doric columns (fig. 35). The following year Philip reached Antwerp, where he was greeted by triumphal arches of Serlian design, similar to those erected in London five decades later.[26]

Conclusion

What are we to make of this suggestive web of connections, and how might they enrich the concept of mannerism as a term of explication for early American furniture? First, connecting furniture to perspective, architecture, and stage design provides an escape from the arbitrary semantics of stylistic nomenclature. In describing the complex field of textual, pictorial, and artifactual novelty at this time as "mannerist," and seeing furniture as inseparable from (rather than derivative of) this field, we can come to grips with the element in the furniture that was most transformative. For mannerism was not just a new language of ornament—though it was that—nor was it really a license to depart willfully from classical form. Though it would be a mistake to think, as Manca seems to, that Anglo-American joiners were not highly literate in classical design, neither does it make sense to define mannerism as a model of liberation from academic propriety, because in Anglo-American culture at this time classicism was not perceived as a rigid canon in the first place. Indeed, in the formal drama of mannerism, classical motifs played a leading role, but not an exclusive one. Strapwork itself is a nonclassical innovation, and many of the features that most strongly characterize mannerist furniture are matters of overall structure rather than decoration. The reason that these forms should be designated as mannerist is not only because of their relation to classical ornament, then, but because they were part of a shift in the nature of design itself. As theater historian John Orrell has written, "a stage design is—at least potentially—a sort of metascene, or perspective of a perspective," and the same could be said of mannerist furniture: it is, at least potentially, metafurniture, which dramatically announces itself as performing a role in its environment. It holds fast to a primary artistic principle of its day, aptly summarized by art historian Mary Ann Caws: "mannerist gesture precisely points to its own pointing." This is emphatically not the same as saying that mannerist furniture drew attention to itself—that is, after all, a feature of highly decorated furniture in any period. Mannerist furniture is distinctive, not for its level of ornament, but in the nature of its ornamental organization. Mannerist American furniture may look deceptively simple in comparison to Continental precedents. But it is still decorated, and its decoration is thematized around its own purpose as decoration. Strapwork boldly announces its own purpose as a framing element; swollen and exaggerated columns, pediments, and moldings are so assertive that they threaten to overwhelm the forms they articulate; perspective effects meet and order the gaze through an aggressively artificial system of forms. Mannerist self-consciousness did take place in America—not at the level of individual workmen's attitudes, but at the level of furniture's participation in a broader culture of conspicuous demonstration.[27]

Historian of American art Sally Promey has recently written of just this sort of demonstration throughout seventeenth-century New England culture as both a literal and a figurative "framing." Promey focuses on Puritan theology, in which particular stress was laid on "the ability to see the self 'in frame' (and especially 'in heavenly frame')," and thus her emphasis is on gravestones, paintings, and theological writings (fig. 36). Yet the habit of

Figure 36 Gravestone of Thomas Call Jr., Malden, Massachusetts, 1678. (Courtesy, American Antiquarian Society, Farber Collection.)

constructing truth, power, and art through the act of framing was hardly confined to the Puritan fringe of Anglo-American culture. The masque itself has been analyzed, in recent scholarship, as a framing of the monarch's axis of vision—the royal vantage, in the typical English masque, being the only one that was perfectly aligned with the perspectival vanishing point of the scene. Shakespeare acknowledged the importance of this gaze in his prologue to *Henry V* (ca. 1599):

> O For a Muse of Fire, that would ascend
> The brightest Heaven of Invention:
> A Kingdome for a Stage, Princes to Act,
> And Monarchs to behold the swelling Scene.

As Stephen Orgel has argued, the perspectival stage can even be seen politically, as an attempt to shore up the security of the court hierarchy during a period of declension. In the Stuart era, as the king's authority became ever

Figure 37 *The Execution of Charles I,* England, 1649. Oil on panel. (Collection of Lord Dalmeny, on loan to the Scottish National Portrait Gallery.)

more tenuous, court masques became ever more elaborate, expensive, and exaggerated in their assertion of royal authority. This story comes to an ironic end, as Samuel J. Edgerton has persuasively argued, in the execution of Charles I (fig. 37). By putting the monarch to death, his enemies effectively asserted that "no man had divine right to the center of the universe," yet in the execution itself they participated in the long-standing tradition of mannerist theatricality and its "emphasis on personification and visual impression." Frank Kermode notes that the selection of the Banqueting House as the site of Charles's execution, where so many masques had taken place, meant that the spectacle hardly had to travel from its accustomed "scaffold" on the stage to that erected for the beheading, with the king remaining (in Andrew Marvell's words) "the royal actor."[28]

Today, a world in which the greatest political event of a lifetime was experienced as theater may seem strangely familiar—a forerunner, perhaps, of our own era of postmodern self-regard. Arnold Hauser, a German art historian who did much to advance the notion of mannerism in the fine arts, might have agreed with such a characterization. He wrote, "Mannerism, which discovered the spontaneity of the mind and recognized art as an autonomous creative activity, developed, in accordance with the spirit of that discovery, the totally new idea of fictitious space." For Hauser, mannerist art opened the door to that most modern way of thinking about representational art: in terms of a dynamic relationship between "the space within and the space without." According to this understanding, the artificiality of depicted space not only was acknowledged by mannerist artists but was transformed by them into an aesthetic in its own right. Even when furniture does not literally resemble a theater set or a strapwork-rich print

Figure 38 Great chair attributed to Thomas Dennis, Ipswich, Massachusetts, ca. 1670. Oak. H. 45", W. 25¾", D. 17½". (Courtesy, Peabody Essex Museum; photo, Gavin Ashworth.)

Figure 39 Friedrich Unteutsch, design for a cartouche illustrated on pl. 50 in *Neues Zieratenbuch den Schreinern Tischlern ofern Küstlern und Bildhauer sehr dienstlich,* 1640–1650. (Courtesy, Victoria & Albert Museum.)

source, it can be quite profitable to see it in these terms. Thus, it is easy to claim the famous Ipswich joined chair illustrated in figure 38 as a presentational mannerist object (pace Manca, who views it as "a rich but not strained application of Renaissance motifs"). Its horizontal strapwork banding above the panel, columnar supports, trapezoidal plan, finials, and figural stile ornaments all suggest connections to theatrical stages, architectural and book frontispieces, or printed cartouches (fig. 39). Its surmounting crest possesses an explosive architectural character and, as a crowning touch to the composition, rivals the gable on a Robert Smythson country house (fig. 40). Yet its underlying mannerist handling of space is not substantially different from that of the chair shown in figures 41 and 42, which

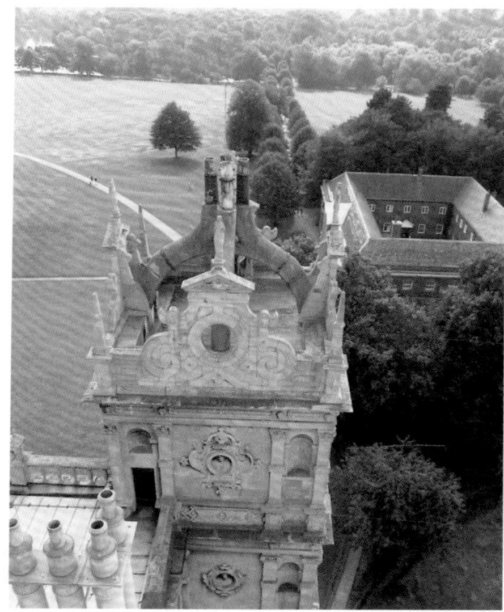

Figure 40 Entrance front gable, Wollaton Hall, Nottinghamshire, 1580–1588.

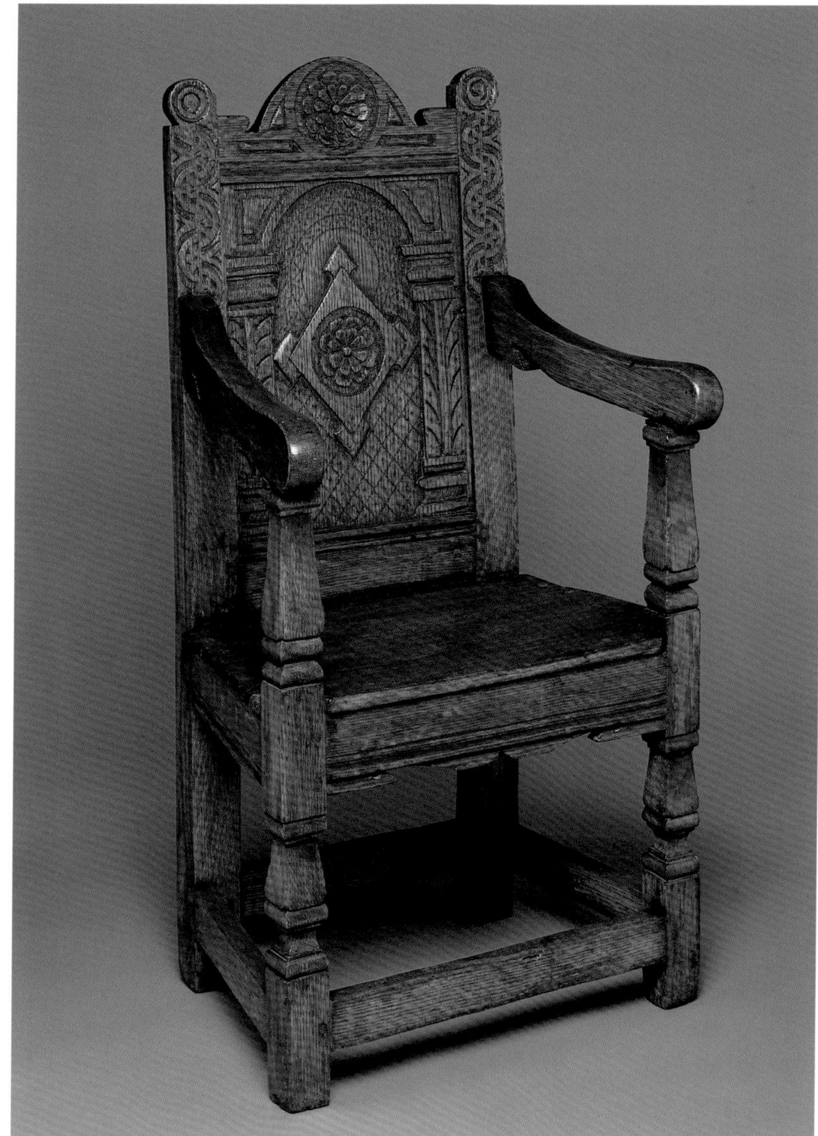

Figure 41 Great chair, probably Middletown, Connecticut, second half of the seventeenth century. Red oak. H. 44¼", W. 22½", D. 19½". (Chipstone Foundation; photo, John R. Glembin.)

Figure 42 Detail of the back of the chair illustrated in fig. 41.

Figure 43 Armchair, Shrewsbury, England, 1662. Oak. Dimensions not recorded. (Reproduced from Victor Chinnery, *Oak Furniture: The British Tradition* [Suffolk, Eng.: Antique Collectors' Club, 1979], fig. 2.11.) Richard Ellis made this chair for the Shrewsbury Drapers' Company.

Figure 44 Armchair, French, sixteenth century. Walnut. H. 55⅜", W. 24⅝", D. 16½". (Courtesy, Worcester Art Museum, Worcester, Massachusetts.)

seems at first a poor cousin: unlovely, and lacking the obvious ornamental cues of the style. Yet even in this artifact, one can see the traces of mannerist theatricality. Its framing columnar legs and its open stance, which is geometrically identical to the Ipswich example, act to funnel compositional force toward the open archway that decorates the back. That archway is lightly incised to suggest a checkerboard floor below and a vault above—the image is naïvely executed, to be sure, but nonetheless manages to convey the sense of an illusionary space. For all its apparent roughness, this chair plays its own demonstrative role no less dramatically than the Ipswich chair. Even if it is not a mannerist masterpiece, it should be seen on a continuum with objects grander than itself—not only stylistically, but conceptually as well (figs. 43, 44). Clearly, there are limits to the degree of influence that mannerism had on New England furniture, which was a complicated blend of new Continental ideas, lingering medievalisms, and technological determination, and it would also be foolhardy to claim that furniture can be "about" representational space to the same extent as a painting or even a theatrical design. But it would be equally inadvisable to deny, prima facie, that provincial New England furniture was in no way in dialogue with its own art historical period. The connections are more than stylistic. The mannerist masque includes its "audience" within itself, enforcing a ratification of courtly order through the structure of the king's gaze. A mannerist civic pageant transforms a cityscape into a teeming affirmation of royalty through the device of a giant theater flat. A mannerist painting, by acknowledging its artificiality, signals the vanity of its own attempt to represent the divine. Mannerist furniture, too, is structured around and through the person looking at it, and it, too, represents an authority that is not negotiable. It is no coincidence that its most typical forms play a dominant role in the home: a court cupboard or a serving table to be laid with silver, or a great chair meant to enthrone the family patriarch. These pieces of furniture were not commodities in the modern sense. They were valuable, of course, and they were part of a system of conspicuous consumption. But like all mannerist art, they also operated above and outside that system. They were premised on the conceit that it was in the theater of power that power itself was made real.[29]

To take Shakespeare's words as a guide one last time, one might reflect on the following exchange from *As You Like It*:

> TOUCHSTONE: Why, if thou never wast at court, thou never sawest good manners; if thou never sawest good manners, then thy manners must be wicked; and wickedness is sin, and sin is damnation. Thou art in a parlous state, shepherd.
>
> CORIN: Not a whit, Touchstone: those that are good manners at the court are as ridiculous in the country as the behavior of the country is most mockable at the court. You told me you salute not at the court, but you kiss your hands: that courtesy would be uncleanly, if courtiers were shepherds.

As always, Shakespeare proves with stunning force that people in the distant past were as capable of self-consciousness just as sophisticated as that of today's knowing postmoderns. At the end of the day, furniture is furniture, not Shakespeare, and one must not expect a richness of content that the medium cannot, by its very nature, possess. (This, too, is an idea that may seem proper to modern formalism but has its roots in a genre of Renaissance and mannerist writing on art called *paragone,* which compared the virtues of one medium against another.) As often, Benno Forman had a provocatively counterintuitive view on this point. "The student of decorative arts history is in a much more enviable position than the student of painting," he wrote, "for objects—even anonymous ones—are often complexly articulated fabrications, the various elements of which are subject to objective analysis." Here Forman points to the signal virtue of furniture as a historical text. It may be difficult, even impossible, to track with absolute precision the process by which the makers of a chair, table, or cupboard absorbed ideas, and similarly, the furniture may yield the traces of those ideas only with difficulty. But it is furniture's very reticence that makes it so compelling: it tends to speak of matters that are deeply embedded in the culture that produced it. Making the case that early American furniture is mannerist requires that historians pick their way back along a torturous chain of cultural influence, compression, and distillation. And in a sense, the messy incompleteness of such a narrative is a more revealing art historical picture than even the most brilliant exegesis of a single painting or masque. In this respect furniture is like the provinces (or the colonies) themselves—which as Shakespeare suggests, have manners every bit as self-conscious as those observed in the city, if one only knows to look for them. The challenge for "connoisseurs" today is the same as it was for Forman: to write furniture history in terms of the mentality of the period maker, remembering that such reconstruction will never be definitive or complete. Forman once noted that "each generation must rewrite history in its own image." And history of any kind, at its best, is always a matter of enlarging the possibilities of interpretation, not closing them down. To the joiners of New England, we owe nothing less.[30]

ACKNOWLEDGMENTS The author would like to thank Joseph Manca for his provocation and subsequent forbearance. Additional thanks are owed to Luke Beckerdite, Victor Chinnery, Edward S. Cooke Jr., Sarah Fayen, Peter Follansbee, Brock Jobe, Ethan Lasser, Alan Miller, Jonathan Prown, Frederick Vogel III, Alicia Volk, Philip Zimmerman, and particularly to Robert F. Trent.

1. A complete bibliography of Forman's published writings can be found in *New England Furniture: Essays in Memory of Benno M. Forman,* edited by Brock W. Jobe (Boston: Society for the Preservation of New England Antiquities, 1987), pp. xv–xvi. Benno M. Forman, *American Seating Furniture, 1630–1730: An Interpretive Catalogue*, edited by Robert F. Trent and Robert Blair St. George (New York: W. W. Norton, 1988), pp. 8, xxiv.

2. Benno M. Forman, "Delaware Valley 'Crookt Foot' and Slat-Back Chairs: The Fussell-Savery Connection," *Winterthur Portfolio* 15, no. 1 (spring 1980): 41–64, at 49; Albert Sack, *The New Fine Points of Furniture, Early American: Good, Better, Best, Superior, Masterpiece* (New York: Crown Publishers, 1993).

3. Joseph Manca, "A Matter of Style: The Question of Mannerism in Seventeenth-Century American Furniture," *Winterthur Portfolio* 38, no. 1 (2003): 1–36, at 1, 5, 8.

4. Calcagnini cited in John Shearman, *Mannerism* (London: Penguin Books, 1967), p. 156; Sebastiano Serlio, *Extraordinario libro di architettura* (1551), pl. 28; Erwin Panofsky, *Idea: A Concept in Art Theory,* translated by Joseph J. S. Peake (1924; reprint, New York: Harper & Row, 1960), pp. 73, 79. Manca, "A Matter of Style," p. 34.

5. Robert F. Trent, "The Concept of Mannerism" and "New England Joinery and Turning before 1700," in *New England Begins: The Seventeenth Century,* edited by Jonathan Fairbanks and Robert Trent, 3 vols. (Boston: Museum of Fine Arts, 1982), 3: 368–412, 501–10. Manca, "A Matter of Style," p. 23.

6. Trent, "The Concept of Mannerism," p. 376. For a detailed account of English borrowings from Serlio, Dietterlin, Vredeman, and de l'Orme, see Anthony Wells-Cole, *Art and Decoration in Elizabethan and Jacobean England: The Influence of Continental Prints, 1558–1625* (New Haven, Conn.: Yale University Press, 1997), pp. 15–18, 27–30, 38–40, 58–88. Wells-Cole shows

that of these figures, Serlio and Vredeman were the most significant. By comparison, the direct influence of Dietterlin and de l'Orme was negligible. Timothy Mowl, *Elizabethan and Jacobean Style* (London: Phaidon Press, 1993), p. 164; see also Benno M. Forman, "Continental Furniture Craftsmen in London," *Furniture History* 7 (1971): 94–120; Neil Kamil, *Fortress of the Soul: Violence, Metaphysics, and Material Life in the Huguenots' New World, 1517–1751* (Baltimore: Johns Hopkins University Press, 2005), chap. 13, passim. Shakespeare's lines are as follows: "Go, write it in a martial hand; be curst and brief; / it is no matter how witty, so it be eloquent and fun / of invention: taunt him with the licence of ink: / if thou thou'st him some thrice, it shall not be / amiss; and as many lies as will lie in thy sheet of / paper, although the sheet were big enough for the / bed of Ware in England, set 'em down: go, about it." *Twelfth Night* (ca. 1601), act 3, scene 2.

7. Thomas Dekker, in a separately published text on the entry festivities, noted that the work crew for the entertainment included eighty joiners, sixty carpenters, six turners, and other artificers, "over whom Stephen Harrison Joyner was appointed chiefe; who was the sole Inventor of the Architecture, and from whome all directions, for so much as belonged to Carving, Joyning, Molding, and all other worke in those five Pageants of the Citie (Paynting excepted) were set downe." Dekker further described "The magnificent entertainment given to King Iames, Queene Anne his wife, and Henry Frederick the Prince, uppon the day of his Maiesties tryumphant passage (from the Tower) through his honourable cittie (and chamber) of London, being the 15. of March. 1603, As well by the English as by the strangers: with the speeches and songs, delivered in the severall pageants." Other civic pageants included the annual lord mayor's inauguration in London and processionals used to entertain royalty on their progresses around England. See *Jacobean Civic Pageants,* edited by Richard Dutton (Staffordshire, Eng.: Keele University Press, 1995); Dutton identifies John Grinkin as another artificer who contributed to such pageants, pp. 10, 141. Timothy Mowl and Brian Earnshaw, *Architecture without Kings: The Rise of Puritan Classicism under Cromwell* (Manchester, Eng.: Manchester University Press, 1995), p. 79. John Peacock, *The Stage Designs of Inigo Jones: The European Context* (Cambridge: Cambridge University Press, 1995), pp. 62–63. See also David Evett, *Literature and the Visual Arts in Tudor England* (Athens: University of Georgia Press, 1990), pp. 95–102. David M. Bergeron, "Pageants, Masques, and Scholarly Ideology," in *Practicing Renaissance Scholarship: Plays, Pageants, Patrons, and Politics* (Pittsburgh, Pa.: Dusquesne University Press, 2000), pp. 164–92, passim, p. 181. Many of the terms Bergeron mentions first appear in English in John Shute's *The First and Chief Grounds of Architecture* (London, 1563). Anthony Wells-Cole points to the oak and plaster hall screen at Burton Agnes, Yorkshire, as "the nearest surviving visual equivalent" of Harrison's monuments. Wells-Cole, *Art and Decoration in Elizabethan and Jacobean England*, p. 173. *Design and the Decorative Arts: Britain, 1500–1900,* edited by Michael Snodin and John Styles (London: V&A Publications, 2001), p. 84.

8. Manca, "A Matter of Style," p. 27; Horace Field and Michael Bunney, *English Domestic Architecture of the XVII and XVIII Centuries* (London: G. Bell and Sons, 1928), p. 15. Mark Girouard, who describes Smythson's architecture as "Elizabethan" rather than mannerist in style, vigorously objects to understanding the period in terms of mistranslation: "Elizabethan architecture at its best is not an undigested mixture, but a true synthesis, a style in its own right." Girouard, *Robert Smythson and the Elizabethan Country House* (New Haven, Conn.: Yale University Press, 1983), p. 162. Manca points to Malcolm Airs, *The Tudor and Jacobean Country House: A Building History* (Bridgend, Eng.: Bramley Books, 1998), as upholding a view of English architecture as a case of ineptitude rather than conscious manipulation of classical norms. David Evett also sees artisans as slowing and modifying the influx of new ideas, a process he refers to as "crafts inertia." Evett, *Literature and the Visual Arts in Tudor England,* p. 11. Manca, seeking to undercut prevailing uses of the concept of mannerism, suggests that Summerson himself had regrets about the choice of the term "artisan mannerism" by the time of his classic work's 1983 edition, but to me this seems unlikely given his continued use of the phrase. Manca, "A Matter of Style," p. 28 n. 33; John Summerson, *Architecture in Britain, 1530–1830,* (1953; rev. ed, New Haven, Conn.: Yale University Press, 1993), pp. 144ff. In any case, Summerson's locution has proved sufficiently useful to win wide currency among historians of British art and architecture, notably Elizabeth Chew, Timothy Mowl, Caroline Van Eck, and Lucy Worsley. Wendell Garrett also adopted the phrase in "The Matter of Consumer's Taste," *Winterthur Newsletter* 15, no. 3 (March–April 1969); see also William N. Hosley, "Regional Furniture/Regional Life," in *American Furniture,* edited by Luke Beckerdite (Hanover, N.H.: University Press of New England for the Chipstone Foundation, 1995), pp. 3–38, 35 n. 12.

9. Manca, "A Matter of Style," p. 27. Henri Zerner is not a recent convert to the limited view of mannerism; already in 1972 he argued against the prevailing scholarly habit, inspired by Shearman's *Mannerism* of using the term to unite disparate media within an overarching "style of civilization." Zerner, "Observations on the Use of the Concept of Mannerism," in *The Meaning of Mannerism,* edited by Franklin W. Robinson and Stephen G. Nichols Jr. (Hanover, N.H.: University Press of New England, 1972), pp. 105–19, at 109. For a detailed account of Shearman's position and Zerner's critique, see Elizabeth Cropper, introduction to Craig Hugh Smyth, *Mannerism and Maniera* (Vienna: Bibliotheca Artibus et Historiae, IRSA Verlag, 1992). Alice T. Friedman, "Did England Have a Renaissance? Classical and Anticlassical Themes in Elizabethan Culture," in *Cultural Differentiation and Cultural Identity in the Visual Arts,* edited by Susan J. Barnes and Walter S. Melion (Washington, D.C.: Center for Advanced Studies in the Visual Arts, 1989), pp. 95–111, 110 n. 3. For a wide-ranging application of the concept of mannerism to other decorative arts of the period, see J. F. Hayward, *Virtuoso Goldsmiths and the Triumph of Mannerism* (London: Sotheby Parke-Bernet, 1976); and Alain Gruber, *The History of Decorative Arts: The Renaissance and Mannerism in Europe* (New York: Abbeville Press, 1993).

10. Jonathan Prown and Richard Miller address the "only marginally rococo" style of Philadelphia furniture in "The Rococo, the Grotto, and the Philadelphia High Chest," in *American Furniture,* edited by Luke Beckerdite (Hanover, N.H.: University Press of New England for the Chipstone Foundation, 1996), pp. 105–36. For more on the inadequacy of stylistic terms to describe decorative arts in the eighteenth century, see Rémy G. Saisselin, *The Enlightenment against the Baroque: Economics and Aesthetics in the Eighteenth Century* (Berkeley: University of California Press, 1992), p. 3. Manca's concept of grammatical correctness might be further complicated by applying the work of art historian Christy Anderson, who has written a compelling analysis of Inigo Jones's classicism as a conscious effort to transform the "language" of architecture, comparable to contemporary efforts to regulate the English language itself. "Within the circle of the court," Anderson argues, "Jones's architecture was equated with the literate and the Latinate, whereas Elizabethan and Jacobean architecture was equivalent to the vernacular use of English." Christy Anderson, "Monstrous Babels: Language and Architectural Style in the English Renaissance," in *Architecture and Language: Constructing Identity in European Architecture, c. 1000–1650,* edited by George Clarke and Paul Crossley (Cambridge: Cambridge University Press, 2000), pp. 148–61, at 153. The relationship between these two competing languages—one learned but static, the other native and inventive, but parochial—is analyzed from several perspectives in *Albion's Classicism: The Visual Arts in Britain, 1550–1650,* edited by Lucy Gent (New Haven, Conn.: Paul Mellon Center Publications, 1995). See also Peter Erickson's review of *Albion's Classicism* in *Art Bulletin* 78, no. 4 (December 1996): 736–39. Erickson comments that the pressing question of method in appraising the English Renaissance is whether classicism and "Albion" (i.e., indigenous British) traditions are to be seen in "sharp contrast" or as a "hybrid mixture."

11. Manca, "A Matter of Style," pp. 27–28. Manca also implies that Anthony Wells-Cole eschews the term "mannerism" in his recent *Art and Decoration in Elizabethan and Jacobean England,* which is not the case; see, for example, pp. 58, 170. Benno M. Forman, "Axioms for Furniture Historians," Benno M. Forman Papers, box 1, Winterthur Library.

12. Arnold Hauser, *The Social History of Art,* 4 vols. (New York: Alfred A. Knopf, 1951), 2: 355–56. Zuccari was in England in the mid-1570s and painted several portraits there; he is quoted in Moshe Barasch, *Theories of Art from Plato to Winckelmann* (New York: New York University Press, 1985), p. 298. See also E. James Mundy, with the assistance of Elizabeth Ourusoff de Fernandez-Gimenez, *Renaissance into Baroque: Italian Master Drawings by the Zuccari, 1550–1600* (Milwaukee: Milwaukee Art Center, 1989); and Panofsky, *Idea,* pp. 75ff.

13. Benno M. Forman, "Axioms for Furniture Historians." Shearman, *Mannerism,* p. 19.

14. Robert F. Trent, *Hearts and Crowns: Folk Chairs of the Connecticut Coast, 1720–1840* (New Haven, Conn.: New Haven Colony Historical Society, 1977), p. 11. For a similar analysis of composition in turned chairs, see Robert F. Trent and Karin Goldstein, "Notes about New 'Tinkham' Chairs," in *American Furniture,* edited by Luke Beckerdite (Hanover, N.H.: University Press of New England for the Chipstone Foundation, 1998), pp. 215–37.

15. Trent, "New England Joinery and Turning before 1700," pp. 504, 505. Manca, "A Matter of Style," p. 36.

16. Forman, "Axioms for Furniture Historians."

17. *As You Like It,* act 2, scene 7. Thomas Hobbes, *Leviathan* (1651), pt. 1, chap. 16. As Manca points out, Shakespeare himself has in the past been called a mannerist author, notably in

John Greenwood, *Shifting Perspectives and the Stylish Style: Mannerism in Shakespeare and His Jacobean Contemporaries* (Toronto: University of Toronto Press, 1988), though this attempt to circumscribe the playwright within a stylistic category has met with some skepticism. For an important early summation of mannerism as a term in literary history, see James V. Mirollo, "The Mannered and the Mannerist in Late Renaissance Literature," in Robinson and Nichols, *The Meaning of Mannerism,* pp. 7–24.

18. Christopher Gilbert, "Oak Furniture from Yorkshire Churches," in Christopher Gilbert, *Selected Writings on Vernacular Furniture, 1966–1998* (Leeds, Eng.: Regional Furniture Society, 2001), p. 9. Victor Chinnery, *Oak Furniture: The British Tradition* (Suffolk, Eng.: Antique Collectors' Club, 1979), pp. 223, 305.

19. Hilary Ballon, "Constructions of the Bourbon State: Classical Architecture in Seventeenth-Century France," in *Cultural Differentiation and Cultural Identity in the Visual Arts,* pp. 135–48, at 136. Although de l'Orme's treatise is known to have been present in England—Thomas Tresham, Francis Willoughby, and Henry Wotton all owned copies—Anthony Wells-Cole notes that direct borrowings from his work are rare among surviving buildings. Wells-Cole, *Art and Decoration in Elizabethan and Jacobean England,* p. 38. The French order appears with great frequency in mannerist objects from the Netherlands, so the route of transmission was likely through objects rather than print.

20. John Dee, introduction to Euclid's *Elements* (London, 1570; translated by Henry Billingsley), quoted in Lily Campbell, *Scenes and Machines on the English Stage during the Renaissance: A Classical Revival* (New York: Barnes and Noble, 1921), p. 80.

21. On Serlio's reception in England, see *Sebastiano Serlio on Architecture,* translated by Vaughan Hart and Peter Hicks (New Haven, Conn.: Yale University Press, 1996), pp. xxxiii–xxxiv; and Wells-Cole, *Art and Decoration in Elizabethan and Jacobean England,* pp. 15–18. Joseph Moxon, *Mechanick Exercises; or the Doctrine of Handyworks* (London, 1678; reprint, Mendham, N.J.: Astragal Press, 1994). For du Brueil, see Simon Jervis, *Printed Furniture Designs before 1650* (Leeds, Eng.: Furniture History Society, 1974). For a discussion of seventeenth-century New England paintings, see Jonathan L. Fairbanks, "Portrait Painting in Seventeenth-Century Boston: Its History, Methods, and Materials," in *New England Begins,* pp. 413–55.

22. Peacock, *The Stage Designs of Inigo Jones,* p. 58.

23. Sebastiano Serlio, *The Book of Architecture,* translated by Robert Peake (London, 1611). On the office of revels, see Campbell, *Scenes and Machines,* pp. 104–5; the quoted passage was originally transcribed in A. Feuillerat, *Documents Relating to the Office of the Revels in the Time of Elizabeth* (Louvain: A. Uystpruyst, 1908), p. 5. Busino is quoted in Allardyce Nicoll, *Stuart Masques and the Renaissance Stage* (New York: Benjamin Blom, 1938), p. 33. On musical instrument makers and geometric theory, see Stephen Birkett and William Jurgenson, "Why Didn't Historical Makers Need Drawings? Part I: Practical Geometry and Proportion," *Galpin Society Journal,* no. 54 (May 2001): 242–84.

24. Jerzy Limon, *The Masque of Stuart Culture* (Newark: University of Delaware Press, 1990), pp. 59–60. *Albions Trivmph: Personated in a Maske at Court* (London, 1631). As is typical of Jones's work, the allegorical figures of Architecture are drawn from Continental pattern books; identical representations of Theory and Practice appear, for example, in the frontispiece to Vredeman de Vries's *Architectura* (Antwerp, 1577).

25. The literature on early American cupboards includes Robert F. Trent, Peter Follansbee, and Alan Miller, "First Flowers of the Wilderness: Mannerist Furniture from a Northern Essex County, Massachusetts, Shop," in *American Furniture,* edited by Luke Beckerdite (Hanover, N.H.: University Press of New England for the Chipstone Foundation, 2001), pp. 1–64; Robert F. Trent and Michael Podmaniczky, "An Early Cupboard Fragment from the Harvard College Joinery Tradition," in *American Furniture,* edited by Luke Beckerdite (Hanover, N.H.: University Press of New England for the Chipstone Foundation, 2002), pp. 228–42; Patricia E. Kane, *Furniture of the New Haven Colony: The Seventeenth-Century Style* (New Haven, Conn.: New Haven Colony Historical Society, 1973); Gerald W. R. Ward, *American Case Furniture in the Mabel Brady Garvan and Other Collections at Yale University* (New Haven, Conn.: Yale University Art Gallery, 1988), pp. 128, 383–87; Gerald W. R. Ward, "Some Thoughts on Connecticut Cupboards and Other Case Furniture," in *New England Furniture: Essays in Memory of Benno M. Forman,* pp. 66–87; Trent, "New England Joinery and Turning before 1700," pp. 530–32; and *Pilgrim Century Furniture: An Historical Survey,* edited by Robert F. Trent (New York: Main Street/Universe Books, 1976), pp. 55–78, 89–94, 122–25. Jonathan Prown has made a similar argument regarding the eighteenth-century desk-and-bookcase form, writing that their interiors "serve as personal theaters where users played out the

dramatic affairs of business and everyday life. . . . Projecting into the foreground and serving as the main point of interaction, the leather-covered writing surface is a stage that is defined on its outer perimeter by a wooden frame." Jonathan Prown and Ronald L. Hurst, *Southern Furniture, 1680–1830: The Colonial Williamsburg Collection* (Williamsburg, Va.: Colonial Williamsburg Foundation, in association with Harry N. Abrams, 1997), p. 445. Shakespeare writes in scene 5 of *Romeo and Juliet* (1592): "Away with the joint-stools; remove the court-cubbord, look to the plate." Benno M. Forman, "Cupboards," Benno M. Forman Papers, box 16, Winterthur Library. Ralph Edwards advanced the idea that "court" might be from the French in *The Shorter Dictionary of English Furniture from the Middle Ages to the Late Georgian Period* (Covent Garden, Eng.: Country Life, 1964), pp. 288–89. Peter Thornton, who initially concurred with this etymology, later revoked the argument in "Two Problems," *Furniture History* 7 (1971): 64; Peter Thornton, *Seventeenth-Century Interior Decoration in England, France and Holland* (New Haven, Conn.: Yale University Press, 1978), pp. 233, 380 n. 37.

26. The Royal Works document is located in the United Kingdom National Archives, Public Record Office, London (E351/3216) and is quoted in John Orrell, *The Human Stage: English Theatre Design, 1657–1640* (Cambridge: Cambridge University Press, 1988), pp. 39–41; Mark A. Meadow, *Hof-, Staats- en Stadsceremonies/Court, State and City Ceremonies* (Zwolle, Netherlands: Uitgeverij Waanders, 1998); George R. Kernodle, *From Art to Theatre: Form and Convention in the Renaissance* (Chicago: University of Chicago Press, 1944), p. 96; *La siège et les fêtes de Binche*, edited by Charles Reulens (Mons, 1878), pp. 116–19; Albert van de Put, "Two Drawings of the Fetes at Binche for Charles V and Philip (II), 1549," *The Journal of the Warburg and Courtauld Institutes* 3, nos. 1–2 (April 1939–July 1940): 49–55.

27. Orrell, *The Human Stage*, p. 209. Mary Ann Caws, *The Eye in the Text: Essays on Perception, Mannerist to Modern* (Princeton, N.J.: Princeton University Press, 1981), p. 59.

28. Sally M. Promey, "Seeing the Self 'in Frame': Early New England Material Practice and Puritan Piety," *Material Religion* 1, no. 1 (March 2005): 10–47. Stephen Orgel, *The Jonsonian Masque* (Cambridge, Mass.: Harvard University Press, 1965). See also Lawrence Stone, *The Crisis of the Aristocracy, 1558–1641* (Oxford: Oxford University Press, 1965); Martin Holbrook, "Courtly Negotiations," in David Bevington and Peter Holbrook, *The Politics of the Stuart Court Masque* (Cambridge: Cambridge University Press, 1998); Jennifer Chibnall, "'To That Secure Fix'd State': The Function of the Caroline Masque Form," in *The Court Masque*, edited by David Lindley (Manchester, Eng.: Manchester University Press, 1984), p. 81. Samuel J. Edgerton, "Maniera and the Mannaia: Decorum and Decapitation in the Sixteenth Century," in *The Meaning of Mannerism*, pp. 67–103, at 67. Frank Kermode, *The Age of Shakespeare* (New York: Random House, 2004), p. 190.

29. Arnold Hauser, *Mannerism: The Crisis of the Renaissance and the Origins of Modern Art* (London: Routledge and Kegan Paul, 1965), p. 279. Manca, "A Matter of Style," pp. 23–24. On the Ipswich chair and its mate, see Trent, *New England Begins*, pp. 514–16; Benno M. Forman, *American Seating Furniture*, pp. 135–36.

30. *As You Like It*, act 3, scene 2. Benno M. Forman, "A Catalogue of Ware Chairs," unpublished typescript, 1973, p. 21, Benno M. Forman Papers, box 11, Winterthur Library. Forman, *American Seating Furniture*, p. xxiv.

David R. Pesuit

Structure, Style, and Evolution: The Sack-Back Windsor Armchair

▼ SEVERAL BOOKS AND scores of articles published over the past seventy years have explored the stylistic development and regional characteristics of the American Windsor chair, but few scholars have considered how the construction of this seating changed over time. Using analytical methods derived from physics and engineering, this article documents stages in the evolution of the sack-back Windsor armchair and its most salient structural and stylistic features: the arm rail, arm supports, hoop, seat, and undercarriage. Engineering concepts and equations are accompanied by explanatory paragraphs, so nontechnical readers may skip the indented sections and still understand the results. As the following arguments reveal, form in Windsor seating followed both function and failure.[1]

Anyone who has shopped for chairs knows that many factors influence the decision to buy. Cost is a major consideration, as are comfort, stylishness, durability, and fitness for intended use. Windsor chair purchasers in the eighteenth and nineteenth centuries probably used the same criteria. Then as now the importance given to each of these concerns depended on priority, purpose, and pocketbook. A chair intended principally for outdoor use may not have functioned well at the kitchen table, and a chair suitable for a meetinghouse or a tavern may have been inappropriate for a formal parlor.

Furniture historians Nancy Goyne Evans and Charles Santore have noted that early Windsors were well suited for use in gardens because they did not obscure the view or block summer drafts, but neither scholar considered how weight may have influenced choice in chairs intended for outdoor use. Early comb-back armchairs, which often weigh at least twenty pounds, are considerably more difficult to move than lighter sack-back armchairs. Obviously, portability was less of a concern in wealthy households, which typically had servants or slaves available for the task, but logic suggests that Windsor purchasers considered size and weight when buying chairs for indoor use. Large comb-back and low-back chairs were extremely comfortable and represented a less expensive alternative to similarly commodious late baroque and rococo seating forms. The same chairs, however, were poorly suited for use around tavern tables or in rows at meetinghouses. Data compiled from chairs illustrated in Santore's *The Windsor Style in America, 1730–1830* indicates that the seat width of Philadelphia comb-back Windsor chairs decreased over time and that weight decreased as a result (see table 1). If his dating is correct, most Windsor chair seats assumed a standard width of approximately 21½ inches between 1765 and 1780. Most later chairs have oval seats instead of D-shaped ones, which provided a further reduction in weight.[2]

Table 1 *Geometric and Other Comparisons between Philadelphia Comb-Back Bent-Arm Armchairs,* taken from information and photographs in Charles Santore, *The Windsor Style in America, Volumes 1 and 2* (1997; reprint, Philadelphia: Courage Books, 1981).

Volume and figure number	Date assigned by Santore	Seat width	Seat depth	Seat depth to width ratio	Medial stretcher type	Medial stretcher placement toward rear	Knuckle arm	Maker
1: 26	1740–1750	25"	16"	.640	late baroque	yes	no	Gilpin
1: 8	1730–1740	24"	16"	.667	late baroque	yes	no	
2: 2	1740–1750	24"	16"	.667	late baroque	yes	no	
1: 20	1740–1770	24½"	17"	.694	late baroque	possibly	no	
2: 1	1740–1750	21"	15"	.714	late baroque	yes	no	Gilpin
2: 4	1750–1770	23¾"	15¾"	.663	late baroque	no?	no	
2: 6	1750–1770	24⅝"	16¾"	.680	late baroque	no?	no	
2: 3	1750–1770	24½"	16¾"	.684	late baroque	no?	no	
1: 29	1760–1775	24½"	17"	.694	bulbous	possibly	no	
1: 30	1760–1775	23"	17"	.739	bulbous	possibly	no	
1: 31	1760–1790	23"	18½"	.804	bulbous	no?	yes	
2: 7	1765–1780	23¾"	17"	.687	bulbous	no	no	
1: 32	1765–1785	24¾"	16¼"	.747	bulbous	no	no	Henzey
2: 12	1765–1790	21¼"	16"	.753	bulbous	no	yes	
2: 10	1765–1780	21½"	16¼"	.756	bulbous	no	yes	
2: 11	1765–1780	21½"	16½"	.767	bulbous	no?	yes	

For some individuals who purchased Windsor chairs, style and comfort were more important considerations than size and weight. This may have been especially true of furniture intended for use in formal settings, like the four Windsor chairs listed in the dining room in Philadelphia banker Charles Norris's 1766 inventory. Judging from room-by-room inventories taken before the Revolution, Windsor furniture often stood in halls or passages, readily accessible as supplementary seating when and where need arose. The 1768 inventory of Norfolk, Virginia, merchant Robert Tucker, for example, lists ten "Windsor chairs" in the passage. It would be difficult to imagine a period context in which the architectonic turnings, carved elements, and paint colors of most early Windsors would have seemed out of place. Indeed, many of the later comb-back chairs illustrated and discussed by Santore have carved arm knuckles similar to those on formal seating (see table 1).[3]

For tavern and meetinghouse owners, strength and durability were probably more important than style in the selection of Windsor furniture because seating in those places was subjected to more frequent and rougher use. Given the fact that Philadelphia had about 20,000 inhabitants in 1760, it is likely that proprietors of many public establishments knew one another. During the course of business discussions, they probably learned whose chairs were holding up and whose were failing; they all understood that furniture repairs and replacement costs affected their bottom line. Since tavern and meetinghouse owners presumably placed large orders for Windsor seating, there must have been considerable competition to build chairs that were as strong and durable as they were pleasing to look at. Before the Revolution, Windsor style and structure may have been influenced as much by the needs of public use as by demand for seating suitable for domestic use.

Shipping records suggest that Philadelphia makers captured a large portion of both markets, exporting thousands of Windsors annually. As early as the 1760s "Philadelphia chairs" were routinely mentioned in the advertisements of merchants from New York to Charleston.[4]

By the 1780s, however, the tone of some advertisements had changed. Makers outside Philadelphia boasted that their products were better than Philadelphia chairs. In the October 14, 1783, issue of the *South Carolina Gazette and Daily Advertiser,* Andrew Redmond reported that he made and sold "Philadelphia Windsor chairs . . . both armed and unarmed, as neat as any imported, and much better stuff." Four years later Daniel Lawrence of Providence, Rhode Island, advertised that he made "all kinds of Windsor Chairs . . . in the newest and best Fashions . . . beautifully painted, after the Philadelphia mode." Lawrence further claimed that his chairs were "warranted of good seasoned materials, so firmly put together as not to deceive the purchasers by an untimely coming to pieces." According to Santore,

Figure 1 Armchair, Philadelphia, Pennsylvania, ca. 1760. Unidentified ring-porous hardwoods, maple, and tulip poplar. H. 38⅜", W. 21⁵⁄₁₆" (seat), D. 15⅜" (seat); seat height: 17⅞"; seat depth/seat width: .721; rail width: .995"; rail thickness: .744"; arm support angle: 6°. (Private collection; photo, Gavin Ashworth.) The hoop is replaced.

"New York and New England chairs of the 1770 to 1790 period were in many ways better than those being produced in Philadelphia. Without realizing it, Philadelphia makers had been seduced by the siren song of the assembly line into producing a standardized, uninspired tapered leg on their chairs."[5]

The problem was actually much more fundamental than Santore realized. Growing demand for Windsor furniture created tensions between style and structure that resulted in failures of several kinds. Study of these failures and how artisans responded to them shows that makers relied as much on applied physics as on hand skills and aesthetics to survive and prosper in the marketplace.

Evidence of damage to early Windors illustrates this point. The arm rail of the Philadelphia sack-back chair illustrated in figures 1–3 is repaired where

Figure 2 Detail of the arm rail repair on the chair illustrated in fig. 1. (Photo, Gavin Ashworth.)

Figure 3 Detail of the underside of the armchair illustrated in fig. 1, showing vestiges of the original green paint on the legs and stretchers. (Photo, Gavin Ashworth.)

it cracked at the rear (fig. 2). A similar example made by William Cox (figs. 4–7) shows evidence of a catastrophic failure, like the "untimely coming to pieces" mentioned in Daniel Lawrence's 1787 advertisement. The arm rail on the Cox chair broke (fig. 5) and its seat cracked between the arm supports and rear legs (fig. 6). A stylish, simply turned Massachusetts Windsor

Figure 4 William Cox, armchair, Philadelphia, Pennsylvania, ca. 1770. Unidentified ring-porous hardwoods, maple, and white pine. H. 36¾", W. 21⅝" (seat), D. 16⅛" (seat); seat height: 16¾"; seat depth/seat width: .751; rounded rail width: 1.042"; rail thickness: .709"; arm support angle: 15°. (Private collection; photo, Martin Schnall.) The underside of the seat is marked "COX" and branded "EGB." The right arm is an early replacement made of maple in the same style as the original.

Figure 5 Detail showing structural failure of the arm rail of the chair illustrated in fig. 4. (Photo, Gavin Ashworth.)

Figure 6 Detail of the underside of the armchair illustrated in fig. 4, showing seat cracks at the arm supports and between the rear legs. (Photo, Gavin Ashworth.)

Figure 7 Detail of the left arm (from the sitter's perspective) of the armchair illustrated in fig. 4. (Photo, Gavin Ashworth.) The laminated sections of the knuckles are thicker than those on most Windsor chairs, and they do not flare outward as is usually the case.

(fig. 8), probably made within a few years of the Cox example, was subjected to some of the same stresses as the early Philadelphia examples, but its damage was less severe: the rear legs broke away but the arm rail did not fail. The detail illustrated in figure 9 documents a subtle but important difference between this chair and the others. The arm rails of the Philadelphia chairs are rounded at the front and back, whereas the arm rail of the Massachusetts chair is squared off at the rear. Since the "flat-back" rail of the latter chair uses more wood, common sense suggests it is stronger. Engineering failure analysis shows this as well.[6]

Figure 8 Armchair, Massachusetts, ca. 1770. Unidentified ring-porous hardwoods, unidentified softwood, and maple. H. 37⅝", W. 20⅞" (seat), D. 14¹¹⁄₁₆"(seat); seat height: 16⅛"; seat depth/seat width: .707; flat-back rail width: 1.003", rail thickness: .612"; arm support angles 7° (right) and 10° (left). (Private collection; photo, Gavin Ashworth.) The hoop has an early repair, and handmade tension rods have been added to strengthen the arm supports. The rear legs and medial stretcher are replaced.

Figure 9 Detail comparing the flat-back arm rail of the armchair illustrated in fig. 8 (left) with the rounded rail of the armchair illustrated in fig. 4 (right). (Photo, Gavin Ashworth.)

The Arm Rail

Children who climb trees learn basic lessons about the flexibility of wood. They discover that dry branches snap, but that green ones can be bent into U shapes or even farther. Windsor craftsmen learned early on—probably from wheelwrights—that lengths of straight-grain hickory and oak could be boiled or steamed and then bent into shapes that retained their form yet remained somewhat pliant after cooling and drying. Those who remember bending tree branches may recall that the branch always begins to break on the outside surface of the U shape, where the wood is most stretched, and that the break progresses through the branch toward the middle. Meanwhile, the inside of the U squeezes together or compresses, at least until the break is most of the way through. Like the tree branch, the outside surface of a Windsor chair arm rail is in tension, and its inside surface next to a sitter is in compression. But there is a difference. The application of steam relieves the tensile and compressive stresses created by bending. The wood fibers stretch and squeeze to accommodate these stresses. Drying and cooling "freeze" the arm in its new shape. Leaning back in a Windsor, like bending the tree branch, puts the outside surface of the U-shaped rail in tension and the inside surface in compression, while pushing out on the hand holds does the exact opposite. It compresses the outside surface of the arm and puts the inside surface in tension.

Although contrary to accepted practice, some letters and symbols have been set in italics to assist those not accustomed to reading engineering analyses.

Stress Analysis: Rounded and Flat-Back Arm Rails

When a tree branch or chair rail is about to break, it has reached its maximum yield stress. Since the branch begins to break at its outside surface, one would expect tensile stress to be greatest at this surface and compressive stress to be greatest at the inside surface. Therefore, we can imagine a surface somewhere in between, where tensile and compressive stresses are neutralized. Engineers use this neutral surface to develop equations relating these stresses to material shapes and properties. The first equation below relates stress at any distance y on either side of this neutral surface to bending force B. It states what common sense suggests, that stress increases with distance y away from this neutral surface and with the size of the bending force, B.[7]

$$\text{stress (y)} = \text{By}/ \qquad \text{(Eq. 1)}$$

$$\text{maximum stress} = \text{By}_{\text{max}}/\text{I} \qquad \text{(Eq. 2)}$$

The "*I*" in the denominator is the focus of this discussion. Engineers know it as a moment of inertia, but it functions as a bending resistance that depends only on cross-sectional geometry. The equations indicate that the greater the moment of inertia, the smaller the stress produced for a given bending force B, and the stronger the arm of the chair. Now imagine for simplicity's sake that the arm rail has a rectangular cross-section. Engineering analysis shows that the moment of inertia of this shape is

$$\text{I} = \text{tw}^3/12 \qquad \text{(Eq. 3)}$$

where w is arm rail cross-sectional width and t is arm rail vertical thickness. In this case the strength of the arm rail depends much more on rail width than on vertical thickness. The equation below shows that if thickness t remains the same, a 10% increase in rail width produces a 33% increase in bending strength. Vertical thickness would have to be increased by one third to obtain the same result.

$$I_2 / I_1 = t\,w_2^3 \;/\; t\,w_1^3 = (1.1\,w_1)^3 \;/\; w_1^3 = 1.33$$

Figure 10 Graph showing the relative strength of flat-back and rounded arm rails. Results are generalized using the dimensionless parameter w/t where w is rail width and t is rail vertical thickness. The flat-back arm rail of the chair illustrated in fig. 8 is 1.004" wide and .612" thick; its w/t ratio is 1.639 and its relative strength ratio is 1.275, making it about 27.5% stronger than a rounded rail of the same size.

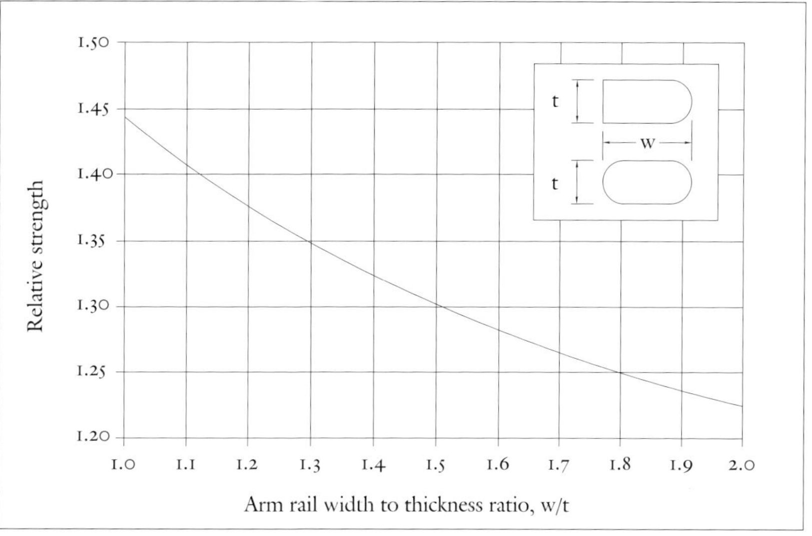

A wide rounded arm rail is also stronger for the same reason. The Cox chair has an especially wide rounded rail. But beyond this, comparisons between various rail shapes become more difficult because the moments of inertia are more difficult to calculate. The graph shown in figure 10 compares the strength of rounded and flat-back rails using w/t, arm rail cross-sectional width-to-thickness ratio. The detailed analysis is found in appendix 1. When w/t tends toward unity (when the arm rail is as wide as it is thick), the graph shows that the rail squared off at rear is almost 45% stronger than the rounded arm rail. Common sense suggests a large difference in this limit because the cross-sectional percentage lost by rounding off is then largest. On the other hand, when w/t is large (when the arm is much wider than it is thick), the percentage gain in cross section from rounded to flat-back becomes smaller. For the Cox chair, whose rail is 1.042 inches wide at rear and .709 inches thick, w/t = 1.468, and the increase in strength gained by squaring off at rear is about 32%. In other words, chair maker Cox lost about one-third of the strength of his arm rail when he rounded its back surface instead of squaring it off (figs. 9, 10). That is quite a loss for a small pile of shavings left on the shop floor.[8]

Charles Santore's photographic inventory of early Windsor chairs can be used to estimate when the transition from rounded rail to the stronger flat-back rail occurred. Most of the fourteen comb-back chairs with steam-bent arms that Santore dates to 1750 or earlier appear to have arms that are rounded along their back surface, but five of the fourteen comb-backs he dates to 1750–1770 appear to have rails that are rectangular or nearly rectangular at the back. The rails of three of these five chairs are also thicker at the center rear than at the arm hold, further evidence that makers were trying to strengthen their chairs. A different situation occurs for sack-backs with steam-bent arms. Sack-backs made before 1750 are not now known, but three of the ten chairs he attributed to the 1750–1770 period have arm rails that appear to be squared off at the rear. However, none of the thirty-one Philadelphia sack-back Windsors collected for Independence Hall or made for Carpenters' Hall during the mid-1770s have flat-back arm rails. This suggests that flat-back arm rails were uncommon in Philadelphia sack-backs, even though they occur on some earlier comb-back chairs.[9]

Figure 11 Armchair, Philadelphia, Pennsylvania, ca. 1765. Unidentified ring-porous hardwoods, maple, and tulip poplar. H. 37", W. 21 3/16" (seat), D. 16 1/4"(seat); seat height: 17 1/2", seat depth/seat width: .770; flat-back rail width: 1.087"; rail thickness: .733"; arm support angle: 11°. (Private collection; photo, Gavin Ashworth.) The maker of this chair and the example illustrated in fig. 12 used seventeen pins and seventeen nails to secure the hoop, each joint of the arm supports, the knuckles of the arms, the legs at the seat, and every other spindle. He did not use fasteners on the stretchers.

Chairs with Flat-Back Arm Rails

Two sack-back armchairs from the same shop (figs. 11, 12) allow an observer to distinguish the maker's intent from later repairs. Although most Philadelphia Windsors were originally made without metal fasteners, both of these chairs have nails securing the spindles to the hoop and the arm rail. The nails at the rear of the rail were driven in from the back, but those at the sides were inserted from the inside to retard arm movement. This intelligent arrangement creates a structural web that flexes less at the arms. Both chairs have wooden pins that secure the arm supports and every other spindle to the seat, even though most Philadelphia chairs have no pins for that purpose. Many knuckle handholds were glued or nailed and have been lost over the years, but the handholds on the two sack-backs are intact. On both chairs, the maker used two small pins to secure the knuckle to the underside of the arm and two more to secure the scrolled arm extender (fig. 13). He

Figure 12 Armchair, Philadelphia, Pennsylvania, ca. 1765. Unidentified ring-porous hardwoods, maple, and tulip poplar. H. 35⅞", W. 21⁷⁄₁₆" (seat), D. 16¼" (seat); seat height: 17⅝"; seat depth/seat width: .764; flat-back rail width: .985", rail thickness: .737"; arm support angle: 10°. (Private collection; photo, Gavin Ashworth.) The medial stretcher is replaced and the legs are extended. The chair retains much of its original green paint.

Figure 13 Detail showing the right arms (from the sitter's perspective) of the chairs illustrated in figs. 11 and 12. (Photo, Gavin Ashworth.) Two pins secure the side laminates and two more secure the lower laminates. The gouge cuts used to define the scroll volutes are slightly different.

Figure 14 Detail of the underside of the armchair illustrated in fig. 11, showing the scribe marks likely used to denote the leg and pin positions. (Photo, Martin Schnall.)

also pinned the legs under the seat (fig. 14) and double-wedged them from above. In total the maker used seventeen pins and seventeen nails in the construction of each chair. These chairs are clearly the products of a sophisticated shop that was especially conservative from a structural point of view.

Further evidence of this shop's sophistication can be seen in figure 15, which shows that the seat blanks of the sack-back chairs were bent before

Figure 15 Side view of the armchair illustrated in fig. 11, showing the bent seat and seat pins. (Photo, Gavin Ashworth.)

they were carved. Although most board components of period furniture have shrunk and/or bowed over time, moisture loss did not create the curvature of these seats. If it had, the side stretchers would have pulled out long ago. This bowing is also not the result of heavier jack-planing, since maximum seat thickness is about the same from front to rear. Seat bowing added a manufacturing step, but it saved wood and weight. Using this process, a maker could reduce blank thickness by one-quarter inch or more and reduce the time and effort required to shape a stylish, comfortable saddle. Few shops made bowed seats for Windsor chairs.

From a manufacturing perspective, the two sack-backs (figs. 11, 12) incorporate standardized pin and nail sizes and spindles drilled and wedged into hoops in the same way (fig. 16). Scribe lines denoting leg positions on the underside of the seats indicate that the maker used templates to lay out his holes and jigs to bore them. Philadelphia chair maker John Lambert

Figure 16 Detail showing the upper surfaces of the right arms (from the sitter's perspective) of the chairs illustrated in figs. 11 and 12. (Photo, Gavin Ashworth.) Similarities in arms indicate that the maker used patterns.

Figure 17 Overall side views of the armchairs illustrated in figs. 11 and 12. (Photos, Gavin Ashworth.) The back and arm rail of the chair on the right (fig. 12) have a more pronounced slope.

advertised "3 Machiens for letting in feet with Propriety and Dispatch." In the production of Windsor furniture, accurate boring is essential.[10]

As was the case with most urban enterprises, the shop that produced the two sack-backs (figs. 11, 12) employed multiple tradesmen. Two different artisans carved the arms. The knuckle edges on one of the chairs become sharp as they spiral, but those on the other chair are rounded (figs. 13, 16). In addition, the rough-carved undersides of these knuckles vary significantly.

The shop responsible for these sack-backs made at least two models, differing primarily in the rake of their rails and the angles of their seat holes (fig. 17). The rear spindles of the chair illustrated in figure 12 are more raked than those on the other Windsor (fig. 11), and the arm rail of the former is nearly twice as raked as that of the latter. Although improper repairs have changed the angles of many surviving Windsors, that was not the case with these sack-backs. Their rails have identical nails and their stretchers are parallel to the floor. The user of the chair shown in figure 11 sits rather upright while the user of the other example (fig. 12) has the option of leaning back. Both chairs could be used at a table, but the example illustrated in figure 12 is more of a lounge chair and may have been made to accommodate a close stool.

The leg splay of these structurally sophisticated sack-backs is greater than that of the Cox chair (figs. 4, 11, 12, 18) but similar to that of small,

Figure 18 Overall side views of the armchairs illustrated in figs. 4 and 12. (Photo, Gavin Ashworth.) The chair on the left (fig. 12) has greater leg splay than the sack-back on the right.

Philadelphia fan-back armchairs with rounded seats (fig. 19). In addition, both sack-backs have rearward medial stretchers like early comb-back Windsors made by Thomas Gilpin and several of his competitors. The master of the shop that produced these sack-backs was clearly familiar with a range of local options for various Windsor forms, and either he or one of his workmen was an exceptional turner. The legs on seating from his shop are considerably more robust than those on most contemporary Philadelphia examples, even though they were made from stock of the same size. Similarly, few sack-back armchairs from that city have comparable handholds (fig. 20). Finely shaped knuckles are more often found on elaborate Philadelphia comb-back Windsors with sawn arms (fig. 21). As the details illustrated in figures 13 and 16 show, the knuckles on the two sack-backs are beautifully modeled with protruding central lobes and deeply relieved volutes. In some respects, the handholds on these chairs are more vigorous than those on formal seating from the same era.[11]

Figure 19 Armchair, Philadelphia, Pennsylvania, ca. 1765. Tulip poplar, maple, oak, and hickory. H. 37", W. 21¼" (seat), D. 16¾" (seat); seat height: 17½"; seat depth/seat width: .741. (Courtesy, Winterthur Museum.)

Figure 20 Armchair, Philadelphia, Pennsylvania, ca. 1765. Oak, hickory, maple, and tulip poplar. H. 37", W. 21¼" (seat), D. 15¼" (seat); seat height: 17½"; seat depth/seat width: .741. (Courtesy, Perseus Books Group. Illustration taken from Charles Santore, *The Windsor Style in America, Volumes 1 and 2* [1997; reprint, Philadelphia: Courage Books, 1981], 2: 94, fig. 75.) Like the chairs illustrated in figs. 11 and 12, this sack-back has arm knuckles with a large central lobe.

Intrinsic and extrinsic evidence strongly suggests that these sophisticated sack-backs (figs. 11, 12) were made in Philadelphia during the 1760s. Their leg splay and major turnings have parallels in early fan-back Windsors from that city, and their arm supports have fat baluster elements related to those on sophisticated ladder-back chairs made in the Delaware Valley region (see fig. 22). Several Lancaster examples have handholds with protruding central lobes, but no recorded chair has a flat-back arm rail like the two sack-backs. In a further departure, most Lancaster chairs have spade feet and knuckles butted to the ends of their arms. A sack-back Windsor armchair attributed to Frederick, Maryland, is one of the closest cognates to the two Philadelphia examples. The former chair has similar scribe lines and pins under the seat, related arm support turnings, and finely shaped knuckles with a prominent central lobe. Despite these parallels, the Frederick chairs appear at least one generation removed from the Philadelphia sack-backs. The more advanced structure of the metropolitan examples suggests manufacture in an intensely competitive environment where various makers were attempting to build superior chairs.[12]

Figure 21 Armchair, Philadelphia, Pennsylvania, ca. 1773. Unidentified ring-porous hardwoods, tulip poplar, maple, and mahogany. H. 53", W. 23" (seat), D. 17½" (seat); seat height: 25"; seat depth/seat width: .761. (Courtesy, Carpenters' Company of Philadelphia; photo, Gavin Ashworth.) This chair was one of the speaker's chairs used at the first Continental Congress when that group met at Carpenters' Hall in 1774. Like the chairs illustrated in figs. 11, 12, and 20, this comb-back has arm knuckles with a large central lobe. The arms are mahogany.

Figure 22 Detail of the Windsor armchair illustrated in fig. 11 and a mid-eighteenth-century Delaware Valley armchair. (Private collection; photo, Gavin Ashworth.)

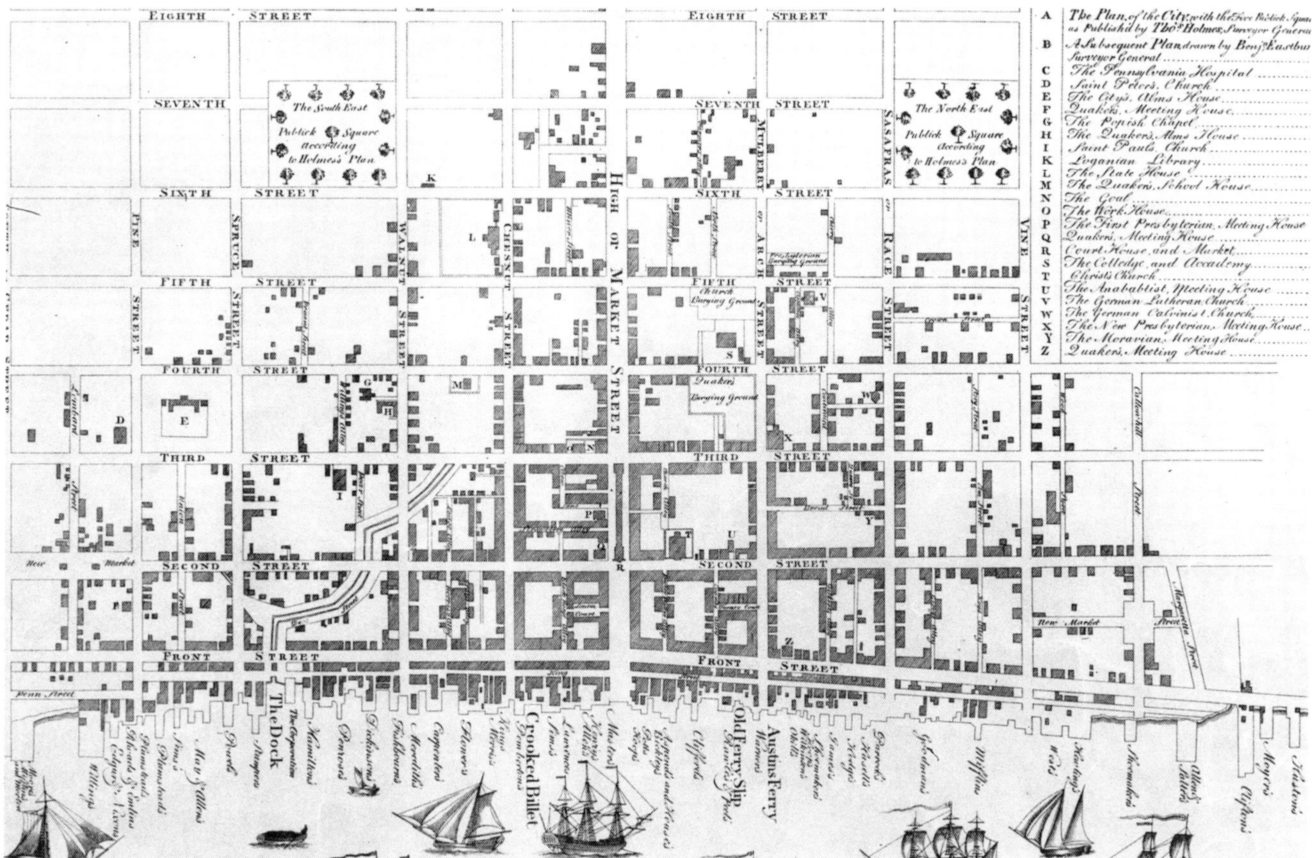

Figure 23 Detail of *Plan of the Improved part of the City [of Philadelphia] surveyed and laid down by Nicholas Scull, Esq. Surveyor General of the Province of Pennsylvania . . . published according to Act of Parliament Novr. 1st 1762 and sold by the Editors Matthew Clarkson, and Mary Biddle in Philadelphia.* (Courtesy, Historical Society of Pennsylvania.)

More than twenty Windsor chair makers plied their trade in Philadelphia before the Revolution. Many of these artisans' addresses are unknown, but several maintained shops in the city's commercial district (fig. 23). William Cox worked on Second Street, Francis Trumble worked on Front and Second Streets, and David Chambers and Josiah Sherald worked nearby. The homes of many wealthy consumers were within easy walking distance. Merchant John Cadwalader and his wife Elizabeth (Lloyd) lived in an enclave of fine houses on Second Street, four blocks south of Market Street and one block from the Delaware River wharves. They purchased a dozen "round top Windsor chairs" and two settees from Trumble on July 19, 1771.[13]

If an eighteenth-century consumer crisscrossed this commercial district in search of Windsors, he or she might encounter a dozen shops offering a variety of choices. Some chair makers may have limited their production to standardized seating, while others offered a variety of options including sculpted seats, carved knuckles, and mahogany arms. A few shops may have produced chairs with different rakes that served different functions but worked well en suite (see figs. 11, 12). Just as today, artisans had to justify their prices. In the absence of documentation, one imagines the conversations and negotiations that took place as patrons and makers addressed issues of cost, strength, durability, comfort, weight, and style.

Stylistic and structural options undoubtedly varied from maker to maker depending on the size and composition of their workforce, patronage, and intended market. Trumble's advertisements, bills, and surviving work indicate that he made several models of Windsors including examples described as "sack-back," "arch top," and "round top." All were available with either "Scrol arms" or "plain" arms. Although Trumble's reference to "Round Top Scrol arm Chairs" adequately describes the sack-backs illustrated in figures 11 and 12, his signed chairs have different leg turnings and construction details. Windsor chair makers and sellers of Trumble's stature may have offered different levels of work—a premium grade for special commissions, a better grade for the local market, and standardized work for export. The fact that Trumble had 1,200 "Windsor chairs" on hand in 1775 suggests that he was engaged in the coastal trade. Like earlier Boston chair makers and merchant upholsterers, Trumble may have purchased piecework from independent turners and assembled chairs from parts made in other shops.[14]

Table 2 lists the names of at least a dozen Windsor furniture makers working in Philadelphia before the Revolution for whom few if any signed chairs are known. Most of these artisans can be considered potential candidates for the maker of the sack-backs illustrated in figures 11 and 12, but several factors make attributions of unlabeled or unbranded Windsor chairs to specific artisans problematic. Many Philadelphia chair makers, including Trumble,

Table 2 *Working Dates and Street Addresses of Philadelphia Windsor Chair Makers Active before 1774*

Maker	*Working Dates*	*Address and Comments*
Black, Robert	1760–1793	
Biggard, John	before 1767	Moved to Charleston in 1767
Chambers, David	1748	Walnut Street; Plumb Street
Covert, Isaac	1772–1786	Apprenticed to Henzey in 1772
Cox, William	1767–1804	Second Street
Freeman, Benjamin	1765–1819	Front Street
Galer (Gayler), Adam	1767–ca. 1773	Working in New York City, 1774–1775
Gilbert, John	1759–1788	
Gilpin, Thomas	ca. 1735–1766	(Evans cites working dates 1752–1767)
Henderson, Peter	1766–1784	
Henzey, Joseph	1767–1796	106 South 8th Street; 76 Almond Street
Kelso, John	before 1774	Moved to New York City in 1774
Lambert, John	ca. 1760–1793	(Evans cites working dates 1786–1793)
Mason, Richard	1764–1793	
Pinkerton, John	1767–1783	Became an ironmonger in 1784
Saul, Joseph	1746–1767	Saul may have worked later; he died in 1773
Sherald, Josiah	1758–1778	Second Street below Dock Bridge
Snowden, Jedediah	1749–1776	Market Street west of Front Street
Trotter, Benjamin	1750s–1768	
Trumble, Francis	1740–1798	Front Street; Second Street
Walker, Robert	1766–1774	
Widdifield, William	1768–1817	Apprenticed to Cox in 1768–1770

Sources: Charles Santore, *The Windsor Style in America, Volumes 1 and 2* (1997; reprint, Philadelphia: Courage Books, 1981), 2: 242; and Nancy Goyne Evans, *American Windsor Chairs* (New York: Hudson Hills Press, in association with the Winterthur Museum, 1996), p. 681.

Cox, Joseph Henzey, and William Widdifield, were members of the Society of Friends. Quaker artisans typically took apprentices of the same faith and often engaged in mutually beneficial business arrangements including buying and selling piecework and collaborating to assemble furniture cargos for export. The Society of Friends also maintained a Windsor chair manufactory on Front Street in the third block north of Market Street, facing the Delaware River (see fig. 23). This enterprise and the aforementioned practices probably promoted standardization of some aspects of Philadelphia Windsor design.[15]

The Rectangular Arm Rail

Although the flat-back rail is considerably stronger than the rounded rail, it was never common in Philadelphia. Not one of the many sack-back chairs collected by Charles Dorman for Independence Hall has flat-back arm rails. Most chairs documented and attributed to the city have rectangular or rounded rails. Since chair rails were carved and shaved from logs split along the grain, those who made them must have known that larger cross-sections were stronger. Therefore, it should come as no surprise that some Philadelphia makers used fully rectangular rails from an early date. The graph in figure 24 summarizes calculations in appendix 1 comparing rounded and

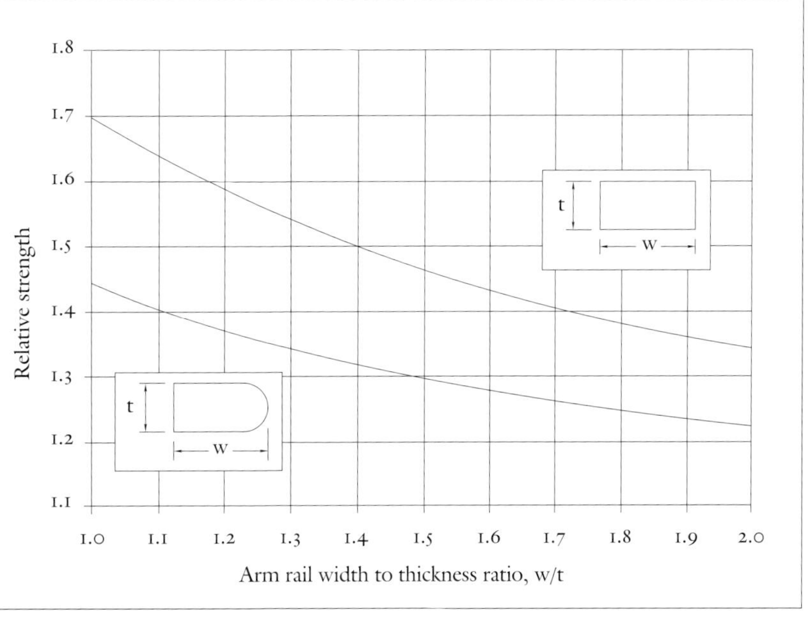

Figure 24 Graph showing the relative strength of flat-back, rectangular, and rounded rails. Results are generalized using the dimensionless parameter *w/t* where *w* is rail width and *t* is rail vertical thickness. The flat-back arm rail of the chair illustrated in fig. 8 is 1.004" wide and .612 " thick; its *w/t* ratio is 1.639 and its relative strength ratio is 1.275, making it about 27.5% stronger than a rounded rail of the same size. Had its rail been rectangular, it would have been about 43% stronger than a rounded rail of the same size.

flat-back rails with rectangular rails. The rounded rail with a width-to-thickness ratio ranging between 1.3 and 1.6 becomes 40–50 percent stronger if its front and rear surfaces are squared off. The rectangular rail was even stronger than the flat-back rail, and it saved labor and cost.

A small group of sack-backs at Carpenters' Hall (fig. 25) indicates that Philadelphia chair makers were producing Windsors with rectangular rails before the Revolution. These chairs are from two sets in use when the First Continental Congress met there in September 1774. The Carpenters'

Figure 25 Armchair, Philadelphia, Pennsylvania, 1773. Unidentified ring-porous hardwoods, tulip poplar, and maple. H. 37¼", W. 21¾"(seat), D. 16" (seat); seat height: 17½"; seat depth/seat width: .737; rectangular rail width: 1.51"; rail thickness: .81"; arm support angle: 15°. Courtesy, Independence National Historic Park; photo, Gavin Ashworth.) The only pins in the chair are those used to secure the hoop to the arm rail. This chair proves that Windsors with wide, strong rails were made in Philadelphia before the American Revolution.

Company paid twenty shillings for the first set—described as "Chares for the Hall"—in January 1773. These Windsors were branded with dates six years later. The second set was probably purchased for the Library Company of Philadelphia, which moved from the Pennsylvania State House into space rented from the Carpenters' Company on September 6, 1773. To furnish the Library Company's new space, the Carpenters' Company also acquired six brass sconces and two chandeliers. The chairs from both sets have very similar handholds and arm supports, and for years were considered a set of five, but four have 21½-inch-wide seats and rectangular rails (see fig. 25) and one has a 20¼-inch-wide seat and a rounded rail.[16]

Quantitative analysis explains why the chairs with rectangular rails survive in greater number. The rectangular rails of the chairs represented by the example illustrated in figure 25 are more than 50 percent wider than the rounded rail of the smaller fifth chair. Since the strength of a rectangular rail varies with the cube of its width (see eq. 3, fig. 24), a 50-percent wider rectangular rail with the same thickness is about 3.375 times stronger ($1.5^3 = 3.375$). The rounded rail of the smaller chair has a width-to-thickness ratio of 1.5 and would have been about 1.5 times stronger had it been rectangular. Therefore, the rails of the four chairs with rectangular rails are roughly five times stronger (3.375 × 1.5) than the rail of the one chair with a rounded rail.

Equation 3 can be used to make a more exact comparison including differences in rail thickness. The rounded rail is 0.656 inches thick and 0.993 inches wide; the rectangular rails are about 0.810 inches thick and 1.510 inches wide.

$$s(y) = By/I = 12By/tw^3$$

At some position *y*,

$$s_2/s_1 = I_1/I_2 = t_1w_1^3 / t_2w_2^3$$
$$= (.656'')(.993'')^3 / (.810'')(1.510'')^3$$
$$= .2303$$

Since the stress at any given point in the wider rectangular rail is about 23% as large as in the smaller one, it is 1/.2303, or 4.34, times stronger. On the other hand, the rounded rail with a width-to-thickness ratio of 1.51 would be 1.47 times stronger according to figure 24 if it had been rectangular. Therefore, according to this more accurate calculation, the rectangular rails on the four wider Carpenters' Hall chairs are 4.34 × 1.47, or 6.37, times stronger than the rail on the single surviving chair with a rounded rail.

The Philadelphia sack-back chairs examined for this study provide statistical insight into the transition from rounded to rectangular rails. Seven of twelve nine-spindle sack-backs have rounded rails, whereas the remaining five have rectangular rails (see table 3). By comparison, thirteen of twenty-three seven-spindle Philadelphia chairs have rectangular or flat-back rails; the remaining ten have rounded rails. In other words, almost 60 percent of the nine-spindle chairs have rounded rails, whereas nearly 60 percent of the seven-spindle chairs have rectangular or flat-back rails. Probability experts are cautious about drawing conclusions from limited samples, but these are not inordinately small; early field trials of experimental drugs use samples of about the same size. The Windsor samples support Evans's assertion that sack-back chairs with seven or nine spindles were made concurrently, but they also suggest that nine-spindle production began earlier because their makers favored the rounded rail used on many nine-spindle comb-backs. The verticality of the nine-spindle sack-back chair illustrated in figure 1 is related to early comb-backs as well.[17]

Although many surviving Philadelphia sack-back Windsors have rounded or partially rounded rails, this is not the case for chairs made elsewhere. All of the early Lancaster area chairs discussed in Evans's and Santore's monographs appear to have rectangular rails, even though most have seats 21–21½ inches wide, like many pre-Revolutionary Philadelphia examples. Rectangular rails are also common on Rhode Island Windsors, which typically have narrower seats. Of the twenty-two sack-backs measured and illustrated in Evans's book, fifteen have rectangular rails and seats 20½ inches wide or less.[18]

With regard to Windsors made in New York City, the situation is much the same. Three sack-backs Santore attributes to that city have bold turn-

Table 3 *Nine-Spindle Philadelphia Windsor Chairs Arranged by Rail Type and Increasing Arm Support Angle*

Chair	Rail type	Seat width	Seat depth to width ratio	Increasing arm support angle	Arm rail width	Arm rail thickness	Hoop diameter	Hoop penetrations 2	3	4	5	6	7	8	Attachments of legs	of arm supports	of stretchers
Henzey, Independence Hall, acc. 3350	rounded	21¾"	.736	2°	0.860	.666	.838	O	O		O		O	O	1w	—	—
Henzey, Independence Hall, acc. 8139	beveled	21¾"	.741	3°	0.936	.634	.840	θ	θ				θ	θ	peen	—	—
Independence Hall, acc. 8458	rounded	21¼"	.735	5°	1.180	.782	.928	θ	θ				θ	θ	1w	—	—
Figure 1	rounded	21¼"	.721	6°	0.995	.744		—	—	Hoop replaced					peen	—	—
Henzey, Winterthur, acc. 1987.19	rounded	21"	.762	7°	0.953	.850	.838	ϕ	ϕ				ϕ	ϕ	2w	—	—
Trumble, Independence Hall, acc. 1019	rounded	20¾"	.753	10°	1.110	.760	.934	ϕ	ϕ	ϕ	θ	ϕ	ϕ	ϕ	1w	—	—
Trumble, Independence Hall, acc. 1087	rounded	20¾"	.783	10	1.105	.738	.914	ϕ	ϕ	ϕ		ϕ	ϕ	ϕ	1w	—	—
Independence Hall, acc. 7394	rectangular	21"	.744	1°	0.906	.736	.792	O	O				O	O	1w	—	—
Independence Hall, acc. 8488	rectangular	21⅛"	.757	7°	1.011	.694	.760	ϕ	ϕ				ϕ	ϕ	1w	—	—
Trumble, Independence Hall, acc. 7884	rectangular	20¾"	.808	10°	1.023	.762	.844	ϕ						ϕ	1w	—	—
E. Evans, Independence Hall, acc. 5841	rectangular	22⅛"	.746	10°	0.978	.722	n.d.	ϕ	ϕ	ϕ	O	ϕ	ϕ	ϕ	1w	—	—
Independence Hall, acc. 8489	rectangular	21¼"	.759	11°	0.992	.690	.796	θ	θ				θ	θ	2w	—	—
Averages					1.004	.731	.848										

Salient measurements are in red. *W* refers to the number of wedges used to secure each leg at the seat.

ings, rectangular rails, and seats nearly 20½ inches wide. He dates these chairs between 1765 and 1780, concurrent with his dates for early Philadelphia sack-backs, but his own work on continuous-armed New York Windsors includes a New York chair with equally robust turnings marked by the firm Hampton and Always, whose short-lived partnership date is documented to 1792. There is reason to believe that these New York sack-backs were made after the Revolution and are later than most Philadelphia examples with wider seats and rounded arms.[19]

Finally, all of the armchairs with 21½-inch seat widths (excluding chairs with D-shaped seats) that Evans attributes to Boston and Rhode Island have rectangular rails. Many of these chairs also have legs with greater splay than similar Philadelphia examples and wide baluster-shaped arm supports with thin, elongated tops. Therefore, it is probable that the makers of at least some of these chairs were familiar with sophisticated sack-backs similar to those illustrated in figures 11 and 12.[20]

Once makers realized that cross-sectional width was much more important to arm rail strength than vertical thickness, arm rails became sleeker in side section and turnings became thinner, especially in New England. The Windsor illustrated in figure 26 is strong enough for daily use, even though it is light and has few of the nails and none of the pins found on some earlier products. Several American artists depicted men and women seated on similar chairs more than a hundred years after their manufacture, a testament to the durability and strength of this seating form (fig. 27).

Figure 26 Armchair, probably Massachusetts, ca. 1790. Unidentified ring-porous hardwoods, unidentified softwood, and maple. H. 38½", W. 20" (seat), D. 15¾6" (seat); seat height: 17"; seat depth/seat width: .787; rectangular rail width: 1.017"; rail thickness: .573"; arm support angle: 17.5°. (Private collection; photo, Gavin Ashworth.) Of all the chair hoops examined for this study, the one on this chair is thickest in the center. The hoop tapers as it approaches the arm rail, which, like the arm supports, is quite thin. The seat does not have the usual channel next to the spindles.

Figure 27 Thomas W. Dewing (1851–1938), *The Carnation,* 1892. Oil on canvas. 20" x 15⅝". (Courtesy, Freer Gallery of Art, Smithsonian Institution, gift of Charles Lang Freer.) The lightness and elegance of chairs like the one illustrated in fig. 26 attracted American painters a century after they were made.

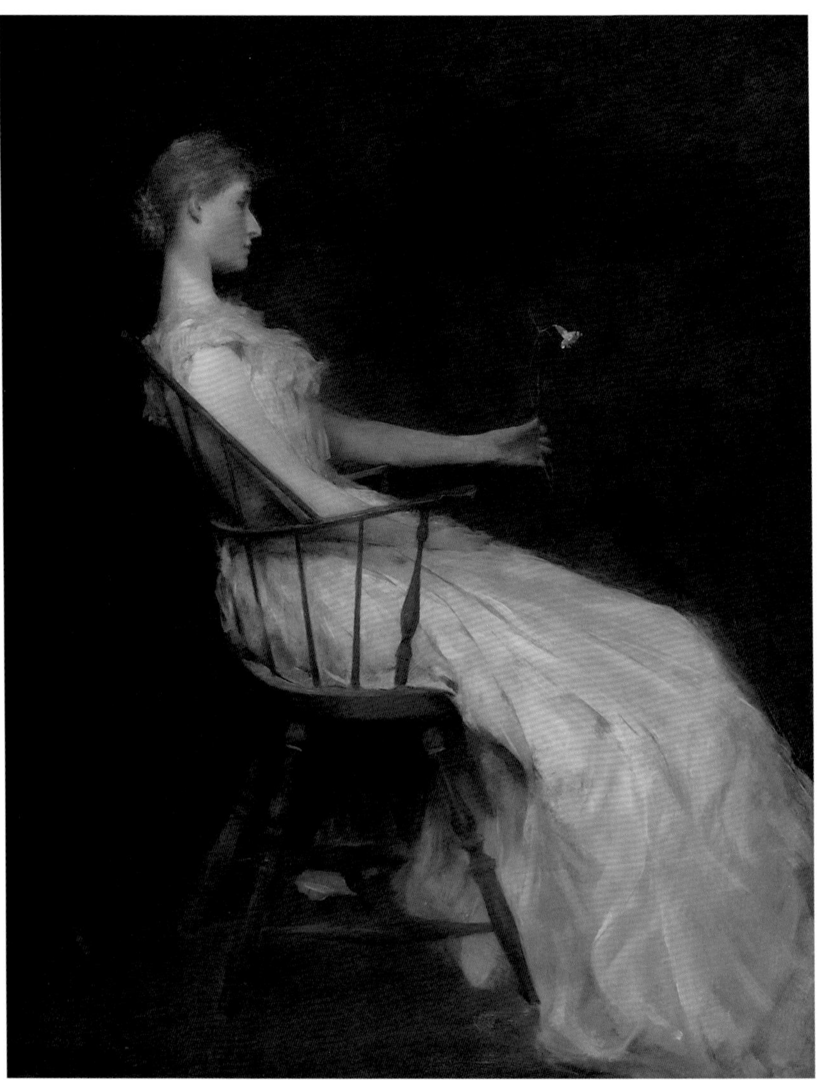

The Locking Arm

Although changes in arm rail strength have been the focus of this article so far, other structural developments occurred as Windsor chair makers sought to prevent an "untimely coming to pieces." The arm support played an important role as the chair evolved from a design with strength based on rigidity toward a design with planned flexibility. The chair illustrated in figure 1 has arm supports that are nearly perpendicular to the seat when seen from the side, like the arm supports on many tall-back and low-back armchairs (fig. 28). By contrast, the chair shown in figure 4 has forward-canted arm supports and hoop anchors placed far forward. Neither Windsor has pins or nails at the tops or bottoms of its short spindles or arm supports, but the arm supports of the chair illustrated in figure 4 are strengthened with handmade metal tensioning bars. When a sitter leans back in such chairs, the hoop and back spindles bend back slightly. Since the hoop is anchored at the rail, the rail is also pulled; the more forward the hoop anchor, the more direct the pull. If the arm supports and short spindles are nearly perpendicular to the seat and not pinned or nailed at the arms, there is nothing save the tightness of the wedged arm supports and short spindles to keep the arms from pulling away and failing. The arm supports of these chairs did pull out at one time. This probably explains why few early sack-backs with nearly vertical arm supports have survived.

To fix this problem, a few Philadelphia chair makers pinned or nailed their arm supports and short spindles, but most craftsmen decided instead to cant the arm support about 10 or 15 degrees forward (fig. 29) and to limit the side splay of the arm (see figs. 1, 4). The forward-canted arm support was a structural advancement because it placed the arm support rail joints in tension created by leaning back on the chair. In other words, forward canting produced an arm lock that became stronger when the chair was sat on. With the arm supports canted to the sides (see fig. 1), the locks are still

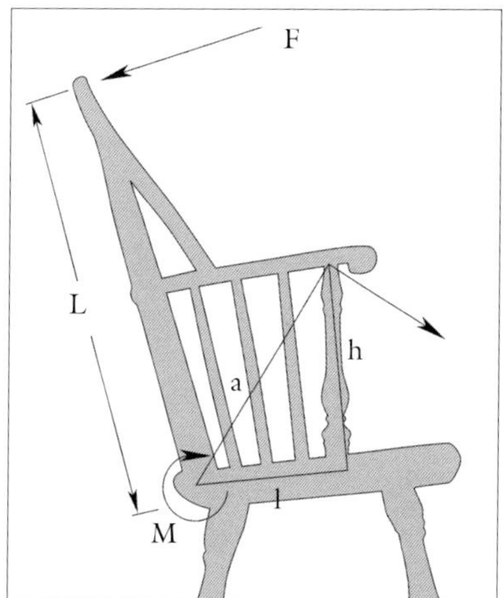

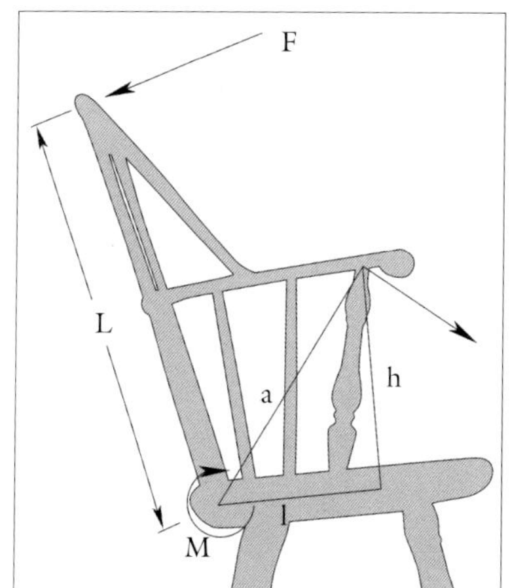

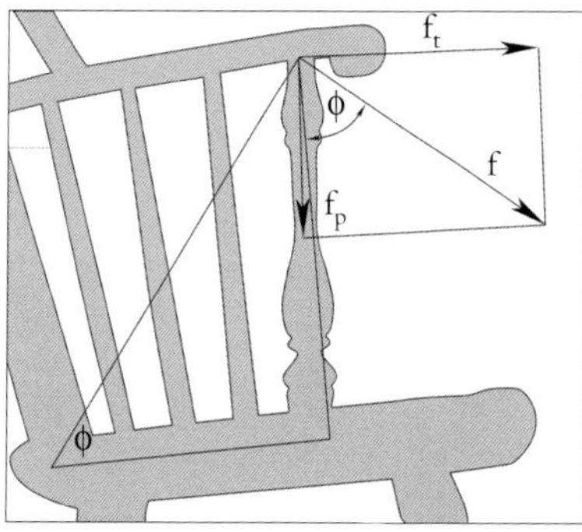

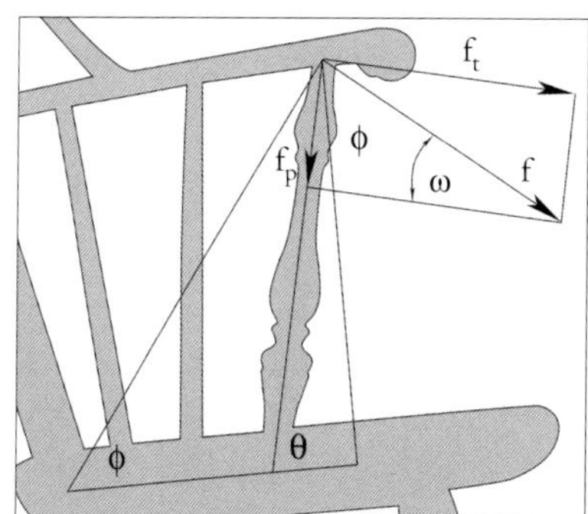

Figure 28 Diagram showing forces and movements created by a sitter leaning back on the chair illustrated in fig. 1. (Artwork, Wynne Patterson, Inc. from drawings by Martin Schnall.)

Figure 29 Diagram showing forces and movements created by a sitter leaning back on the chair illustrated in fig. 4. (Artwork, Wynne Patterson, Inc. from drawings by Martin Schnall.)

present, but pushing the arm rail to the side when a sitter rises partially circumvents them and may damage the chair.

Moment Analysis and Arm Support Pullout

An engineering moment balance addresses these points and others. In this analysis, forces act at various distances from a point of rotation, called a fulcrum or a hinge. Two forces of the same magnitude equidistant from the hinge, acting on opposite sides and in opposing directions, balance, just like two children of the same weight sitting equally distant from the balance point on a seesaw. A smaller force farther away from the fulcrum can balance a bigger force, like a smaller child sitting farther out on the seesaw, but a third child sitting on the balance point has no effect, no matter how much that child weighs. When a person leans back on any armchair, forces are created along the back of the chair (see figs. 28, 29). The force distribution depends on sitter height and posture, but since the force most distant from the seat is potentially most destructive, the situation can be simplified using a single resultant force F acting at the top of the hoop at distance L from the fulcrum; the greater the lean back, the greater the force. This force creates a moment M at the base of the back of the chair, but the back of the chair resists this moment; the more rigid the spindles and the greater their number, the greater the countermoment. Net rearward bending force F_n is less than the applied force F created by leaning back because of the resistance to bending offered by the rear of the chair.

$$FL - M = F_n L$$

If the chair is not to pull apart, other forces must keep the arm supports and side spindles from pulling out; their moments must balance the net rearward bending moment. With reference to the diagrams illustrated in figures 28 and 29:

$$FL - M - f\,a = 0;$$
$$FL - M - f\,(l^2 + h^2)^{1/2} = 0.$$

Or, with rearrangement,

$$f = [FL - M] / (l^2 + h^2)^{1/2}$$
$$= F_{net}\, L / (l^2 + h^2)^{1/2} \qquad \text{(Eq. 4)}$$

Since hoop height L is about twice as large as arm support distance l along the seat (see figs. 28, 29), and since rail height h is about the same length as l, this equation shows that when one leans back on a sack-back Windsor, the force acting on the arm supports is about 1.5 times greater than the net force created by leaning back on the chair.

$$f \approx F_{net}\, 2l / \sqrt{2}l \approx \sqrt{2}F_{net}$$

In other words, the difference in moment arm lengths has amplified the net force acting on the back of the chair.

The force f acting at the top of the arm supports can be resolved into two components, one acting along the arm supports to pull them out (f_p), and a second acting along the arms to pull them back. If the arm supports have little or no forward cant (see fig. 28), the force f_p acting to pull them out becomes

$$f_p = f\cos\varphi = \sqrt{2}F_{net}\cos\varphi$$

But since h and l are about the same length, φ is about 45° and $\cos\varphi$ is about $1/\sqrt{2}$.

$$f_p \sim \sqrt{2}F_{net} / \sqrt{2} = F_{net}$$

For chairs with little or no forward cant to their arm supports, the force acting to pull out the arm supports is about the same as the net force acting on the back of the chair. If, on the other hand, the arm support is canted forward, the diagram in figure 29 shows that the force component acting along the arm supports to pull them out is

$$f_p = f \sin \varpi,$$

where ϖ is defined by the perpendicular from vector f to the arm support. But since geometry shows that $\varpi = \theta - \varphi$,

$$f_p = f \sin \varpi = f \sin (\theta - \varphi). \qquad \text{(Eq. 5)}$$

Now compare the pullout force f_p generated in uncanted and variously canted arm supports. If subscript c refers to canting and subscript u refers to uncanted supports,

$$f_{pu} = f \cos\varphi = f \sin (90° - \varphi) \qquad \text{(Eq. 6)}$$

$$f_{pc} = f \sin \varpi = f \sin (\theta - \varphi)$$

$$f_{pc} / f_{pu} = \sin (\theta - \varphi)/ \sin (90° - \varphi)$$

Since θ is less than 90° for the forward cant, $\sin (\theta - \varphi)$ is smaller than $\sin (90° - \varphi)$, and the pullout force generated in a canted arm support is smaller than the pullout force generated in an uncanted arm support. This is demonstrated graphically in the diagrams shown in figures 28 and 29. The f_p vector for the canted case in figure 28 is shorter than the f_p vector for the uncanted case in figure 29, even though the two f vectors are of the same length.

Equation 6 can be used to compare the size of the pullout force for various arm support cants. Since φ is about 45° for most sack-backs, the pullout force with a 10° forward cant is approximately $\sin 35°/ \sin 45°$, or 81% of the pullout force for an arm support without canting. With a 20° forward cant, the pullout force is about $\sin 25°/ \sin 45°$, or 60% of the pullout force without canting. With a 20° forward cant, the force acting to pull out the arm support is almost halved. As the diagrams in figures 28 and 29 show, the greater the forward cant the greater the force pulling back on the arm rail to keep it locked in place.

These equations are simplifications. The lean-back force should be evenly distributed in some reasonable way, and the short side spindles under the arm should be included. But little can be gained by doing so at this time because the resulting equations cannot be solved. There is no quantitative information regarding the relative strength of joints with single and double wedges. One can only surmise that joint strength depends on the number of wedges, on wedge angle relative to the grain, and on joint contact area.

Arm Lock Development

The analysis above shows that the arm support with greater forward cant is stronger. With a 10-degree cant, the pullout force generated at the top of the arm support by leaning back is reduced by about 20 percent. With a 20-degree cant, the force is almost halved. Arm lock strength is also affected by the thickness of the arm rail where the support is tenoned in place. The 12-degree lock on the Philadelphia chair illustrated in figure 4 is no more susceptible to pullout failure than the 18-degree lock on the armchair shown in figure 26 because the former chair has a thicker rail (fig. 30). Most Philadelphia makers used a thicker rail and a less canted support to address the pullout problem.

Figure 30 Diagram showing how an increase in the cant of the arm support increases the size of the barriers (*a*) the arm rail must clear before failing. Increasing arm rail thickness also increases the size of the barriers. (Artwork, Wynne Patterson from drawings by Martin Schnall.)

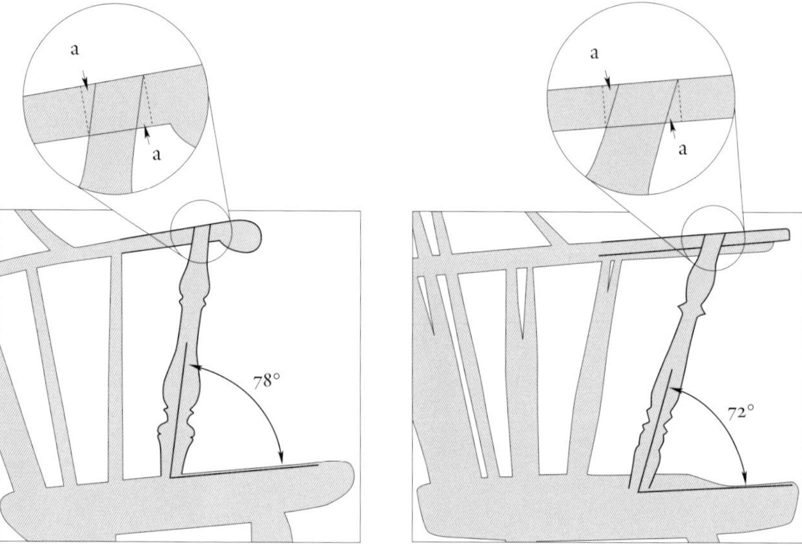

Figure 31 Armchair, probably Philadelphia, Pennsylvania, ca. 1760. Unidentified ring-porous hardwoods, tulip poplar, and maple. H. 35", W. 20½" (seat), D. 15" (seat); seat height: 16½"; seat depth/seat width: .736; rounded rail width: .924", rail thickness: .769" increasing to 1.099" near the middle spindle; arm support angle: 20.5°. (Courtesy, Independence National Historic Park; photo, Gavin Ashworth.) The only pins in the chair are those used to secure the hoop to the arm rail. This chair proves that Windsors with strongly canted arm supports were made early on in Philadelphia or its environs.

Figure 32 Thomas Blackford, armchair, Boston, Massachusetts, ca. 1785. Maple, oak, and hickory. H. 45", W. 21½" (seat), D. 15⅞" (seat); seat height: n.d.; seat depth/seat width: .718; rectangular rail width: .903"; rail thickness: .657"; arm support angle: 5–6°. (Courtesy, Winterthur Museum.) This chair, which was inspired by Philadelphia seating, indicates that Windsors with unpinned, nearly vertical arm supports were still made in Boston in the 1780s.

Figure 33 Lewis Bender, armchair, Philadelphia, Pennsylvania, ca. 1795. Oak, hickory, maple, and tulip poplar. H. 36½", W. 20⅜" (seat), D. 15" (seat); seat height: 17", seat depth/seat width: .736; rounded rail width, rail thickness, and arm support angle not recorded. (Private collection; courtesy, Perseus Press.) This chair shows that Windsors with rounded arm rails and weakly canted arm supports were still being made in Philadelphia in the 1790s. On the other hand, the supports are relatively thin where they enter the seat, which reduces the risk of seat cracking.

The thirty-five sack-backs sampled to determine when and how the transition from rounded to rectangular rails occurred provide insights into how Philadelphia chair makers laid out their arm supports. In the case of arm rails, either makers used rectangular ones or they did not, but with arm supports the situation was different; forward cants range from almost nil to nearly 20 degrees. However, patterns do emerge. Several of the nine-spindle chairs with rounded rails in this sample have arm supports canted less than 5 degrees, and none has supports canted more than 10 degrees. One of the seven-spindle chairs with rounded rails has supports with a slight cant, but most have supports canted 10 degrees or more. On the other hand, half of the seven-spindle chairs with rectangular rails have supports canted nearly 10 degrees, while the others have supports canted 15 degrees or more.

The chairs in this sample document a chronological transition from nine-spindle chairs with rounded rails and near-vertical arm supports to seven-spindle chairs with stronger rectangular rails and 15-degree arm supports, but variations along the way suggest that other influences were at work. Some early Philadelphia chairs with blunt arrow feet have strongly canted arm supports (see fig. 31), as do Windsors from both sets made for Carpenters' Hall (see fig. 25). In contrast, a few late eighteenth-century chair makers including Lewis Bender and Thomas Blackford, who moved from Philadelphia to Boston in the mid-1780s, used supports with little cant (see figs. 32, 33). A chair made by Bender in the mid-1790s also has a rounded rail. All of the Joseph Henzey chairs in this sample have near-vertical arm supports (see fig. 34 and table 3), but this structural shortcoming apparently had little effect on the appeal of his products. He had a very successful career.[21]

Figure 34 Joseph Henzey, armchair, Philadelphia, Pennsylvania, ca. 1785. Unidentified ring-porous hardwoods, unidentified softwood, and maple. H. 37¾", W. 21¾" (seat), D. 16" (seat); seat height: 17¾"; seat depth/seat width: .736; rounded rail width: .919"; rail thickness: .703"; arm support angle: 5°. (Courtesy, Independence National Historic Park; photo, Gavin Ashworth.) Henzey's Windsors are known for long baluster turnings, short tapered feet, and finely shaped seats, but structural analysis indicates that his chairs are weaker because their arm rails are rounded and arm support angles are weak. Since Henzey did not set up a large shop until after the Revolution, this chair and others suggest that he was using weaker construction methods after the war.

The Hoop

Three factors have been discussed in relation to arm support pullout failures in early Windsors: arm support cant angle, arm thickness at the arm support, and arm rail width. In summary, the smaller the arm support forward cant, the smaller the horizontal tension on the arm support and the greater the risk that leaning back and pulling on the arm will pull it away from the chair. But for any arm support cant, thicker arms provide greater physical barriers to arm support pullout, and wider arms reduce the flex that could allow these physical barriers to be overcome. There is a fourth factor for chairs without pins or nails at the tops of their arm supports: the taller the hoop or bow, the greater the risk that leaning back will generate a force sufficient to pull the arms away from their supports.

Back Height and Arm Pullout

A moment balance is used to develop this height relationship. If equations 4 and 5 are combined, pullout force f_p is related to lean-back force F for any arm support forward cant θ, hoop height L, and spindle stiffness M.

$$
\begin{aligned}
f_p &= f \sin(\theta - \varphi) \\
&= F_{net} L \sin(\theta - \varphi) / (l^2 + h^2)^{1/2} \qquad \text{(Eq. 7)}
\end{aligned}
$$

Since l and h are relatively fixed for most armchairs (see figs. 28, 29), and since φ is $tan^{-1}(h/l)$, f_p is a direct function of hoop height L for any spindle stiffness M and arm support forward cant θ. Therefore, for any sack-back chair, this equation provides the result that would be expected intuitively: the taller the hoop, the greater the pullout force on the arm supports and the greater the risk of arm support pullout failure.

The makers of sack-back Windsors had three ways to reduce the risk of arm support pullout caused by tall hoops. They could pin or nail the arm supports, top and bottom; they could thicken the arms to increase the size of the locking lip (see fig. 30); or they could keep hoop height low. The sack-back armchairs with flat-back rails illustrated in figures 11 and 12 have wrought sprigs at the tops of their arm supports and short spindles, and pins at the bases of two of their four short spindles and their arm supports. Chairs like these were uncommon, however; only two of the Philadelphia-area examples in this study have pins or nails securing the tops of their arm

Figure 35 Armchair, possibly Philadelphia, Pennsylvania, ca. 1765. Unidentified ring-porous hardwoods, unidentified softwood, and maple. H. 35", W. 20½" (seat), D. 11¾" (seat); seat height: 16"; seat depth/seat width: .709; rectangular rail width: .953"; rail thickness: .582"; arm support angle: 12°. (Courtesy, Independence National Historic Park; photo, Gavin Ashworth.) This chair has one of the shallowest seats of any object examined for this study. Like the sack-back illustrated in fig. 31, this chair shows that some early makers deviated from the Philadelphia standard.

Figure 36 Anthony Steel, armchair, Philadelphia, Pennsylvania, ca. 1800. Unidentified ring-porous hardwoods, unidentified softwood, and maple. H. 37½", W. 21¼" (seat), D. 15⅝" (seat); seat height: 16¾"; seat depth/seat width: .927; rectangular rail width: .927"; rail thickness: .814", arm support angle: 9°. (Courtesy, Independence National Historic Park; photo, Gavin Ashworth.) The chair is branded "A. STEEL." The spindles are nailed at five places on the seat and three places on the rail. Nails are also found at the tops and bottoms of the arm supports and stretcher joints. If these nails are original, the chair proves that Windsors with stronger reinforced joints were being made in Philadelphia near the end of the eighteenth century.

supports (figs. 35, 36). The earlier chair (fig. 35) has a shallower seat than the Windsor shown in figure 1 and unusually bold baluster turnings. The later example (fig. 36) bears the brand of Anthony Steel, who did not begin work until 1790 or 1791. With regard to arm rail thickness, tables 3 and 4 show that it did not change much; the average for twelve nine-spindle chairs is .731 inches, while the average for twenty-three seven-spindle chairs is .723 inches. Most Philadelphia makers chose instead to keep hoop heights relatively low.

Chair makers who did use pins or nails to secure their arm supports could create tall sack-backs with pullout-resistant rails. A chair found in Easton, Pennsylvania (figs. 37–39), has a very tall hoop, wide arm splay, and a very shallow seat. Evans and Santore illustrate other tall-back Windsors from Lancaster, Pennsylvania, and New England. Since the hoops of these tall chairs are about 40 percent higher than most and their spindles are about average in diameter, equation 7 shows that leaning back on one of them

Figure 37 Armchair, possibly Easton, Pennsylvania, ca. 1765. Unidentified ring-porous hardwoods and maple. H. 39⅝", W. 21$^{5}/_{16}$" (seat), D. 15½" (seat); seat height: 16½"; seat depth/seat width: .676; rectangular rail width: .995"; rail thickness: .744"; arm support angles: 6 and 8°. (Private collection; photo, Gavin Ashworth.) This early, simply turned chair is stronger than most comparable Philadelphia examples. The tops and bottoms of the arm supports and all of the stretcher joints are pinned, and the spindles penetrate the seat like those on the Massachusetts chair illustrated in fig. 8. The fact that few Philadelphia makers used pins to reinforce their arm supports may explain why no tall sack-backs comparable to this example are known to have been produced in that city.

Figure 38 Detail showing the pins securing the right arm (from the sitter's perspective) support of the chair illustrated in fig. 37. (Photo, Gavin Ashworth.)

Figure 39 Detail of pinned stretcher joints on the armchair illustrated in fig. 37. (Photo, Gavin Ashworth.)

Figure 40 Armchair, Philadelphia, Pennsylvania, ca. 1765. Unidentified ring-porous hardwoods, unidentified softwood, and maple. H. 37½", W. 21½" (seat), D. 16⅞" (seat); seat height: 17½"; seat depth/ seat width: .736; rounded rail width: .985"; rail thickness: .674"; arm support angle: 10°. (Private collection; photo, Gavin Ashworth.) This stylish chair displays the same structural weaknesses and damage found on the chairs illustrated in figs. 1 and 4: the hoop and rounded arm rail are cracked. The stretchers of this chair are not pinned. The feet have been extended.

creates much more pullout force at the arm support than would usually be expected. Since most Philadelphia sack-backs lack pegged or nailed arm supports, it is not surprising that no tall-back example is known. Evans suggests that tall-back chairs were made for invalids and the elderly who would not subject them to heavy use.[22]

Equation 7 is not completely valid for comb-back armchairs because there is no direct link between the tall spindles at the rear and the arm supports. But there is an indirect link; the more rigid and plentiful the tall spindles, the more direct the pull on the arm at the arm support when a sitter leans back on the chair. Therefore, early comb-back Windsors probably suffered from the same arm support pullout problems. Evidence supports this. Seven of the nine comb-back armchairs at Independence Hall are pinned at the tops of their arm supports. Most of those chairs have pins at the tops of some short spindles as well.[23]

Hoop Spindle Penetration Cracks

Most hoop failures are cracks where the spindles penetrate the hoop and reduce its cross section by 40 percent or more. Such cracks typically occur at the rear of the spindle because the rear of the hoop, like the rear of the arm rail, is in tension when a user leans back. Although hoop cracks are not catastrophic failures like arm support pullouts or seat breaks, they weaken the superstructure and make the chair unsatisfactory for public display and use.

Physical evidence suggests that many Philadelphia chair makers believed the fewer the spindle penetrations, the smaller the risk of hoop failure, because the hoop then remains more whole. Some early Windsors, like the one illustrated in figure 31, have only five spindles, whereas others have only one or two spindles penetrating the hoop. Most Philadelphia makers used four penetrating spindles. With seven-spindle chairs, the penetrations are typically at the 2, 3, 5, and 6 positions, and with nine-spindle chairs they are typically at the 2, 3, 7, and 8 positions. The end spindles rarely penetrate the hoop. Most makers drove a wedge into the end of each penetrating spindle perpendicular to the grain, but some used wedges set parallel to the grain or on the bias, and others peened the ends of the spindles. The following chart illustrates common penetration patterns for nine- and seven-spindle chairs. Symbols used here are repeated in tables 3 and 4.

Philadelphia nine-spindle hoops	1	2	3	4	5	6	7	8	9
Wedges parallel to the grain		θ	θ				θ	θ	
Wedges perpendicular to the grain		ϕ	ϕ				ϕ	ϕ	
With a small central penetration		ϕ	ϕ		o		ϕ	ϕ	
Peened, not wedged		O	O				O	O	

Philadelphia seven-spindle hoops	1	2	3	4	5	6	7
Wedges perpendicular to the grain		ϕ	ϕ		ϕ	ϕ	
With a central penetration and a crack		ϕ	ϕ[c]	O	ϕ	ϕ	

Concerns over diminished hoop integrity may explain why some Philadelphia chair makers used nails to reinforce their spindle penetrations. The strong seven-spindle sack-backs with flat-back arm rails shown in figures 11 and 12 have five penetrations—three in the middle and one at each end—rather than four as do most Philadelphia examples. For added strength, the maker of those sack-backs wedged the spindles on the bias and secured them with small wrought sprigs nailed in from the rear. A few Philadelphia chairs with seven spindle penetrations and no nails are also known.

1	2	3	4	5	6	7
n		n	n	n		n
ø		ø	ø	ø		ø

The hoop-spindle attachments for all of the Philadelphia sack-backs in this study are shown in tables 3 and 4. Most of the nine-spindle chairs have spindles that penetrate the hoop at the 2, 3, 7, and 8 positions and are secured by wedges driven in perpendicular to the grain. All of Joseph Henzey's nine-spindle chairs have penetrating spindles at the 2, 3, 7, and 8 positions, whereas two of Francis Trumble's three chairs have six or seven penetrating spindles. Most of the seven-spindle sack-backs also have four spindle penetrations, but there are exceptions. Several have five penetrations securing the ends of the hoop like the flat-back armchairs or across the middle, five in a row, whereas two of the chairs have seven penetrations. Other variations can be observed in the Windsors made for Carpenters' Hall. The chairs from the set with strong, wide rectangular rails (see fig. 25) have only four hoop penetrations, whereas the single example with a much weaker rounded rail has five hoop penetrations like the stronger chairs with flat-back arm rails.

Rather than indicating whether some chairs are weaker or stronger than others, the data in tables 3 and 4 reveals fundamental, even philosophical, differences among Philadelphia makers regarding how best to secure the hoops of their sack-back chairs. Surviving Windsors with cracked hoops provide some insight (see fig. 40). Three of the four Philadelphia chairs in this study with four spindle penetrations and rounded rails have one or more hoop cracks, whereas none of the chairs with seven spindle penetrations made in Philadelphia or elsewhere has cracked hoops.[24]

Engineering analysis suggests why hoop cracks are less common with seven hoop penetrations and rectangular rails, provided that the hoop diameter is not undersized. Calculating the stresses on a given system of hoop spindle joints for a given sitter is beyond the scope of this article and falls within the purview of mechanical engineering finite element analysis. Nevertheless, one can develop a mental picture of these stresses based on geometry and an understanding of structural properties.[25]

When a hoop cracks at a spindle penetration, the wood has been subjected to a local stress greater than it can bear. If, as is often the case, the hoop has a constant diameter along its length where the spindles intersect, this failure-inducing stress is not the result of reduced hoop cross-section; the cross sections are all about the same. What remains for consideration are bending stresses that occur when a sitter leans back or flexes the chair arms—the same stresses discussed earlier in reference to tree branches bending until they break. If the hoop is penetrated and wedged at all positions, bending stress is evenly distributed and not localized at any one spindle. If the hoop is penetrated and wedged at only four positions, however, stress may be localized at some point or points along the hoop, and failure may occur.

Contrary to common sense, a hoop with fewer spindle penetrations is weaker. With more penetrations, the arm and the hoop above it are more locked together, and they move as a unit when the chair is sat on. This structure has engineering antecedents in the king and queen post trusses found in medieval and later buildings and cognates in modern suspension bridge design (fig. 41).

Solving the Hoop Crack Problem

Flexing the arms of a sack-back from side to side also produces a focused flex in a hoop not fully penetrated by spindles. When the arms move sideways, the ends of the hoop move with them, and the hoop must flex to accommodate this movement; the more forward the ends of the hoop, the greater

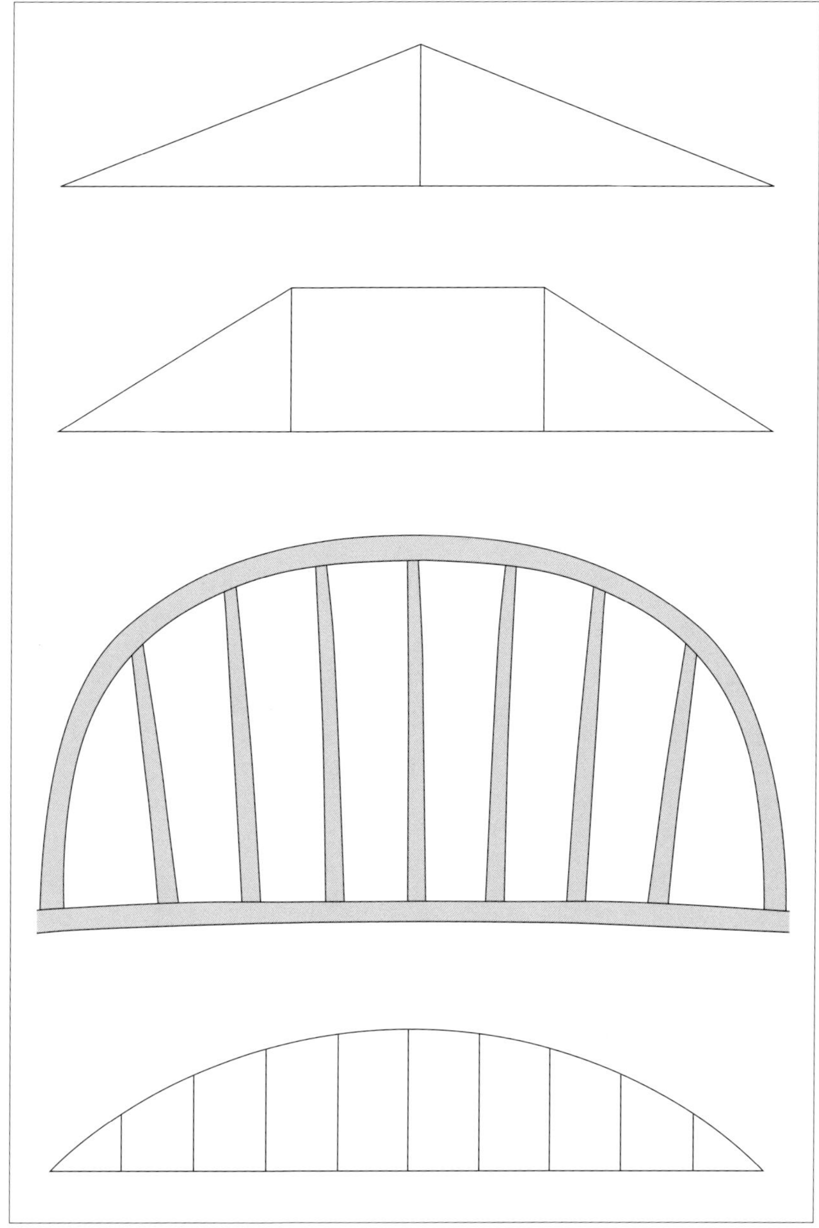

Figure 41 Drawing comparing the structures (from top to bottom) of a king post, queen post, Windsor hoop and spindle, and suspension truss. (Artwork, Wynne Patterson from drawings by Martin Schnall.)

the flex. If the spindles penetrate the hoop at the 2, 3, 5, and 6 or the 2, 3, 7, and 8 positions, bending stress will probably concentrate near the middle of the hoop because the ends of the hoop are in sitting tension and the spindles in between are fairly well tied down. Therefore, the working relationship is that the weaker the arm rail, the greater the arm flexibility and the greater the hoop movement. This probably explains why surviving chairs with stronger rectangular rails have fewer cracked hoops.

Since hoops are made of green wood, they are pliant and supple at first. Over time, the wood dries out and becomes susceptible to cracking. The rate at which this happens depends on how well the hoop is protected by paint or varnish and where the chair is used. The hoop of a sack-back with four penetrations (see fig. 4) did not crack until recently, but there is evidence that eighteenth-century Philadelphia makers knew that hoops were prone to cracking and sought ways to remedy the problem. Some chair makers, including Francis Trumble and Ephraim Evans, made sack-back Windsors with seven penetrating spindles, whereas Anthony Steel used five fully penetrating spindles across the back in a row (see table 4). Evans worked in Philadelphia between 1779 and 1785, while Steel's career lasted from about 1790 until his death in 1817, but Trumble began work in about 1760 and made chairs for forty years. Therefore, Trumble's chairs may document a transition from few hoop penetrations to many penetrations over the course of his career (see tables 3, 4). In contrast, most New England sack-backs have only penetrating spindles (see table 5), as do many comparable Windsors made in the southwest of England.[26]

Figure 42 Armchair, Newport, Rhode Island, ca. 1770. Unidentified ring-porous hardwoods, unidentified softwood, and maple. H. 34⅝", W. 21½" (seat), D. 15⅝" (seat); seat height: 14⅝"; seat depth/seat width: .721; rectangular rail width: .941"; rail thickness: .633"; arm support angle: 20°. (Private collection; photo, Gavin Ashworth.) This chair has pins or nails at all major stress points. All of the tall spindles penetrate the hoop and are wedged. The oversize rectangular hoop of this chair suggests that some early makers were aware of the problems of cracking hoops.

Use of seven or nine penetrating spindles was not the only way to reduce the risk of hoop cracking. An early New England armchair with an outsize rectangular-sectioned hoop (fig. 42) was probably made in response to this problem. The hoop is about 1.125 inches wide and one-quarter inch thick, and it looks as though someone trained as a wheelwright made it. Since the

Table 4 *Seven-Spindle Philadelphia Windsor Chairs Arranged by Rail Type and Increasing Arm Support Angle*

Chair	Rail type	Seat width	Seat depth to width ratio	Increasing arm support angle	Arm rail width	Arm rail thickness	Hoop diameter	Hoop penetrations 1	2	3	4	5	6	7	Attachments of legs	of arm supports	of stretchers
Henzey, Independence Hall, acc. 1084	rounded	21¾"	.736	5°	0.919	.703	.768			ϕ				ϕ	1w	—	pins
Independence Hall, acc. 1041	beveled	21⅞"	.731	7°	0.903	.620	.823		ϕ	ϕ		ϕ	ϕ		1w	—	—
Independence Hall, acc. 8353	rounded	22¼"	.702	8°	0.920	.749	.879		ϕ	ϕ		ϕ	ϕ		n.d.	—	—
Independence Hall, acc. 8522	rounded	21¼"	.753	10°	1.000	.708	.809		ϕ	ϕ		ϕ	ϕ		1w	—	—
Figure 40	rounded	21½"	.762	10°	0.985	.674	.834		ϕ	ϕ		ϕ	ϕ		2w	—	—
Independence Hall, acc. 8558	rounded	21¼"	.753	11°	0.893	.701	.769		ϕ	ϕ		ϕ	ϕ		1w	—	—
Independence Hall, acc. 7777	rounded	21¼"	.765	11.5°	0.976	.711	.819		ϕ	ϕ		ϕ	ϕ		1w	—	—
Carpenters' Hall	rounded	20¼"	.833	12.5°	0.993	.656	.704	ϕ		ϕ	ϕ	ϕ		ϕ	1w	—	—
Figure 2	rounded	21½"	.750	15°	1.025	.706	.864		ϕ	ϕ	ϕ	ϕ	ϕ		2w	—	—
Averages:					0.957	.692	.808										
Figure 11	flat-back	21⅛"	.772	11°	1.008	.691	.827	Ø		Ø	Ø	Ø		Ø[a,b,c,d]	2w	2n	—
Figure 12	flat-back	21⅜"	.760	10°	0.998	.747	.817	Ø		Ø	Ø	Ø		Ø[a,b,c,d]	2w	2n	—
Independence Hall, acc. 5788	rectangular	21¼"	.835	8°	0.838	.782	.828		ϕ	ϕ		ϕ	ϕ		1w	—	—
Independence Hall, acc. 8366	rectangular	21"	.726	9°	0.890	.631	.789		ϕ	ϕ	O	ϕ	ϕ		1w	—	—
Independence Hall, acc. 1106	rectangular	21"	.762	9°	0.966	.720	.872		ϕ	ϕ		ϕ	ϕ		1w	—	—
Figure 36	rectangular	21¼"	.735	9°	0.927	.814	.892		ϕ	ϕ	ϕ	ϕ	ϕ[b,d]		n.d.	2n	nails
Independence Hall, acc. 4938	rectangular	20"	.763	10°	1.066	.866	.910		ϕ	ϕ	O	ϕ	ϕ		nails	—	nails
Figure 35	rectangular	20¼"	.709	12°	0.953	.582	.917	ϕ	ϕ	ϕ	ϕ	ϕ	ϕ	ϕ[d]	1w	1pt	—
Independence Hall, acc. 1088	rectangular	21"	.780	14°	0.889	.643	.849		ϕ	ϕ	ϕ	ϕ	ϕ		1w	—	—
Figure 25	rectangular	21⅜"	.737	15°	1.510	.810	.870		ϕ	ϕ		ϕ	ϕ		1w	—	—
Independence Hall, acc. 8616	rectangular	21"	.726	16°	0.959	.847	.917		ϕ	ϕ	O	ϕ	ϕ		1w	—	—
Independence Hall, acc. 8617	rectangular	21"	.738	16°	1.102	.809	.907		ϕ	ϕ	ϕ	ϕ	ϕ		1w	—	—
Independence Hall, acc. 1020	rectangular	21"	.750	17°	1.011	.777	.886	ϕ	ϕ	ϕ	ϕ	ϕ	ϕ	ϕ	1w	—	—
Averages:					1.010	.753	.876										

Salient measurements are in red. [a] Spindles are nailed at the hoop, [b] spindles are nailed or pinned at the arm rail, [c] short side spindles are nailed at the arm rail, and [d] spindles penetrate the seat or are nailed or pinned to it. *W* refers to the number of wedges used to secure each leg at the seat; 2n refers to nails at the top and bottom of each arm support; 1pt refers to one pin at the top.

Figure 43 Detail of the pins securing the hoop and arm support on the left side (from the sitter's perspective) of the chair illustrated in fig. 42. (Photo, Gavin Ashworth.)

Figure 44 Armchair, Massachusetts, ca. 1770. Unidentified ring-porous hardwoods, unidentified softwood, and maple. H. 34", W. 21¾" (seat), D. 16" (seat); seat height: 16⅛"; seat depth/seat width: .724; rectangular rail width: .839"; rail thickness: .68"; arm support angle: 15°. (Private collection; photo, Gavin Ashworth.) This chair originally had pins or nails at all major stress points. All of the tall spindles penetrate the hoop and are wedged. The hoop has extra length at the sides and becomes thinner as it tapers into the arm rail. The arm rail becomes thicker as it approaches the handholds, which provides additional strength and wood thick enough to shape the knuckles from the solid.

penetrating spindles remove a small percentage of its cross section, the risk of cracking is greatly reduced. The detail illustrated in figure 43 shows that the hoop is original to the chair. Its locking pin is the same size and shape as the pin holding the arm support, and the paint layers in both areas are undisturbed. Few American chair makers used rectangular hoops, but some makers used hoops that were thicker near the center for additional strengthening. Other makers tapered the hoop near the arm rails so it would flex near the ends instead of at the spindles, where so much wood had been drilled away (fig. 44). The chair illustrated in figure 26 has both features; the example shown in figure 44 has a hoop that tapers and turns near the arm rail terminations, creating an extra length of hoop that keeps bending stresses away from the relatively weak hoop-spindle penetrations. Tapering of the hoop near the arm rail may have been a structural advance when the chairs were made, but it created cracking problems near the arm rail if the wood dried out and became brittle over time.

The Seat and Undercarriage

Most eighteenth-century Windsor chair seats are thick boards pierced by legs with one or two wedges to keep them snug. Some seats are blind-socketed, especially those on Rhode Island and eastern Connecticut chairs. Blind-socketed seats are aesthetically pleasing because the upper surface is unmarred by construction details; they are strong because they are usually made of a hard wood like maple, and the legs are often pinned through the rear or sides of the seat. By contrast, through-socketed seats are easier to make and more receptive to adjustments in leg splay during manufacture, especially when softer woods are used. Through-socketed seats are also self-locking. When a chair with through-socketed legs is in use, sitting weight pushes down on the seat around the legs and tightens it against the sides of the pierced leg joints. Today, the legs of some early chairs protrude one-eighth of an inch or more. This self-locking capability is analogous to the self-locking arm created by the forward-canted arm support discussed above.[27]

Although one might expect thick one-board seats to be strong, seat cracks and breaks are common in early Windsors. As the chairs illustrated in figures 1 and 4 suggest, this type of damage is usually found at the arm supports or between the rear legs (see figs. 3, 6). Since the seats of most early armchairs are more than twenty-one inches wide, cost-conscious chair makers had no choice but to orient the wood grain from side to side if they wanted to avoid the added effort of wood matching and gluing. Most Philadelphia makers chose tulip poplar for their seats, whereas most New England makers chose white pine. Tulip poplar is relatively dense; early sack-back Windsors with seats made of that wood typically weigh about fifteen pounds. With white pine seats, chair weight could be reduced about 10 percent, but that wood's lower density made the seat weaker and more susceptible to cracking. Philadelphia makers rarely, if ever, used elm, which is common in English Windsor seats. This comes as no surprise, given their access to less brittle and more easily worked woods.

Post Thickness and Seat Failure

A pry bar analogy helps to explain why Windsor chair seats crack at the arm supports. Since Philadelphia arm supports are relatively thick and therefore rigid, sitting forces that pull back on the arm rail are directly transmitted into the seat at the bottom of the arm support. With early chairs like the one shown in figure 1, the arm support is wide where it enters the seat, but with later chairs (see fig. 4), the support is smaller.

> From an engineering perspective, figure 29 shows that the horizontal prying force created by leaning back is greater when the arm support is more canted:
>
> $$f_t = f_{pry} = f \cos \varpi = f \cos (\theta - \varphi)$$
>
> Since φ is about 45°,
>
> $$f_{pry} = f \cos (\theta - 45°)$$
>
> The greater the forward cant of the arm support, the smaller the value of θ and the greater the value of $f \cos (\theta - 45°)$, the force acting on the pry bar. This and the use of pine for the seat help to explain why the seat of the Cox chair (figs. 4–7) cracked at its arm supports.

Some Windsor chair makers found ways to reduce or eliminate damage from pry bar forces that did not compromise the arm lock created by forward canting. The arm supports of the Philadelphia chair illustrated in figure 33 have relatively thin lower sections that reduce the risk of pry bar failure because seat holes are smaller; the pry bar force is the same, no matter what the diameter of the rigid arm support, but the seat is stronger because less of it is taken away. Likewise, the seemingly underdeveloped supports of the New England chair shown in figure 26 are even more structurally advanced because they are thinner throughout their length. The arm support flexes with the spindles as one sits back instead of transmitting pry bar forces directly into the seat of the chair.

The pry bar analogy also holds for Windsor chair legs. Thicker legs need wider seat holes; the thicker the leg joint, the greater the risk that the seat will crack if a side stretcher fails when a sitter leans back on the chair. Therefore, thinner legs, like those of the chair illustrated in figure 26, were also a structural step forward, provided that seat thickness remained comparable and that reduction in leg thickness did not cause other structural problems. Intuition suggests that the greater the leg splay, the greater the force the stretcher joints must bear if the chair is to remain intact. Engineering failure analysis confirms this and demonstrates that the chair with stretchers higher off the floor may be the weaker chair.

> *Leg Splay and Stretcher Failure*
>
> If a sitter's weight W is evenly distributed on a Windsor chair seat, each leg bears $W/4$, provided that the chair sits flat on the floor. A moment balance at the point where a leg enters the seat relates this weight to the tensile force f_s pulling on the side stretcher below it (fig. 45). The balance is written around this point because the leg would start to hinge around it and pry on the seat if the stretcher let go. Since the chair does not move

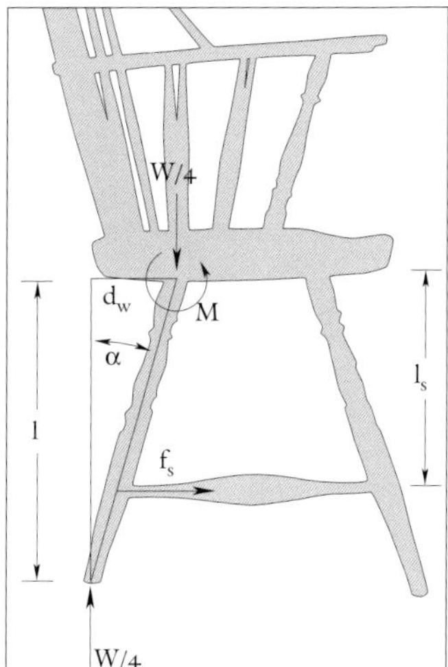

Figure 45 Diagram showing moments created in the undercarriage of a Windsor chair. (Artwork, Wynne Patterson, Inc. from a drawing by Martin Schnall.)

when it is on a level floor, the only other force to consider is provided by Sir Isaac Newton's First Law of Motion: for every action there is an equal and opposite reaction. The weight pushing down on each leg is balanced by a reaction force of equal magnitude pushing up from the floor. With reference to figure 45,

$$\begin{aligned} W\,d_w/4 &= M + f_s l_s \\ W\,l\tan\alpha/4 &= M + f_s\,l_s \\ f_s &= W\,l\tan\alpha/4l_s - M/\,l_s \qquad \text{(Eq. 8)} \end{aligned}$$

where d_w is the shortest perpendicular distance between the fulcrum or hinge and the resistance force *W/4* on the floor, l_s is the shortest perpendicular distance between the fulcrum and the force f_s pulling out on the stretcher, and *M* is the resistive moment offered by the leg joint at the seat, much like the resistance offered by the back spindles in the lean-back analysis above. The weight acting at the top of the leg does not enter the equation because it sits on the fulcrum, like a child sitting on the balance of a seesaw. This is the tensile or pulling force on one side stretcher joint. If the weight on the seat is evenly distributed and the front and back legs have the same splay, the force on each side stretcher joint is doubled. Since the typical seat bottom is about 14½ inches above the floor and the typical stretcher is about four inches above the floor, l_s is 14.5 – 4, or 10.5, and

$$\begin{aligned} f_s &= 14.5W\tan\alpha/42 - M/10.5 \\ &\approx W\tan\alpha/3 - M/10.5 \end{aligned}$$

The value of the resistive moment offered by the seat joint is unknown, but the equation shows that it lessens the tensile force on the stretcher, and that its contribution is reduced by a factor of ten. It is not disregarded, however; experience shows that the legs of Windsors with loose stretchers can bear a sitter's weight without hinging out and failing if the seats are thick and dense. Therefore, a net stretcher tensile force is defined that includes the moment contribution made by the seat joint, in the same way that a net rearward force was defined in the above arm support analyses. Again, with reference to figure 45,

$$\begin{aligned} W\,d_w/4 &= M + f_s l_s = f_{sn} l_s \\ W\,l\tan\alpha/4 &= f_{sn}\,l_s \\ f_{sn} &= W\,l\tan\alpha/4l_s \qquad \text{(Eq. 9)} \end{aligned}$$

If the height of the underside of the seat is about 14½ inches above the

Figure 46 Overall views showing the armchairs illustrated in figs. 1, 4, 8, 11, and 26 from the side and rear. (Photo, Gavin Ashworth.)

floor and the stretcher is about 10 inches below the seat as with many Philadelphia examples,

$$f_{sn} = 14.5W \tan/40 = W \tan/2.75 \qquad \text{(Eq. 10)}$$

Equation 10 allows one to consider the range of leg splay found on most Windsors. If the legs splay approximately 10°, about 25% of the weight on each leg produces tension in the side stretchers, but if the legs splay approximately 20°, about 50% of the weight on each leg produces tension in the side stretchers.

$$f_{s10^\circ} \approx W \tan 10^\circ/2.75 = .064W = .256\ (W/4)$$
$$f_{s20^\circ} \approx W \tan 20^\circ/2.75 = .13W = .532\ (W/4)$$

In other words, stretcher pullout forces are doubled when leg splay is doubled. All other things being equal, engineering analysis shows what intuition would tell us, that the stretchers on a chair with less leg splay are less likely to fail.

Leg splay changed as the American Windsor developed (see fig. 46). On

Figure 47 Armchair, probably Boston, Massachusetts, ca. 1770. Unidentified ring-porous hardwoods, unidentified softwood, and maple. H. 36", W. 21 3/16" (seat); D. 16 3/8" (seat); seat height: 16 3/4"; seat depth/seat width: .740; rectangular rail width: .936"; rail thickness: .676"; arm support angle: 10°. (Private collection; photo, Gavin Ashworth.) Although this chair was inspired by pre-Revolutionary Philadelphia seating, it has a fully rectangular rail, swelled feet, and a sculpted hoop above the arm rail. This chair also has equal leg splay like the New England Windsors illustrated in figs. 8 and 26.

the early Philadelphia sack-back chairs illustrated in figures 1 and 4, the front legs splay about 14 degrees to the side and 12 degrees forward, and the rear legs splay about 10 degrees to the side and 18 degrees rearward. By contrast, the sack-back Windsors shown in figures 11 and 12 have front legs that splay about 20 degrees forward and 20 degrees to the side, and rear legs that splay approximately 20 degrees rearward and 15 degrees to the side. The leg splay angles on the New England chairs illustrated in figures 8 and 26 are about 15

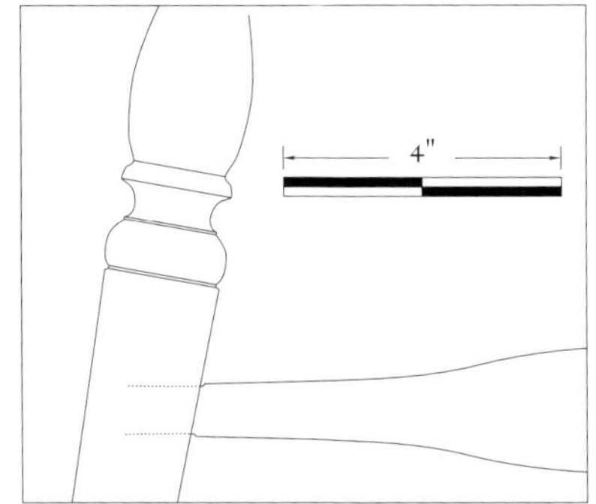

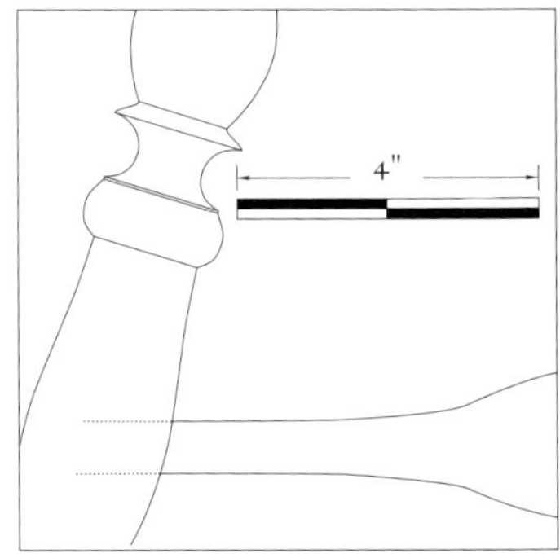

Figure 48 Drawing comparing the tapered and swelled foot. (Artwork, Wynne Patterson, Inc. from a drawing by Martin Schnall.) The swelled foot was more than a New England stylistic convention. It allowed approximately 10 percent greater stretcher penetration and 10 percent greater stretcher diameter, which increased joint contact surface by about 20 percent.

degrees in all directions. Their leg angles relate more closely to the chairs shown in figures 11 and 12 than conventional Philadelphia sack-backs.

If these chairs are representative, the undercarriages of many early Philadelphia sack-backs followed a rather standard form, with postlike front legs having little splay and stool-like back legs splayed less to the side to protect the medial stretcher and more to the rear to improve stability. The chairs illustrated in figures 11 and 12 follow this rule but with more dramatic leg splay reminiscent of some Philadelphia fan-back armchairs (see fig. 19). The maker of these sack-backs apparently understood that greater leg splay creates greater stress at the stretcher joints. He compensated by double-wedging the legs from above and pinning them below the seat (see fig. 14).

Windsors with postlike front legs and stool-like rear legs were also made in New England, but chairs with equally splayed legs are much more common (see figs. 26, 47). The leg splay on most New England sack-backs is about 5 degrees less than that of the chairs shown in figures 11 and 12, and stretcher pullout stresses are about 25 percent smaller (see eq. 10). However, the medial stretchers of chairs with all four legs splayed 15 degrees receive about 50 percent more stress than those on early Philadelphia chairs.

$$f_{S10^\circ} \approx 4W \tan 10^\circ/2.75 = .256\ W;$$
$$f_{S15^\circ} \approx 4W \tan 15^\circ/2.75 = .390\ W;$$
$$f_{S15^\circ}/f_{S10^\circ} = 1.5$$

Although identical leg splays increase the pullout force on the medial stretcher, they reduce manufacturing effort because the angles for the leg holes are all the same.

Stretcher Height and the Swelled Foot

All other things being equal, chairs with higher stretchers are more likely to fail. The analysis below demonstrates this using the same moment balance developed to relate stretcher pullout force to leg splay. A two-inch rise in stretcher height increases stretcher pullout force by about 25 percent.

The analysis begins with equation 9, which relates leg splay angle α, height l of the underside of the seat above the floor and vertical distance l_s between the underside of the seat and the stretcher to the tensile force f_s created in one side stretcher joint by an evenly distributed weight W on all four legs. With reference to that equation and figure 45,

$$f_{sn}\, l_s \approx W d_w/4 \approx W\, l \tan\alpha/4$$
$$f_{sn} \approx W(l / l_s)(\tan\alpha/4)$$

This rearrangement shows that for any fixed leg splay angle α, net stretcher tensile force f_{sn} depends on the ratio of l, the height of the underside of the seat, to l_s, the vertical distance between stretcher and seat bottom. If, as is often the case, the bottom of the seat is about 14½ inches off the floor and the stretcher is about 4½ inches off the floor, the ratio is about 14.5/(14.5 – 4.5), or 1.45. But if the stretcher is 1 inch higher, the ratio increases to 14.5/(14.5 – 5.5), or 1.611. Therefore, all other things being equal, a 1-inch increase in stretcher height increases net stretcher tensile force by about 1.61 / 1.45, or 11%, independent of leg splay angle α. Using the same equation, a 2-inch increase in stretcher height increases net stretcher tensile force by about 25%.

Table 5 *New England and Pennsylvania Chairs with Fully Penetrated Hoops Arranged by Increasing Seat Depth to Width Ratio*

Chair	Rail type	Seat width	Increasing seat depth to width ratio	Arm support angle	Arm rail width	Arm rail thickness	Hoop diameter	Hoop penetrations 1	2	3	4	5	6	7	Attachments of legs	of arm supports	of stretchers
Figure 37 (Pennsylvania)	rectangular	21⅝"	.676	6–8°	0.933	.771	.855	ϕ	ϕ	ϕ	ϕ	ϕ	ϕ	ϕ[d]	1w	2p	pins
Figure 35 (Pennsylvania?)	rectangular	20¼"	.709	12°	0.953	.582	.917	ϕ	ϕ	ϕ	ϕ	ϕ	ϕ	ϕ[d]	1w	1pt	—
Figure 42 (Rhode Island)	rectangular	21½"	.721	20°	0.941	.633	—	ϕ	ϕ	ϕ	ϕ	ϕ	ϕ	ϕ[b,c]	1w	1pt	n.d.
Figure 44 (Massachusetts)	rectangular	21¾"	.724	15°	0.839	.680	.804	ϕ	ϕ	ϕ	ϕ	ϕ	ϕ	ϕ[c]	1w	2n	nails
AWC 6.40 ("Rhode Island")	rectangular	21¼"	.729	14°	0.913	.769	.857	ϕ	ϕ	ϕ	ϕ	ϕ	ϕ	ϕ[c]	—	1pt	nails
AWC 6.126 (Connecticut)	rectangular	19½"	.782	15°	0.930	.657	.896	ϕ	ϕ	ϕ	ϕ	ϕ	ϕ		no	—	—
AWC 6.132 (Connecticut or Rhode Island)	rectangular	21"	.786	10°	1.052	.728	.728	ϕ	ϕ	ϕ	ϕ	ϕ	ϕ	ϕ[a]	1w	—	—
AWC 6.47 ("Rhode Island")	rectangular	21¼"	.788	10°	0.862	.657	.687	O	O	O	O	O	O	O[c]	1w	2p	—
Figure 26 (Massachusetts)	rectangular	20"	.788	17.5°	1.115	.572	.872	ϕ	ϕ	ϕ	ϕ	ϕ	ϕ	ϕ	1w	2n	nails
Chair nearly identical to fig. 26	rectangular	20"	.787	15°	1.089	.515	.867	ϕ	ϕ	ϕ	ϕ	ϕ	ϕ	ϕ	1w	2n	nails

Salient measurements are in red. *AWC* refers to Nancy Goyne Evans, *American Windsor Chairs* (New York: Hudson Hills Press, in association with Winterthur Museum, 1996). *AWC* 6.126 is a six-spindle chair. Superscript abbreviations are: [a] spindles are nailed or pinned at the hoop, [b] long spindles are nailed (pinned) at the arm rail, [c] short side spindles are nailed at the arm rail, and [d] spindles penetrate the seat or are nailed or pinned to it. 1w and 2w refer to the number of wedges used to secure each leg at the seat; 2n refers to two nails at the top and bottom of each arm support; 1pt is one pin at the top.

Since chairs with relatively high stretchers are fairly common in New England, it should not be surprising that many Yankee makers reinforced all of their stretcher joints with pins or nails (see table 5). Some New England makers used another technique to strengthen leg connections. The New England sack-back illustrated in figure 47 is closely related to classic Philadelphia examples. No pins or nails secure the stretchers, the arm supports cant forward about 10 degrees to lock in a relatively thick arm, the seat and the hoop are precisely sculpted, and the spindles penetrate the hoop at the 2, 3, 5, and 6 positions. At the same time, the chair has a rectangular arm rail and swelled feet like many other New England examples. As the drawing shown in figure 48 indicates, swelled feet allowed stretcher joint diameter to increase by 10 percent or more and joint length to increase by about 15 percent, giving a 25 percent or greater increase in cylindrical joint surface contact area. Therefore, the swelled foot is more than a New England stylistic variant. It is a structural innovation that made stretcher joints stronger and allowed makers to build chairs with more leg splay and higher stretchers than their Philadelphia contemporaries without using nails or pins.

Optimizing Stretcher Strength

Early Windsor chairmakers capitalized on the properties of green wood to shape their stock and strengthen the joints of their furniture. Green wood was cheaper than dried wood and much easier to turn on a low-speed lathe. As the legs shrank, they squeezed the side stretcher tenons and made strong connections; the greener the wood, the greater the shrinkage and the stronger the hold. Contemporary chair makers often glue their joints or use construction techniques that have not been documented in period Windsor construction. Michael Dunbar, for example, turns two rings in each stretcher tenon so that leg shrinkage creates a locking ring between them, a practice he observed while repairing an old ladderback chair. Dunbar also uses oversize tenons and dries them in hot sand so that they shrink less after assembly. Finally, he makes his side stretchers about one-quarter inch longer than the distance between the legs before stretcher installation would dictate, which pushes the stretchers against the legs and makes them more difficult to pull out even when loose. This practice creates a truss because the legs are well anchored in the thick seat. Nevertheless, Dunbar does not think much of socketed leg-stretcher connections:

> Socket joints are not the best way to secure two parts together. In fact, in the whole spectrum of ways in which wood is joined, there are few that are less satisfactory. As surely as wood shrinks and swells in reaction to the moisture in the air, a socket joint will loosen. It will loosen no matter what is done to prevent it from doing so. A nail, screw or dowel driven into the joint only prevents it from coming apart. These fasteners cannot keep the joint tight. More esoteric solutions, such as compressing an oversized tenon before inserting it into the socket or injecting a liquid to swell these tenons, do not last much longer.[28]

Despite Dunbar's assertions, many socketed leg joints have survived more than two centuries without loosening, because early makers had tricks of their own in addition to those described above. Contemporary craftsmen drill side stretcher sockets perpendicular to the leg grain, whereas some period artisans drilled them at a 45-degree angle. Makers who used the latter method obtained a double off-angle cinch when the legs shrank: the cinch every Windsor maker obtains because the leg is at an angle to the side stretcher, and a second cinch because the grain of the legs is at an angle to the side stretchers. The second off-angle cinch is more easily documented in refinished chairs.

The situation with regard to the medial stretcher is more complicated because the pullout forces are greater and the stretchers commonly fail. While two legs pull on each side stretcher joint, all four legs pull on the medial stretcher; the greater the splay, the greater the pull. Since few early Philadelphia chairs have pinned stretchers (see tables 3, 4), Philadelphia makers relied on the shrinkage of the side stretchers to hold the medial stretcher. There is no data on the relative strength of such joints, but it appears that long-term strength improves as the size and gradual swell of the side stretchers increase. The angle of the side stretchers relative to the medial stretcher may also be important. If the sockets for the medial stretcher are drilled at a nonperpendicular angle to the grain of the side stretchers, additional cinching is obtained.[29]

Since the medial stretcher often failed, it would have been a logical place for makers to have used wide-ended tenons like those found in some seventeenth-century chairs or blind wedges that would have expanded and tightened the joints. Furniture historian Thomas Ormsbee reported that he had seen Windsor stretchers fitted with blind wedges, but no contemporary scholars or conservators have made a similar claim in reference to stretchers on Windsor furniture. Were stretcher failures the "coming to pieces" reported in the 1787 Rhode Island advertisement? That seems doubtful, given the confidence Philadelphia makers had in this aspect of their production. Few of the Philadelphia sack-backs cited in tables 3 and 4 have pins or nails reinforcing the stretcher joints. Given his propensity for pinning and nailing, the maker of the sophisticated sack-backs illustrated in figures 11 and 12 would almost certainly have reinforced his stretcher joints if contemporary chairs regularly failed in those locations.[30]

A New Methodology for the Study of Windsor Furniture

Aesthetic analysis tends to emphasize the distinctive or unusual, and often says more about modern preferences than period tastes. Conversely, structural analysis tends to be more objective. Connoisseurs and scholars of Windsor furniture have spent lifetimes separating chairs into regional categories, developing chronologies, and debating the skill reflected in carefully shaped arm supports, turnings, and other details. Although such considerations are important, a purely stylistic approach overlooks a salient fact: the Windsor chair was an engineering innovation—possibly one of the most significant of the eighteenth century. When evaluating Windsor furniture, period purchasers probably considered how well it worked of equal or greater importance to how well it looked.

This study introduces some of the tools needed for in-depth structural analysis and uses these tools to identify several steps in the development of the American Windsor armchair as it evolved from a rigid, failure-prone object into a lighter, stronger, and more flexible one. Some of these structural developments have been used to group and date these chairs in ways not possible using stylistic analysis. Specific failure modes have been identified and analyzed, and new criteria have been established to help determine when one chair is better made than another. Style and condition are important, but the long-term intrinsic value of a piece of furniture should depend in no small way on its ability to perform the tasks for which it was made.[31]

ACKNOWLEDGMENTS For assistance with this article the author thanks Karie Diethorn, Brock Jobe, Jane Kolter, Martin Edward Schnall, and especially Philip Zea, who asked me to think beyond the arm rail and who read many drafts. This work would not have been possible without the earlier scholarship and contributions of many students of Windsor furniture, including Charles Dorman, Nancy Goyne Evans, Wallace Nutting, Thomas Ormsbee, and Charles Santore. The article is dedicated to the late Alonzo Lee Nichols, who gave me the ability to know what I was looking at and the courage to follow my eye, and to my wife, Elaine Ulman, who started me down a long twisting path when she refused to have chairs that might come to pieces in our living room.

1. Please email comments to d.pesuit@verizon.net.

2. Nancy Goyne Evans, *American Windsor Chairs* (New York: Hudson Hills Press, in association with the Winterthur Museum, 1996), pp. 38–50. Charles Santore, *The Windsor Style in America, 1730–1830* (Philadelphia: Running Press, 1981), pp. 32–35. Santore published a second volume with the same title in 1987. Both volumes were reissued as a single book in 1992.

3. William MacPherson Hornor, *Blue Book: Philadelphia Furniture* (Philadelphia: By the author, 1935), p. 298. Inventory of Robert Tucker taken September 5, 1768, and recorded February 1770, Norfolk County Appraisments, no. 1, 1755–1783, pp. 117a–120. The author thanks Robert Leath, Curator of Historic Interiors, Colonial Williamsburg Foundation, for providing this reference.

4. *New York Gazette,* January 4, 1762, as quoted in Evans, *American Windsor Chairs,* p. 67; and Rita Susswein Gottesman, *The Arts and Crafts in New York, 1726–1776* (New York: New-York Historical Society, 1938), p. 123. In 1766 the *South Carolina Gazette* reported that the mercantile firm Sheed and White had imported Philadelphia Windsor chairs in the brig *Philadelphia Packet,* as quoted in Harrold E. Gillingham, "The Philadelphia Windsor Chair and Its Wanderings," *Pennsylvania Magazine of History and Biography* 55 (1931): 301–32.

5. *South Carolina Gazette and General Advertiser,* October 14, 1783, as quoted in Santore, *Windsor Style,* 1: 44, and Evans, *American Windsor Chairs,* p. 598. *United States Chronicle* (Providence, Rhode Island), July 19, 1787, as quoted in Irving Whitall Lyon, *The Colonial Furniture of New England: A Study of the Domestic Furniture in Use in New England in the Seventeenth and Eighteenth Centuries* (1891; reprint, New York: E. P. Dutton, 1977), pp. 180–81; Santore, *Windsor Style,* 1: 44, and Evans, *American Windsor Chairs,* pp. 272–73. Santore, *Windsor Style,* 1: 44.

6. A chair similar to the one shown in figure 8, with a long history of ownership in the Edward Littlefield family of Andover, Massachusetts, appeared at auction in 1999 (*Antiques and the Arts Weekly,* November 12, 1999, p. 82). This chair had sold on the North Shore of Massachusetts several years earlier.

7. Both equations are based on the assumption that the material is homogeneous, that its properties do not vary significantly from one cross section to another or within the cross section itself.

8. For more information pertaining to equations 1 and 2, see Ferdinand Beer and E. Russell Johnston, *Mechanics of Materials,* 3rd ed. (New York: McGraw Hill, 1981), p. 156.

9. For the comb-back chairs with steam-bent arms and rounded rails dated 1750 or earlier, see Santore, *Windsor Style,* 1: figs. 8, 20–22, 25–28, and 2: figs. 1–6. For the five examples with rectangular back rails dated 1750–1770, see ibid., 1: figs. 7, 9, 10, and 2: figs. 31, 34. The three chairs with squared-off arm rails dated 1750–1770 are illustrated in ibid., 1: figs. 94–97, and 2: figs. 75–80.

10. As quoted in Horner, *The Blue Book of Philadelphia Furniture,* p. 300.

11. Small Philadelphia fan-back Windsors with rounded seats are illustrated in Evans, *American Windsor Chairs,* figs. 3-29, 3-34, and Santore, *Windsor Style,* 1: fig. 81. Chairs with Gilpin's brand are illustrated in Evans, *American Windsor Chairs,* figs. 3-3, 3-4, 3-5, and Santore, *Windsor Style,* 1: fig. 26. Philadelphia chairs with boldly shaped handholds are illustrated in Santore, *Windsor Style,* 1: fig. 8, 2: figs. 14, 16. For comparisons with the handholds of formal chairs, see Harold Sack and Deanne Levison, "American Roundabout Chairs," *Antiques* 139, no. 5 (May

1991): 934–47, or their "Queen Anne and Chippendale Armchairs in America," *Antiques* 137, no. 5 (May 1990): 1166–77. For an even closer cognate, compare these handholds with the crests of a few formal Philadelphia chairs in J. Michael Flanigan, *American Furniture in the Kaufman Collection* (Washington, D.C.: National Gallery of Art, 1986), p. 28, or Helen Comstock, *American Furniture: A Complete Guide to Seventeenth, Eighteenth and Early Nineteenth Century Styles* (New York: Viking Press, 1962), no. 263.

12. A representative Lancaster chair is illustrated in Evans, *American Windsor Chairs,* fig. 3-58. The Frederick armchair is illustrated and discussed in ibid., pp. 120–21, fig. 3-84.

13. Trumbull's bill is reproduced in Nicholas B. Wainwright, *Colonial Grandeur in Philadelphia: The House and Furniture of General John Cadwalader* (Philadelphia: Historical Society of Pennsylvania, 1964), p. 58.

14. Nancy A. Goyne, "Francis Trumble of Philadelphia, Windsor Chair and Cabinetmaker," *Winterthur Portfolio* 1 (1964): 239.

15. *The Branded Furniture of Independence National Historic Park,* edited by Jane B. Kolter and Lynne A. Leopold-Sharp (Philadelphia: Independence National Historical Park, 1981), p. 7.

16. Santore, *Windsor Style,* 1: 67. An entry in the Carpenters' Hall account book notes that members of the company paid for the chairs, but it does not identify the maker: "N.B. the Chairs are not allowed as all the members that furnished them made no charge." None of the members is known to have made chairs. The author thanks Ruth O'Brien, director of Carpenters' Hall, for the following information from the Carpenters' Hall Building Records Database, transcribed from Charles E. Peterson, "Carpenters Hall," *Transactions of the American Philosophical Society* 43, part 1 (1953): "When Carpenters' Hall was about half completed, the Library Company of Philadelphia . . . was offered the opportunity of renting part of it. The library, then in the State House, was particularly short of space for its 'philosophical apparatus' . . . Agreement was reached on October 26, 1772, and the Carpenters' Company proceeded to 'furnish the house ready for the Library Company to move in.' The latter appointed a committee for fitting up the new quarters, and Thomas Nevell of the Carpenters' Company was engaged to do the joinery. The minute book shows that . . . a dozen Windsor chairs, six brass sconces and two chandeliers were also provided. The Library Company moved in September 6, 1773."

17. Evans, *American Windsor Chairs,* p. 97.

18. Santore attributes eight Windsors with steam-bent arms to Rhode Island (*Windsor Style,* 1: figs. 106, 114, 118, 2: figs. 107–111). If chairs with D-shaped seats are excluded, four of the remaining five chairs have rectangular rails.

19. Santore, *Windsor Style,* 1: figs. 107, 108; 2: fig. 87. For more on the Hampton and Always chair, see Charles Santore, "The New York Windsor," *Maine Antique Digest,* July 1987, p. C-10, fig. 5. According to Santore, Hampton and Always were in partnership in 1792, but Evans dates the beginning of the partnership to 1795–1796 (Evans, *American Windsor Chairs*).

20. For the armchairs with 21½-inch seat widths attributed to Boston and Rhode Island, see Evans, *American Windsor Chairs,* figs. 6-33, 6-37, 6-40, 6-42, 6-47, 6-50, 6-131, 6-132, 6-146, 6-194, and 6-199. For chairs with greater leg splay, see ibid., figs. 6-33, 6-37, 6-40, 6-42, 6-47, 6-50, and 6-132.

21. For more on Blackford, see ibid., p. 350, fig. 6-194.

22. For Windsors with tall backs from Lancaster, Pennsylvania, and New England, see ibid., figs. 3-62, 3-65 3-66, 6-37, 6-81, 6-101, and 6-132. For more on seating for invalids and the elderly, see ibid., p. 112.

23. The author thanks Karie Diethorn, curator at Independence National Historical Park, for this information.

24. See figs. 1, 4, and 40 in this article and table 5.

25. Saeed Moveni, *Finite Element Analysis, Theory and Application with ANSYS* (New York: Prentice Hall, 2003).

26. For more on Ephraim Evans, see Evans, *American Windsor Chairs,* p. 692. For more on Windsors made in the southwest of England, see Bernard D. Cotton, *The English Regional Chair* (Woodbridge, Suffolk: Antique Collectors' Club, 1990), p. 274.

27. Michael Dunbar, *Make a Windsor Chair with Michael Dunbar* (Newton, Conn.: Taunton Press, 1984).

28. Ibid., p. 27.

29. Ibid., p. 24. Dunbar is probably following an old tradition when he dries the medial stretcher before installation to minimize shrinkage after it is installed.

30. For more on the construction of early turned chairs, see Benno M. Forman, *American Seating Furniture, 1630–1730* (New York: W. W. Norton & Co., 1988), p. 105. Thomas H. Orms-

bee, *The Windsor Chair* (New York: Deerfield Books, 1962), p. 30. Santore, *Windsor Style,* p. 198.

31. Although this work presents a new methodology, it leaves many questions unanswered while opening new avenues for further research. The tension between style and strength should be examined in the development of Windsor seating from every colony and state. There are also questions regarding very early American Windsors and their relation to British antecedents and seminal Philadelphia work. Since the Philadelphia Society of Friends ran a Windsor chair manufactory where members apprenticed their sons and relatives, the minutes of monthly meetings might reveal a great deal about Philadelphia makers and the conflicts among them. Similarly, the minutes of early Friends meetings in Massachusetts and Rhode Island might provide insights into who made some of the stronger unsigned New England chairs "after the Philadelphia mode." The technological tricks that have allowed some Windsors to survive daily use without repair for more than two centuries should also be tested and compared. The relative strength of single- and double-wedged joints, strength of stretcher joints, and effect of joint length and diameter deserve special attention. Failure tests comparing early assembly methods would provide a strong basis for further analytical work.

Appendix 1

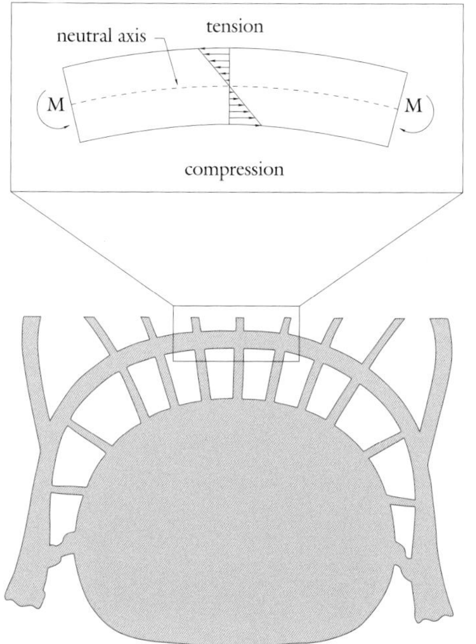

Figure A1

Relative Strength of Windsor Arm Rails

For any bar in bending as on the chair illustrated in fig. A1 an equation may be written to relate stress, σ_y at any distance *y* from its neutral surface to bending moment or flexure, *M.*

$$\sigma_y = My/I$$

In this equation *I* is the second moment of inertia of the bar's cross section, the integral of y^2dA. Since *y* reaches a maximum at point *c* in the figure, stress also reaches a maximum.

$$\sigma_{max} = Mc/I \qquad \text{(Eq. 1)}$$

The ratio *c/I* depends only on cross-sectional geometry.

Equation 1 may be used to compare maximum stresses in the rails of two Windsors experiencing the same bending moment. If the first chair has moment of inertia I_1 and the second chair has moment of inertia I_2,

$$\frac{\sigma_{max1}}{\sigma_{max2}} = \frac{Mc_1/I_1}{Mc_2/I_2}$$

But since both rails experience the same flexure,

$$\frac{\sigma_{max1}}{\sigma_{max2}} = \frac{c_1/I_1}{c_2/I_2} \qquad \text{(Eq. 2)}$$

Square vs. Round Rail Cross-Sections

Although sack-back Windsor rails are neither perfectly round nor perfectly square, they are considered first because the equations are relatively simple. Since the rails have the same overall dimensions, equation 2 is simplified.

$$\sigma_{max1}/\sigma_{max2} = I_2/I_1 \qquad \text{(Eq. 3)}$$

The formula for a rectangular cross-section can be used to provide a moment of inertia for the square cross-section

$$I_1 = tw^3/12 = w^4/12 \text{ o } t^4/12$$

where *t* is rail vertical thickness and *w* is cross-sectional width. But since $t = 2R$ and $w = 2R$,

$$I_1 = 4R^4/3$$

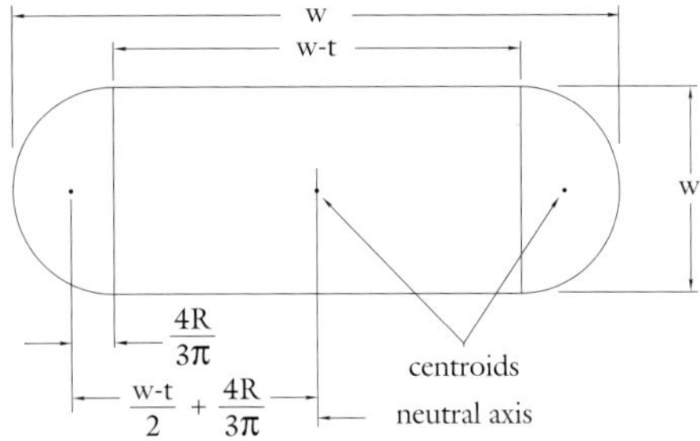

Figure A2 Rounded armrail

For the circular cross-section,

$$I_2 = pR^4/4$$

Therefore, the stress experienced by the square cross-section compared with the circular cross-section is

$$\sigma_{max1}/\sigma_{max2} = 3\pi/16 = 0.589$$

The square cross-section sees .589 times as much stress for the same applied moment or flexure. In other words, if the woods are the same, the square cross-section is about 1/.589 or 1.7 times stronger than a circular cross-section of the same size.

Rectangular vs. Rounded-End Cross Sections

A strength comparison can also be made for rails that are wider than they are thick. The second moment of the rectangular rail is known from above, but the second moment of the rail with two rounded ends is more difficult to calculate. That shape is in effect two half-rounds with a rectangular cross-section in between.

The parallel axis theorem allows us to obtain this moment of inertia. It says that the second moment of inertia of a body removed some distance from its neutral axis is its moment around that axis plus the product of its area and the square of the distance by which it is removed. With reference to figure A2,

$$I_{\text{rounded end}} = I_{\text{half-round}} + d^2A_{\text{half-round}}$$

Since the second moment of a half-round around its neutral axis or centroid is $.11R^4$, since the distance of that centroid above the base is $4R/3\pi$, and since $R = t/2$,

$$I_{\text{rounded end}} = .11R^4 + \pi R^2[(w-t)/2 + 4R/3\pi]^2/2$$

$$= .03936t^4 - .11292wt^3 + .09817w^2t^2$$

The above polynomial will be referred to as I_{end} for the moment. Since the rounded rail has two such ends and a rectangle with thickness *t* and width $(w-t)$ in between,

$$I_{\text{rounded arm}} = t(w-t)^3/12 + 2I_{\text{end}}$$

With the moment for the rounded rail in hand, relative strength is determined as before. Since the maximum distance, *c* from the neutral axis in equation 2, is the same for both rails, equation 3 applies. If subscript *1* refers to the rectangular cross-section,

$$\sigma_1/\sigma_2 = \frac{t(w-t)^3/12 + 2I_{\text{end}}}{tw^3/12}$$

where I_{end} is defined above. This result can be simplified and generalized for any w/t ratio:

$$\text{Rel strength} = 1 - .6439(t/w) + .290(t/w)^2 - .0554(t/w)^3$$

This equation shows that the rail with a rectangular cross-section is indeed stronger than the rail with a rounded cross-section, but that the difference diminishes as the rail becomes wider. In the limit w/t becomes unity, the equation provides the same result as the circular vs. square analysis above.

Rectangular vs. Squared Off at Rear

The rail whose cross section is squared off at rear is considered last because its equations are the most complicated.

In the analysis above the neutral axis was also the axis of symmetry. The moments of inertia of the half-rounds were determined and then translated to the center of the rectangular area. But in this case the neutral axis must be determined before the moments can be translated. This axis passes through the center of gravity of the whole cross-section, c_g.

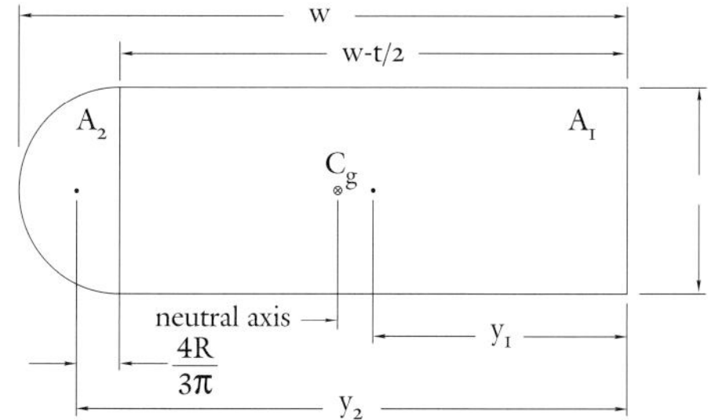

Figure A3 Flat-back armrail

$$c_g = \frac{\Sigma_i y_i A_i}{\Sigma_i A_i}$$

Or, with reference to figure A3,

$$c_g = \frac{A_1 y_1 + A_2 y_2}{A_1 + A_2}$$

Figure A3 is now used to evaluate each of these terms in turn.

$$A_1 = t(w - t/2)$$

$$A_2 = \pi R^2/2 = \pi t^2/8$$

$$y_1 = (w - t/2)/2$$

$$y_2 = w - t/2 + 4R/3\pi$$

$$= w - t/2 + 2t/3\pi$$

The terms are then combined using the center-of-gravity equation.

$$c_g = \frac{2(2wt - t^2)(w - t/2) + \pi t^2(w - t/2 + 2t/3\pi)}{8wt - 4t^2 + \pi t^2}$$

With reference to figure A3 this neutral line lies between y_1 and y_2.

Having determined the neutral axis, the moments of inertia can be translated using the parallel axis theorem as before. Again, with reference to figure A3,

$$\begin{aligned} I_1 &= bh^3/12 + A_1 d_1^{\,2} \\ &= bh^3/12 + A_1(c_g - y_1)^2 \\ &= t(w - t/2)^3/12 + (wt - t^2/2)(c_g - (2w - t)/4)^2 \\ I_2 &= .11R^4 + A_2 d_2^{\,2} \\ &= .11(t/2)^4 + A_2(y_2 - c_g)^2 \\ &= .11(t/2)^4 + (\pi t^2/8)(w - t/2 + 2t/3\pi - c_g)^2 \end{aligned}$$

The moment of inertia for the flat-back arm rail can now be calculated,

$$I_{\text{flat-back}} = I_1 + I_2$$

where I_1 and I_2 are defined in terms of c_g and the above equations. With this moment of inertia, relative strength can be determined as before. Since the maximum distance, *c* from the neutral axis in equation 2, is not the same for the rectangular and flat-back arm rails, that distance must be included in the analysis. The results are not amenable to elegant simplification, as in the example above.

Figure 24 in the text shows the results of these analyses. The flat-back arm rail is a great deal stronger than the rounded arm rail, but not quite as strong as the rectangular rail.

Appendix 2

Notes on Chair Measurements

Since measurements play an important role in this work, it is important to know how they were made. Each arm rail width and thickness measurement is usually the average of two or more micrometer measurements at the center spindle. If rail dimensions change significantly near the center spindle, it is noted in the text or the captions. Seat width, seat depth, seat height, and overall height were measured to the nearest sixteenth of an inch. Seat heights were measured to the top of the central pommel. Arm support splay angles were obtained using a protractor flush with the seat at the center of the arm support. Leg splay angles were obtained using vertical and horizontal distances defined by the center of each leg where it met the floor

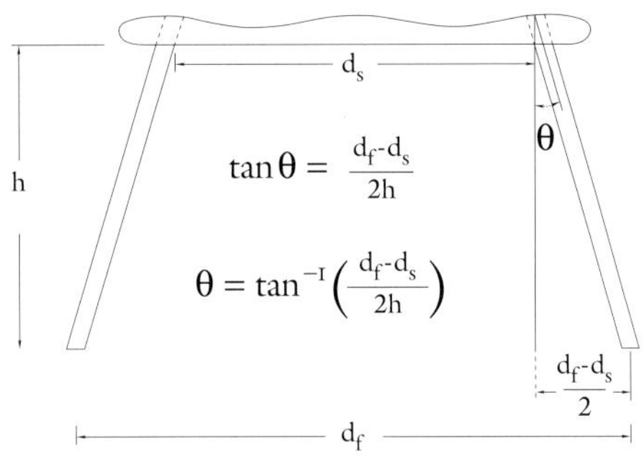

Figure A4 Symmetric leg splay measurement

and a plumb bob dropped from the center of the leg flush with the underside of the seat. Left and right refer to a person sitting on a chair.

Since plumb bobs are not found in most furniture measurement kits, a simplified leg splay measurement technique may be substituted if opposing legs are symmetrical. The technique provides an incorrect average angle for Windsors whose rear legs splay more than their front legs. First the following definitions: d_s is the horizontal distance between the centers of the legs under the seat, d_f is the horizontal distance between the centers of the legs at the floor, and h is the height of the underside of the seat at the top of the leg. Therefore, with reference to the figure, leg splay angle θ is defined by the right triangle whose height is h and whose base is $(d_f - d_s)/2$.

$$\tan\theta = (d_f - d_s)/2h; \quad \theta = \tan^{-1}(d_f - d_s)/2h$$

The tan^{-1} (inverse tangent) function is found on most engineering calculators. To check calculator operation, enter 1.0 and press the tan^{-1} function. If the calculator is working in degrees, it will show 45 degrees. If one of the legs is low and the legs are symmetrical, the measurement technique is still valid. Measurements are then made to and along the stretcher instead of to and along the floor.

Philip D. Zimmerman

New York Card Tables, 1800–1825

▼ CARD TABLES DEMONSTRATE great range and expression in design, construction, and materials despite their functional simplicity. Because large numbers of them survive, they invite comparisons and hold the promise of documentation to maker, place, and/or time of manufacture. This article surveys the development of card tables in New York during the first quarter of the nineteenth century, a period marked by New York's ascendancy as an urban community and, more specifically, as a leading center of furniture making. By 1805 David Longworth reported in his *Almanack* that the city supported sixty-six cabinetmakers, nineteen chair makers, fifteen carvers and gilders, and nine joiners. The number of furniture-making artisans increased exponentially over the next few decades. At about this time, New York surpassed Philadelphia as the largest city in the United States. New York artisans amalgamated designs and technical innovations and spread them throughout the United States via a substantial export trade.[1]

Despite the great numbers of early nineteenth-century card tables and other furniture forms ascribed to New York City artisans, no federal card tables documented to have been made before 1800 have come to light. New York furniture makers' price books published in 1796 and 1802 help fill this void, but they must be interpreted with care. Created to establish labor prices between journeymen and shop masters for all kinds of tasks, the first editions drew heavily from London prototypes. As furniture historian Patricia Kane observed, *The New-York Book of Prices for Cabinet & Chair Work, agreed upon by the Employers* (1802) introduced a few local preferences and omitted other entries from the London books. This trend toward more representative descriptions continued in the New York price books of 1810 and 1817, as well as in interim supplements. Given this cautionary note, the price books nonetheless document the dominant card table forms, which compare favorably with anonymous survivals that may be identified as New York products with reasonable assurance based on favorable comparisons of their physical features with other documented New York furniture. Card table headings in the 1802 price list itemize "square" (rectangular in plan), "circular" (half-round or demilune), and "ovalo corner" (inset quarter-round corner) forms, each described as either solid or veneered in reference to construction of the hinged tops.[2]

Inlay patterns and techniques, the presence of églomisé, and the five-leg design combine to suggest that the engaging and provocative card table illustrated in figure 1 was made in New York City. Its central églomisé panel

Figure 1 Card table, probably New York City, ca. 1801. Mahogany with white pine and walnut. H. 29 3/16", W. 36", D. 17 1/8" (closed). (Courtesy, Winterthur Museum, gift of Henry Francis du Pont.) This table is one of a pair.

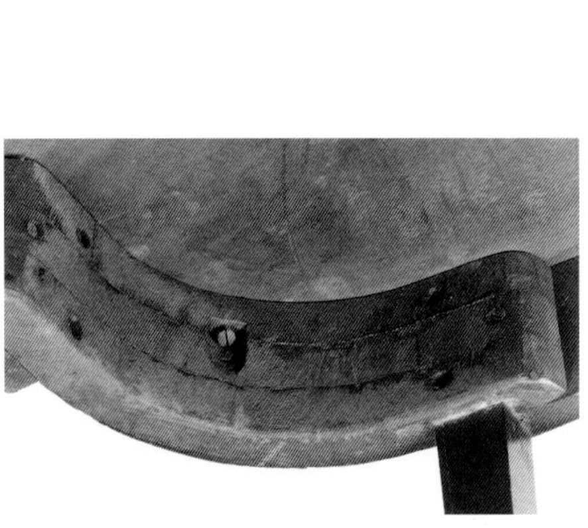

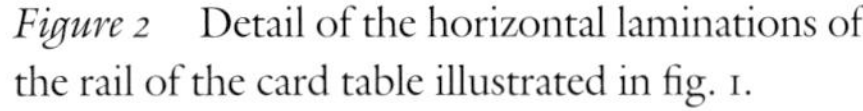

Figure 2 Detail of the horizontal laminations of the rail of the card table illustrated in fig. 1.

depicts an eagle and shield bearing the names of Thomas Jefferson and Aaron Burr. A tie between those men in the Electoral College left the outcome of the presidential race of 1800 in doubt until the House of Representatives resolved the matter in Jefferson's favor on February 17, 1801. Given the contentiousness of national politics, the card table likely commemorates the start of Jefferson's administration and was probably made in early 1801. It is rectangular with ovolo front corners, a popular table and sideboard treatment also called "sash" in period manuscripts. The curved portion of the frame is made of three horizontal layers of white pine glued together with the grain oriented at oblique angles to the adjoining layers (fig. 2). This general technique was used on all sorts of curved surfaces, such as the popular half-round table frame represented by the New York card table illustrated in figure 3. When curved rail sections joined straight sections, as in ovolo card tables, just the curved sections were laminated and usually glued and screwed to the boards of the straight sections. Some secondary woods are difficult to identify, but white pine predominates. Although the thickness of individual laminates and the consequent number of layers varied, the result did not. Lamination produced a strong shape that resisted warping and splitting along the "short grain." A few New York card tables of this period, including that shown in figure 3, had round corners constructed of four or five vertically laminated boards, which resemble modern plywood (fig. 4). Another technique, associated with Duncan Phyfe's work of circa 1820 and later, used two vertically laminated boards, each slit with saw cuts, or "kerfs," about every half inch, then bent to shape and saturated

Figure 3 Card table, probably New York City, 1795–1805. Mahogany with unidentified secondary woods. H. 28½", W. 35¾", D. 18" (closed). (Courtesy, New-York Historical Society.) The top of this table is unusual in being made from solid wood. The name "Edward Rogers" is inscribed in chalk on the underside of the fixed leaf.

Figure 4 Detail of the vertically laminated rail of the card table illustrated in fig. 3.

Figure 5 Detail showing the kerfed and laminated corners of a card table attributed to Duncan Phyfe, New York City, 1830–1840. (Courtesy, Northeast Auctions.)

with glue (fig. 5). Still other techniques, such as single kerfed boards bent to shape and backed with canvas, were used at the time but are not associated with New York tables.[3]

One of the more recognizable features of New York federal card tables is the fifth leg, hinged to the left side of the rear rail so that it can swing out to support the folding table leaf. Most American card tables, including a few New York examples, have four legs, one of which was also hinged to support the folding top. Reasons for this regional preference are unclear. Any advantage in stability gained by five legs was diminished by the unbalanced appearance of the extra leg in the closed position. A few New York card tables were made with a sixth leg on the right side, but on some examples this additional leg was fixed. This resolution seems only to have increased cost and complicated use, since sitters had to contend with yet another leg. Regardless, the fifth leg was a well-established New York tradition, having been the norm in eighteenth-century cabriole-leg card tables. The 1802 New York price book described basic card table forms as having "four fast legs, and one fly leg." This wording clarified the 1796 New York price book entry that specified "one fly foot, square edge to the top, four plain legs, all solid," which left unresolved whether the fly leg was one of or in addition to the four plain legs. The 1802 wording carried through the 1810 and 1817 New York price book editions. In contrast, the Philadelphia *Journeymen Cabinet and Chair-Makers' Book of Prices* (1811) called for only three fixed and one swing leg.[4]

The 1802 price list distinguished veneered from solid card tables by noting "three joints in each top; clamp'd and veneer'd; the edges cross or long banded." All table frames that incorporated curves were veneered, regardless of how the top leaves were constructed. The 1810 New York price book listing for "an elliptic veneered card table," a new and typically New York shape, is slightly more descriptive and affords a convenient example for detailed discussion of construction features: "the rail veneered, a bead or band on the lower edge; three joints in each top, and clamp'd slip'd on the back edges, and veneered on three sides, or the inside lip'd for cloth, the edges banded." The elliptic shape of the top and conforming frame differed from the simpler circular or half-round shape, which had a constant radius. Double and triple elliptic alternatives introduced multiple curves (fig. 6). All of these card table forms had conforming curved frame rails constructed of two or more laminates, three and four layers being most common. However complex its shape, the table frame was always veneered. Veneers were integral to ornamental schemes, but they also masked all of the different construction techniques and materials. Veneered frames ended in a "bead or band on the lower edge," as noted in the price-book description. Beads were strips of wood applied to the underside of the frame with a projecting half-round profile (cock bead) that marked the bottom of the frieze and protected the edge of the veneer from damage and helped prevent peeling. Some makers used a narrow strip of cross-banding rather than a bead (fig. 6), but the former was purely decorative and afforded almost no protection for the rail veneer. Typically, the banding was carried across the solid mahogany legs as well.[5]

Unlike the solid tops of card tables made elsewhere in the United States, New York tops were typically veneered on a solid core of secondary wood. The 1810 price book called for veneer "on three sides," namely the top surface visible when the table was closed and the two inside surfaces visible when open. Many makers used brilliant crotch veneer for the top and less figured cuts of similar color and character for the interior surfaces. Tables veneered with matching pieces of plum-pudding mahogany or other exotically figured woods were exceptional (fig. 7). Relatively few New York card tables had broadcloth or leather on the inside surfaces, even though *The*

Figure 6 John T. Dolan, card table, New York City, 1809–1813. Mahogany with white pine and cherry. H. 30⅛", W. 35¾", D. 36⁵⁄₁₆" (open). (Courtesy, Museum of the City of New York.) This triple elliptic table bears Dolan's label.

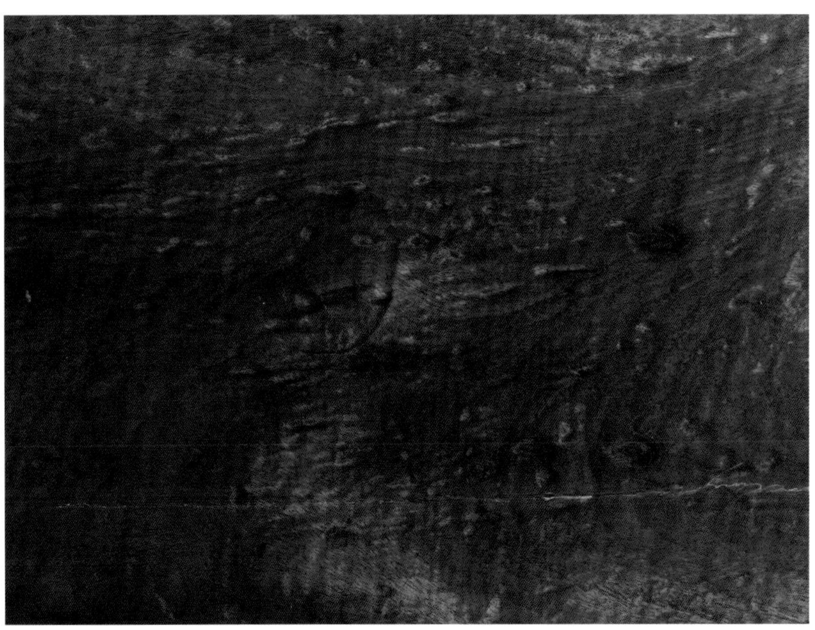

Figure 7 Detail of the plum-pudding mahogany veneer on the top of the card table illustrated in fig. 13. (Photo, Gavin Ashworth.)

New-York Revised Prices for Manufacturing Cabinet and Chair Work (1810) indicated that "inside[s] lip'd for cloth" represented no additional cost.[6]

Some New York card tables have unvarnished mahogany veneers on the undersides of the fixed table leaf. *The New-York Book of Prices for Manufac-*

Figure 8 Bed steps, New York City, 1815–1830. Mahogany with white pine and tulip poplar. H. 24½", W. 19", D. 24". (Courtesy, Boscobel Restoration; photo, Gavin Ashworth.)

Figure 9 Detail showing the "slipped" rear edge of the upper leaf of the card table illustrated in fig. 13. (Photo, Gavin Ashworth.) The joint between the one-quarter-inch veneer and core is visible inside the mortise.

Figure 10 Detail showing the "slipped" top edge of a veneered drawer front. (Photo, Gavin Ashworth.)

turing Cabinet and Chair Work (1817) included a special notation in the introduction that described this practice as "veneering under side of card table beds." A set of New York neoclassical bed steps displays similar veneering (fig. 8). The inner veneers would have been visible only when the sliding steps were removed completely in order to clean the chamber seat. Interior veneers may have been intended to reduce the possibility of warping, a concern that Thomas Sheraton raised in his *Cabinet Dictionary* of 1803. Warped sides would have restricted the sliding movement of steps, just as a warped fixed leaf would have made the top of a card table uneven and unsightly. However, card tables that combine underside veneers with cloth or leather playing surfaces complicate this interpretation.[7]

In New York, the standard method for constructing the tops of card tables was to frame the leaves using secondary woods and to cover the cores entirely with mahogany veneers and banding. As specified in the price books, the front and side edges of each leaf were cross-banded, an application that easily conformed to curves and—more important—hid all the white pine edges and framing joints. The back edge was sometimes not worked, exposing the sandwich of veneers and secondary wood, but it was usually covered with a thin strip of mahogany, typically about one-quarter-inch thick but sometimes only the thickness of the veneer (fig. 9). Contemporary price books described this practice as "slip'd on the back edges." The origin of this terminology is obscure, but it likely derived from a slip of wood. The tops of mahogany-veneered drawer fronts of all kinds were also routinely slipped with mahogany to disguise the white pine cores (fig. 10). The 1802 price list used that term along with "long banding" to denote veneers laid along tabletop edges with the grain "long," or parallel, in contrast to the more common alternative of cross-banding, in which the grain lay perpendicular to the core wood.[8]

Slipped back edges of tabletops give the impression that the leaves were veneered on solid mahogany cores. Such encasing obscures much evidence of construction, but the unveneered undersides of fixed leaves on some New York tables as well as small but consistent clues elsewhere are telling. Exposed undersides show that cores were made of two, three, or four longitudinal white pine boards glued edge to edge. Although evidence is hidden, these joints are probably simple butt joints, as in many late eighteenth-century tabletops and chest tops made throughout America of walnut, cherry, and other primary woods. Use of single, full-width pine boards in New York tabletops was very rare. Battens, called "clamps" in the price books, secured each end by tongue-and-groove joints. Tenons or other joining techniques may also have been used, but none has yet been recorded among the relatively few examples where these joints are exposed. Because the grain of the battens was oriented perpendicular to the other core boards, battens countered warping and protected end grain from splitting and fracturing, just as they did in the lids of slant-top desks. In shaped card-table tops, notably double- or triple-elliptic varieties, the battens were angled so that the multiple-curve cuts were taken out of the single board. Occasionally, the battens of tabletops were made of mahogany in combination with white pine longitudinal boards. Mahogany is a dense, hard wood that resists warping and can maintain a more stable edge profile than conifers and other secondary woods. Its use in these hidden areas indicates a commendable level of concern for durability on the part of the furniture maker.[9]

For table leaves completely encased by veneers and banding, the most obvious evidence of construction lies in patterns of splits in the large sheets of veneer. Shrinkage of the boards within the core, combined with good adhesion of the veneer, resulted in consistent splitting along the seams (fig. 11). These splits occur in the middle of the leaves but do not extend to

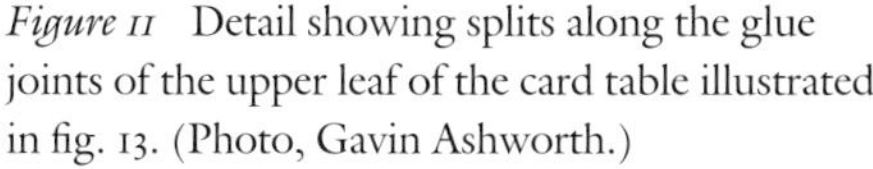
Figure 11 Detail showing splits along the glue joints of the upper leaf of the card table illustrated in fig. 13. (Photo, Gavin Ashworth.)

the edges because they do not pass over the cross grain of the clamps at each end. Moreover, most splits do not follow grain patterns in the mahogany veneer, responding instead to the movement of the core woods underneath. Types of woods used in the top leaf must be extrapolated from evidence on the underside of the fixed leaf, which is usually white pine.[10]

Entries for veneered card tables in the 1802 and subsequent New York price lists also called for "three joints in each top," a requirement omitted in descriptions of solid card tables. Contemporary artisans must have understood this terminology, but for modern students, reference to the 1796 price list is helpful. This early publication specifies "glueing up tops, either solid or to veneer on, at per joint, 0.0.3," confirming that the "three joints in each top" were glue joints between the boards. Thomas Sheraton's *Drawing Book* (1793) advised makers to "rip up dry deal, or faulty mahogany, into four inch widths, and joint them up." Four four-inch boards yielded three joints and approximated the width of most tabletops. The battens or clamps, which were listed separately in the New York price books, represented additional glue joints, as did the slipped back edge. Despite the unambiguous language in these documents, examination of surviving New York card tables confirms variation in the numbers of joints between the longitudinal boards—ranging from none (a full-width board) to the requisite three joints for a four-board top. In practical terms, the price list provision merely established a norm.[11]

American card tables had long been made with mortise-and-tenons set into the back edges of tops to align the leaves in the open position. All New York tables beginning in the 1790s appear to have at least one alignment tenon—called a "rear leaf-edge tenon" in other studies—and some have as many as four (fig. 12). The 1817 New York price list addressed this feature

Figure 12 Detail of an alignment tenon and mortise on the rear edge of the top of the card table illustrated in fig. 13. (Photo, Gavin Ashworth.)

with an introductory note that specified "Card table tops to start with two mortises and tongues." Here again, the price list offered only a general guideline that was probably ignored as often as it was followed. Lack of consistency in the numbers of alignment tenons extended to their placement on either the folding or the fixed leaf. In two nearly identical card tables (Winterthur Museum), one has a single alignment tenon on the fixed leaf whereas the other has two tenons on the hinged leaf. Still other tables of this and similar design (suggesting roughly similar times of manufacture) have the targeted number of three tenons. On a five-legged table, the two outside tenons are on the fixed leaf whereas the center tenon is on the hinged leaf.[12]

The use of white pine as the dominant secondary wood in the tops of New York card tables defines a regional practice, but the mere presence of that wood does not readily distinguish New York work from that of several other furniture-making centers, since white pine was used extensively throughout the Northeast and elsewhere. Woods used for the rear swing or "fly" rails are more diagnostic. Swing rails, attached by a wood hinge to a stationary half (which in turn was attached to an inner fixed rail, often of white pine or similar wood), received appreciable use and wear and were often made of stronger woods. Most New York outer rear rails were made of cherry or maple. In contrast, New England swing rails were commonly made of birch, maple, or white pine, and those in Philadelphia and farther south were made of oak, ash, or yellow pine.[13]

New York furniture makers boldly combined a double- or triple-elliptic card-table top with a pillar-and-claw base to produce a distinctive card table with a narrow, sometimes absent, frame (fig. 13). Aesthetics aside, the most

Figure 13 Card table, New York City, 1805–1815. Mahogany with cherry, tulip poplar, and white pine. H. 28½", W. 36", D. 17¾" (closed). (Courtesy, Boscobel Restoration; photo, Gavin Ashworth.)

Figure 14 Detail showing the operation of flies linked to the swinging rear legs of the card table illustrated in fig. 13. (Photo, Gavin Ashworth.)

significant design problem was to support the hinged top without the benefit of a swinging leg. Part of the solution was to use a pair of small brackets, called flies, which were attached to the rear rail with wood hinges—a support system already in use for Pembroke tables. A second aspect of the problem concerned the center of gravity, which shifted when the folding top was opened. Without a swing leg to compensate, the table would fall over in the direction of the cantilevered and weighty hinged leaf. This matter was resolved in pillar-and-claw bases by hinging the two rear feet so that they pivoted backward, thereby reconfiguring the stance of the tripod base to hold the open tabletop in balance (fig. 14). The 1810 New York price book provides the first American evidence of these "mechanical"

Figure 15 Card table, New York City, 1815–1825. Mahogany with white pine. H. 30", W. 36", D. 18" (closed). (Courtesy, Boscobel Restoration; photo, Gavin Ashworth.) The swivel top rotates, exposing a well.

tables. It described the complex action simply as "three claws, two of ditto to turn out with the joint rail." As constructed, each fly at the back rail was linked by a system of metal rods running through the pillar to the rear legs, which swung back a few inches. This modest adjustment worked, but any additional weight added to the hinged leaf—such as a stack of books or tray with a tea or coffee service—endangered the balance of the table. Within a few years, card tables with folding tops that swiveled replaced these aesthetically elegant but functionally awkward tables.[14]

Swivel tops solved the balance problem associated with mechanical pillar-and-claw card tables (fig. 15). The pair of hinged tops turned ninety degrees on an off-center axis so that when open, the two leaves remained centered on the table frame and over the central support. Because there was no change in the center of gravity, legs could be fixed, freeing cabinetmakers to address matters of appearance without compromising stability. The first use of a swivel top in America may be in the card table designed by architect Benjamin Henry Latrobe as part of a larger suite of drawing room seating and tables made for a house he designed and had built for William Waln of Philadelphia (fig. 16). Latrobe first mentioned the suite in an August 26, 1808, letter in which he complained to Waln that he had ordered "another pattern" to replace the first attempt at realizing his chair design, which he dismissed as "the ugliest thing I ever saw." In a letter of September 8, 1809, Latrobe informed Dolley Madison, for whom he was also designing seating furniture, that the Waln drawing room "will not be furnished this winter." Furniture historians have always assumed that the Waln suite predated the Madison furniture, but this reference to delay suggests that it may not have been completed before 1810. A painted console table inscribed "Made

Figure 16 Card table designed by Benjamin Henry Latrobe and possibly made by Thomas Wetherill, Philadelphia, Pennsylvania, ca. 1811. Mahogany with tulip poplar and white pine. H. 29½", W. 36", D. 17⅞" (closed). (Collection of Mrs. George M. Kaufman; photo, Gavin Ashworth.) This table has a swivel top.

Figure 17 George Wright, console table, Philadelphia, Pennsylvania, 1811. White pine. H. 29½", W. 73", D. 23¼" (closed). (Courtesy, Philadelphia Museum of Art, gift of the Associate Committee of Women, 1913.) This early photograph shows the console table below a later looking glass and frame.

for W. Waln . . . By Geo G Wright whilst foreman for Mr J. B. Barry & Son . . . October 10th 1811" provides a further cautionary note (fig. 17). Although the relation of this object to the painted tables and chairs still awaits resolution, the console table was clearly made for Waln's new house if not for the same room as the Latrobe furniture.[15]

Dating the Waln card table 1810 or 1811 places it in the vanguard of design for swivel-top card tables. One of the earliest documentary references to this form is in an 1810 bill from English furniture maker George Oakley, which lists "a calamander wood circular loo table upon pedestal and claws." The following year, *The London Cabinet-Makers' Union Book of Prices* described card-table tops "made to turn around on an iron center, fix'd to a cross rail." Significantly, swivel tops are not mentioned in either the 1805 London *Supplement to the Cabinet-Makers' Union Book of Prices* or the 1797 London *Prices of Cabinet Work*. The French-trained New York cabinetmaker, or "ebenist," Charles Honoré Lannuier made two different swivel-top card tables and marked them with his second label, which furniture scholars have dated between 1805 and 1812 or later, while acknowledging the need for conjecture (fig. 18).[16]

Figure 18 Charles Honoré Lannuier, card table, New York City, 1810–1815. Mahogany with mahogany. H. 29½", W. 36¼", D. 18⅛" (closed). (Courtesy, White House Historical Association; photo, Bruce White.) This swivel-top table bears Lannuier's label and is one of a pair.

The early Latrobe and Lannuier card tables notwithstanding, the date of 1810 (and sometimes 1805) commonly used to mark the beginning of American swivel-top card tables is too early. A large and diverse body of evidence suggests that production was delayed for at least a few years. Swivel tops were not mentioned in the seventy-two-page 1810 New York price list. An undated twelve-page supplement entitled *Additional Revised Prices* lists "a swivel top, with piece framed between the rails for ditto" under a heading for card tables. This little booklet was probably issued shortly before or soon after another supplement entitled *Additional Prices Agreed Upon by the New-York Society of Journeymen Cabinet Makers* and dated July 1815. Swivel tops formed part of the furniture headings in the 1817 New York price book, affirming widespread acceptance of the technique by that date. Firmly datable American examples commence about 1815. Duncan Phyfe made a pair of swivel-top card tables for James Lefferts Brinckerhoff of New York in

May 1816. Among the earliest datable New England examples is the "pr of Grecian card-tables" that Thomas Seymour made for Peter Chardon Brooks, also in 1816. Recent dating of the Edward Lloyd family swivel-top card table to circa 1812 is conjectural. Assuming its attribution to Baltimore furniture maker Edward Priestley is correct, it is not specified in any of several documented payments, one of which was made in 1812. Another unspecified payment in 1817 for $43.50 seems to be a more reasonable time frame for this table. In October of that year, Stephen Girard bought his stylish pair of dolphin-carved swivel-top card tables from Henry Connelly of Philadelphia.[17]

Figure 19 Joseph Brauwers, card table, New York City, 1814 or later. Mahogany with white pine and tulip poplar. H. 29", W. 36", D. 18" (closed). (Courtesy, Winterthur Museum, gift of David Stockwell.) This table bears Brauwers's label.

Design flexibilities inherent in swivel-top technology accommodated other card table features that may also be dated independently to circa 1815. An early swivel-top card table bears the label of New York cabinetmaker Joseph Brauwers, self-described as another "ebenist, from Paris" (fig. 19). Brauwers was listed at the address printed on the label in 1814, but how long he remained there or used that label is unknown. His card table combines a swivel top and a frame with canted corners on a base of four small columns gathered in the center above a platform supported on "swept" legs, which are often referred to today as saber legs. Canted corners were described in the undated *Additional Revised Prices* supplement and were among the few entries noted, but not described, in the 1815 *Additional Prices* amendment to the 1810 edition, in which canted corners were not mentioned. The wording in the undated supplement was unchanged in the 1817 price book: "Canted corners, the rail glued up in thicknesses or dovetailed, ditto veneered and

Figure 20 Detail showing the construction of a canted corner on the card table illustrated in fig. 19.

Figure 21 Card table, probably New York City, 1815–1825. Mahogany with white pine, tulip poplar, and cherry. H. 29⅞", W. 36", D. 17¾" (closed). (Courtesy, Winterthur Museum, bequest of Henry Francis du Pont.)

Figure 22 Detail showing the laminated construction of a canted corner of the card table illustrated in fig. 21.

mitred on the corners, extra from square solid table." The frame of the Brauwers table is made of solid mahogany boards, dovetailed at the corners (fig. 20). Its construction is unusual in the use of mahogany rather than white pine as the secondary wood. It also differs in having a thin, one-quarter-inch thick casing of mahogany laminated over the inner frame and underneath the outer figured mahogany veneer. Canted card tables "glued up in thicknesses" described laminated frames, but the laminations were horizontal rather than vertical as they are on this table. A typical example has three laminated layers of white pine that stagger at the cants like brickwork (figs. 21, 22). An informal survey of New York canted frames suggests that laminated construction was less common than dovetailed boards.[18]

The laminated table frame illustrated in figure 21 rests on a lyre base, in turn supported on a platform into which four swept legs are dovetailed. The front façade of the paired lyres forming the base is carved and ornamented with iron strings (which are usually made of brass or wood). The rear lyre is blank. Although New York card tables with lyres and lyre-back chairs are popularly dated as early as 1810, evidence suggests that these particular motifs, as with swivel tops, came into use about 1815. Unequivocal evidence for such designs begins in late 1815, when Duncan Phyfe sketched and executed lyre-back chairs, which he sold to Charles N. Bancker of Philadelphia in January of the following year (fig. 23). Later in 1816, Phyfe sold two more sets of lyre-back side chairs (one caned and one upholstered, the same com-

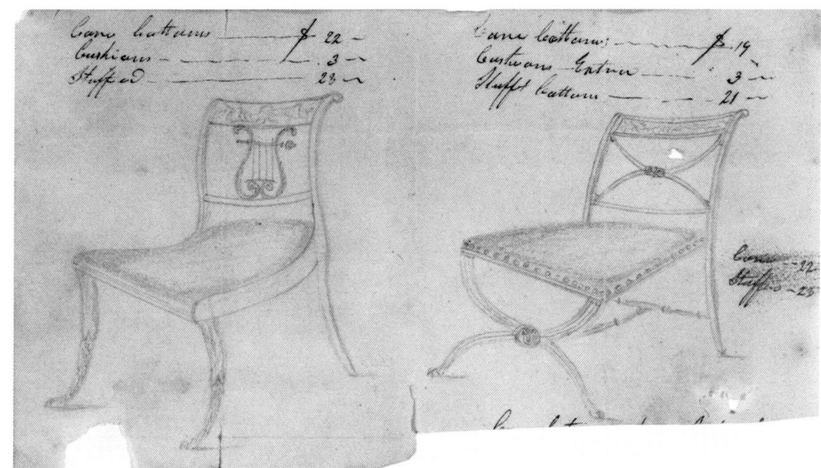

Figure 23 Sketches of a lyre-back chair and a Grecian cross-front chair attributed to Duncan Phyfe, New York City, ca. 1815. Pencil and ink on paper. (Courtesy, Winterthur Museum Library.)

bination as noted on the Bancker drawing) and a lyre-end sofa to James Lefferts Brinckerhoff of New York.[19]

Lyres as furniture motifs first entered American price lists in the 1817 *New York Book of Prices*. As illustrated in a plate in the back of that and other publications and as observed in several tables, lyres were made in halves and tenoned into the table bed above and the platform below (fig. 24). In some elegantly constructed tables, the lyres "crossed at right angles," producing a sculptural pillar (fig. 25). The four legs had dovetailed ends that slid into the canted corners of the platform, termed the "octagon block." These blocks were either thick boards laminated horizontally or built up of two

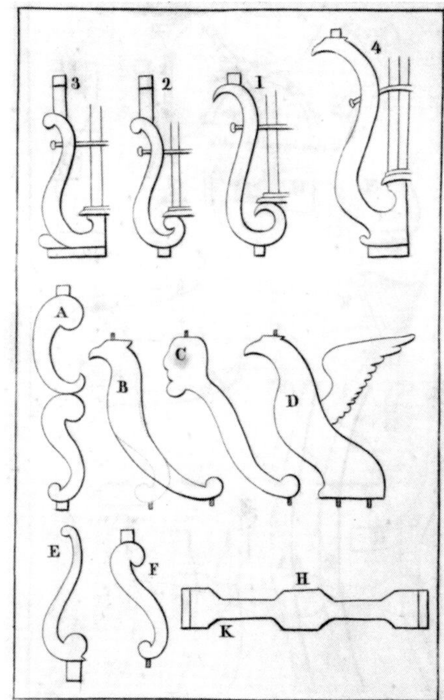

Figure 24 Plate 5 from the 1817 *New York Book of Prices*. (Courtesy, Winterthur Museum Library.)

Figure 25 Card table, New York City, 1815–1825. Mahogany and ebony with white pine. H. 30½", W. 35¾", D. 18" (closed). (Courtesy, Winterthur Museum, bequest of Henry Francis du Pont.)

Figure 26 Detail of the lapped block with triangular in-fills on the card table illustrated in fig. 15. (Photo, Gavin Ashworth.)

thick boards oriented on end that crossed with a lap joint. Triangular blocks filled out the sides (fig. 26). The small printed supplement to the 1810 New York price list, undated but probably about 1815, described the laminated technique as "glueing up the block long and cross way." The supplement also specified that the grain be set at oblique angles—"lapp'd and the corners filled in"—to minimize warping and splitting. Iron straps screwed into the undersides of the legs and the block held the legs in place, relieving some of the downward stress on the joints and preventing the dovetail mortises from splitting apart.[20]

As with lyre motifs, canted corners were not new in the early nineteenth century. Tables with octagonal tops had been made a hundred years earlier, and case pieces with narrow, canted corners became popular by the 1730s. Tables with canted corners were included in the 1796 price lists for New York and Philadelphia furniture, each of which resembled the other and borrowed heavily from the London price list of 1788 and subsequent editions of the 1790s. The 1796 New York price list included entries for a "Canted Corner Work Table" and a "card table with canted corners to be the same price as circular." "Rounding or canting the corners of the flaps" was also mentioned as the least expensive of several decorative options for Pembroke tables. As price tables in the back of these publications indicate, however, these canted corners were fundamentally different from those of 1815 and later. The earlier canted corners were narrow, ranging from "one

Figure 27 Duncan Phyfe, card table, New York City, 1816. Mahogany with white pine and tulip poplar. H. 30", W. 36", D. 18" (closed). (Private collection; photo courtesy Robert Mussey Associates.)

Figure 28 Detail showing the attachment of colonnettes to two crossbars dovetailed into the frame of the card table illustrated in fig. 27.

inch and a quarter [on the flat]" to three inches. In contrast, canted corners on tables made after 1815 are usually at least six inches wide, a dimension that created a markedly different table shape. The listing for narrow canted corners continued in the 1802 New York edition, but thereafter lapsed in that city and elsewhere in the United States. No mention of canted corners occurs in either the 1810 New York price book or the 1811 Philadelphia one. However, with the advent of swivel tops and the design freedom they allowed, New York furniture makers needed to add the new canted shape in 1815, when references and documented instances of use occur with increasing frequency.[21]

The card tables that Phyfe made for Brinckerhoff attest to the dynamic and evolving nature of New York furniture design after 1815. In addition to swivel tops and canted corners, these tables have four, widely spaced, turned and fluted colonnettes set onto a broad platform with concave sides and four hocked animal feet with gilded acanthus carving (fig. 27). The platform is horizontally laminated in the same fashion as the octagonal blocks of card tables with four clustered columns. Whereas most tables of this form have clustered columns socketed up into a single, wide crosspiece supporting the table bed, the more widely separated column pairs of the Brinckerhoff tables fit into separate crossbars dovetailed into the bed (fig. 28). However, the most important aspect of this design was the range of creative opportunity that lay within the platform concept. Lannuier realized these possibilities more fully than anyone else, producing tables similar to Brinckerhoff's as well as those with a carved and gilded caryatid (fig. 29), dolphins, or broad lyres in place of the two forward columns. Variations by other makers

Figure 29 Charles Honoré Lannuier, card table, New York City, 1817. Mahogany with ash, tulip poplar, white pine, cherry, and basswood. H. 31⅛", W. 36", D. 17⅞" (closed). (Courtesy, Metropolitan Museum of Art.)

Figure 30 Michael Allison, card table, New York City, 1817 or later. Mahogany with tulip poplar and cherry. H. 31", W. 37¾", D. 18½" (closed). (Courtesy, Bernard & S. Dean Levy.)

included tables with carved eagles or inverted cornucopia forming the front legs, or scrolled front legs in combination with a rear lyre, all on similar platform bases. Several of these features were illustrated in plate 5 of the 1817 New York price list (fig. 24). Michael Allison labeled yet another canted-corner card table of this general plan that had four ornately carved cyma-curved supports and eagle-headed feet (fig. 30). The label on this table bears the printed date of January 1817.[22]

A group of swivel-top card tables that Lannuier labeled before his death in 1819 suggests that he played a crucial role in developing that form. According to furniture historian Peter Kenny, Lannuier may have taken the idea of swivel tops from prototypes made in post-Revolutionary France. Several details remain unresolved, however. If Lannuier learned about swivel tops before leaving France for New York in 1803, why did the technique remain dormant for so long? When, in fact, can swivel tops be documented in French furniture? If swivel tops did originate in France, what was the role of other French-trained furniture makers working in New York, such as Joseph Brauwers? Latrobe's role also deserves more scrutiny.[23]

Lannuier's familiarity with swivel tops and his proclivity to experiment with various designs led to the production of tables with incurved or concave corners. Examples with this feature from New York and elsewhere in the United States are very rare except in his work. The first specifically dated use of concave corners occurs in two nearly identical pairs of gilded figural card tables made for William Bayard of New York City in 1817 (fig. 29). Another pair of tables with concave corners was among work Lannuier shipped to Cuba shortly before he died in 1819. A card-table-size New York serving table (Boscobel Restoration) and an inlaid card table are the only other examples with similar corner treatment. Although these tables are anonymous, they establish that cabinetmakers other than Lannuier produced this concave-corner form. As with canted corners, care must be taken to distinguish these corner treatments from narrower hollows found on some tables and case pieces. Similarly, an engraved plate that appeared in the 1811 *London Book of Prices* illustrates a tabletop with "hollow ends," not incurved corners. Moreover, that shape seems not to have been used much if at all in the United States.[24]

Lannuier and other New York furniture makers combined canted-corner tops with other card table design features to extend their range of offerings. Lannuier's design of a pair of monochromatic mahogany swivel-top card tables is remarkably subdued in comparison to his gilded figural furniture from the same period, namely 1815 to 1819 (fig. 31). The turned and reeded

Figure 31 Charles Honoré Lannuier, card table, New York City, 1815–1819. Mahogany with white pine, tulip poplar, and cherry. H. 29¾", W. 36", D. 17¾" (closed). (Courtesy, Winterthur Museum.) This table bears Lannuier's third label.

Figure 32 John Budd, card table, New York City, 1817 or later. Mahogany with white pine. H. 29⅝", W. 35⅝", D. 17¾" (closed). (Courtesy, Daughters of the American Revolution Museum.) This table bears Budd's 1817 label.

front legs join the middle of the cant and are marked on the outside by a raised panel or plinth. A similar swivel-top table bears the label of John Budd (active 1817–1840) with the engraved date of May 1817 (fig. 32). This table differs in having twist- or rope-turned legs, a decorative treatment that seldom appeared before this date except in card tables from Lannuier's shop. A more imaginative interpretation occurs in a pair of canted-corner tables with bandy legs, carved waterleaf ornament, and animal feet (fig. 33). As with the turned-leg tables, these front legs intersect the center of the canted corner, marked by a carved panel. Canted-corner card tables with a variety of bases continued to be made through the 1820s.[25]

Figure 33 Card table, probably New York City, 1815–1820. Mahogany with white pine, cherry, and tulip poplar. H. 29⅞", W. 36", D. 18⅛" (closed). (Courtesy, Mabel Brady Garvan Collection, Yale University Art Gallery.)

Figure 34 Card table, probably New York City, 1815–1820. Mahogany with white pine. H. 31", W. 37⅜", D. 20" (closed). (Collection of Mrs. George M. Kaufman; photo, Dirk Baker.)

Some bases for card tables were the same as those made for contemporary Pembroke tables and sofa tables. One of the more elegant designs features an octagon block raised on four swept legs (figs. 34, 35). On the table illustrated in figure 34 the block supports four turned and carved colon-

Figure 35 Michael Allison, Pembroke table, New York City. Mahogany with white pine and ash. H. 30", W. 21⅝" (closed), D. 37 13/16". (Courtesy, Museum of the City of New York, gift of Estelle de Peyster in memory of Julia de Peyster Martin.)

Figure 36 Pembroke table, probably New York City, 1810–1820. Mahogany with ash, maple, tulip poplar, and white pine. H. 30", W. 22⅜" (closed), D. 35¾". (Courtesy, Boscobel Restoration.)

nettes set close to one another and a carved finial in the center. In contrast, the classic pillar-and-claw Pembroke base with a single urn-shaped and waterleaf-carved pillar above four swept legs was seldom, if ever, used on swivel-top card tables (fig. 36). The urn-shaped base was used consistently on mechanical, three-legged card tables, although questions of stability seem to have truncated its longevity. By the time pillar-and-claw bases were practical for card tables, the fashion for urn shapes seems to have passed in favor of more complex carved supports. Although there were many intersections in card table and Pembroke table design, some bases were not suitable for both forms. Large pillars had been used on Pembroke tables since the 1790s, but they were not a viable option for folding-top card tables,

Figure 37 Card table, probably New York City, 1815–1825. Mahogany with white pine. H. 29½", W. 35½", D. 18" (closed). (Courtesy, Mabel Brady Garvan Collection, Yale University Art Gallery.)

Figure 38 Duncan Phyfe, card table, New York City, 1820 or later. Woods and dimensions not recorded. (Courtesy, Decorative Arts Photographic Collection, Winterthur Museum.) This table bears Phyfe's August 1820 label.

which had changing centers of gravity. Similarly, some front-facing platform-base designs for swivel-top card tables were not appropriate for the in-the-round design of Pembrokes. The boldly carved eagles with outswept wings supporting a canted-corner frame on a pair of card tables relate to pier tables instead (fig. 37). In general, however, card and Pembroke table designs moved in tandem, and the two table forms were sometimes made en suite.[26]

A pillar-and-claw card table with the August 1820 printed label of Duncan Phyfe demonstrates how fully card table designs had blended with Pembroke designs (fig. 38). Four leaf-carved legs rise to a boldly turned pillar beneath a D-shaped top. A highly decorated pillar on a firm, four-claw base supported Pembroke table frames as readily as card tables. Carved and uncarved versions dominated table designs of the 1820s. Two more Phyfe card tables with the same label use paired pillars spaced at each end of a trestle base. Whereas the single turned pillar updated an existing base design, the two-column trestle-base design has no obvious prototypes (figs. 39, 40). On one table the hexagonally faceted pillars taper downward. On the other, the turned pillars are architecturally rendered columns with brass-mounted capitals and bases. Curved and carved legs form each leg unit, which are connected by a stretcher.[27]

Figure 39 Duncan Phyfe, card table, New York City, 1820 or later. Mahogany with unidentified secondary wood. H. 29¼", W. 36", D. 18" (closed). (Courtesy, Israel Sack, Inc.) This table bears Phyfe's August 1820 label.

Figure 40 Duncan Phyfe, card table, New York City, 1820 or later. Mahogany with unidentified secondary wood. H. 31½", W. 36", D. 18" (closed). (Courtesy, Sotheby's.)

Card tables of the 1820s and later continued to express the creativity of their makers while marking broader changes in fashion and taste. Yet increasing popularity of center tables and accompanying shifts in furnishing arrangements diminished the importance of the card table—used for all sorts of functions but designed to stand against the wall—relative to other furniture forms. In classic understatement, the authors of *An Encyclopedia of Domestic Economy* (1845) foretold the bland future of these tables. After extolling the "modern and improved" swivel-top design, they observed, "these card-tables are, therefore, capable of every kind of embellishment as well as any occasional tables, and there is nothing in their appearance to distinguish them particularly from other tables." Gradually, card tables blended into the seemingly endless array of tables made for mid-nineteenth-century living.[28]

1. David Longworth, *Longworth's American Almanack, New-York Register, and City Directory* (New York, 1805), p. 111. Margo C. Flannery reports that about one thousand furniture makers were listed in New York City directories between 1795 and 1825 in "Richard Allison and the New York City Federal Style," *Antiques* 103, no. 5 (May 1973): 1001. Marilynn A. Johnson, "John Hewitt, Cabinetmaker," *Winterthur Portfolio* 4 (1968), pp. 185–205. Peter M. Kenny, "From New Bedford to New York to Rio and Back: The Life and Times of Elisha Blossom, Jr., Artisan of the New Republic," in *American Furniture,* edited by Luke Beckerdite (Hanover, N.H.: University Press of New England for the Chipstone Foundation, 2003), pp. 238–69.

2. A demilune card table with the label of New Yorker George Shipley (active 1791–1795) is identified as a Providence, Rhode Island, product; the Charles Courtright label on another demilune card table, probably of New York manufacture, is called spurious in Benjamin A. Hewitt, Patricia E. Kane, and Gerald W. R. Ward, *The Work of Many Hands: Card Tables in Federal America, 1790–1820* (New Haven, Conn.: Yale University Art Gallery, 1982), nos. 32, 39. Patricia E. Kane, "Design Books and Price Books for American Federal-Period Card Tables," in ibid., p. 46.

3. Charles F. Montgomery, *American Furniture: The Federal Period* (New York: Viking Press, 1966), no. 297. The mate to the commemorative table shown in figure 1 was sold in Sotheby's, *Important Americana,* New York, January 21–22, 2000, lot 730. "Ovalo" corners, commonly spelled "ovolo" today, appear throughout *The Journeymen Cabinet & Chair Makers' New-York Book of Prices* (New York: T. & J. Swods, No. 99 Pearl-Street, 1796) and *The New-York Book of Prices for Cabinet & Chair Work, agreed upon by the Employers* (New York: Southwick and Crooker, September 1802). The term was dropped from *The New-York Revised Prices for Manufacturing Cabinet and Chair Work* (New York: Southwick and Pelsue, 1810) and later price books. Between 1800 and 1806 New York cabinetmaker John Hewitt shipped "inlaid sash cornered" sideboards to Savannah, which seems to be this shape. Johnson, "John Hewitt," pp. 186–88. For more on the woods used in card tables made in New York, see Hewitt, Kane, and Ward, *Many Hands,* chart 12, p. 194. For another card table similar to the example illustrated in figure 3, see ibid., pp. 89–91, no. 37. According to David L. Barquist, the vertically laminated ovolo corners of the card table shown in figure 3 are made of tulip poplar (*American Tables and Looking Glasses in the Mabel Brady Garvan and Other Collections at Yale University* [New Haven, Conn.: Yale University Art Gallery, 1992], no. 108). Philip D. Zimmerman, "The Architectural Furniture of Duncan Phyfe, 1830–1845," in *The Richard and Beverly Kelly Collection* (Portsmouth, N.H.: Northeast Auctions, April 3, 2005), p. 15, fig. 7. Hewitt, Kane, and Ward, *Many Hands,* chart 12, p. 194.

4. For a New York six-leg card table with two swinging legs and a Rhode Island six-legged table with one swing leg, see J. Michael Flanigan, *American Furniture from the Kaufman Collection* (Washington, D.C.: National Gallery of Art, 1986), nos. 64, 68. *New-York Book of Prices* 1802, p. 20. *New-York Book of Prices* 1796, p. 35. *New-York Revised Prices* 1810, p. 24; and *The New-York Book of Prices for Manufacturing Cabinet and Chair Work* (New York: J. Seymour, 1817), p. 34. *The Journeymen Cabinet and Chair-Makers' Pennsylvania Book of Prices* (Philadelphia: Printed for the Society, 1811), p. 33.

5. *New-York Book of Prices* 1802, p. 21.

6. For a table with matched veneers, see Berry B. Tracy, *Federal Furniture and Decorative Arts at Boscobel* (New York: Boscobel Restoration and Harry N. Abrams, 1981), no. 28. *New-York Revised Prices* 1810, p. 26.

7. For card tables with unvarnished veneer on the underside of the stationary leaf, see Montgomery, *American Furniture,* nos. 314, 319, 320; and Tracy, *Federal Furniture,* no. 27. *New-York Book of Prices* 1817, p. 3. Tracy, *Federal Furniture,* no. 52; white pine boards are used elsewhere in the bed steps. Thomas Sheraton, *The Cabinet Dictionary,* 2 vols. (1803; reprint, New York: Praeger Publishers, 1970), 1: 129–30. For a card table with a leather playing surface and a fixed leaf with underside veneer, see Montgomery, *American Furniture,* no. 318.

8. *New-York Book of Prices* 1802 states, "All straight drawers the top edge slip'd with mahogany" (p. 3), and "the top edge of the drawer fronts slipt with mahogany" (p. 9). *New-York Book of Prices* 1796, p. 9, includes an entry for "Slipping drawer sides, and rounding the slips," which may be more representative of London practices. *New-York Book of Prices* 1802, p. 21.

9. For a New York card table with a full-width, single-board top, see *The Taft Museum: The History of the Collections and the Baum-Taft House,* edited by Edward J. Sullivan (New York: Hudson Hills Press, 1995), p. 103. Glue joints between the boards are sometimes difficult to detect.

10. Core woods of some top leaves are visible through mortises cut through the slipped back edges for alignment tenons.

11. *New-York Book of Prices* 1796, p. 36. Thomas Sheraton, *The Cabinet-Maker and Upholsterer's Drawing-Book* (1793; reprint, New York: Dover Publications, 1972), p. 161. Sheraton recommended 3½" widths in his *Cabinet Dictionary,* 1: 129.

12. The term "rear leaf-edge tenon" is used in Hewitt, Kane, and Ward, *Many Hands,* chart 12, p. 194. Only 2 of the 27 New York tables in Hewitt's study had three rear leaf-edge tenons, but this author knows of many others. Some card tables from other regions do not have any alignment tenons, and only those made in New York are known to have four. *New-York Book of Prices* 1817, p. 3. The two nearly identical tables (acc. nos. 57.722 and 57.723) are installed as a pair in the Phyfe Room. One (57.723) is illustrated in Montgomery, *American Furniture,* no. 315. See card table 1932.8 in *Taft Museum,* p. 103.

13. For comparative uses in card tables, see Hewitt, Kane, and Ward, *Many Hands,* chart 11, p. 194. Several visual identifications recorded as white pine may actually be other, visually similar woods, such as Atlantic white cedar, but reliable evidence confirms widespread use of white pine in furniture making. The card table illustrated in figure 1 has a walnut outer rear rail, which is an exception. A similar exception occurs in the walnut hinged supports, or "flies," of a New York Pembroke table at Winterthur labeled by George Woodruff. See Montgomery, *American Furniture,* no. 331.

14. This early generation of the form was produced only in New York and, to a lesser degree, in Philadelphia. For a Philadelphia example, see Philip D. Zimmerman et al., *Sewell C. Biggs Museum of American Art: A Catalogue,* 2 vols. (Dover, Del.: Biggs Museum, 2002), 1: 51, no. 34. *New-York Revised Prices* 1810, p. 25. Some tables are so closely balanced, especially when closed, that the direction of pivoting rear-leg casters determines whether the table will stand unsupported.

15. As quoted in Jack L. Lindsey, "An Early Latrobe Furniture Commission," *Antiques* 139, no. 1 (January 1991): 212. Lindsey dates the card table circa 1808. As quoted in Beatrice B. Garvan, *Federal Philadelphia, 1785–1825: The Athens of the Western World* (Philadelphia: Philadelphia Museum of Art, 1987), p. 91. The undated Latrobe designs for the Madison seating, which are believed to be circa 1809 based on correspondence, show chairs that have elaborate stretchers on deeply curved front and rear legs, in contrast to the bold, stretcherless designs of the Waln chairs. Arguments can be advanced to support either set as the earlier. The author thanks Christopher Storb for providing further information. George Wright is listed in Deborah Ducoff-Barone, "Philadelphia Furniture Makers, 1800–1815," *Antiques* 145, no. 5 (May 1991): 995.

16. Ralph Edwards, *The Shorter Dictionary of English Furniture: From the Middle Ages to the Late Georgian Period* (London: Country Life, 1964), pp. 526–27, fig. 31. As quoted in Barquist, *American Tables,* p. 220. *Prices of Cabinet Work, with Tables and designs . . . revised and corrected by a committee of Master Cabinet Makers.* These two price books are in the British Library. The author thanks Adam Bowett for bringing them to his attention and checking their contents. Peter M. Kenny, Frances F. Bretter, and Ulrich Leben, *Honoré Lannuier: Cabinetmaker from Paris* (New York: Metropolitan Museum of Art, 1998), nos. 57–58, 61, pp. 150–52. Peter Kenny dates the label on the basis of style between 1810 and 1812. Written and other evidence does not

allow precise dating for the Lannuier card tables, the labels, or documented or attributed Lannuier furniture related to these card tables. The original owner of the pair of card tables also owned a bedstead, which bears the third Lannuier label, stylistically dated from after 1812 to 1819.

17. *Additional Revised Prices,* p. 3, Hirsch Library, Museum of Fine Arts, Houston; and *Additional Prices Agreed Upon by the New-York Society of Journeymen Cabinet Makers* (July 1815), Winterthur Library. Jeanne Vibert Sloane, "A Duncan Phyfe Bill and the Furniture It Documents," *Antiques* 131, no. 5 (May 1987): 1109, fig. 6. Robert D. Mussey Jr., *The Furniture Masterworks of John and Thomas Seymour* (Salem, Mass.: Peabody Essex Museum, 2003), no. 113. The date range of 1808–1815 assigned to card table no. 112 is too early. Jonathan L. Fairbanks and Elizabeth Bidwell Bates dated it circa 1818 in *American Furniture: 1620 to the Present* (New York: Richard Marek Publishers, 1981), p. 256; and Richard H. Randall Jr. dated it 1815–1825 in *American Furniture in the Museum of Fine Arts, Boston* (Boston: Museum of Fine Arts, 1965), no. 105. Alexandra Alevizatos Kirtley, "Survival of the Fittest: The Lloyd Family's Furniture Legacy," in *American Furniture,* edited by Luke Beckerdite (Hanover, N.H.: University Press of New England for the Chipstone Foundation, 2002), p. 35; Alexandra A. Alevizatos, "'Procured of the Best and Most Fashionable Materials': The Furniture and Furnishings of the Lloyd Family, 1750–1850" (master's thesis, University of Delaware, 1999), p. 221. The author dates the table 1810–1815 and 1810–1820 in earlier studies: Alexandra Alevizatos Kirtley, "A New Suspect: Baltimore Cabinetmaker Edward Priestley," in *American Furniture,* edited by Luke Beckerdite (Hanover, N.H.: University Press of New England for the Chipstone Foundation, 2000), pp. 113–15; and Alevizatos, "'Procured of the Best and Most Fashionable Materials,'" pp. 335–37. Robert D. Schwarz, *The Stephen Girard Collection* (Philadelphia: Girard College, 1980), no. 23.

18. Montgomery, *American Furniture,* no. 318. A similar card table also labeled by Brauwers is no. 16 in *Classical America, 1815–1845* (Newark, N.J.: Newark Museum Association, 1963). *Additional Revised Prices,* p. 3; *Additional Prices* 1815, p. 5; and *New-York Book of Prices* 1817, p. 34. Another construction feature that distinguishes the Brauwers table from other New York work is visible on the underside of the fixed top leaf: it combines mahogany veneer on secondary wood longitudinal boards with unveneered solid mahogany clamps. Montgomery, *American Furniture,* no. 319. The laminations on this table frame are unusual in having wood grain oriented in parallel rather than at oblique angles.

19. A much earlier and isolated exception can be found in an undated Philadelphia-made armchair with a lyre-shaped back splat. Perhaps one of twelve belonging to George Washington, the chair resembles a set made between 1792 and 1797 by Adam Haines of Philadelphia. See Deborah D. Waters, *Delaware Collections in the Museum of the Historical Society of Delaware* (Wilmington, Del.: Historical Society of Delaware, 1984), no. 11; Kathleen Catalano and Richard C. Nylander, "New Attributions to Adam Haines, Philadelphia Furniture Maker," *Antiques* 117, no. 5 (May 1980): 1112, 1114. An apparent second member of the lyre-back set, not examined by the author, differs in its finials and other small decorative details, which may represent later changes to either of the two surviving chairs. See Sotheby Parke-Bernet, *American Heritage Auction of Americana,* New York, January 27–30, 1982, lot 1094. Montgomery, *American Furniture,* pp. 124, 126–28, nos. 72–73. The Phyfe drawing is on a separate piece of paper from the Bancker bill and is not dated but is presumed to be related to the bill. Sloane, "A Duncan Phyfe Bill," p. 1109, pl. II, fig. 7.

20. Mention of lyres is absent from the 1810 *New-York Revised Prices* and the 1811 *Pennsylvania Book of Prices.* For examples with crossed lyres, see Montgomery, *American Furniture,* no. 320; Kenny, Bretter, and Leben, *Honoré Lannuier,* nos. 62–63; and Tracy, *Federal Furniture,* no. 27. *Additional Revised Prices,* p. 4. Peter Kenny identifies this little booklet, a copy of which is in the Library of the Museum of Fine Arts, Houston, as pre-1815, in Kenny, Bretter, and Leben, *Honoré Lannuier,* p. 82 n. 90. See also p. 179.

21. *New-York Book of Prices* 1796, pp. 33, 36, 62, table 17. An obscure circumstance occurred in 1806 when furniture maker James Linacre of Albany charged Peter E. Elmendorf "To repairing a tabel and cuting the corners." A rectangular, Marlborough-leg Pembroke table with large cants at the corners of the drop leaves survives with other Elmendorf furniture and may be this table. See Anne Ricard Cassidy, "Furniture in Upstate New York, 1760–1840: The Glen-Sanders Collection" (master's thesis, University of Delaware, 1981), p. 38.

22. Sloane, "A Duncan Phyfe Bill," p. 1109, fig. 6. Veneer covers the tops and sides, but splitting patterns reveal the inner structure of a near mate to the Brinckerhoff table. Kenny, Bretter, and Leben, *Honoré Lannuier,* nos. 64–87. Barquist, *American Tables,* no. 120; *American Furniture with Related Decorative Arts, 1660–1830: The Milwaukee Art Museum and the Layton Art Col-*

lection, edited by Gerald W. R. Ward (New York: Hudson Hills Press, 1991), no. 97; and Kenny, Bretter, and Leben, *Honoré Lannuier,* figs. 52, 93. Bernard & S. Dean Levy, Inc., photo files.

23. Kenny, Bretter, and Leben, *Honoré Lannuier,* p. 178.

24. Collections of the Metropolitan Museum of Art and the Albany Institute of History and Art. Kenny, Bretter, and Leben, *Honoré Lannuier,* nos. 70–73. Peter M. Kenny, "Opulence Abroad: Charles-Honoré Lannuier's Gilded Furniture in Trinidad de Cuba," in *American Furniture,* edited by Luke Beckerdite (Hanover, N.H.: University Press of New England for the Chipstone Foundation, 2004), pp. 239–64, figs. 6, 11. Tracy, *Federal Furniture,* no. 39; and Israel Sack, Inc., *Opportunities in American Antiques,* brochure 39 (June 1, 1984), p. 66, no. P5554. For the *London Book of Prices* engraving, see Montgomery, *American Furniture,* p. 359.

25. Kenny, Bretter, and Leben, *Honoré Lannuier,* nos. 55–56. The circa 1810 date assigned to no. 306 in Montgomery, *American Furniture,* is too early. In Hewitt, Kane, and Ward, *Many Hands,* no. 41, the authors call the swivel-top tables "the earliest known documented example of this simple construction" yet provide no dating beyond Lannuier's birth and death. Elisabeth Donaghy Garrett, *The Arts of Independence: The DAR Museum Collection* (Washington, D.C.: National Society, Daughters of the American Revolution, 1985), p. 117, nos. 115, 116. Barquist, *American Tables,* no. 117.

26. For Pembroke tables with a single urn-shaped and waterleaf-carved pillar above four swept legs, see Montgomery, *American Furniture,* no. 332; Tracy, *Federal Furniture,* no. 35; and Nancy McClelland, *Duncan Phyfe and the English Regency, 1795–1830* (New York: William R. Scott, 1939), pls. 133, 137. Barquist, *American Tables,* no. 119.

27. Another Phyfe-labeled card table of this form is in Kenny, Bretter, and Leben, *Honoré Lannuier,* fig. 104. Israel Sack, Inc., *Opportunities in American Antiques,* brochure 43 (July 1, 1988), no. P6037; and Christie's, *Important American Furniture,* New York, October 8, 1997, lot 86.

28. T. Webster and Mrs. Parkes, *An Encyclopedia of Domestic Economy* (1845; New York: Harper & Brothers, 1848), p. 261.

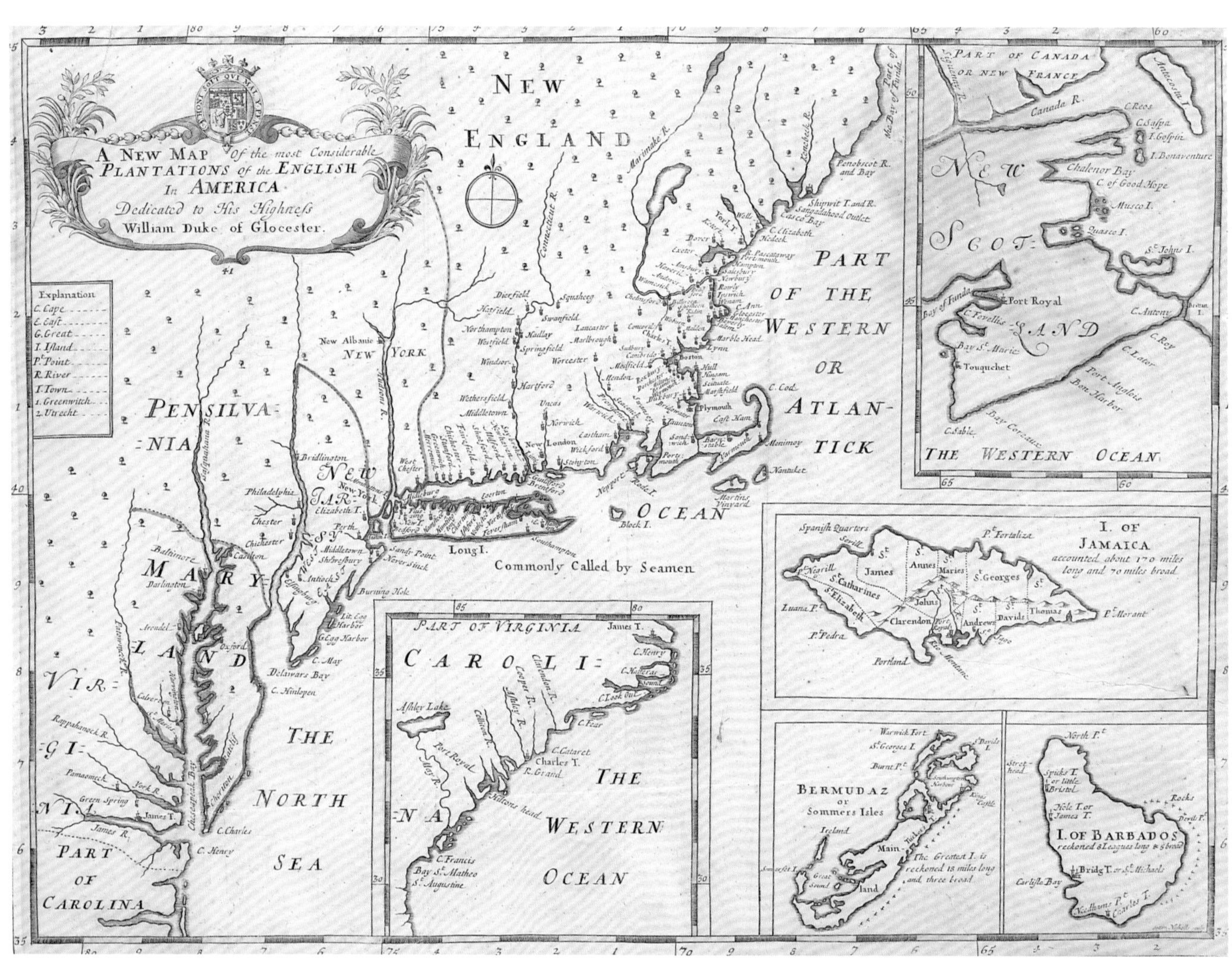

Figure 1 Edward Wells, *A New Map of the Most Considerable Plantations of the English in America,* Oxford, England, 1700–1730. Engraving with watercolor on paper. 13 11/16 x 18 5/8". (Courtesy, Historic Deerfield, Inc., Albert and June Lauzon Collection, gift of Mrs. June Lauzon.)

Joshua W. Lane and Donald P. White III

Fashioning Furniture and Framing Community: Woodworkers and the Rise of a Connecticut River Valley Town

▼ IN 1614 DUTCH ADVENTURER Adriaen Block sailed up the Connecticut River, observing a fertile landscape of forests and floodplains dotted with settlements of Native Americans with whom he hoped to establish trade (fig. 1). Nearly two hundred years later Reverend Timothy Dwight, of Northampton, Massachusetts, traveled through the same region noting gardenlike farms and woodlots punctuated by the white spires of churches where Indian villages once stood. Whereas Block encountered an alien world of cultural difference, Dwight saw the Connecticut River Valley as an idealized arcadian vale peopled with pious citizen-farmers. In his posthumously published *Travels in New England and New York* (1821–1822), Dwight observed that the "inhabitants of this valley may be said . . . to possess a common character." Failing, or refusing, to recognize evidence of a society divided by class and racial distinctions, conflicted over access to, and uses of, the land and its resources, and exposed to the financial vagaries of an industrializing economy, he struck a nostalgic note in describing a world that never was. In 1836 Thomas Cole visually reinforced Dwight's assessment in his landscape painting of the Connecticut River Valley of central Massachusetts, *The Oxbow* (fig. 2).[1]

As more recent historians of the region's early history have found, the area's first European settlers were more attuned to perceived ethnic, cultural, and religious differences than to any sense of "common character." Slavery, warfare, and class divisions—expressed most starkly by the unequal distribution of land to the rich—and religious disagreements over such issues as ministerial authority and qualifications for church membership, cleaved inhabitants one from another in the first several decades of European settlement. First- and second-generation English colonists were as likely to move away from one another as a means of resolving conflict as they were to seek compromises to remain together in their original settlements. Yet, by 1650 arrival of settlers from outside the region had slowed to a trickle, and after 1680 mobility rates dropped, as the children and grandchildren of the region's original settlers grew into adulthood, intermarried, and populated the region's towns with families of their own. By the end of the seventeenth century, extended kin networks linked individuals in communities up and down the Connecticut River and gave shape to a collective "civic culture" among middle- and upper-class whites, characterized by what historian Robert Blair St. George termed "regional consciousness."[2]

Inhabitants who participated in this "civic culture" manifested regional consciousness in their foodways, agricultural practices, social customs, and,

Figure 2 Thomas Cole, *The Oxbow,* 1836. Oil on canvas. 51½" x 76". (Courtesy, Metropolitan Museum of Art, gift of Mrs. Russell Sage, 1908.)

Figure 3 Detail of the tulip-and-leaf decoration on the chest illustrated in fig. 5. (Photo, Gavin Ashworth.)

Figure 4 Detail of the carved center panel of the chest illustrated in fig. 63. (Photo, Gavin Ashworth.)

Figure 5 Chest, Hatfield or Hadley, Massachusetts, 1715–1720. Soft maple, chestnut, and oak with white pine. H. 44¾", W. 45⅝", D. 19⅞". (Courtesy, Historic Deerfield, Inc., gift of Dr. Ogden B. Carter Jr.; photo, Gavin Ashworth.) The paint is not original.

more enduringly, the architecture of their houses and public buildings, gravestones, furniture, and other artifacts of material culture. Collectors and furniture historians have focused on approximately 220 case pieces with relief-carved tulip-and-leaf motifs made in towns from Suffield to Deerfield (fig. 3) and approximately 80 joined case forms decorated with relief-carved flower heads and applied half-columns, bosses, and moldings thought to originate in a Hartford County shop currently associated with Wethersfield woodworker Peter Blinn (1649–1725) (fig. 4) as material expressions of a uniquely American identity that emerged in the region during the late seventeenth and early eighteenth centuries (figs. 5, 6). Although much is now known about this furniture and its makers, little attention has been given to contemporary regional work that diverged from these traditions. Furniture made by craftsmen working outside these two groups raises important questions about the geographic contours of regionalism in the

Figure 6 Cupboard, Hartford County, Connecticut, ca. 1680. Red oak, white oak, white pine, cedar, poplar, and maple. H. 56", W. 49¼", D. 20$^{5}/_{16}$". (Courtesy, Yale University Art Gallery, gift of Charles Wyllys Betts.)

Connecticut River Valley and the development of regional identity over time. This study examines examples of furniture that several of the 215 woodworkers who lived and practiced their trade in Windsor made between 1635 and 1715 to address the following questions. What kinds of furniture did joiners working in the Connecticut River Valley's primary woodworking center of Windsor, between Suffield and Wethersfield, produce? How did generations of Windsor woodworkers contribute to the development of a regional aesthetic? What did these joiners' preferences in construction methods, decorative techniques, and designs suggest about their, and their clients', assumptions concerning cultural propriety, craft proficiency, and self-identity?[3]

Much of the historiography of regionalism in the Connecticut River Valley explores the role that elites—acting in their overlapping capacities as public figures and private consumers—played as arbiters of taste. Some scholars have argued that furniture and other "artifacts of regional consciousness" were part of a dialectical exchange between elites and commoners. The elites sought to distance themselves from those of lesser wealth and status while maintaining their grasp on power by emphasizing their mutual interests with commoners. Commoners, for their part, resented and resisted the power of the elites at the same time that they sought to emulate them. In the Connecticut River Valley, wealthy magistrates, merchants, and ministers acquired furniture as props to create "a theater of dominance that separated them from their less wealthy neighbors" without alienating them. But what was the role of the craftsman in this ongoing drama? The lives and products of Windsor's woodworkers reveal much about what furniture historian Edward Cooke has termed the "social economy" of the seventeenth-century Connecticut River Valley—the making and exchanging of household goods within a specific social context of family relations, barter, political favors, and patronage that the town's woodworkers relied on in practicing their trades. Within this social economy, their furniture rose above the status of marginal props in a drama played out between elites and commoners and became constitutive of the very culture that defined both.[4]

Historical, Cultural, and Aesthetic Context

In the mid-1630s English colonists moving from earlier settlements in eastern Massachusetts established the towns of Wethersfield, Hartford, and Windsor in Connecticut and Springfield in Massachusetts (fig. 7). Although they came variously from all regions in England as merchant-adventurers, Indian traders, Puritan religious idealists, farmers, and craftsmen, they shared a single-minded ambition to own enough farmland to feed their families and produce marketable surpluses. The colonists who arrived in 1635 from an initial settlement in Dorchester, Massachusetts (fig. 8), were typical: they imme-

Figure 7 Detail of Tobias Conrad Letter, *A Map of the Most Inhabited Part of New England,* Augsburg, Germany, 1776. Engraving with watercolor wash on paper. 39½" x 42". (Courtesy, Historic Deerfield, Inc.) This map was based on another map drawn by Braddock Mead (alias John Green) and published by Thomas Jefferys, London, 1755.

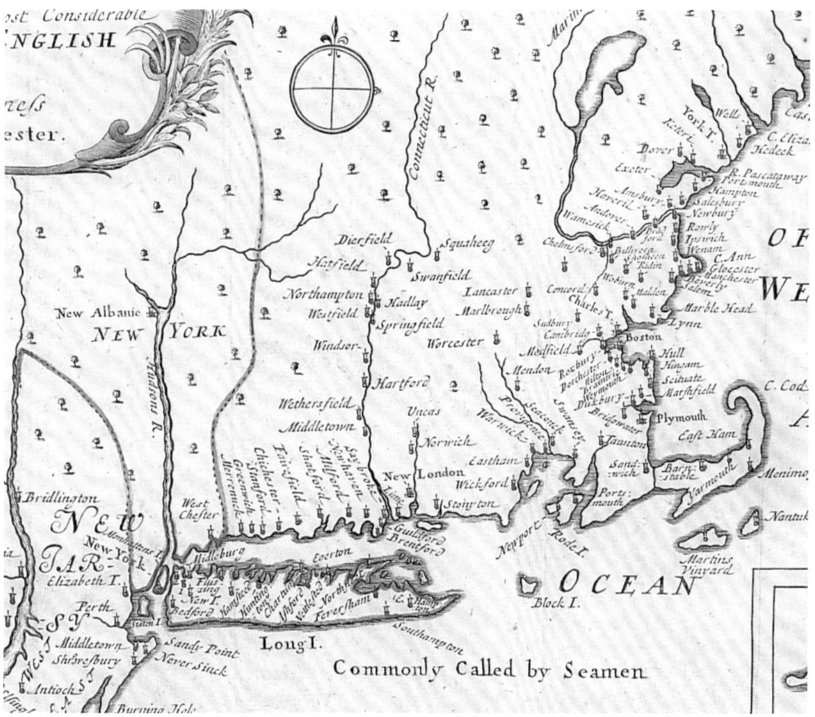

Figure 8 Detail of the map illustrated in fig. 1.

diately set about the task of claiming the land and apportioning it to the male heads of households among them. What set the majority of Windsor's settlers apart from those in the other three Connecticut River Valley towns were their interconnected family backgrounds in England, their circumscribed regional English origins, and their collective religious experience. As natives of towns and villages in England's southwest counties of Devon, Dorsetshire, Somersetshire, and Wiltshire, all within a forty-mile radius of Dorchester, Dorset, many in this group had come to know one another as followers of charismatic Puritan preacher and colonial promoter Reverend John White (1575–1648), rector of Holy Trinity Church in Dorchester. In 1628 and 1629 White had recruited a dozen young single men and twenty-seven married couples with seventy-two children among them to establish a settlement in New England. Perhaps drawing on his experiences both in the rebuilding of Dorchester after a devastating fire destroyed the town in 1613 and in an earlier failed colonial project, White targeted craftsmen, particularly woodworkers, as critical to the success of his settlement.[5]

On the eve of their departure for Massachusetts in 1630, White helped his recruits covenant as an oceangoing congregation and presided over their installation of his young colleague Reverend John Warham (1595–1670) as minister. The group departed aboard the ship *Mary and John* on March 29, 1630, landed in Massachusetts Bay on June 14, then traveled overland to settle at Mattapan, the future site of Dorchester. By 1635 other newcomers, these from East Anglia, not only claimed land that members of Reverend Warham's group had counted on for their own families but also clashed with them over politics and religion. These factors prompted Warham and many members of his original shipboard congregation to resettle in Windsor.[6]

On their arrival in Windsor, Warham's congregation confronted two other groups with competing claims to the land. One group consisted of settlers from Plymouth Colony, who had set up an Indian trading post in Windsor's Great Meadow bordering the Connecticut River. The other group included woodworkers whom the master carpenter Francis Stiles had hired to help fulfill a contract that English nobleman and colonial investor Sir Richard Saltonstall had negotiated with him to improve land that Saltonstall had been granted in Windsor. Members of the Dorchester group occupied the land surrounding the trading post and eventually bought out the Plymouth settlers' interests in the venture. They also claimed the land Stiles had been sent to improve, obstructing Stiles and his workers and arrogating Saltonstall's land for redistribution among themselves. Although they allowed Stiles and his workmen to remain in Windsor, they apparently relegated them to the margins of society. The Dorchester group had acted quickly to solidify their claims to the land and to define and dominate town government. Once assured of power, they set out to create a community grounded in their Congregationalist faith that, in their view, both corrected the social and economic ills that had followed passage of the Enclosure Acts throughout England and preserved traditional order and social hierarchy.[7]

Windsor's settlers defined propriety and prosperity primarily in terms of land-ownership. In England, as much as 30 percent of the rural population had consisted of the landless poor, and so it was with added significance that Windsor's inhabitants measured their success by the quality, type, and value of their acreage and by the houses, barns, outbuildings, pens, and fences that they erected on those lands. Through their acquisition of home lots, woodlots, fields, and pastures, Windsor's freemen—resident, landowning male heads of households—provided not only for their families' immediate wants but also for their sons' future needs: their land represented their male heirs' inheritances. However, they also prized material possessions. For the convenience and comfort of their large families, Windsor's wealthier landowners furnished their homes with an assortment of housewares and textiles as well as boxes, chests, cupboards, tables, benches, chairs, bedsteads, and other wooden furniture made from sawn boards nailed together and from riven components assembled with mortise-and-tenon joints. These objects, especially textiles and furniture, represented movable wealth customarily willed to female heirs. Whereas these middling and wealthy farmers owned similar furniture forms, household inventories indicate that the wealthy both purchased furniture in greater quantities than their less-wealthy neighbors and commissioned a few expensive, stylish forms not seen in poorer neighbors' homes, such as large oak cupboards, possibly decorated with moldings, carving, and turned columns in their upper cases. With case furniture constructed from durable oak and yellow pine, embellished with carved and painted surfaces, and secured with locks, Windsor residents symbolically set themselves apart from the poor landless whites they had left behind in England, from the Native Americans who had helped them through their initial years of settlement in Windsor, and from the "white Indians"—traders, hunters, landless vagrants—they occasionally encountered in the region. Case furniture fitted with locks and keys conveyed values of security, stability, and materialism that must have contrasted sharply with the impermanence and profligacy ascribed to poor whites, "white Indians," and Native Americans.[8]

Windsor woodworkers used red and white oak as the primary material for joined case furniture. A single laborer working with a wedge, beetle, and froe could split all of the stock required for joinery, an important consideration since the town did not have a water-powered sawmill until 1687. Durable and resistant to rot and insect damage when dry, riven oak displays large transverse rays. This grain pattern satisfied the prevailing late Renaissance taste for woodwork with visually complex, patterned surfaces. Settlers accustomed to furniture constructed from English oak, which was usually of poor quality and mill-sawn to reduce waste, must have appreciated the vibrant pattern and superior grain of riven American variants. In a similar vein, Windsor furniture makers and their patrons evidently preferred yellow pine over less durable conifers and softwoods. Readily pit-sawn into clear, wide boards, yellow pine was well suited for lids, panels, drawer interiors, and board furniture. Its high pitch content may also have deterred insects, which would have been advantageous in furniture intended to store textiles.

Like English craftsmen elsewhere, Windsor's woodworkers used oak for both practical and cultural reasons. Expressing ideas about wood that had been circulating in English culture since medieval times, Randall Holme noted that oak was "the strongest of Trees, . . . apt for mighty Buildings . . . [and] the emblem of Protection and Safety, Force, Strength, and long Life."

A wreath of oak leaves symbolized "Valour and safety . . . and therefore may not unfitly be termed the Garland of Honour and Protection." Oak appeared as a literary conceit in other contexts, reinforcing and enlarging on the symbolic meanings Holme set forth in *The Academy of Armory, or, A Storehouse of Armory and Blazon* (1688). In his journal, Windsor woodworker Matthew Grant captured the text of a sermon that Reverend Thomas Hooker, minister at Hartford, Connecticut, delivered from the pulpit of Windsor's church as a guest preacher, sometime in the 1640s. Drawing from Matthew 12:18–20, Hooker described "God's children" as "bruised reeds before their conversion" and urged the unconverted in his audience to recognize their innately sinful natures—to "know themselves to be reeds and not oakes." By contrast, Hooker compared the full church members in his audience to oaks. For the woodworkers whom Reverend John White had recruited to build a model community and Windsor's Christian faithful, oak was a potent symbol of Puritan style and ideology. Literally it constituted the material from which plain-style furniture was made; rhetorically it served as a metaphor for the converted; and figuratively it evoked spiritual reflection.[9]

Oak was imbued with yet other meanings. It figures centrally in Aesop's "The Oak and the Reed," a fable that English antiquarian Philip Ayres included in his *Mythologia ethica, or, Three centuries of Æesopian fables in English* (1689). In this story, a stalwart oak is blown down in a gale while the humble reed survives unscathed. Ayres's version repeated Aesop's characterization of oak as rigid and inflexible, and further portrayed it as an ancient tree rooted in history and resistant to the winds of change. By 1689 riven oak furniture was quickly passing out of fashion in urban centers on both sides of the Atlantic. That Connecticut River Valley inhabitants continued to favor oak for furniture well into the eighteenth century attests to their selective attachment to and recycling of the past.[10]

Windsor furniture makers offered a variety of options including architectural moldings, painted decoration, and carving that merged the visual tradition of Britain's pre-Christian past with Renaissance classical designs. Incorporating abstract geometric, architectural, and naturalistic imagery, this carving resembled and may have been inspired by printed textile design books that circulated throughout Europe beginning in the 1550s (figs. 9, 10). In the construction and decoration of their furniture, Windsor's wood-

Figure 9 Embroidery patterns illustrated in Giovanni Andre Valvassore's *Esemplario di lavrio* (Venice, 1552) and Giovanni Ostaus's *Vera perfettiono del desegno* (Venice, 1557). (Private collection; photo, Gavin Ashworth.)

Figure 10 Elizabeth White, sampler, Hatfield, Massachusetts, before 1688. Wool on linen. 13¾" x 6¾". (Courtesy, Historic Deerfield, Inc.)

workers attempted to fulfill their patrons' expectations regarding workmanship, artifice, aesthetics, and symbolism. Acquired in the expectation that it would be handed down to later generations, this furniture provided its owners with a sense of continuity and community. Furniture rooted in regional English traditions reminded settlers of the Old World and, through ownership and inheritance, ramified connections with family living abroad and in the Connecticut River Valley. As historian Laurel Thatcher Ulrich has shown, material possessions, especially case furniture carved with the initials of their female owners' maiden names, also denoted gender and lineage within the blended family lines that increasingly defined regional culture at the end of the seventeenth century.[11]

Woodworking Traditions

Twenty-seven immigrant woodworkers plied their trade in seventeenth-century Windsor. Of the eight shop traditions that can be identified today, only a few persisted intact for more than three generations. Others disappeared more quickly as woodworkers created hybrid styles by combining traditional practices and designs with techniques and motifs that they learned while collaborating on public building projects and working for one another. The lives of the masters and the choices they made in practicing their trades determined their success as well as the influence their shop exerted on woodworking in the region. Furniture made by members of the Barber family offers historical insights into some of the factors that defined a shop's place within the community and the wider network of woodworking shops spread across the region.

The Barber Shop

A joined, carved chest that probably belonged first to Nicholas Hoyt (1622–1655) may represent the work of Thomas Barber Sr. (1614–1662), a carpenter from Bedford, in the English Midlands (figs. 11, 12). Barber was not related to Hoyt by marriage, and since they immigrated with different

Figure 11 Chest attributed to Thomas Barber Sr., Windsor, Connecticut, 1640–1662. Oak with yellow pine and oak. H. 23¾", W. 54", D. 23¼". (Courtesy, Pocumtuck Valley Memorial Association, gift of Mrs. Catherine W. Hoyt; photo, Gavin Ashworth.) The stiles have been shortened and the lid and till are missing.

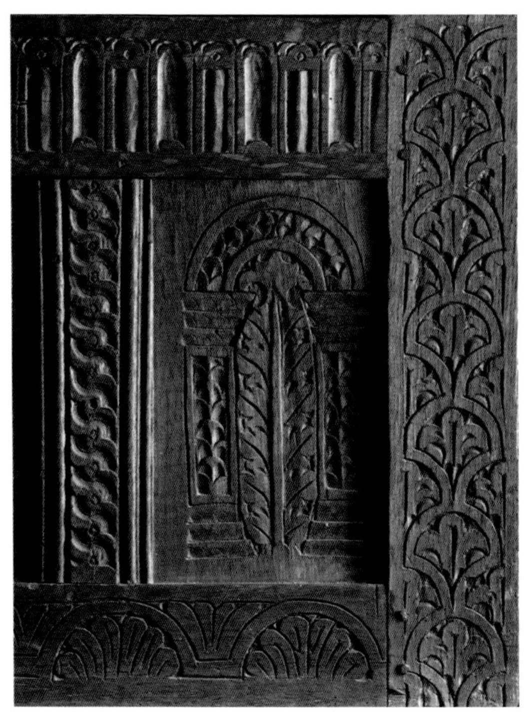

Figure 12 Detail of the carving on the façade of the chest illustrated in fig. 11. (Photo, Gavin Ashworth.)

Figure 13 Chest attributed to Thomas Barber Jr., Windsor or Simsbury, Connecticut, ca. 1662. Oak with yellow pine and oak. H. 28⅝", W. 55½", D. 24¼". (Courtesy, Connecticut Historical Society; photo, Gavin Ashworth.)

groups, it is unlikely that they had encountered each other in England. The chest's attribution is based on its close similarity to a chest that Barber's son and apprentice Thomas (1644–1711) probably made for his father-in-law, cooper William Phelps (1599–1672), in 1663 or thereafter (fig. 13).[12]

Both chests have oak panels and framing members assembled with double-pinned mortise-and-tenon joints. The Hoyt chest has four back panels, whereas the Phelps chest has only three. The floor of the Hoyt chest is constructed in the same manner as that of the Phelps chest: the boards are oriented longitudinally, joined with a spline (a long, thin strip of wood slotted into grooves on the boards' inner edges), and set into grooves in the stiles and all four lower rails. Both floorboards of the Hoyt chest are composed of pit-sawn yellow pine. The floor of the Phelps chest has a single pine board at the back and a pit-sawn oak board at the front. The size and grain of the oak board suggest that the maker cut it from the same log as the lid. Although the original lid of the Hoyt chest is missing, it may have been composed of two oak boards joined with a spline and attached to the case with three snipe-bill hinges, as in the lid of the Phelps chest (fig. 14). The carving on the two chests is clearly by different hands. The decoration on the Hoyt example extends to the sides of the case and is the most complex and fully developed work associated with the Barber shop (see fig. 12). This carving is fresher and more vivid than that on the Phelps chest (figs. 15, 16) and best reflects the distinctive character of the shop's English regional origin.[13]

Figure 14 Detail showing a spline used to join the lid boards of the chest illustrated in fig. 13. (Photo, Gavin Ashworth.)

Figure 15 Detail of the carving on the left stile of the chest illustrated in fig. 13, showing the tesselated trefoil found in the same locations on all examples attributed to the Barber shop. (Photo, Gavin Ashworth.)

Figure 16 Detail showing the carving on the upper rail and molding on the muntins and lid of the chest illustrated in fig. 13. (Photo, Gavin Ashworth.)

The carving on the front stiles of these chests and the two related examples consists of trefoils set within a spade-shaped border (see figs. 12, 15). Similarly, the Hoyt chest and one of the related examples have façade muntins with chain motifs composed of S-curves flanking a circular punched design and upper rails with gouge-cut arcades separated by flutes and surmounted by circular punched designs and gouge strikes. In addition to these analogues in carved ornament, all four chests have various configurations of a single set of moldings. The molding (bead-fillet-step-half-round-groove) on the edges of the façade and side muntins of the Hoyt chest is repeated on the edges of the façade muntins and lid of the Phelps chest (fig. 16). A simpler variant of this molding (step-groove-half-round) is on the edges of the side muntins, inner edges of the side rails, and till of the Phelps chest and on several components of one of the related chests.

As a young man, Thomas Sr. may have moved to nearby Millbrook, Bedfordshire, to apprentice with master carpenter Francis Stiles (1602–1660). By March 1635 Stiles, his five siblings, including woodworkers Henry Stiles (1593–1651) and Thomas Stiles (b. 1612), and Barber had moved to London and assembled a group of thirteen additional men to "prepare a house" and fence land patented by Sir Richard Saltonstall in Windsor, Connecticut. In lieu of cash, Saltonstall had agreed to give these workmen 1,100 acres from his original grant. Francis Stiles was to receive an additional 419½ acres for his work and oversight of the project. Stiles's group reached Windsor on December 30, 1635, but the following year brought only disappointment as the newly arrived group from Dorchester took possession of Saltonstall's land and persuaded the Connecticut General Court to nullify his grant. After years of bitter litigation, Saltonstall gave up on his patent.[14]

Probably fearing that Francis Stiles was planning to leave Windsor and abandon his workmen, the Connecticut General Court bound Barber and two other young woodworkers to him, effectively forcing Stiles to honor the terms of their original indenture. This order and a series of further legal actions that Stiles had initiated to reclaim his land kept him in Windsor until 1647, when he moved to Stratford, Connecticut. Considering Barber's association with Stiles, the furniture attributed to the former's shop may represent an extension of the Midlands tradition in which his master worked. Because of the General Court's order, Barber would also have been exposed to the stylistic vocabularies and working methods of the other men Stiles had been instructed to train: eighteen-year-old Thomas Cooper (1617–1675) from Hingham, Norfolk, in East Anglia, and nineteen-year-old George Chapple (1616–1682) from Barnstaple, Devon. From the seventeenth century on, cross-pollination of design was a hallmark of Connecticut River Valley regional style.[15]

Grudgingly the Dorchester group accepted Stiles's men into their settlement, primarily viewing them as candidates for service in the militia-like train band and the Pequot War of 1637. The town fathers provided Stiles's men with land, but not in the amount or location that they felt they deserved. Saddled with small home lots in the hinterlands and deterred from holding town offices or joining the church, Stiles's men lived on the geographic and social fringe of Windsor. Apparently anxious about possible legal challenges to the legitimacy of their own land claims, many members of the Dorchester group may have never fully overcome their initial suspicion and resentment. They harassed Stiles's men with lawsuits, and by 1660 only Barber remained. He lived on a thirty-acre grant on the edge of town, far from Windsor's center.[16]

The residents of Windsor appear to have ostracized Barber. Although the town's freemen elected him a sergeant in the militia, they stripped him of his rank in 1649 as punishment for striking his superior officer, woodworker and train band captain Aaron Cooke. Barber never held a town office, never became a full member of the church, and never received any town work contracts, which forced him to seek work in other Connecticut River Valley towns. In 1649 he spent five weeks in Springfield building a sawmill and gristmill for William Pynchon, the founder of Springfield, Massachusetts, and between 1658 and 1661 he built a house, barn, and cider press, hewed timber for the construction of a prison house, and did agricultural labor for William's son John. In 1661 Barber agreed to move to Northampton, Massachusetts, after the selectmen of the town offered him a lot and twenty acres of farmland. Unfortunately, their arrangement never came to pass, for Barber died in Windsor the next year. At the time of his death, Barber's estate was valued at £132. That figure placed him in the bottom 20 percent for his profession and well below the £496 median estate value for Windsor's twenty-four other immigrant-generation woodworkers.[17]

The townspeople of Windsor were kinder to Barber's children, who gained community acceptance at an early age. In 1661, at the unusually young age of seventeen, Barber's son Thomas married Mary Phelps (1644–1725), daughter of William Phelps, one of Windsor's deputies to the Connecticut General Court. This marriage to a magistrate's daughter allied Thomas Jr. with a large network of woodworkers who were related by marriage to Phelps's family. Several months later, Thomas Jr.'s father and mother, Jane Coggins (1619–1662) died, leaving him and his five siblings as orphans. As a result, the Connecticut General Court bound nine-year-old Josiah Barber (1653–1729), "according to his desire," to one of Windsor's most successful woodworkers, John Moore Sr. Thomas Barber Sr. had willed half his woodworking tools, seventeen acres of meadow and upland, and a mare to his eldest son, eighteen-year-old Thomas Jr., and the other half of his tools to his fourteen-year-old son, Samuel (1648–1708), whom he had started to train as a woodworker. To ensure that Samuel also continued with his training, the Connecticut General Court bound him as an apprentice to Thomas Jr.[18]

By October 1668 Thomas Jr. had finished training Samuel and moved his family to Massaco, a satellite community on Windsor's western border (incorporated as a separate town in 1668 and renamed Simsbury in 1672). He quickly became the town's leading woodworking craftsman and a central figure in local government. He served as ensign and lieutenant in the militia and was elected one of three selectmen on December 1, 1681. Barber's neighbors apparently trusted him and his fellow selectmen so thoroughly that they subsequently voted to dispense with regular elections for selectmen and allowed the three to serve until the town decided that another election was required. For Thomas Jr., this policy resulted in a twenty-two-year term. He received many of the town's building contracts, including construction of the meetinghouse in 1674 (for which he received 240 acres of meadow in payment) and the rebuilding of the meetinghouse in 1682, after it was destroyed by fire during King Philip's War. He also built the gristmill

Figure 17 Chart showing the genealogy of the Barber family.

BARBER FAMILY						
Marriage Date	Name	Dates	Birth location	Death location	Marriage location	Occupation/note
Generation 1						
	Thomas Barber	1614–1662	Bedford, Bedford, Eng.	Windsor, CT	Windsor, CT	Woodworker
1640	Jane Coggins	1619–1662	Bedford, Bedford, Eng.	Windsor, CT		Aunt of wife of Peter Buell (1644–1729)
Generation 2						
Children of Thomas Barber 1614 and Jane Coggins						
	John Barber	1642–1712	Windsor, CT	Suffield, CT	Springfield, MA	
1663	Bathsheba Coggins	1644–1688	Windsor, CT	Springfield, MA		Sister of wife of Peter Buell (1644–1729)
1689	Hannah Gardener	1642–1711	Springfield, MA	Suffield, CT		
	Thomas Barber	1644–1711	Windsor, CT	Simsbury, CT	Windsor, CT	Woodworker
1663	Mary Phelps	1644–1725	Windsor, CT	Simsbury, CT		Daughter of William Phelps (1599–1672); owner of the chest illustrated in fig. 13
	Sarah Barber	1646–?	Windsor, CT	Windsor, CT	Windsor, CT	
1663	Timothy Heald	1638–?	Ardley, Cheshire, Eng.	Windsor, CT		
	Samuel Barber	1648–1708	Windsor, CT	Windsor, CT	Windsor, CT	Woodworker
1670	Mary Coggins	1648–1676	Windsor, CT	Windsor, CT		Sister of wife of Peter Buell (1644–1729)
1676	Ruth Drake	1657–1731	Windsor, CT	Windsor, CT	Windsor, CT	Daughter of John Drake II (1622–1688)
	Mary Barber	1651–1725	Windsor, CT	Simsbury, CT	Windsor, CT	Mother of 2nd wife of Peter Buell (1644–1729); possible owner of the box illustrated in fig. 18
1667	John Gillett	1644–1699	Windsor, CT	Simsbury, CT		Woodworker
	Josiah Barber	1653–1729	Windsor, CT	Windsor, CT	Windsor, CT	Woodworker; apprentice of John Moore I (1614–1677)
1677	Abigail Loomis	1659–1700	Windsor, CT	Windsor, CT		Sister of Nathaniel Loomis (1656–1733)
1701	Sarah Porter	1655–1730	Windsor, CT	Windsor, CT	Windsor, CT	Daughter of John Porter (1622–1688)
Generation 3						
Children of Thomas Barber 1644 and Mary Phelps						
	John Barber	1664–1712	Windsor, CT	Simsbury, CT	Simsbury, CT	
1701	Mary Holcomb	1676–1745	Windsor, CT	Simsbury, CT		Daughter of Joshua Holcomb (1640–1690)
	Joanna Barber	1667–1739	Windsor, CT	Windsor, CT	Windsor, CT	
1719	Benjamin Colt	1669–1739	Hartford, CT	Windsor, CT		Brother of Abraham Colt (1666–1730)
	Sarah Barber	1669–1748	Simsbury, CT	Simsbury, CT	Simsbury, CT	
1701	Andrew Robe	1662–1735	Simsbury, CT	Simsbury, CT		Woodworker; probable apprentice of Thomas Barber Jr. (1644–1711)
	Thomas Barber	1671–1713	Simsbury, CT	Simsbury, CT	Simsbury, CT	Woodworker
1699	Abigail Buell	1673–1727	Windsor, CT	Simsbury, CT		Daughter of Peter Buell (1644–1729)
	Anna Barber	1672–1722	Simsbury, CT	Simsbury, CT	Simsbury, CT	
1701	Jonathan Higley	1675–1716	Simsbury, CT	Simsbury, CT		
	Samuel Barber	1683–1725	Simsbury, CT	Simsbury, CT	Simsbury, CT	Woodworker
1712	Sarah Holcomb	1691–1787	Simsbury, CT	Simsbury, CT		Daughter of Nathaniel Holcomb (1644–1713)

	Mary Barber	1683–1712	Simsbury, CT	Simsbury, CT	Simsbury, CT	
1702	Ephraim Buell	1683–?	Simsbury, CT	Simsbury, CT		Son of Peter Buell (1644–1729)
Children of Samuel Barber 1648 and Mary Coggins						
	Samuel Barber	1673–1758	Windsor, CT	Simsbury, CT	Windsor, CT	Woodworker
1713	Martha Ponder	1677–?	Windsor, CT	Windsor, CT		
	John Barber	1676–1767	Windsor, CT	Windsor, CT	Windsor, CT	Woodworker
1717	Jane Alvord	1699–?	Windsor, CT	Windsor, CT		Sister of Jeremiah Alvord (1696–1738)
Children of Samuel Barber 1648 and Ruth Drake						
	William Barber	1678–1704	Windsor, CT	Windsor, CT		Woodworker
	Joseph Barber	1681–1748	Windsor, CT	Windsor, CT	Windsor, CT	Woodworker
1713	Mary Loomis	1691–1786	Windsor, CT	Windsor, CT		Sister of Nathaniel Loomis (1656–1733)
	Ruth Barber	1683–1747	Windsor, CT	Windsor, CT	Windsor, CT	
1706	William Phelps	1669–1733	Windsor, CT	Windsor, CT		Woodworker
	Elizabeth Barber	1684–1717	Windsor, CT	Windsor, CT	Windsor, CT	
1709	Daniel Loomis	1682–1754	Windsor, CT	Windsor, CT		Woodworker; nephew of Nathaniel Loomis (1656–1733)
	Mary Barber	1685–1719	Windsor, CT	Windsor, CT	Windsor, CT	
1704	Peter Brown	1666–1724	Windsor, CT	Windsor, CT		Woodworker
	Sarah Barber	1688–1742	Windsor, CT	Westfield, MA	Windsor, CT	
1711	Stephen Palmer	1686–?	Windsor, CT	Westfield, MA		Brother of John Palmer (1693–1756)
	Benjamin Barber	1690–?	Windsor, CT	Windsor, CT	Windsor, CT	
1720	Hannah Loomis	1689–?	Windsor, CT	Windsor, CT		Daughter of Samuel Loomis (1666–1754)
Children of Josiah Barber 1653 and Abigail Loomis						
	Abigail Barber	1678–?	Windsor, CT	Windsor, CT	Windsor, CT	
1701	Cornelius Brown	1672–1747	Windsor, CT	Windsor, CT		Son of Peter Brown (1632–1692)
	Elizabeth Barber	1684–1717	Windsor, CT	Windsor, CT	Windsor, CT	
1704	Enoch Drake	1683–1776	Windsor, CT	Windsor, CT		Grandson of John Drake II (1622–1688)
	Rebecca Barber	1687–1768	Windsor, CT	Windsor, CT	Windsor, CT	
1707	Nathaniel Drake	1685–1769	Windsor, CT	Windsor, CT		Grandson of John Drake II (1622–1688)
	Jonathan Barber	1694–1720	Windsor, CT	Windsor, CT	Windsor, CT	
1720	Rachel Gaylord	1704–1778	Windsor, CT	Windsor, CT		Daughter of Nathaniel Gaylord (1656–1720)

and sawmill in 1678, minister Reverend Dudley Woodbridge's house in 1691, and, with woodworkers Peter Buell and Nathaniel Holcomb (1644–1713), the minister's barns in 1697. In 1706 Thomas Jr. constructed buildings at Simsbury's copper and graphite mines in return for a financial stake in their future profits. These grants, additional real estate purchases, fees collected from the saw- and gristmills, and profits from the copper and graphite mines made Thomas Barber Jr. rich. When he died in 1712, he was the town's largest landowner and wealthiest citizen, leaving an estate valued at £448. That figure represents a 270 percent increase over the value of his father's estate. In contrast, the median estate value for contemporary woodworkers in Windsor was £218, a 56 percent decrease from the previous generation.[19]

Several of Thomas Jr.'s children married into other Windsor woodworking families (fig. 17). Thomas Barber III (1671–1713) married Peter Buell's daughter Abigail (1673–1727) in 1699. Both Thomas Jr.'s first- and third-born sons forged familial bonds with the Holcombs. In 1701 John Barber (1664–1712) married Mary Holcomb (1676–1745), whose father, Joshua (1640–1690), was a Simsbury woodworker. Eleven years later Samuel Barber (1683–1725) married Nathaniel Holcomb's daughter Sarah (1691–1787). Thomas Jr.'s daughters also established links with woodworking craftsmen. In 1701 Sarah Barber (1669–1748) married Simsbury woodworker Andrew Robe (1662–1735). Robe, whose family was not active in any woodworking trade, may have been Barber's apprentice, as he received half of the tools in his father-in-law's estate, including a hack saw, three files, beetle rings and wedges, a shave, a drawing knife, and cooper's adz. Thomas Barber Jr. willed the other half of his tools to Thomas III. Thomas Jr.'s youngest daughter, Mary (1683–1712), followed in her brother Thomas III's footsteps in solidifying the connection between the Barber and Buell families. In 1702 she married Peter Buell's son Ephraim (b. 1683).[20]

Figure 18 Box attributed to Thomas Barber Sr., Windsor, Connecticut, before 1663. Oak. H. 4⅜", W. 8⅝", D. 5¼". (Private collection; photo, Gavin Ashworth.) The lock is missing.

Figure 19 Detail showing the waxed linen lining on the bottom board of the box illustrated in fig. 18. (Photo, Gavin Ashworth.)

A recently discovered box made of thinly riven oak sheds additional light on furniture from the Barber family shops (fig. 18). The sides are rabbeted to receive the front and back and secured with a small wrought nail driven through each corner, and the lower inside edges of all four boards are rabbeted to receive the rabbeted upper edges of the bottom boards. Before the maker assembled the box, he glued waxed, indigo-dyed linen to the bottom board (fig. 19). During the seventeenth century, waxed linen was used throughout Europe to line clerical vestments. The top of the box has a step-ogee molding on the front and sides and is attached with elaborately cut, sheet brass cotter-pin hinges. Evidence for at least two lock mechanisms and a carrying handle (probably brass) survive on the box.[21]

The outer and inner surfaces of the lid and the front, sides, and back of the box are decorated with interlocked arcades set within scribed borders (figs. 20, 21). The individual arcs forming the arcades are the products of two cuts made with a small quarter-round gouge rather than a single cut made with a larger tool. Barber's tool kit included more small gouges than the kits of many of his contemporaries. The arcades and scribed lines frame the major carved elements, which consist of broad, convex lobes with rounded ends, separated by smaller lobes with hollowed ends and circular

Figure 20 Back of the box illustrated in fig. 18. (Photo, Gavin Ashworth).

Figure 21 Detail showing the carving on the inner surface of the lid of the box illustrated in fig. 18. (Photo, Gavin Ashworth.)

and spade-shaped designs at either end (see figs. 18-21). Most of these motifs appear in similar contexts on the façade of the Hoyt chest (see figs. 11, 12) and the box illustrated in figure 22. The spade-shaped elements relate

Figure 22 Box attributed to Thomas Barber Sr., Windsor, Connecticut, before 1663. Woods and dimensions not recorded. (Wallace Nutting, *Furniture Treasury*, 2 vols. [Framingham, Mass.: Old America Co., 1928], 1: fig. 163.)

directly to the motifs set between the lunettes on the top rail of the Phelps chest. The inner and outer faces of the lid of the box illustrated in figure 18 and façade of the box illustrated in figure 22 are further decorated with circular flower heads. Although the patterns of motifs on these boxes do not exactly replicate those on any other furniture attributed to Barber, the individual elements, composition, and execution of the carving strongly suggest that they are from his shop.

Small boxes often appear in seventeenth-century New England inventories, but few have survived. The example illustrated in figure 18 may have resembled the "Smal Carv^{d} box" valued at 1s. 2d. in the 1713 inventory of Thomas Barber Jr.'s estate. The recovery history of this box provides a further link to Thomas Barber Sr. Recently discovered in an early nineteenth-century house built by Henry Austin (1770–1829) in Owasco, Cayuga County, New York, this box descended from his father, Joab (1740–1820). A native of Suffield, Connecticut, Joab was the fourth-generation descendant of John Gillett (1644–1699), a Windsor woodworker who, in 1667, married Thomas Barber Sr.'s second daughter, Mary (1651–1725). Shortly after their marriage, the couple left Windsor to settle in Suffield.[22]

The Buell Shop

A group of three related boxes can be attributed to the shop of William Buell (1614–1681), a woodworker who emigrated from Chesterton, Huntingdon, England. All of these objects have similar rosettes accentuated with gouge strikes and notches, and in some instances the rosettes appear in the intersections of strapwork in a horizontal guilloche pattern. The only object in this group with a reliable provenance is a box that family tradition maintains Buell made for himself (fig. 23). Constructed from stock more than one inch thick, the boxes attributed to Buell are among the largest examples from New England. Each has a two-inch-high board nailed to the top of the back. The round projecting ends of the board engage holes drilled in cleats

Figure 23 Box attributed to William Buell, Windsor, Connecticut, 1640–1681. Oak with pine. H. 8½", W. 27", D. 18". (Courtesy, Oneida Historical Society, gift of Dr. Wales Buel.)

attached to the underside of the lid, forming a modified pintal hinge. To lay out the carving, the maker used a grid of eight equal sections marked off in a rectangular border on the front and a grid of four equal sections marked off in a rectangle on the sides. Each of the rectangles is bordered by a half-inch-wide scribed band containing paired alternating gouge cuts flanking circular punches. This band occurs on the projecting edges of the bottom board and on the front and sides of the lid. Alternating half-inch and quarter-inch notches are gouged on the outer edges of the front and back boards, the edges of the lid, and the edges of the board nailed to the back. Ornament also extends to the sides and to surfaces not readily visible, including the undersides of the cleats, which feature alternating circular and cruciform punches, and the outer edges of the back board and applied secondary board, which are finished with alternating horizontal and vertical notches.[23]

As indicated by his precision and attention to detail, Buell was a very skilled tradesman. A woodworker who specialized in finish-carpentry, he immigrated to Windsor in 1638 with his mother's cousin, Reverend Ephraim Huitt, whom Reverend John Warham later accepted as an assistant to occupy the teaching position in Windsor's church. In addition to making furniture, Buell produced woodwork for various public buildings. In 1661 he received £32 for three high pews to accommodate the deacons, the town magistrates, and their wives in Windsor's first church. The following year the selectmen of Springfield, Massachusetts, hired Buell and his eldest son and apprentice Samuel (1641–1721) to produce interior components for the town meetinghouse. This work included installing pillars to support the pulpit and fabricating the gallery and pews.[24]

Buell's career differed markedly from that of Thomas Barber Sr. and most other immigrant woodworkers in Windsor. Like Barber, most of these men supplemented their income by hewing timber, splitting fence rails, riving shingles, doing farmwork, or performing other tasks. However, there is no evidence that Buell worked in any capacity other than his primary trade. His only contract for heavy carpentry was for stocks made for the town of Windsor in 1664. Buell's skill and patronage allowed him to charge a higher wage (seven shillings per day) than any of his contemporaries and five shillings more than the two-shilling cap imposed by the Connecticut General Court on woodworkers and other craftsmen in 1641.[25]

It is surprising that Buell's shop did not exert a more lasting influence on the woodworking trades of the Connecticut River Valley. He appears as an

BUELL FAMILY

Marriage Date	Name	Dates	Birth location	Death location	Marriage location	Occupation/note
Generation 1						
	William Buell	1614–1681	Chesterton, Huntingdon, Eng.	Windsor, CT	Windsor, CT	Woodworker
1640	Mary Post	1616–1688	Dorchester, Dorset, Eng.	Windsor, CT		
Generation 2						
Children of William Buell 1614 and Mary Post						
	Mary Buell	1642–1718	Windsor, CT	Windsor, CT	Windsor, CT	
1659	Simon Mills	1637–1683	Windsor, CT	Windsor, CT		
	Samuel Buell	1641–1721	Windsor, CT	Killingworth, CT	Windsor, CT	Woodworker
1662	Deborah Griswold	1646–1717	Windsor, CT	Killingworth, CT		
	Peter Buell	1644–1729	Windsor, CT	Simsbury, CT	Windsor, CT	Woodworker
1670	Martha Coggins	1648–1689	Windsor, CT	Simsbury, CT		Niece of wife of Thomas Barber Sr. (1614–1662)
1698	Mary Gillett	1667–1734	Windsor, CT	Simsbury, CT	Simsbury, CT	Daughter of John Gillett (1644–1689) and Mary Barber (1651–1725)
	Hannah Buell	1647–1704	Windsor, CT	Windsor, CT	Windsor, CT	
1668	Timothy Palmer	1647–1704	Windsor, CT	Windsor, CT		Woodworker
	Hepzibah Buell	1649–1704	Windsor, CT	Deerfield, MA	Windsor, CT	
1673	Thomas Wells	1652–1691	Wethersfield, CT	Deerfield, MA		Woodworker
1698	Daniel Belding	1648–1732	Wethersfield, CT	Hadley, MA		Woodworker
Generation 3						
Grandchildren of William Buell 1614 and Mary Post, Children of Samuel Buell 1641 and Deborah Griswold						
	Samuel Buell	1663–1732	Killingworth, CT	Killingworth, CT	Killingworth, CT	Woodworker
1688	Judith Stevens	1668–1732	Killingworth, CT	Killingworth, CT		
	Mary Buell	1669–?	Killingworth, CT	Windsor, CT	Windsor, CT	
1688	Samuel Bissell	1668–1698	Windsor, CT	Windsor, CT		Son of Samuel Bissell (1635–1698)
1700	Hezekiah Porter	1673–1757	Windsor, CT	Windsor, CT		Son of John Porter (1622–1688)
	John Buell	1672–1746	Killingworth, CT	Windsor, CT	Windsor, CT	Woodworker
1695	Mary Loomis	1672–1769	Windsor, CT	Killingworth, CT		
	Hannah Buell	1674–1761	Killingworth, CT	Windsor, CT	Windsor, CT	
1699	Joseph Porter	1675–1741	Windsor, CT	Windsor, CT		Son of John Porter (1622–1688)
	David Buell	1679–1750	Killingworth, CT	Killingworth, CT	Stonington, CT	Woodworker
1701	Phoebe Fenner	1673–?	Saybrook, CT	Killingworth, CT		
	Josiah Buell	1681–?	Killingworth, CT	Killingworth, CT	Killingworth, CT	
1716	Martha Sesson	1680–?	Killingworth, CT	Killingworth, CT		
	Mehitable Buell	1682–1704	Killingworth, CT	Lebanon, CT	Killingworth, CT	
1701	Nathaniel Porter	1680–1709	Hadley, MA	Lebanon, CT		Son of Samuel Porter (1635–1689)
Children of Peter Buell 1644 and Martha Coggins						
	Abigail Buell	1673–1727	Windsor, CT	Simsbury, CT	Simsbury, CT	
1699	Thomas Barber	1671–1714	Simsbury, CT	Simsbury, CT		Woodworker
	Martha Buell	1675–1760	Windsor, CT	Simsbury, CT	Simsbury, CT	
1695	Nathaniel Holcomb	1673–1766	Springfield, MA	Simsbury, CT		Woodworker
	Mary Buell	1677–1727	Simsbury, CT	Simsbury, CT	Simsbury, CT	
1696	Joshua Holcomb	1672–1727	Simsbury, CT	Simsbury, CT		Son of Joshua Holcomb (1640–1690)
	Ephraim Buell	1683–?	Simsbury, CT	Simsbury, CT	Simsbury, CT	
1702	Mary Barber	1683–1712	Simsbury, CT	Simsbury, CT		Daughter of Thomas Barber Jr. (1642–1712)
1712	Mary Holcomb	1676–1745	Windsor, CT	Simsbury, CT	Windsor, CT	Daughter of Joshua Holcomb (1640–1690)
	Samuel Buell	1686–1741	Simsbury, CT	Simsbury, CT	Simsbury, CT	
1710	Hannah Holcomb	1680–1740	Windsor, CT	Simsbury, CT		Daughter of Joshua Holcomb (1640–1690)

Figure 24 Chart showing the genealogy of the Buell family.

enigmatic figure among Windsor's woodworkers. Like Thomas Barber Sr., he apparently held no public office and had little to do with town affairs. He neither served in the militia nor joined the church, although his wife, Mary Post (1616–1688), became a member in 1643. Buell maintained a small shop and is not known to have taken any apprentices other than his two sons. His estate was appraised at £148, placing him in the bottom 10 percent for woodworkers of his generation. However, since Buell probably gave much of his real estate to his five children before he died, he may have occupied a higher economic position.[26]

After completing their training, Buell's two sons, Samuel and Peter (1644–1729), moved away from Windsor to establish shops in newly settled communities in the colony (see fig. 24). In 1662 Samuel married Deborah Griswold (1646–1717), the daughter of the Kennilworth, Warwick, carpenter Edward Griswold (1607–1697), and the couple moved with Edward to south-central Connecticut to help establish the town of Killingworth. Five subsequent generations of Samuel Buell's family practiced woodworking trades there (fig. 24). In 1667 Samuel's brother received one of the initial allotments of land in Massaco. In the years that followed, Peter served as Simsbury's longest-sitting selectman along with Thomas Barber Jr., and he worked with Barber on a number of public and private construction projects. Peter married Barber's cousin Martha Coggins (1648–1689) in 1670 and Mary Gillett Bissell (1667–1734) in 1698. The latter marriage occurred within months of the death of Mary's husband, Jacob Bissell Jr. (1664–1698).[27]

Apart from the three boxes, little is known about furniture produced by Buell and his sons. Although their present whereabouts are unknown, a chest illustrated in figure 11 of Luke Vincent Lockwood's *Colonial Furniture in America* (1921) and a box initialed "ED" and illustrated in figure 158 in Wallace Nutting's *Furniture Treasury* (1928) may shed further light on the work of these tradesmen (figs. 25, 26). Pioneer collector Henry Wood Erving owned both objects at the time they were published, raising the possibility that he obtained them from the same source. The chest has three panels in the façade and two at each side, and all the observable joints are double-pinned except those of the thin side muntins, which are single-

Figure 25 Chest, Windsor or Killingworth, Connecticut, ca. 1660. Woods and dimensions not recorded. (Luke Vincent Lockwood, *Colonial Furniture in America*, 2 vols. [New York: Castle Books, 1921], 1: 27, fig. 11.)

Figure 26 Box, Windsor or Killingworth, Connecticut, ca. 1660. Woods and dimensions not recorded. (Wallace Nutting, *Furniture Treasury*, 2 vols. [Framingham, Mass.: Old America Co., 1928], 1: fig. 158.)

pinned. As on Buell's boxes, the cleats securing the lid of the chest terminate in a scrolled element, and the carving extends from the façade to the sides. The carving on each of the front panels consists of gouge-accented petal forms quartered by a cruciform motif and linked by strapwork to four satellite pinwheels. With only slight variation, this pattern replicates, on a larger scale, the central ornament on a box attributed to the Buell shop (Yale University Art Gallery).[28]

The carving on the front boards of all the boxes (see figs. 23, 26) is contained within a scribed border that consists of alternating gouge cuts and circular and cruciform punches flanked by lines scored with a marking gauge. The alternating horizontal and vertical notches on the front edges of the ED box also relate to similar patterns of notches on the other boxes and are a distinctive characteristic of furniture from the Buell shop tradition. On all of these objects, the carving extends over to the sides. On the ED box, the side ornament consists of four convex circles arranged in a cruciform pattern. An identical carving scheme also appears on a Buell shop box at the Metropolitan Museum of Art. The ED box also has two details not found on the other examples: fluted arcades enclosing incised foliage and three-dimensionally modeled flower heads surmounting incised hearts and bird forms resembling roosters in the upper left and right corners.[29]

Anonymous Shop

A chair and four joined chests, one of which belonged to Windsor resident Anne Millington (b. 1647), represent the products of an anonymous Windsor shop (figs. 27, 28). All of these objects have framing members wrought from unusually massive stock. The stiles are rectangular in cross section and the rails are nearly two inches thick (fig. 29). In contrast, most contemporary Connecticut joiners used thinner rails and stiles that were pentagonal in cross section—a shape that resulted naturally from the riving process. The bottoms of the four chests consist of a single, thick yellow pine board butted and nailed to all four lower rails, leaving the edges of the board visible. On one of the later chests, all four floor rails are secured to the stiles with two pins. The Millington chest and its two close cognates have only one pin at each of these joints, while all of the other joints are double-pinned. This idiosyncratic and structurally dubious configuration seems to be an early relic of shop practice abandoned by craftsmen working later in the tradition. The carved panels of all the chests are decorated with similar designs con-

Figure 27 Chest, Windsor, Connecticut, before 1662. Woods and dimensions not recorded. (Luke Vincent Lockwood, *Colonial Furniture in America,* 2 vols. [New York: Castle Books, 1921], 1: 27, fig. 10.)

Figure 28 Chest, Windsor, Connecticut, ca. 1660. Oak. H. 24½", W. 48¼", D. 19¾". (Private collection; photo, Gavin Ashworth.) The lid and floor boards are replacements.

Figure 29 Detail showing the cross section of the left front stile of the chest illustrated in fig. 28. (Private collection; photo, Gavin Ashworth.)

sisting of incised, gouged, and relief-carved elements arranged in a diamond pattern and set within a rectangle. The edges of the framing members next to the panels are worked with half-round, scratch-stock molding highlighted with a pattern of opposing gouge strikes with notched lead-ins. Lunettes carved with a V-shaped parting tool and accented with gouge cuts adorn the top rail of each chest. Rather than being first struck with the aid of a compass, the arc that forms each lunette was simply cut freehand. Consequently the lunettes are remarkably crude and irregular in execution.[30]

A woodworker trained in this shop tradition may also have made an idiosyncratic joined chair. Rather than the typical large single panels seen in most joined chairs, the back of this chair is composed of two rows of turned spindles separated by a central horizontal rail (fig. 30). Traveling up the center lines of each of the front faces of this chair's rear stiles is a band of opposing gouge strikes with notched lead-ins identical in size and sequence to the notches worked around the front and side panels of the Millington chest and its three related examples. Since this carving appears on the center of a framing member rather than on its edge, it is worked within a scribed bor-

Figure 30 Great chair, Windsor, Connecticut, ca. 1660. Oak. H. 47½", W. 23⅝", D. 17¾". (Courtesy, Museum of Fine Arts, Boston, gift of Aimee and Rosamond Lamb.) The feet, stretchers, and seat are replacements, and the paint is modern.

der rather than on the convex surface of a molding. Further aligning this chair with the four chests, the front seat rail and the three horizontal rails framing the back are carved with gouge-accented freehand lunettes. Although none of the carving on the chair is an exact match with that on the chests, the techniques used to execute this work were similar.

The Rockwell Shop

A board chest that belonged to Josiah Rockwell (1678–1742) of Windsor is a keystone for attributing a small group of furniture with angled, convex crease moldings to members of his family (fig. 31). Known woodworkers include his great-uncle John Rockwell I (1588–1662), father, Samuel Rockwell Sr. (1631–1711), uncle John Rockwell II (1627–1673), brother Samuel Rockwell Jr. (1667–1725), and cousin John Rockwell III (1663–1746) (fig. 32). The maker of Josiah's chest decorated the front with a one-inch-wide angled convex molding, applied scrolled brackets, and painted designs—a sawtooth motif on the upper edge; abstract, geometric design flanked by stylized flower heads and Maltese crosses in the middle; interconnected undulating lines in the corners; and large lunettes on the lower edge. The lid has a complex, compound molding on the front edge, gouged notches on the sides, and oak cleats with incised molding and bracket-shaped ends. The chest's feet are separated at each side by ornamental cutwork voids. While this type of foot shaping is typical in English and New England work, the cutouts on the Josiah Rockwell chest and other related examples are distinctive enough to support attributions to this shop tradition. The voids on Josiah's chest appear as long, horizontally oriented rectangles surmounted by acute triangles, creating bifurcated feet that resemble the side profiles of the stiles of a joined chest.

Originally from Fitzhead, Somerset, Josiah's grandfather William Rockwell (1591–1640) and his wife, Susannah Capen (1602–1666), joined Reverend John Warham's congregation in the 1620s. In the initial division of

Figure 31 Chest attributed to John Rockwell III, Windsor, Connecticut, ca. 1700. Yellow pine and oak with yellow pine. H. 27", W. 49", D. 18". (Courtesy, Historic Deerfield, Inc., gift of Thomas C. Frary in memory of Margery Collins Frary.)

Figure 32 Chart showing the genealogy of the Rockwell family.

ROCKWELL FAMILY						
Marriage Date	Name	Dates	Birth location	Death location	Marriage location	Occupation/note
Generation 1						
	John Rockwell	1563–1637	Fitzhead, Somerset, Eng.	Fitzhead, Somerset, Eng.	Fitzhead, Somerset, Eng.	
1585	Honor Newton	1564–1637	Fitzhead, Somerset, Eng.	Fitzhead, Somerset, Eng.		
Generation 2						
Children of John Rockwell 1563 and Honor Newton						
	John Rockwell	1588–1662	Fitzhead, Somerset, Eng.	Windsor, CT	Fitzhead, Somerset, Eng.	Woodworker
1619	Wilmot Cade	1587–1662	Fitzhead, Somerset, Eng.	Windsor, CT		
	William Rockwell	1591–1640	Fitzhead, Somerset, Eng.	Windsor, CT	Dorchester, Dorset, Eng.	
1624	Susannah Capen	1602–1666	Dorchester, Dorset, Eng.	Windsor, CT		2nd wife of Matthew Grant (1601–1681)
Generation 3						
Children of John Rockwell 1588 and Wilmot Cade						
	Mary Rockwell	1624–1689	Fitzhead, Somerset, Eng.	Windsor, CT	Windsor, CT	
1646	Robert Watson	1620–1689	Stepney Parish, London, Eng.	Windsor, CT		Grandfather of Nathaniel Watson (1663–1690)
	Thomas Rockwell	1625–1656	Fitzhead, Somerset, Eng.	Windsor, CT		
Children of William Rockwell 1591 and Susannah Capen						
	Joan Rockwell	1625–1665	Dorchester, Dorset, Eng.	Windsor, CT	Windsor, CT	
1642	Jaffrey Baker	1623–1655	Dorchester, Dorset, Eng.	Windsor, CT		Woodworker
	John Rockwell	1627–1673	Dorchester, Dorset, Eng.	Windsor, CT	Windsor, CT	Cooper, joiner
1651	Sarah Ensign	1630–1659	Chilkham, Kent, Eng.	Windsor, CT		
1662	Deliverance Haynes	1640–1710	Dorchester, MA	Windsor, CT	Windsor, CT	
	Samuel Rockwell	1631–1711	Dorchester, MA	Windsor, CT		Woodworker, rope maker, cooper
1658	Mary Norton	1630–?	Dean, Bedford, Eng.	Windsor, CT		
	Ruth Rockwell	1633–1683	Dorchester, MA	Windsor, CT	Windsor, CT	
1652	Christopher Huntington	1624–?	St. Andrew, Norwich, Eng.	Windsor, CT		Woodworker
Generation 4						
Children of John Rockwell 1627 and Deliverance Haynes						
	John Rockwell	1663–1746	Windsor, CT	Windsor, CT	Windsor, CT	Woodworker
1682	Elizabeth Weed	1666–?	Stamford, CT	Windsor, CT		
Children of Samuel Rockwell 1631 and Mary Norton						
	Mary Rockwell	1662–1738	Windsor, CT	Lebanon, CT	Windsor, CT	
1683	Josiah Loomis	1661–1755	Windsor, CT	Lebanon, CT		Woodworker; brother of Nathaniel Loomis (1656–1733)
	Samuel Rockwell	1667–1725	Windsor, CT	East Windsor, CT	East Windsor, CT	Carpenter, cooper, rope maker, sawyer, turner

1694	Elizabeth Gaylord	1669–1721	Windsor, CT	East Windsor, CT		Sister of Nathaniel Gaylord (1656–1720)
	Joseph Rockwell	1668–1742	Windsor, CT	Windsor, CT	Windsor, CT	
1694	Elizabeth Drake	1677–1731	Windsor, CT	Windsor, CT		Daughter of Job Drake (1651–1733)
	Abigail Rockwell	1676–1741	Windsor, CT	East Windsor, CT	East Windsor, CT	
	Josiah Rockwell	1678–1742	Windsor, CT	East Windsor, CT	East Windsor, CT	Owner of the chest illustrated in fig. 31
1713	Rebecca Loomis	1682–?	Windsor, CT	East Windsor, CT		Sister of Nathaniel Loomis (1656–1733)
Generation 5						
Children of Samuel Rockwell 1667 and Elizabeth Gaylord						
	Elizabeth Rockwell	1695–1781	Windsor, CT	East Windsor, CT	East Windsor, CT	
1722	Tahan Grant	1692–1769	Windsor, CT	East Windsor, CT		Great-grandson of Matthew Grant (1601–1681)
	James Rockwell	1704–1776	Windsor, CT	Litchfield, CT		
	Matthew Rockwell	1708–1782	Windsor, CT	Windsor, CT		

Windsor's land, William received a home lot and a sizable grant in the Great Meadow. He served as one of two church deacons and one of three selectmen empowered to lay out land grants and oversee the settlement's civic affairs. His older brother, John Rockwell, John's wife, Wilmot Cade (1587–1662), and their three young children joined the Dorchester group and accompanied William to Windsor. John also received land on which he built a house and where he earned a comfortable living as a farmer and a woodworker. John left an estate valued at £240 when he died in 1662. Tools listed in his inventory—a pair of cooper's compasses, a tapping auger, turning tools, a rabbeting plane, ten plain irons and stocks, a bench, vice, and screws—indicate that he practiced multiple trades including joinery, cooperage, and turning.[31]

William Rockwell died in 1640, survived by his widow and five children. It is likely that John Rockwell I trained William's sons John and Samuel, but there is no evidence that he helped them or his own children forge links with the local community. Like William Buell, the elder John did not hold any town office, did not join the local church, and did not receive any town contracts. Rockwell seems to have avoided other woodworkers and made no effort to encourage kinship ties with their families.[32]

Five years after William Rockwell's death, his wife Susannah married woodworker Matthew Grant (1601–1681), a native of Roxbury, Yorkshire, and one of Reverend John White's original recruits for the Dorchester colony. Unlike her brother-in-law John Rockwell I, Grant had developed close connections to members of the community—woodworkers and non-woodworkers alike. As a surveyor, he assisted in the distribution of town lands, and as a carpenter he collaborated with other woodworkers on public building projects. He kept the church's records as its official scribe, and, starting in 1651, he assumed similar duties as town clerk, a position he held until his death. He also oversaw the marriage of his children to other members of the woodworking community. At age forty-four, with four teenaged and adult children of his own, Grant was at the height of his career. Susannah Rockwell must have understood the advantages her marriage to Grant would afford to her sons and grandsons (fig. 33). Through this union, she forged kinship connections to the woodworking community that her brother-in-law and sons' master had been unable, or unwilling, to establish.[33]

Unlike the sons of Thomas Barber Sr. and William Buell, who left Windsor to start woodworking careers in newly settled communities where their skills were in demand, John Rockwell II and Samuel Rockwell Sr. both remained in Windsor. Not only had their mother's marriage to Matthew Grant integrated them into the woodworking community but also, after his only son and heir, Thomas (1625–1656), died, their uncle John Rockwell I had bequeathed them his woodworking tools and much of his land. Like his uncle, John Rockwell II possessed multiple woodworking skills, including those of cooper and turner. His son and apprentice John III also prospered, leaving an estate valued at £1,160. The itemized inventory of the

Figure 33 Chart showing the genealogy of the Grant family.

GRANT FAMILY

Marriage Date	Name	Dates	Birth location	Death location	Marriage location	Occupation/note
Generation 1						
	Matthew Grant	1601–1681	Roxbury, York, Eng.	Windsor, CT	Woodbridge, Dorset, Eng.	Woodworker, surveyor
1625	Priscilla Gray	1601–1644	Barbridge, Leicester, Eng.	Windsor, CT		
1645	Susannah Capen	1602–1666	Dorchester, Dorset, Eng.	Windsor, CT	Windsor, CT	Wife of William Rockwell (1591–1640)
Generation 2						
Children of Matthew Grant 1601 and Priscilla Gray						
	Samuel Grant	1631–1718	Dorchester, MA	Windsor, CT	Windsor, CT	Woodworker; probable owner of the table illustrated in fig. 41
1658	Mary Porter	1637–?	Windsor, CT	Windsor, CT		Sister of John Porter (1622–1688)
	Tahan Grant	1634–1693	Dorchester, MA	Windsor, CT	Windsor, CT	Blacksmith
1663	Hannah Palmer	1640–?	Windsor, CT	Windsor, CT		Sister of Timothy Palmer (1647–1704)
	John Grant	1642–1684	Windsor, CT	Windsor, CT	Windsor, CT	Woodworker
1660	Mary Hall	1648–1720	Windsor, CT	Windsor, CT		
Generation 3						
Children of Samuel Grant 1631 and Mary Porter						
	Samuel Grant	1659–1710	Windsor, CT	Windsor, CT	Windsor, CT	Woodworker
1683	Anna Filley	1664–1686	Windsor, CT	Windsor, CT		
1688	Grace Minor	1670–1753	Woodbury, CT	Windsor, CT	Windsor, CT	
	John Grant	1664–1695	Windsor, CT	Windsor, CT	Windsor, CT	Woodworker
1696	Elizabeth Skinner	1669–1707	Windsor, CT	Windsor, CT		
	Matthew Grant	1666–1734	Windsor, CT	Windsor, CT		Shoemaker
1690	Hannah Chapman	1671–1752	Windsor, CT	Windsor, CT		
Children of Tahan Grant 1634 and Hannah Palmer						
	Tahan Grant	1665–1693	Windsor, CT	Windsor, CT	Windsor, CT	Blacksmith
1689	Hannah Bissell	1671–1704	Windsor, CT	Windsor, CT		Daughter of Nathaniel Bissell (1640–1713)
Generation 4						
Children of Tahan Grant 1665 and Hannah Bissell						
	Tahan Grant	1692–1769	Windsor, CT	Windsor, CT	Windsor, CT	
1722	Elizabeth Rockwell	1695–1781	Windsor, CT	Windsor, CT		Daughter of Samuel Rockwell (1667–1725)

younger Rockwell's tools indicates that he was one of the best-equipped woodworkers of his generation.[34]

Samuel Rockwell Sr. worked principally as a cooper and rope maker and received a good deal of business from the town. Matthew Grant counted him as one of only fourteen men admitted to the church in 1661. From his home in Windsor's settlement on the east side of the Connecticut River, where he moved his family in 1672, he sporadically served in various town offices such as way warden, fence viewer, bounds goer, and assessor. Unlike his uncle, he took an active role in town government and became a full member of the church in 1658. His woodworking skills enabled him to live comfortably, and Windsor tax records indicate that he occupied a middle rung on the town's economic ladder.[35]

In 1688 Samuel Rockwell Jr. finished an apprenticeship as a cooper and rope maker with his father and established himself on the east side of the Connecticut River. From the beginning of his career, he kept an account book in which he recorded transactions with more than one hundred individuals. This document provides rare insight into the social economy of woodworking within the family kinship network that his grandmother established through her marriage to Matthew Grant. It also documents his acquisition of specialized skills subsequent to his apprenticeship that enabled him to expand and diversify his craft practices and products over the course of his career.[36]

Rockwell provided inhabitants of Windsor's east side settlement with a range of staved vessels in four sizes as well as a range of miscellaneous goods such as paddles, oars, turned trenchers, and, at ten times the cost of a trencher, "knot dishes" carved from burls. For Matthew Grant's grandsons Samuel Jr. (1659–1710) and Matthew (1666–1734), who were a woodworker and shoemaker respectively, Rockwell produced shingles and wooden shoe heels and lasts. In addition to these craft activities, he maintained an orchard, from which he produced cider that he sold in the casks and barrels he made. Rockwell hired Samuel Grant Jr. to build his house on February 27, 1693, just months before his marriage to Elizabeth Gaylord (1669–1721), the daughter of woodworker William Gaylord and sister of woodworker Nathaniel Gaylord. Rockwell may have helped with the work, thereby avoiding the expense of hiring additional workmen and enabling him to learn house carpentry. By 1702 his brother Joseph (1668–1742) apparently felt confident enough in Samuel's house-carpentry skills to hire him to frame, raise, and shingle his dwelling. Although the percentage of time that Rockwell devoted to carpentry is difficult to determine, he worked in that trade as late as 1722, when he built a new, larger house to live in. During his career, Rockwell maintained business relations with several local tradesmen. Windsor woodworker John Moore III turned the spigots that he used to tap his barrels and casks and made furniture, including two turned chairs, for Rockwell's house. In return, Rockwell provided Moore with hooped wheel rims, oak timber that the latter used to make chests and boxes, and skilled labor. In 1697 Rockwell worked for five days in Moore's shop as partial payment for the aforementioned chairs.[37]

Rockwell probably developed furniture-making skills by observing the workmen in Moore's shop as well as other craftsmen from whom he purchased furniture. His kinsman woodworker Nathaniel Loomis Jr. made four window frames and furniture including a chest, a box, and two bedsteads for Rockwell's newly constructed house between 1691 and 1694. Similarly, woodworker Thomas Ellsworth (1665–1750) constructed a table for Rockwell's sister Abigail (1676–1741) on his behalf. In 1702 Rockwell made turned chairs for his father and Matthew Grant, and the following year he produced a table for Abigail. By 1714 Rockwell was making furniture for neighbors and members of his extended family on a more regular basis.[38]

As Rockwell gained new skills, he also invested in equipment and resources. In 1698 he paid Samuel Grant Sr. ten pounds for his share of the sawmill that Grant and his partner Nathaniel Bissell had constructed in the Windsor settlement east of the river. Rockwell's acquisition of additional skills and investments paid off. On his death in 1725, his estate was valued at £823 and contained land worth £655. Appraised at more than twice the £405 mean estate value held by third-generation Windsor and East Windsor residents, Rockwell's personal fortune placed him among the top twenty of Windsor's wealthiest inhabitants and established him as the sixth wealthiest man living in the community east of the Connecticut River during the early eighteenth century. Following the example set by his grandfather, he joined Windsor's Second Church and was installed as deacon in 1716. His wealth and status enabled him to send his son Matthew (1708–1782) to Yale College. After obtaining his divinity degree, Matthew returned to East Windsor, where he was ordained minister of his father's church in 1748, succeeding the church's first minister, Reverend Timothy Edwards.[39]

Two joined chests can be attributed to the Rockwell shop tradition based on the presence of one-inch-wide angled convex moldings that relate to similar molding on the Josiah Rockwell board chest (figs. 31, 34-36). Hartford, Connecticut, collector Irving W. Lyon, onetime owner of the carved

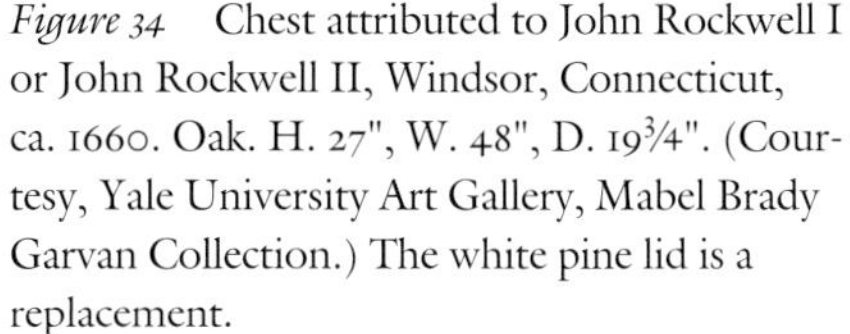

Figure 34 Chest attributed to John Rockwell I or John Rockwell II, Windsor, Connecticut, ca. 1660. Oak. H. 27", W. 48", D. 19¾". (Courtesy, Yale University Art Gallery, Mabel Brady Garvan Collection.) The white pine lid is a replacement.

Figure 35 Chest attributed to John Rockwell I or John Rockwell II, Windsor, Connecticut, ca. 1660. Oak. H. 26¼", W. 48½", D. 20½". (Private collection; photo, Gavin Ashworth.) The lid is a replacement.

Figure 36 Detail of the chest illustrated in fig. 35, showing the angled convex molding and incised chevrons on the muntins of the façade.

example, noted that he "Bought the chest about 1880, in Windsor, Conn., from Havens family." Windsor's vital records record the 1886 marriage of Horatio Nelson Havens (b. 1846) to Florence Amanda Barber (b. 1845), a direct descendant of Windsor woodworkers Thomas Barber Sr. and his son Josiah Barber, either of whom probably obtained it from a craftsman trained in the Rockwell shop tradition. Perhaps this was the couple from whom Lyon acquired the chest. The other joined chest, recently discovered in a barn in the vicinity of Hartford, Connecticut (fig. 35), relates in construction and incised molded decoration to the Havens joined chest and the Josiah Rockwell board chest.[40]

Angled, convex molding is run on the primary framing members of each chest's façade and is enlivened by paired chevrons, incised with straightedge chisel cuts and separated by two small circular punches flanking the molding's apex (fig. 36). Similarly decorated molding (though without the circular punches) appears on the muntins of the chest found in the Hartford area. The floor rail of the Havens family chest has angled, convex molding more elaborately decorated with alternating five-eighths-inch chip cuts and gouge strikes on either side of a row of small circular punches. With its distinctive and well-executed carving, the Havens chest stands as one of the most fully realized examples of West Country joinery produced in the Connecticut River Valley. The top and floor rails of the less-developed Hartford-area example are embellished with two parallel bands of three-quarter-inch-wide channel molding. Single courses of this channel molding also adorn the midline of the front stiles, taking the place of the angled, convex molding that appears in the same place on the Havens chest. The angled, convex molding on the Hartford-area chest runs the length of each façade muntin and is accented with incised paired chevrons. The right façade muntin is oriented with these paired chevrons pointing in a direction opposite to the other two. When the maker of the Hartford-area chest miscalculated the placement of the mortises for the front floor rails, cutting them too low, he

Figure 37 Chest, probably Hartford County, Connecticut, ca. 1720. Tulip poplar. H. 23", W. 46", D. 17½". (Private collection; photo, Nathan Liverant & Son Antiques, Inc.)

cut a second set, leaving the first set visible. These irregularities are likely the result of either haste or carelessness on the part of its maker.

All of the framing members of the façade are constructed with mortise-and-tenon joints secured with delicate double pins. Whereas the façade of the Hartford-area chest is framed with four panels, the façade of the Havens chest has three panels. The use of three wide panels obviated the need for two mortise-and-tenon joints, although their large size and the difficulty in locating and extracting sufficiently large stock probably added to the chest's costliness and desirability. Separating the two panels framing the sides of each chest is a thin, single-pinned muntin. The backs of both examples are framed with four panels. On the Havens chest, the back frame members are idiosyncratically pinned: two pins secure the joints between the center muntin and the top and floor rails, whereas one pin secures the joints between the two outer muntins and the top and floor rails.

The floorboards of both chests are constructed in a similar manner. Seven thin transverse riven oak boards are fitted together at their edges with V-shaped joints and set into a groove in the front floor rail, set into a rabbet in the side floor rails, and butted and nailed to the back rail. The backs of these floorboards were trimmed to fit flush with the back of the case, as indicated by the presence of kerf marks produced by a handsaw on the floor rails of both chests.

A board chest carved with the initials "IW" shows how decorative elements characteristic of the Rockwell tradition and those made popular by other shops in Hartford County and the Connecticut River Valley merged in response to the new and increasingly popular baroque aesthetic in the region (fig. 37). One of four related examples, the IW chest probably postdates the Josiah Rockwell chest (fig. 31) by twenty years (its simple, thumb-molded lid with unadorned pine cleats offers one indication of its later date). Yet its two horizontal courses of angled, convex molding, each of which is flanked by double-groove molding along its upper and lower edges, directly relates to the molding on the Josiah Rockwell chest. Gone from the front of the IW chest are the applied brackets found on the Josiah Rockwell chest. Instead, the IW chest's front board has been lengthened and drawn into deep, stepped cyma curves to form a sweeping skirt. Although the side boards of the IW chest terminate in cutwork feet similar to those on the Josiah Rockwell chest, the forward outer edge of each foot is scrolled to mirror the curves of the skirt. Three other Rockwell shop board chests with analogous configurations of angled, convex, profile-incised moldings, curvilinear skirts, and cutwork feet with projecting front profiles survive. Each of these chests has central incised initials and stylized relief carving. At least twelve other decorated chests with curvilinear skirts produced by other shops are known. Originating in Wethersfield and Hartford and later produced in the Connecticut River Valley of western Massachusetts, these examples antedate the IW chest and were likely made contemporaneously with the Josiah Rockwell chest. The combination of decorative elements such as both scratch-stock and plane-generated moldings, relief carving, gouged decoration along the front edges, shaped skirt and feet created a bold aesthetic statement not before seen in the region.

Documents that survive with the chest identify John White (1745–1787) of Hebron as the original owner, but it more likely belonged first to his father, Jonathan White (1701–1748) of Hatfield, Massachusetts. Jonathan was the brother-in-law of Windsor woodworker Daniel White III (1698–1786), who married Jonathan White's sister Elizabeth (1705–1770) in 1726. Daniel White III probably trained with his father, Daniel Jr. (see fig. 69), who left Hatfield for Windsor in 1696 to marry Sarah Bissell, daughter of woodworker Thomas Bissell. After Sarah Bissell died in 1703, Daniel Jr. married her cousin, Ann Bissell, daughter of woodworker John Bissell. Before he settled in Hebron in 1728, Jonathan White lived briefly with Daniel White III in Windsor, where he likely acquired the chest.

The Moore Shop

Two chests, a table, and approximately fifteen boxes form the largest body of extant furniture produced by a single woodworking shop in seventeenth-century Windsor. These objects serve as a material record of the tools, techniques, and stylistic conventions employed by multiple generations of woodworkers trained in Windsor's preeminent shop tradition—that of immigrant craftsman John Moore I (1614–1677). These objects share similar structural traits and carved decoration featuring squat, tulip-form flower heads attached to meandering vines. Through his woodworking practices, participation in civil and church leadership, and social and kinship ties, Moore emerged as Windsor's principal woodworker and one of the town's most influential craftsmen. Well into the eighteenth century, craftsmen continued to construct furniture that reflected select structural traits and decorative motifs characteristic of Moore's shop tradition even as they integrated new construction methods into their products.[41]

A large carved box initialed "HS" may be the earliest surviving product of the Moore shop (fig. 38). The craftsman responsible for this box laid out

Figure 38 Box attributed to John Moore I, Windsor, Connecticut, ca. 1670. Oak with yellow pine. H. 8½", W. 29", D. 15½". (Courtesy, Metropolitan Museum of Art, gift of Mrs. Russell Sage.)

the shallow relief carving by dividing a rectangle into four equal sections with three vertical scribe lines. Working outward from a roughly wedge-shaped vertical stem aligned on the centerline and alternating from side to side as the pattern progressed, the craftsman used gouge cuts of varying sizes to form the individual leaves and petals of the foliate carving. This method enabled him to replicate any unintentional variation in reverse on the corresponding quadrant, thereby maintaining the pattern's overall symmetry. Small gouge cuts on either side of the centerline form a pattern of linked diamonds carved in relief and extending half the overall height of the relieved field. Whereas this component constitutes the only additional ornament on the raised foliate pattern of this box, other Moore shop products exhibit additional embellishment. In many instances each leaf from a tulip-form flower head was further defined near its tip by an upward oriented gouge strike surmounting a small circular punch. Although not in evidence on this example, the relieved grounds on many Moore shop products feature surfaces textured with a multitoothed punch.[42]

Whereas seventeenth-century New England boxes often have repetitive, gouge-cut notches on the edges of the front boards, top, and lid, those attributed to the Moore shop tradition have angular notches produced by converging cuts made with a straight chisel. In addition to employing similar carving techniques, the craftsmen responsible for these boxes and the aforementioned chests made their cleats the same way. Composed of oak, the cleats taper from back to front in both depth and cross section and terminate in curved notches at either end. The boxes also share an even more distinctive feature: small square notches (approximately three-quarters-inch high, five-eighths-inch wide, and one-quarter-inch deep) occupy one of the upper rear corners of the interior. Although these notches serve no apparent structural purpose, they may have held small rods used to prop open the lids (fig. 39).[43]

Figure 39 Detail showing the notch cut in the upper inside face of the back board of the box illustrated in fig. 38.

John Moore's origins are obscure. He was born in the seafaring community of Southwold, Suffolk, England. That town supported a craft community that supplied shipbuilding and repair services, cooperage, and other essential woodworking skills to a thriving fishing industry. John's father was probably Thomas Moore, who immigrated with him in 1630. Several members of the extended Moore family of Suffolk County joined Puritan colonists who settled in eastern Massachusetts. Thomas, his wife (probably Elizabeth Goode [b. 1588]), and their children, John and Hannah (1616–

1686), appear to have been among the East Anglian families who sailed with Reverend John Warham from Dorset to Massachusetts Bay and who subsequently moved to Windsor. Thomas Moore established a farm on a home lot granted him in the initial division of the Windsor community's lands.[44]

Moore's home lot was located in a section of town populated by an elite group that historian Frank Thistlethwaite has dubbed "Windsor's clerisy." Residents of this neighborhood included one of the church's ruling elders, John Witchfield, members of Dorset's minor gentry, and investors in the Dorchester group's colonizing endeavors: Thomas Newberry and his son Benjamin Newberry (1614–1688), the family of wealthy East Anglian linen draper Joseph Loomis (1615–1687), and Reverend John Warham. Thomas Moore's receipt of a lot located at the social and geographic heart of Windsor indicates that the town's religious leaders and some of its prominent citizens held him in high regard. Although John Moore was only twenty-one when his family settled in Windsor in 1635, he was a fully covenanted member of the church, prepositioned for a role of leadership in the new community's civil, social, and ecclesiastical affairs. In the 1640 division of the town's lands he profited even more than his father did. John received a six-acre home lot (between the lots of his father and John Witchfield) in Windsor's geographic heart, five acres of rich meadowland, forty acres of tillage, a thirty-acre woodlot, and a three-mile-long strip of alluvial floodplain on the east side of the Connecticut River. This single allotment, in excess of eighty-one acres, gave him the resources he needed to succeed as a craftsman and husbandman.[45]

It is difficult to determine when and with whom John Moore trained. He was approximately twelve when his family moved from Southwold to temporary quarters in Dorchester, Dorset; he was sixteen when his family settled in Dorchester, Massachusetts; and he was twenty-one when he arrived in Windsor. Given that John Moore's early life was punctuated by a sequence of moves, it is likely that he apprenticed with his father. Although there is no documentary evidence that Thomas Moore had woodworking skills, he was the only adult male present in John's life long enough to have trained him.[46]

With his apprenticeship completed and his position in Windsor crystallizing, John Moore moved to establish his household and family. In 1637 he married Abigail Pinney (1618–1677). Like her husband, Abigail was one of the Dorchester immigrants on the *Mary and John* and, like John Moore, one of a small number of Windsor residents who had been admitted to full membership in Windsor's First Congregational Church. Together, they would raise five children. With this union, Moore forged kinship ties with other woodworking craftsmen and influential families in the Windsor community, including Abigail's brother Nathaniel (d. 1676), who occasionally collaborated with Moore and his sons on large construction projects. The marriage also enabled Moore to establish alliances with his neighbor Joseph Loomis and William Gaylord, a woodworker from Pittminster, Somerset, and a deacon of Windsor's church. Other ties to the community developed as a result of Moore's friendships, collaborative projects with other craftsmen, and participation in civil affairs. Moore had a long friendship with an immigrant from Yarcomb, Devon, woodworker (and his next-door neighbor) Benjamin Newberry. Newberry collaborated with Moore on such projects as the construction of Windsor's second schoolhouse in 1667 and the framing and raising of a house for the brother-in-law of Moore's sister, Job Drake, in 1669. Newberry also helped Moore obtain several lucrative contracts. As captain of the train band and as major of Hartford County's forces during King Philip's War, Newberry was in charge of the town's military requisitions and supplies. He contracted with Moore to provide the hafts for thirty-six broad pikes made by blacksmith Thomas Burnham for Windsor's troop of dragoons of which Newberry was captain and Moore's son John II was a member. The marriages of Moore's children and other family members linked him and his family to members of other transplanted regional English woodworking traditions (fig. 40). His sister Hannah, for example, married woodworker John Drake Jr. in 1644. John was the son and apprentice of immigrant John Drake Sr., the founder of a shop tradition with roots in Devon, England.[47]

Like many of his peers, John Moore I supplemented his craft production with farming, serving his own interests, the needs of the community, and its growing infrastructure. His accounts with private individuals and with the town of Windsor indicate that he worked as a house carpenter, joiner, wheelwright, shipwright, and turner. Proficiency in these trades—each associated with distinct tools, techniques, and technologies—allowed him to raise house frames; produce chests, boxes, cradles, and other furniture; construct cart wheels and spinning wheels; build boats; make paddles and oars; and turn hafts and handles for a variety of tools and edged weapons. In 1659 he contracted with the town to install sills and underpinnings for a second meetinghouse and to construct a new ferryboat. Through this work he gained a lifelong monopoly on further construction, continuing maintenance, and the manufacture of oars, paddles, and other equipment for Windsor's ferryboat.[48]

In 1642 the freemen of Windsor elected Moore one of five townsmen (selectmen), a position that reflected the community's confidence in his leadership. Although a decade-long gap exists in the surviving town records beginning that year, Moore was reelected in 1652 and served continuously for twenty-one more years. The following year Moore and Newberry were chosen to serve as Windsor's two deputies to the General Court at Hartford, and in 1656 the town's freemen elected Newberry to serve with his neighbor as townsman. Moore's influence on local affairs grew in 1660, when he was chosen moderator of Windsor's town meetings. Both he and Newberry served as moderator and selectman until 1673. In that year Newberry declined to accept his own nomination, and Moore, having just stood reelection, declared that he, too, "desired freedom" from the office. Whereas Newberry served the town and militia, Moore served the town and the church, undergoing ordination as deacon on January 11, 1652. In this capacity, he administered the sacraments from 1669 to 1677 during a period of conflict in the church. Through the years, the community came to rely

Figure 40 Chart showing the genealogy of the Moore family.

MOORE						
Marriage Date	Name	Dates	Birth location	Death location	Marriage location	Occupation/note
	Thomas Moore	1584–1645	Southwold, Suffolk, Eng.	Windsor, CT	Southwold, Suffolk, Eng.	
1614	Elizabeth Goode	1588–?	Southwold, Suffolk, Eng.	Windsor, CT		
Children of Thomas Moore 1584 and Elizabeth Goode						
Generation 1						
	John Moore	1614–1677	Southwold, Suffolk, Eng.	Windsor, CT	Windsor, CT	Carpenter, housewright, millwright, wheelwright
1637	Abigail Pinney	1618–1677	Devonshire, Eng.	Windsor, CT		
	Hannah Moore	1616–1686	Southwold, Suffolk, Eng.	Windsor, CT	Windsor, CT	
1648	John Drake	1622–1689	Wiscombe, Devonshire, Eng.	Windsor, CT		Carpenter, wheelwright
Generation 2						
Children of John Moore 1614 and Abigail Pinney						
	Elizabeth Moore	1638–1728	Windsor, CT	Windsor, CT	Windsor, CT	
1654	Nathaniel Loomis	1626–1688	Braintree, Essex, Eng.	Windsor, CT		
1652	Abigail Moore	1639–1728	Windsor, CT	Windsor, CT	Windsor, CT	
1655	Thomas Bissell	1628–1689	Somerset, Eng.	Windsor, CT		Carpenter, joiner, turner
	Mindwell Moore	1643–1682	Windsor, CT	East Windsor, CT	Windsor, CT	
1662	Nathaniel Bissell	1640–1713	Windsor, CT	East Windsor, CT		Carpenter, millwright, sawyer
	John Moore	1645–1718	Windsor, CT	Windsor, CT	Windsor, CT	Carpenter
1664	Hannah Goffe	1644–1697	Cambridge, MA	Windsor, CT		
1701	Martha Farnsworth	1680–?	Windsor, CT	Windsor, CT	Windsor, CT	
	Andrew Moore	1649–1719	Windsor, CT	Windsor, CT	Windsor, CT	Joiner
1671	Sarah Phelps	1653–1732	Windsor, CT	Windsor, CT		
Generation 3						
Children of John Moore 1645 and Hannah Goffe						
	John Moore	1665–1752	Windsor, CT	East Windsor, CT	Windsor, CT	Carpenter, turner, wheelwright
1693	Abigail Strong	1667–1738	Northampton, MA	East Windsor, CT		
	Thomas Moore	1667–1734	Windsor, CT	Windsor, CT	Windsor, CT	Carpenter, joiner, miller, millwright, sawyer
1695	Deborah Griswold	1674–1756	Windsor, CT	Windsor, CT		
	Samuel Moore	1669–1733	Windsor, CT	Windsor, CT	Windsor, CT	
1702	Damaris Strong	1674–1751	Northampton, MA	Windsor, CT		
	Edward Moore	1674–1729	Windsor, CT	Windsor, CT	Windsor, CT	
1703	Mary Taintor	1685–1760	Windsor, CT	Windsor, CT		
	Joseph Moore	1679–1713	Windsor, CT	Windsor, CT	Windsor, CT	
1701	Sarah Brown	1681–1774	Windsor, CT	Windsor, CT		Owner of the box illustrated in fig. 46
	Josiah Moore	1679–1751	Windsor, CT	Windsor, CT		Cooper
Children of John Moore 1645 and Martha Farnsworth						
	Martha Moore	1705–1768	Windsor, CT	Windsor, CT	Windsor, CT	
1730	Job Drake	1678–1712	Windsor, CT	Windsor, CT		
Children of Andrew Moore 1649 and Sarah Phelps						
	Sarah Moore	1673–?	Windsor, CT	Windsor, CT	Windsor, CT	
1690	Thomas Winchell	1669–?	Windsor, CT	Windsor, CT		
	Andrew Moore	1674–1752	Windsor, CT	Windsor, CT	Windsor, CT	

1698	Mary Sanders	1677–?	Windsor, CT	Windsor, CT		
	Deborah Moore	1677–1734	Windsor, CT	Simsbury, CT	Simsbury, CT	
1697	Samuel Forward	1671–?	Simsbury, CT	Simsbury, CT		
	Thomas Moore	1678–1754	Windsor, CT	Windsor, CT		Carpenter, joiner, wheelwright
	Jonathan Moore	1679–1770	Windsor, CT	Salisbury, CT	Simsbury, CT	
1708	Hannah Large	1692–?	Windsor, CT	Salisbury, CT		
	Abigail Moore	1682–1709	Windsor, CT	Simsbury, CT	Simsbury, CT	
1705	William Stratton	1680–1709	Windsor, CT	Simsbury, CT		
	William Moore	1684–1780	Windsor, CT	East Granby, CT	Simsbury, CT	
1710	Elizabeth Case	1684–1739	Simsbury, CT	Simsbury, CT		
1740	Damaris Phelps	1688–?	Simsbury, CT	East Granby, CT		
	Rachel Moore	1690–1745	Windsor, CT	Windsor, CT	Windsor, CT	
1707	Timothy Phelps	1671–?	Simsbury, CT	Windsor, CT		
	Benjamin Moore	1693–1745	Windsor, CT	Westfield, MA	Windsor, CT	
1716	Eunice Phelps	1688–1732	Windsor, CT	Westfield, MA		
	Amos Moore	1698–1783	Simsbury, CT	Simsbury, CT	Simsbury, CT	
1720	Martha Owen	1698–1780	Windsor, CT	Simsbury, CT		
Generation 4						
Grandchildren of John Moore 1645 and Hannah Goffe, Children of John Moore 1665 and Abigail Strong						
	John Moore	1694–1752	East Windsor, CT	East Windsor, CT	Windsor, CT	Carpenter
1720	Abigail Stoughton	1704–?	East Windsor, CT	East Windsor, CT		
	Ebenezer Moore	1697–1781	East Windsor, CT	East Windsor, CT	East Windsor, CT	
1733	Esther Birge	1697–?	Windsor, CT	East Windsor, CT		
	Elizabeth Moore	1702–1800	East Windsor, CT	East Windsor, CT	East Windsor, CT	
1727	Abraham Foster	1698–1784	East Windsor, CT	East Windsor, CT		
Children of Thomas Moore 1667 and Deborah Griswold						
	Hannah Moore	1697–1793	Windsor, CT	Windsor, CT	Windsor, CT	
1716	Isaac Skinner	1691–1762	Windsor, CT	Windsor, CT		
	Keziah Moore	1708–?	Windsor, CT	Windsor, CT	Windsor, CT	
1729	James Woodruff	1704–?	Windsor, CT	Windsor, CT		
	Deborah Moore	1710–1801	Windsor, CT	Windsor, CT	Hatfield, MA	
1729	Daniel Kellogg	1707–1773	Hatfield, MA	Hadley, MA		
	Thomas Moore	1718–1805	Windsor, CT	Windsor, CT	Windsor, CT	
1743	Hannah Gillett	1719–1805	Windsor, CT	Windsor, CT		
Children of Samuel Moore 1669 and Damaris Strong						
	Esther Moore	1710–1747	Windsor, CT	Windsor, CT	Windsor, CT	
1735	Daniel Hayden	1703–1790	Windsor, CT	Windsor, CT		
	Samuel Moore	1715–1774	Windsor, CT	Windsor, CT	Windsor, CT	
1738	Elizabeth Elmer	1718–1798	Windsor, CT	Windsor, CT		
Children of Joseph Moore 1679 and Sarah Brown						
	Deborah Moore	1705–?	Windsor, CT	Windsor, CT	Windsor, CT	
1727	Phineas Drake	1706–1776	Windsor, CT	Windsor, CT		
	Phoebe Moore	1707–1753	Windsor, CT	Simsbury, CT	Windsor, CT	
1730	John Soper	1708–1749	Durham, CT	Simsbury, CT		
	Joseph Moore	1712–1790	Windsor, CT	Windsor, CT	Windsor, CT	
1735	Elizabeth Allyn	1713–1790	Windsor, CT	Windsor, CT		
Children of Edward Moore 1674 and Mary Taintor						
	Mary Moore	1707–1747	Windsor, CT	Windsor, CT	Windsor, CT	
1730	Caleb Phelps	1708–1781	Windsor, CT	Windsor, CT		
	Hannah Moore	1717–?	Windsor, CT	Windsor, CT	Windsor, CT	
1737	Nathaniel Filley	?	Windsor, CT	Windsor, CT		

on Moore for his woodworking skills and entrusted him with the governance of their spiritual and civil affairs.[49]

John Moore I's position at the head of Windsor's civil leadership brought him greater power and influence in the community. On March 22, 1669, the General Court in Hartford appointed him to oversee the further division of the community's landholdings and the initial division of its outlands, which were to become the satellite communities of Windsor, on the east side, and Simsbury. Newberry frequently assisted him in the performance of these duties. Together, these immigrant artisans controlled Windsor's essential resources. Their duties included dividing the shares of land allotted to Windsor's inhabitants in the fertile planting and grazing grounds of the Great Meadow: "the sum of every mans portion laid out by Deacon moore and capt Newberry." In 1668 Moore and Newberry received rights to sell and distribute all of Windsor's lands on the east side of the Connecticut River. When residents began to plan a settlement in that area four years later, these men apportioned much of the land to Moore's family members and apprentices, particularly his son John II and his second apprentice, Nathaniel Bissell (1640–1713). Favoritism through land distribution was a recurrent pattern in John Moore I's life.[50]

John Moore I probably began to expand his shop during the early 1640s. He may have taken Thomas Bissell (1628–1689), son of Somerset husbandman John Bissell (1591–1677), as an apprentice between 1640 and 1642. Like Moore, Bissell had been one of the original immigrants who moved from Dorchester, Massachusetts, to Windsor. Thomas probably completed his apprenticeship in 1649, three years before cementing his ties to his master by marrying Moore's second daughter, Abigail (1639–1728), in 1652. Thomas Bissell's production of furniture is documented in the 1689 inventory of his estate, which listed "in the shop . . . table frames not finished and chests not finished and turning tools." Like Moore, Bissell had the skills of a turner.[51]

Moore apparently took Bissell's twelve-year-old brother Nathaniel as an apprentice in 1652. Like his brother before him, Nathaniel solidified ties with his master by marrying Moore's third daughter, Mindwell (1643–1682), in 1662. Bissell became Windsor's principal millwright and went on to build the first sawmill on the east side of the Connecticut River in 1668, the first sawmill in Simsbury in 1674, and finally, with woodworker Samuel Grant Jr., the first sawmill in Windsor in 1687.[52]

John Moore I probably required additional help as his patronage grew. He may have begun training his eldest son, John, in 1657, and his second son, Andrew, in 1662. Although neither son's furniture production is documented, a great table that stood until the twentieth century in the Grant family homestead in East Windsor Hill—a mid-eighteenth-century house built on land that carpenter Samuel Grant Sr. (1631–1718) had acquired from his father, town clerk and surveyor Matthew Grant—may represent the work of either John Moore II or his son John III (1665–1752) (fig. 41). A "great table" valued at thirty shillings appears in the 1751 probate inventory of Samuel Grant Sr.'s grandson Samuel III (1691–1751). Neither Samuel Sr. nor the sons that he trained as carpenters appear to have owned a lathe or

Figure 41 Table attributed to John Moore II or John Moore III, Windsor, Connecticut, ca. 1680. Oak. H. 31", W. 70", D. 32¾". (Courtesy, Connecticut Historical Society, gift of Harold G. Holcombe; photo, Gavin Ashworth.) The top, pendants, and most of the brackets are replacements.

Figure 42 Detail of an end rail of the table illustrated in fig. 41, showing a flower head design laid out with gouge strikes. (Photo, Gavin Ashworth.)

made furniture, whereas John Moore III's estate listed augers, gouges, chisels, plain irons, a jointer, a bench, turner's bits, and a screw—all the tools needed to construct and finish the Grant family table. Furthermore, Samuel Rockwell Jr. documented John Moore III's production of turned furniture in his 1697 account book entry crediting Moore for two chairs valued at 5s.6d. An additional clue, concealed on the inner surface of the table frame, strengthens the attribution of this object to a woodworker from the Moore shop tradition. Squat tulip-shaped flower heads similar to those on the box and chest illustrated in figures 38 and 41 are found in a random pattern on the inner surfaces of the end rails (fig. 42).[53]

In addition to supervising his apprentices, John Moore I oversaw the work of at least one journeyman. Anthony Hoskins (1636–1706), son of Beaminster, Dorset, husbandman John Hoskins. Anthony was among several craftsmen hired to refurbish Windsor's meetinghouse. On August 29, 1678, he received credit for providing cedar timber and installing sleepers and floor joists. Not surprisingly, Hoskins's inventory listed a variety of carpenter's tools. John Moore I's final apprentice was Josiah Barber. Unlike the other non-family apprentices taken by Moore, Barber came from a woodworking family. As mentioned previously, Josiah's father, Thomas, was one of the thirteen woodworkers Francis Stiles had hired to build Sir Richard Saltonstall's estate. When Thomas's estate was divided and settled on February 4, 1663, the General Court in Hartford bound Josiah Barber to Moore to ensure the former's care and maintenance until he reached his majority. However, this arrangement was not entirely the work of the General Court. The court document recorded that "Josias Barber according to his desire is placed w^{t}h deacon John moore until he accomplish ye age of Twenty one yeares and Jo: Moore engageth to instruct him in his trade." Even after his apprenticeship ended, Barber remained an active participant in the Moore shop tradition. In 1676 he and John Moore II boarded the walls of Windsor's meetinghouse, and the following year Josiah Barber married Abigail Loomis (1659–1700), John Moore I's granddaughter. As a result of this marriage, Barber and Nathaniel Loomis Jr. (1656–1733), likely the first apprentice of John Moore II, became in-laws.[54]

Figure 43 Chest attributed to Nathaniel Gaylord, Windsor, Connecticut, ca. 1680. Oak with yellow pine. H. 30¾", W. 46", D. 18⅞". (Courtesy, Old Sturbridge Village; photo, Gavin Ashworth.)

If Thomas Bissell trained with John Moore I, it is only logical to assume that the stylistic and structural conventions introduced by Moore were passed on to Bissell and his apprentices. Thomas probably took Nathaniel Gaylord (1656–1720) as his first apprentice between 1668 and 1670. Like his master before him, Gaylord finalized his term by marrying Bissell's daughter Abigail (1658–1723) in 1677. Although no furniture has yet been attributed to Bissell, a joined chest with drawer that Gaylord made for his own use survives (fig. 43). The angled vertical scribe lines at the center of the middle and lower front rails are similar to marks on carved boxes from the Moore shop tradition (fig. 44). The placement of the lines on the Gaylord chest suggest that the maker initially conceived of a symmetrical design, but changed his mind and carved an asymmetric undulating vine on the middle rail and left the bottom rail plain—a pattern repeated on the box illustrated in figure 38.

Figure 44 Detail showing the layout lines and carving on the drawer and façade rails of the chest illustrated in fig. 43. (Photo, Gavin Ashworth.)

A related chest with drawers that appears to predate the Gaylord chest may represent the work of a first- or second-generation craftsman from the Moore shop tradition (fig. 45). Whereas the façade and back of the Gaylord chest have three large panels, the front and rear sections of the chest illustrated in figure 45 have four smaller panels—a feature common on earlier joined chests. The earlier example features drawer sides that are nailed into rabbets in the edges of the drawer front and are cut with grooves to receive drawer guides nailed to the case. In contrast, the drawer sides of the Gaylord chest are attached to the front with half-dovetails, and the drawer is configured to slide on its bottom. Indicative of a shift in joinery practices in the Moore shop tradition, these innovations in drawer construction herald the incorporation of new cabinetmaker's techniques in traditional joined furniture of the region. If the mistakes and hesitancy in the chest's construction indicate inexperience on the part of its maker, then it probably dates from the beginning of Gaylord's career and may be a seminal example of third-generation furniture from the Moore shop tradition.

Like Gaylord, Nathaniel Loomis Jr. may also have been a third-generation woodworker in the Moore shop tradition. Loomis's grandfather Joseph was a linen draper from Braintree, Essex, and his father, Nathaniel Sr. (1626–1688), was a husbandman. In 1654 the elder Nathaniel married John Moore I's eldest daughter, Elizabeth (1638–1728), making the younger Loomis John Moore II's nephew. Nathaniel Loomis Jr.'s training as a woodworker probably began in 1670, when he turned fourteen, the customary age when young men began their apprenticeships. That year, his uncle John Moore II would have been twenty-five, about the age when John Moore I took Thomas Bissell as his first apprentice. Since John Moore II's eldest son, John III, was only five years old in 1670, Loomis may have been the former's first apprentice. During the 1690s Nathaniel Loomis Jr. became the most active furniture craftsman in Windsor's east side settlement. He built and maintained two sawmills and was repeatedly described as a "joyner" in civil documents. His accounts with cooper Samuel Rockwell Jr. illuminate the range of products that Loomis produced. Loomis made case furniture, two bedsteads, and joined window frames for Rockwell's new house between 1691 and 1694. He charged Rockwell eight shillings for a chest in 1691 and 6s.6p. for a box the following year. It is likely that both chest and box bore the emblematic carved motif of the Moore shop tradition—squat tulip-form flower heads linked to an undulating vine (see figs. 38, 43).[55]

The provenances of two boxes with abstract foliate motifs point to John Moore I as the progenitor of that carving style in Windsor (figs. 46, 47). Moore's grandson Joseph Moore (1679–1713) and his wife, Sarah Brown (1681–1774), originally owned the smaller of the two boxes (fig. 46). Joseph's uncle John Moore II or either of his two cousins John Moore III

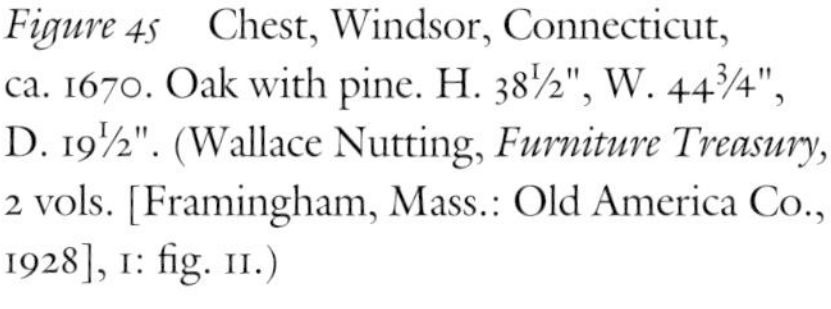

Figure 45 Chest, Windsor, Connecticut, ca. 1670. Oak with pine. H. 38½", W. 44¾", D. 19½". (Wallace Nutting, *Furniture Treasury*, 2 vols. [Framingham, Mass.: Old America Co., 1928], 1: fig. 11.)

Figure 46 Box, Windsor, Connecticut, 1670–1710. Oak. H. 8⅝", W. 30⅜", D. 15⅞". (Courtesy, Windsor Historical Society, loan of Grace Episcopal Church.) The lid and bottom board are replacements.

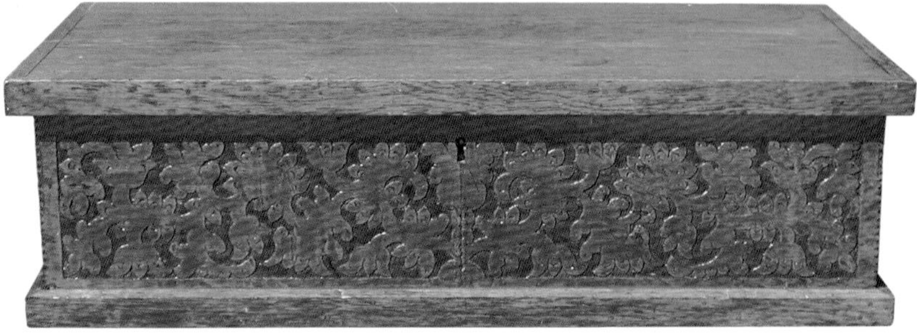

or Thomas Moore may have made the box as a wedding gift for the couple when they married in 1700. A "flowered box," valued at two shillings and listed in Thomas Moore's 1734 probate inventory, suggests that Moore was capable of producing carved forms. By the time he died, Moore had amassed one of the largest arrays of joiner's tools recorded in the possession of a Windsor woodworker of his generation. The larger box with the initials "EB" (fig. 47) belonged to Elizabeth Barber Loomis (1684–1717), daughter of Samuel Barber and his second wife, Ruth Drake (1657–1731). Ruth was daughter of woodworker John Drake Jr. and Hannah Moore (John Moore I's sister). It is likely that Ruth Drake's nephew Josiah Bar-

Figure 47 Box, Windsor, Connecticut, 1670–1710. H. 9", W. 28½", D. 15¼". Oak with pine. (Courtesy, Farmer's Museum, Inc.)

ber made the box as a wedding gift for Elizabeth when she married Daniel Loomis, son of Sergeant Daniel Loomis and Mary Ellsworth. Sergeant Daniel's uncle Nathaniel Loomis married John Moore I's daughter Elizabeth Moore. Their daughter Abigail Loomis (Sgt. Daniel Loomis's cousin) married Josiah Barber, making Elizabeth Barber's husband, Daniel Loomis, Abigail Loomis's first cousin once removed. In this complex web of extended kinship, Elizabeth Barber's husband, Daniel Loomis, and Josiah Barber's wife, Abigail Loomis, were both related to John Moore I (fig. 48).[56]

In both their lives and trades, John Moore I's sons and grandsons assumed the mantle of responsibility worn by their father. They successively oversaw an active multigenerational shop tradition while fulfilling positions of leadership in their communities. John Moore II served as one of Windsor's townsmen from 1676 to 1693. John Moore III served consecutively with his father, from 1686 to 1713, and was town clerk from 1705 to 1715. They trained five apprentices each, solidifying the dominance and vitality of the Moore shop and the continuity of the woodworking tradition introduced by John I into the eighteenth century.

Figure 48 Chart showing family genealogies pertinent to the box illustrated in fig. 47.

ELIZABETH BARBER BOX						
Marriage Date	Name	Dates	Birth location	Death location	Marriage location	Occupation/note
LOOMIS						
Generation 1						
	Joseph Loomis	1588–1659	Braintree, Essex, Eng.	Windsor, CT	Shalford, Essex, Eng.	
1614	Mary White	1590–1652	Shalford, Essex, Eng.	Windsor, CT		
Generation 2						
	John Loomis	1622–1688	Braintree, Essex, Eng.	Windsor, CT	Windsor, CT	
1638	Elizabeth Scott	1623–1696	Rattelsden, Suffolk, Eng.	Windsor, CT		
	Nathaniel Loomis	1625–1689	Braintree, Essex, Eng.	Windsor, CT	Windsor, CT	
1654	Elizabeth Moore	1638–1728	Windsor, CT	Windsor, CT		Daughter of John Moore I (1614–1677)
Generation 3						
Children of John Loomis 1622 and Elizabeth Scott						
	John Loomis	1649–1715	Windsor, CT	Windsor, CT	Windsor, CT	Woodworker
1696	Sarah Boltwood	1649–1726	Wethersfield, CT	Windsor, CT		
	Joseph Loomis	1651–1699	Windsor, CT	Windsor, CT	Hartford, CT	Woodworker
1675	Hannah Marsh	1658–1699	Hartford, CT	Windsor, CT		Sister of John Marsh (1643–1727)
	Thomas Loomis	1653–1688	Windsor, CT	Hatfield, MA	Hatfield, MA	
1680	Sarah White	1662–?	Hatfield, MA	Windsor, CT		Sister of Daniel White (1671–1726)
	John Bissell	1661–?	Windsor, CT	Lebanon, CT	Windsor, CT	Son of John Bissell (1630–1693)
	Daniel Loomis	1656–1740	Windsor, CT	Windsor, CT	Windsor, CT	Woodworker
1680	Mary Ellsworth	1660–1749	Windsor, CT	Windsor, CT		Sister-in-law of Nathaniel Loomis (1656–1733); sister of Josiah Ellsworth (1664–1749)
	Timothy Loomis	1661–1710	Windsor, CT	Windsor, CT	Windsor, CT	Woodworker
1689	Rebecca Porter	1666–1750	Windsor, CT	Windsor, CT		Daughter of John Porter (1622–1688)
	Nathaniel Loomis	1663–1732	Windsor, CT	Bolton, CT	Windsor, CT	Woodworker
1689	Ruth Porter	1671–1753	Windsor, CT	Windsor, CT		Daughter of John Porter (1622–1688)
	Samuel Loomis	1666–1754	Windsor, CT	Colchester, CT	Windsor, CT	Woodworker
1689	Elizabeth White	1667–1736	Hatfield, MA	Windsor, CT		Sister of Daniel White (1671–1726)
1738	Elizabeth Noble	1716–?	Westfield, MA	Colchester, CT		
	Mary Loomis	1672–1769	Windsor, CT	Killingworth, CT	Windsor, CT	
1695	John Buell	1671–1746	Killingworth, CT	Killingworth, CT		Son of Samuel Buell (1641–1721)
Children of Nathaniel Loomis 1625 and Elizabeth Moore						
	Elizabeth Loomis	1655–1717	Windsor, CT	Hartford, CT	Windsor, CT	
1671	William Burnham	1652–1730	Hartford, CT	Hartford, CT		
	Nathaniel Loomis	1656–1733	Windsor, CT	Windsor, CT	Windsor, CT	Woodworker; possible apprentice of John Moore II (1645–1718)
1680	Elizabeth Ellsworth	1657–1743	Windsor, CT	Windsor, CT		Aunt of Elizabeth Barber (1684–1717)
	Abigail Loomis	1659–1700	Windsor, CT	Windsor, CT	Windsor, CT	
1677	Josiah Barber	1653–1733	Windsor, CT	Windsor, CT		Woodworker; son of Thomas Barber (1614–1662); apprentice of John Moore I (1614–1677)

1701	Sarah Porter	1655–1730	Windsor, CT	Windsor, CT	Windsor, CT	Daughter of John Porter (1622–1688)
	Josiah Loomis	1661–1735	Windsor, CT	Lebanon, CT	Windsor, CT	
1683	Mary Rockwell	1662–1738	Windsor, CT	Lebanon, CT		Daughter of Samuel Rockwell (1631–1711)
	Jonathan Loomis	1664–1707	Windsor, CT	Windsor, CT	Windsor, CT	
1688	Sarah Graves	1666–1699	Hartford, CT	Windsor, CT		Daughter of George Graves (1633–1692)
	David Loomis	1667–1751	Windsor, CT	Windsor, CT	Windsor, CT	Woodworker
1692	Lydia Marsh	1667–1751	Hadley, MA	Windsor, CT		Daughter of John Marsh (1643–1727)
	Hezekiah Loomis	1669–1758	Windsor, CT	Windsor, CT	Windsor, CT	
1690	Mary Porter	1672–1752	Windsor, CT	Windsor, CT		Daughter of John Porter (1622–1688)
	Mindwell Loomis	1673–1767	Windsor, CT	Windsor, CT	Windsor, CT	
1696	Jonathan Brown	1670–1747	Windsor, CT	Windsor, CT		Woodworker; son of Peter Brown (1632–1692)
	Mary Loomis	1691–1786	Windsor, CT	Windsor, CT	Windsor, CT	
1708	Joseph Barber	1681–1748	Windsor, CT	Windsor, CT		Son of Samuel Barber (1648–1708)
	Rebecca Loomis	1682–?	Windsor, CT	Windsor, CT	Windsor, CT	
1713	Josiah Rockwell	1678–1748	Windsor, CT	Windsor, CT		Son of Samuel Rockwell (1631–1711)
Generation 4						
Children of Daniel Loomis 1656 and Mary Ellsworth						
	Daniel Loomis	1682–1754	Windsor, CT	Windsor, CT	Windsor, CT	
1709	Elizabeth Barber	1684–1717	Windsor, CT	Windsor, CT		Owner of the box illustrated in fig. 47
	Job Loomis	1686–1765	Windsor, CT	Windsor, CT	Windsor, CT	
1710	Joanna Alvord	1701–1801	Windsor, CT	Windsor, CT		Daughter of John Alvord (1655–1709)
	Isaac Loomis	1694–1752	Windsor, CT	Windsor, CT	Windsor, CT	
1716	Hannah Eggelston	1692–1752	Windsor, CT	Windsor, CT	Windsor, CT	Daughter of James Eggelston (1656–1746)
	Abraham Loomis	1696–1761	Windsor, CT	Torrington, CT	Windsor, CT	
1718	Isabel Eggelston	1697–?	Windsor, CT	Torrington, CT		Daughter of James Eggelston (1656–1746)
BARBER						
Generation 1						
	Thomas Barber	1614–1662	Bedford, Bedfordshire, Eng.	Windsor, CT	Windsor, CT	Woodworker
1640	Jane Coggins	1619–1662	Bedford, Bedfordshire, Eng.	Windsor, CT		
Generation 2						
Children of Thomas Barber 1614 and Jane Coggins						
	John Barber	1642–1712	Windsor, CT	Suffield, CT	Springfield, MA	
1663	Bathsheba Coggins	1644–1688	Windsor, CT	Springfield, MA		Sister-in-law of Peter Buell (1644–1729)
1689	Hannah Gardener	1642–1711	Springfield, MA	Suffield, CT		
	Thomas Barber	1644–1711	Windsor, CT	Simsbury, CT	Windsor, CT	Woodworker
1663	Mary Phelps	1644–1725	Windsor, CT	Simsbury, CT		Daughter of the owner of the chest illustrated in fig. 13
	Samuel Barber	1648–1708	Windsor, CT	Windsor, CT	Windsor, CT	Woodworker
1670	Mary Coggins	1648–1676	Windsor, CT	Windsor, CT		Sister-in-law of Peter Buell (1644–1729)
1676	Ruth Drake	1657–1731	Windsor, CT	Windsor, CT	Windsor, CT	Daughter of John Drake (1622–1689)
	Mary Barber	1651–1725	Windsor, CT	Simsbury, CT	Windsor, CT	
1667	John Gillett	1644–1699	Windsor, CT	Simsbury, CT		Woodworker
	Josiah Barber	1653–1729	Windsor, CT	Windsor, CT	Windsor, CT	Woodworker; apprentice of John Moore I (1614–1677)

1677	Abigail Loomis	1659–1700	Windsor, CT	Windsor, CT		Granddaughter of John Moore I (1614–1677)
1701	Sarah Porter	1655–1730	Windsor, CT	Windsor, CT	Windsor, CT	Daughter of John Porter (1622–1688)
Generation 3						
Children of Josiah Barber 1653 and Abigail Loomis						
	Abigail Barber	1678–?	Windsor, CT	Windsor, CT	Windsor, CT	
1701	Cornelius Brown	1672–1747	Windsor, CT	Windsor, CT		Son of Peter Brown (1632–1692)
	Elizabeth Barber	1684–1717	Windsor, CT	Windsor, CT	Windsor, CT	Owner of the box illustrated in in fig. 47
1709	Daniel Loomis	1682–1754	Windsor, CT	Windsor, CT	Windsor, CT	
	Rebecca Barber	1687–1768	Windsor, CT	Windsor, CT	Windsor, CT	
1707	Nathaniel Drake	1685–1769	Windsor, CT	Windsor, CT		Grandson of John Drake (1622–1689)
	Jonathan Barber	1694–1720	Windsor, CT	Windsor, CT	Windsor, CT	
1720	Rachel Gaylord	1704–1778	Windsor, CT	Windsor, CT		Daughter of Nathaniel Gaylord (1656–1720)

The Drake Shop

When John Moore I's sister Hannah married Wiscomb, Devon, native John Drake Jr., she reinforced and deepened Moore's association with a family of woodworkers whom the Moores had first met as fellow recruits for Reverend John White's planned colony in Massachusetts. John Drake Sr. (ca. 1592–1659) and his wife, Elizabeth Rogers (1581–1661), had started a family in the 1620s, and at the time of their transatlantic crossing in 1630 were raising five children: Elizabeth (1620–1716), Jacob (1621–1689), John Jr. (1622–1688), Job (1623–1689), and Mary (1625–1683). Five years later, as their children were entering their teenage years, the Drakes settled for the last time in Windsor, receiving a seven-acre home lot situated between those of John Moore I and Henry Wolcott (1578–1655), one of the principal investors in the Dorchester settlement and a magistrate in the Connecticut General Court at Hartford.[57]

The Drakes would come to know their neighbors very well. In 1644 Jacob Drake married Mary Bissell (1628–1689), whose two brothers had trained with John Moore I and had married their master's daughters; in 1646 Job Drake married the Wolcotts' daughter Mary (1622–1689); and in 1648 John Drake Jr. married John Moore I's sister. Further cementing John Drake Sr.'s familial links to other Windsor woodworkers, his daughter Elizabeth married Pitminster, Somerset, woodworker William Gaylord, and his daughter Mary married William's brother John (1621–1689). At the time of Elizabeth's marriage, William Gaylord and John Moore were deacons of Windsor's church.[58]

After William Gaylord died, Elizabeth Drake married Norwich, Connecticut, millwright John Elderkin (d. 1687), an itinerant craftsman who received contracts throughout the region. A contract drawn up by Elderkin and dated June 24, 1662, reveals that he hired Elizabeth's brothers John and Jacob to help build a mill in Norwich. In exchange for unspecified labor, Elderkin transferred to his brother-in-laws a gristmill and dam, land, two oxen, and a feather bed and bedstead that he made. Like the Drakes, Elderkin was a native of Wiscomb, England. He may have known John

Drake Sr. before immigrating, and it is possible that both men trained in the same woodworking tradition. If the latter is true, it might explain why Elderkin hired the Drake brothers, despite the geographic distance between Windsor and Norwich, since he could depend on the quality, consistency, and character of their work.[59]

Whereas Windsor's church and civic records document extensive intermarriages among the Drakes and other woodworking families, they reveal little about John Drake Sr.'s activities in town. When woodworker Matthew Grant took over the post of town clerk in the early 1650s, he noted in the minutes for Windsor's 1653 town meeting Drake's election as one of two constables—a position that the latter held until his death in 1659. There is no evidence that Drake received town woodworking contracts, yet he amassed an estate valued at £324.13, a figure that established him as the third wealthiest immigrant-generation woodworker in Windsor.[60]

Drake's sons reaped tangible benefits from their family alliances with the Moores and Wolcotts. In 1662 the General Court in Hartford appointed John Moore and Benjamin Newberry to lay out Windsor's western territory, known as Massaco, "to such inhabitants in Windsor as desire and need it." Six years later, on October 8, 1668, the General Court granted a petition from John Moore I, Benjamin Newberry, and Henry Wolcott's son Simon (1624–1687), requesting permission to establish a plantation at Massaco, separate from Windsor. The General Court granted them authority to divide and dispense the lands for settlement. Wolcott, Moore, and Newberry set aside the largest parcels for themselves and divided the rest among approximately eighteen other men, granting Job Drake (Wolcott's brother-in-law) and John Drake Jr. (Moore's brother-in-law) the next-largest parcels. These apportionments dramatically illustrate the advantages that kinship ties afforded the town's leading woodworkers. Windsor's selectmen appointed Moore and Newberry to survey and lay out Job Drake's lands in 1669, and later that same year contracted with them to frame, raise, and finish a house for Job Drake in Massaco. In 1675 Native Americans fighting in King Philip's War sacked Massaco (which had recently been incorporated as the town of Simsbury) and Job returned to Windsor. John, however, remained in Simsbury until the end of his life.[61]

Like their father, the Drake brothers received few woodworking contracts from the town of Windsor. Their documented public work consisted of a single account with Jacob Drake for making a pair of stocks in 1679. The brothers must have received numerous private commissions, however, since they were among the wealthiest individuals in Windsor and Simsbury. All three men had considerable estates, and their inventories listed a variety of woodworking tools: John Drake Jr. owned wheelwright's tools, carpenter's tools, and several unfinished spinning wheels; Jacob Drake had carpenter's tools; and Job's workshop included a workbench, a joiner's stock, and a wide range of chisels and gouges.[62]

Before his death, it is likely that John Drake Sr. took John Bissell Jr. (1630–1693) as an apprentice. Bissell's older and younger brothers, Thomas and Nathaniel, had trained with John Moore I, and his sister Mary married

Jacob Drake in 1644. At the time of their marriage, John Bissell Jr. was fourteen—the age at which young men typically began serving apprenticeships—and John Drake Sr.'s youngest son, Job, was twenty-one—the age at which young men traditionally completed their terms. Bissell probably established his own shop during the early 1650s. In 1658 he married Isabel Mason (1640–1665), whose father, John, led the Connecticut military forces during the Pequot War. Bissell apparently enjoyed much success. His shop in Windsor remained active through two subsequent generations and included at least eight woodworkers.

Following his father's lead, John Drake Jr. appears to have trained his sons as well as several apprentices. John III (1649–1724) moved to Simsbury with his father in 1668 and may have taken over his shop. In 1718/19 Simsbury appointed John III to make coffins for the townspeople, and at the time of his death he owned woodworking tools, "a small chest not finished," and 360 feet of boards. John III's younger brothers Job (1651–1733) and Joseph (1657–1730) worked as carpenters and joiners in Windsor, stocking guns, framing houses, and supplying sawn lumber. John Jr. may have admitted at least three other woodworkers into the Drake shop tradition. In 1671 his eldest daughter, Hannah (1653–1694), married John Higley Jr. (1649–1715), son of a husbandman from Frimley, Surrey, England, who had newly arrived in Windsor in 1653 and had moved to Massaco as one of the community's original settlers. Higley remained in Simsbury, built the town's second sawmill and gristmill in 1698, and trained his own three sons as woodworkers. Two half brothers, Joseph Loomis III (1649–1715) and James Loomis (1669–1750), married two of John Drake Jr.'s daughters, Lydia (1661–1702) and Mindwell (1671–1736), respectively, raising the possibility that James and Joseph had been John Jr.'s apprentices. Referred to in town records as "Joseph Loomis and James Loomis carpenters," both men lived in Windsor, where they had been granted liberty to build a sawmill in 1692. As John Higley Jr., John Drake III, and Joseph Loomis were all born in 1649, it is possible that John Drake Jr. may have trained them simultaneously.[63]

Two boxes serve as keystones for attributing furniture to the Drake shop (figs. 49, 50). Both objects have large cove base moldings on all four sides and bottom boards that are nailed into rabbets in the front and side boards and set flush with the lower edges of the case. The lid of the box with the initials "EB" (fig. 49) has an integral half-round fillet and applied quarter-round molding on the front and side edges. Although the lid on the other box is fragmentary, the surviving portion indicates that it was constructed like the lid of the EB box. The EB box displays a central shield-shaped reserve flanked by asymmetrical leaves with shaped stems. The edges of the leaves are articulated with gouge cuts and punched designs. These features are comparable to the shield-shaped reserves and carved tulip-and-leaf motifs that adorn boxes and chests attributed to an unidentified Springfield shop (fig. 51). The relieved areas on both boxes are painted. Although the blue and pink paint adorning the ground of the EB box is a twentieth-century enhancement, it may have been added to refresh an earlier paint

Figure 49 Box attributed to Jacob Drake, Windsor, Connecticut, ca. 1680. Oak. H. 9⅝", W. 24¼", D. 20¼". (Private collection; photo, Gavin Ashworth.) The hinges are replaced, and the paint may be a modern re-creation of the original scheme.

Figure 50 Box, Windsor, Connecticut, ca. 1670. Oak. H. 9¼", W. 24½", D. 18⅞". (Courtesy, Antiquarian and Landmarks Society, Inc.; photo, Gavin Ashworth.)

Figure 51 Box, probably Springfield, Massachusetts, ca. 1700. Oak with yellow pine. H. 9¼", W. 25¼", D. 16¼". (Courtesy, Historic Deerfield, Inc.; photo, Gavin Ashworth.)

scheme applied when the box was made. Examples of similarly carved and painted boxes, chests, and fixed woodwork have been found in England's southwestern counties.[64]

The initials "EB" may stand for Elizabeth Bissell (1666–1688), daughter of John Moore I's probable first apprentice, Thomas Bissell, and his wife, Abigail Moore, and niece of woodworkers John, Samuel (1635–1697), and Nathaniel Bissell. It is possible that Job Drake made the box for Elizabeth. A provision in Job's 1689 will that conveyed to his "gr. Child . . . a Chest marked E.D.," probably for his daughter, Esther Drake (1662–1691), indicates that he owned, and possibly made, joined case furniture with carved initials. Job may have made the box as a wedding gift for his niece Elizabeth on her marriage in 1682 to East Windsor woodworker John Stoughton, son of Suffolk County immigrant woodworker Thomas Stoughton Jr. (fig. 52). An even more likely candidate for the maker of the EB box is Jacob Drake, who married Elizabeth Bissell's aunt Mary Bissell (1628–1689). Despite their skills and close relation to Elizabeth, it is doubtful that her father, one of her uncles, or her brother-in-law—all of whom worked in the Moore shop tradition—made the EB box. The same can be said of her husband and father-in-law, who worked in the Stoughton shop tradition. The EB box differs enough from furniture associated with these two shops to suggest that it was made by a member of the Drake family working in a southwest country regional style. The three principal motifs of the carved decoration—three-dimensionally modeled flower heads; asymmetrical leaves accentuated with punches, alternating gouge cuts, shallow gouge strikes; and scrolling line work—are found on furniture from Devon. Similar carving also occurs on furniture attributed to joiner Thomas Dennis (1638–1706). He apparently moved from Ottery St. Mary, near the Drakes' and Elderkins' hometown of Wiscomb, to settle in Portsmouth, New Hampshire, and subsequently relocated to Ipswich, Massachusetts. A chest that Dennis may have made for John and Margaret Staniford in 1676 features three-dimensionally modeled flower heads and asymmetric, gouge-accented leafage that relate to comparable motifs carved on the EB box (see figs. 49, 53).

Figure 52 Chart showing family genealogies pertinent to the box illustrated in fig. 49.

Marriage Date	Name	Dates	Birth location	Death location	Marriage location	Occupation/note
ELIZABETH BISSELL BOX						
BISSELL						
Generation 1						
	John Bissell	1591–1677	Somerset, Eng.	Windsor, CT	Somerset, Eng.	
1627	Elizabeth Thompson	1596–1641	Somerset, Eng.	Windsor, CT		
Generation 2						
Children of John Bissell 1591 and Elizabeth Thompson						
	Mary Bissell	1627–1689	Somerset, Eng.	Windsor, CT	Windsor, CT	
1649	Jacob Drake	1621–1689	Wiscomb, Devon, Eng.	Windsor, CT		Woodworker; possible maker of the box illustrated in fig. 49
	Thomas Bissell	1628–1689	Somerset, Eng.	Windsor, CT	Windsor, CT	Woodworker; probable apprentice of John Moore I (1614–1677)
1652	Abigail Moore	1639–1728	Windsor, CT	Windsor, CT		Daughter of John Moore I (1614–1677)
	John Bissell	1630–1693	Somerset, Eng.	Windsor, CT	Windsor, CT	Woodworker; possible apprentice of John Drake I (1592–1659) or John Drake II (1621–1688)
1658	Isabel Mason	1640–1665	Saybrook, CT	Windsor, CT		
	Samuel Bissell	1635–1697	Somerset, Eng.	Windsor, CT	Windsor, CT	Woodworker; probable apprentice of Thomas Holcomb (1608–1657)
1658	Abigail Holcomb	1639–1688	Windsor, CT	Windsor, CT		Daughter of Thomas Holcomb (1608–1657)
	Nathaniel Bissell	1640–1713	Windsor, CT	Windsor, CT	Windsor, CT	Woodworker; probable apprentice of John Moore I (1614–1677)
1662	Mindwell Moore	1643–1682	Windsor, CT	Windsor, CT		Daughter of John Moore I (1614–1677)
	Joyce Bissell	1641–1690	Windsor, CT	Windsor, CT	Windsor, CT	
1665	Samuel Pinney	1635–1681	Dorchester, MA	Windsor, CT		Brother of Nathaniel Pinney (1641–1676)
Generation 3						
Children of Thomas Bissell 1628 and Abigail Moore						
	Thomas Bissell	1656–1738	Windsor, CT	Windsor, CT	Windsor, CT	
1678	Esther Strong	1661–1726	Northampton, MA	Windsor, CT		
	Abigail Bissell	1658–1723	Windsor, CT	Windsor, CT	Windsor, CT	
1677	Nathaniel Gaylord	1656–1720	Windsor, CT	Windsor, CT		Woodworker; owner of the chest illustrated in fig. 43
1677	Joseph Bissell	1663–1689	Windsor, CT	Windsor, CT	Windsor, CT	Woodworker
1687	Sarah Strong	1666–1739	Northampton, MA	Windsor, CT		Daughter of Thomas Strong (1638–1689)
	Elizabeth Bissell	1666–1688	Windsor, CT	Windsor, CT	Windsor, CT	Owner of the box illustrated in fig. 49
1682	John Stoughton	1657–1712	Windsor, CT	Windsor, CT		Woodworker; son of Thomas Stoughton (1624–1689)
	Benjamin Bissell	1669–1698	Windsor, CT	Windsor, CT		Woodworker
	Sarah Bissell	1672–1703	Windsor, CT	Hatfield, MA	Hatfield, MA	
1696	Daniel White	1671–1726	Hatfield, MA	Windsor, CT		Woodworker; probable maker of the chest illustrated in fig. 69

DRAKE						
Generation 1						
	John Drake	1592–1659	Wiscomb, Devon, Eng.	Windsor, CT	Wiscomb, Devon, Eng.	Woodworker
1620	Elizabeth Rogers	1581–1661	Wiscomb, Devon, Eng.	Windsor, CT		
Generation 2						
Children of John Drake 1592 and Elizabeth Rogers						
	Elizabeth Drake	1620–1716	Wiscomb, Devon, Eng.	Windsor, CT	Windsor, CT	
1653	William Gaylord	1616–1656	Pitminster, Somerset, Eng.	Windsor, CT		Woodworker; father of Nathaniel Gaylord (1656–1720)
1660	John Elderkin	1616–1687	England	Norwich, CT		Woodworker
	Jacob Drake	1621–1689	Wiscomb, Devon, Eng.	Windsor, CT		Woodworker; possible maker of the box illustrated in fig. 49
1644	Mary Bissell	1628–1689	Somerset, Eng.	Windsor, CT		Aunt of the owner of the box illustrated in fig. 49
	John Drake	1622–1688	Wiscomb, Devon, Eng.	Simsbury, CT	Windsor, CT	Woodworker
1648	Hannah Moore	1633–1686	Southwold, Suffolk, Eng.	Simsbury, CT		Daughter of John Moore I (1614–1677)
	Job Drake	1623–1689	Wiscomb, Devon, Eng.	Windsor, CT	Windsor, CT	Woodworker
1646	Mary Wollcott	1622–1689	Tolland, Somerset, Eng.	Windsor, CT		
	Mary Drake	1625–1683	Wiscomb, Devon, Eng.	Windsor, CT	Windsor, CT	
1655	John Gaylord	1621–1689	Pitminster, Somerset, Eng.	Windsor, CT		

Although Dennis employed a similar lexicon of carved ornamental form, his method for constructing boxes differed from that of the Drakes.[65]

The related box, collected in the twentieth century from the Suffield, Connecticut, house of Thomas and Elizabeth Dewey Noble, reinforces the Drake family attribution (see fig. 50). A member of the latter family, probably Job Drake, may have made it for Elizabeth Dewey (1677–1757), daughter of carpenter Thomas Dewey Jr. (1640–1690) of Windsor and Westfield. Just as the Drakes and Bissells were interconnected by marriage, the Deweys, Drakes, and Bissells were intertwined in a geographically larger network of towns encompassing Windsor, Suffield, Springfield, and Westfield (figs. 52, 55). Elizabeth Dewey's cousin Margaret Dewey (1673–1712), daughter of Jedediah Dewey, married Elizabeth Bissell's brother Daniel Bissell (1663–1738), and Job Drake's daughter Abigail Drake (b. 1648) married Thomas Dewey's brother Israel Dewey (1645–1678). It is possible that members of the Dewey family trained with members of the Drake family.

The ornament on these two boxes appears to prefigure that associated with Hampshire County, Massachusetts, suggesting that the woodworking tradition introduced by John Drake Sr. continued as part of the confluence of English-derived carving styles manifest in later joined case furniture from the Connecticut River Valley. A chest of drawers probably made for Thank-

Figure 53 Chest attributed to Thomas Dennis, Ipswich, Massachusetts, 1676. Red and white oak. H. 31$^{11}/_{16}$", W. 49$^{5}/_{8}$", D. 22$^{5}/_{8}$". (Courtesy, Winterthur Museum.)

Figure 54 Chest, probably Suffield, Connecticut, ca. 1730. Woods and dimensions not recorded. (Clair Franklin Luther, *The Hadley Chest* [Hartford, Conn.: Case, Lockwood & Brainard Co., 1935], p. 103, no. 62.

ful Noble (b. 1714) around the time of her marriage to John Leonard in 1735 illustrates the recycling of motifs from the Drake shop tradition in later furniture produced in towns north of Windsor and raises questions about the links between carving styles and family identity (fig. 54). Thankful Noble was linked to the Drake family through marriage. Her father, Thomas Noble Jr. (1666–1750), had married Elizabeth Dewey, daughter of Thomas Dewey Jr. and Constance Hawes (1642–1702) (fig. 55).

The construction of the Noble chest is similar to that of so-called Hadley chests (see fig. 5), which feature three front panels embellished with the distinctive gouge-accented tulip-and-leaf motif; however, the panels on the Noble chest have a central, three-dimensionally modeled rosette below a gouged flower shape—motifs that depart from the flat relief carving elsewhere on the chest and that closely resemble the flower heads on the Drake shop carved boxes. Might these specific motifs, imported into an altogether different carving scheme, have served to identify the Drake family shop tradition and, by extension, the Drake family line, in Thankful Noble's heritage? Perhaps this central panel offered a reminder of the Noble and Dewey family's possible craft connections to the Drakes as apprentices as well as their connection to them as in-laws.

The Cook Shop

A native of Bridport, Devon, Aaron Cook (1614–1690) immigrated to New England with his mother, Elizabeth Charde Cook Ford (1586–1643), stepfather Thomas Ford (d. 1676), and cousin Nathaniel Cook (1625–1688). Ford, a merchant of Simonsbury, Dorset, had been a member of Reverend John White's Holy Trinity Church, Dorchester, and had joined the group of settlers White had organized to establish a colony in Massachusetts. A member of his stepfather's household from the age of two, Aaron Cook continued to rely on his connection with the Ford family to succeed in life. In Windsor, Cook received a nine-acre home lot and one of only ten small plots within the palisade walls of the town. A trained woodworker, he built himself a house by 1637, where he lived with Nathaniel, who was eleven years his junior and his probable ward. Aaron quickly expanded his household when, in 1637, he married Mary Ford (1612–1645), possibly Thomas Ford's daughter and therefore his stepsister. Together, he and Mary started a family, which had grown

Figure 55 Chart showing family genealogies pertinent to the chest illustrated in fig. 54 and the box illustrated in fig. 50

ELIZABETH DEWEY BOX / THANKFUL NOBLE CHEST						
Marriage Date	Name	Dates	Birth location	Death location	Marriage location	Occupation/note
DRAKE						
Generation 1						
	John Drake	1592–1659	Wiscomb, Devon, Eng.	Windsor, CT	Wiscomb, Devon, Eng.	Woodworker
1620	Elizabeth Rogers	1581–1661	Wiscomb, Devon, Eng.	Windsor, CT		
Generation 2						
Children of John Drake 1592 and Elizabeth Rogers						
	Elizabeth Drake	1620–1716	Wiscomb, Devon, Eng.	Windsor, CT	Windsor, CT	
1653	William Gaylord	1616–1656	Pitminster, Somerset, Eng.	Windsor, CT		Woodworker
1660	John Elderkin	1616–1687	England	Norwich, CT		Woodworker
	Jacob Drake	1621–1689	Wiscomb, Devon, Eng.	Windsor, CT		Woodworker
1644	Mary Bissell	1628–1689	Somerset, Eng.	Windsor, CT		
	John Drake	1622–1688	Wiscomb, Devon, Eng.	Simsbury, CT	Windsor, CT	Woodworker
1648	Hannah Moore	1633–1686	Southwold, Suffolk, Eng.	Simsbury, CT		
	Job Drake	1623–1689	Wiscomb, Devon, Eng.	East Windsor, CT	Windsor, CT	Woodworker
1646	Mary Wollcott	1622–1689	Tolland, Somerset, Eng.	East Windsor, CT		
Generation 3						
Children of John Drake 1622 and Hannah Moore						
	John Drake	1649–1724	Windsor, CT	Windsor, CT	Windsor, CT	Woodworker
	Job Drake	1651–1733	Windsor, CT	Windsor, CT	Windsor, CT	Woodworker
	Hannah Drake	1653–1694	Windsor, CT	Simsbury, CT	Windsor, CT	
1671	John Higley	1649–1715	Frimley, Surrey, Eng.	Simsbury, CT		Woodworker
	Joseph Drake	1657–1730	Windsor, CT	Windsor, CT	Windsor, CT	Woodworker
1696	Ann Morton	1678–1717	Windsor, CT	Windsor, CT		
	Ruth Drake	1657–1731	Windsor, CT	Windsor, CT	Windsor, CT	
1676	Samuel Barber	1648–1708	Windsor, CT	Windsor, CT		Woodworker; son of Thomas Barber (1614–1662)
	Lydia Drake	1661–1702	Windsor, CT	Windsor, CT	Windsor, CT	
1681	Joseph Loomis	1649–1715	Windsor, CT	Windsor, CT		Woodworker
	Mindwell Drake	1671–1736	Windsor, CT	Windsor, CT	Windsor, CT	
1696	James Loomis	1669–1750	Windsor, CT	Windsor, CT		Woodworker
Children of Job Drake 1623 and Mary Wollcott						
	Abigail Drake	1648–1696	Windsor, CT	Northampton, MA	Windsor, CT	
1668	Israel Dewey	1645–1678	Windsor, CT	Northampton, MA		Woodworker; uncle of the owner of box illustrated in fig. 50
	Job Drake	1652–1711	Windsor, CT	Windsor, CT	Windsor, CT	Woodworker
1677	Elizabeth Clark	1651–1729	Windsor, CT	Windsor, CT		Daughter of Daniel Clark (1622–1710)

DEWEY						
Generation 1						
	Thomas Dewey	1603–1648	Sandwich, Kent, Eng.	Windsor, CT	Windsor, CT	
1638	Frances Randall	1611–1690	Allington, Dorset, Eng.	Windsor, CT		
Generation 2						
Children of Thomas Dewey 1603 and Francis Randall						
	Thomas Dewey	1640–1690	Windsor, CT	Westfield, MA	Dorchester, MA	Woodworker
1663	Constance Hawes	1642–1702	Dorchester, MA	Westfield, MA		
	Josiah Dewey	1641–1732	Windsor, CT	Lebanon, CT		Woodworker
	Israel Dewey	1645–1678	Windsor, CT	Lebanon, CT	Windsor, CT	Woodworker
1668	Abigail Drake	1648–1696	Windsor, CT	Windsor, CT		
	Jedediah Dewey	1647–1718	Windsor, CT	Westfield, MA	Farmington, CT	Woodworker
1672	Sarah Orton	1652–1711	Farmington, CT	Westfield, MA		
Generation 3						
Children of Thomas Dewey 1640 and Constance Hawes						
	Hannah Dewey	1669–1745	Westfield, MA	Westfield, MA	Westfield, MA	
1690	Matthew Noble	1668–1744	Springfield, MA	Westfield, MA		
	Elizabeth Dewey	1677–1757	Westfield, MA	Westfield, MA	Westfield, MA	Owner of the box illustrated in fig. 50
1695	Thomas Noble	1666–1750	Springfield, MA	Westfield, MA		
Children of Jedediah Dewey 1647 and Sarah Orton						
	Margaret Dewey	1673–1738	Windsor, CT	Windsor, CT	Windsor, CT	
1692	Daniel Bissell	1663–1738	Windsor, CT	Windsor, CT		Woodworker; son of John Bissell (1630–1693)
	Abigail Dewey	1694–1758	Westfield, MA	Westfield, MA	Westfield, MA	
?	Joseph Noble	1691–1753	Westfield, MA	Westfield, MA		
NOBLE						
Generation 1						
	Thomas Noble	1632–1704	Roxbury, MA	Westfield, MA	Springfield, MA	
1660	Hannah Warriner	1643–1721	Springfield, MA	Westfield, MA	Northampton, MA	Wife of Medad Pomroy (1638–1716)
Generation 2						
Children of Thomas Noble 1632 and Hannah Warriner						
1695	Thomas Noble	1666–1750	Springfield, MA	Westfield, MA	Westfield, MA	
	Elizabeth Dewey	1677–1757	Westfield, MA	Westfield, MA		Owner of the box illustrated in fig. 50
	James Noble	1667–1712	Westfield, MA	Westfield, MA	Westfield, MA	
1704	Katherine Higley	1679–1760	Simsbury, CT	Westfield, MA		Daughter of John Higley (1649–1715)
	Matthew Noble	1668–1744	Springfield, MA	Westfield, MA	Westfield, MA	
1690	Hannah Dewey	1669–1745	Westfield, MA	Westfield, MA		
Generation 3						
Children of Thomas Noble 1666						
	Thankful Noble	1714–?	Westfield, MA	Westfield, MA		Owner of the chest illustrated in fig. 54
Children of Matthew Noble 1668						
	Joseph Noble	1691–1753	Westfield, MA	Westfield, MA	Westfield, MA	
?	Abigail Dewey	1694–1758	Westfield, MA	Westfield, MA		
HIGLEY						
Generation 1						
	John Higley	1649–1715	Frimley, Surrey, Eng.	Simsbury, CT	Windsor, CT	Woodworker
1671	Hannah Drake	1653–1694	Windsor, CT	Simsbury, CT		
Generation 2						
Children of John Higley 1649 and Hannah Drake						
	John Higley	1673–1714	Simsbury, CT	Simsbury, CT		Woodworker
	Katherine Higley	1679–1760	Simsbury, CT	Westfield, MA	Westfield, MA	Aunt of the owner of the chest illustrated in fig. 54
1704	James Noble	1667–1712	Westfield, MA	Westfield, MA		
	Brewster Higley	1685–1760	Simsbury, CT	Simsbury, CT		Woodworker
	Samuel Higley	1687–1737	Simsbury, CT	Simsbury, CT		Woodworker

to include four children by the time she died in 1645. Cook soon married Johanna Denslow (1627–1676), with whom he had two more children.[66]

Aaron Cook's life in Windsor, until his departure for Massaco (Simsbury) on the town's western border in 1662, was marked by continual conflict with neighbors. On more than twenty occasions between 1642 and 1661, magistrates of the Particular Court at Hartford found him guilty of such offenses as unlawful impounding of hogs, threat of physical violence, breach of peace, and defamation in open court. No written record of his woodworking practices exists, and it is likely that his contentious behavior prevented him from receiving town contracts and serving in local government. Unlike the majority of his woodworking peers, he neither held civil offices nor joined the church. Windsor's townspeople apparently saw his volatile temperament as suited to only one arena, the militia. They may have felt that Cook's pugnacious spirit—when directed toward perceived enemies such as the Dutch and Native Americans—made him an effective leader of the town's train band. He rose through the militia's ranks to become lieutenant by 1649, commander in 1653, and, by overwhelming vote, captain in 1655.[67]

In 1653 Cook and his stepfather received grants for fifty acres each in Massaco. As was the case in Windsor proper, Cook soon became embroiled in conflicts. In 1660 the Connecticut General Court at Hartford demanded that he cease improvements to his home and farmlands and shortly thereafter rescinded his grant. At the time his grant was rescinded, the multiple judgments rendered against him by the Connecticut General Court totaled £120, an enormous sum for the time. Cook moved his family to Northampton, Massachusetts, in 1660, once again in the company of his stepfather, apparently filling the role of master woodworker (the town had previously attempted to attract Thomas Barber Sr., but he died before he could move). Cook's skills found ready demand. In 1662 he signed Northampton's church covenant, and the following year the town awarded him the exclusive contract to build the meetinghouse. Recognizing his military experience, the town also selected him captain of the militia. Like other woodworkers in the Connecticut River Valley, Cook augmented his trade with farming, real estate dealings, land speculation, tavern keeping, and pursuit of public office. In 1666 he received a fifty-acre grant as a proprietor of Warranoco (later incorporated as the town of Westfield, Massachusetts) and moved to the new settlement in 1668. From 1668 to 1672 he operated Warranoco's tavern. After 1672 he apparently lived briefly in Hadley, then Hatfield. He moved back to Northampton before 1676, the year his second wife, Johanna Denslow died. In 1676 he married Elizabeth Nash (1632–1687), and four years later he received an appointment as associate justice of the Court of General Sessions of the Peace, a position he held until his death. Elizabeth died in 1687, and Cook immediately married his fourth wife, Rebecca Foote (1635–1701). The following year he received a commission from Massachusetts Bay Colony Governor Andrus appointing him major of Hampshire County forces.[68]

Over the years of his adult life in Windsor, Simsbury, and Hampshire County, Massachusetts (the western frontier of the Bay Colony), Cook moved his household and shop at least five times. His mobility was more typical of the region's adult male population at large than it was for his woodworking peers, a remarkably sedentary group. Whereas between 1635 and 1715 approximately 38 percent of the Connecticut River Valley's adult males lived in more than one location during their lives, only 17 percent of woodworkers moved between the region's towns and settlements. For Cook, such movement paid off. At the time of his death, his estate was valued at £526 and included a house and home lot in Northampton, together with thirty-six acres of meadow, a homestead in Windsor, a homestead in Westfield, three hundred acres in Hartford and "a silver bowl . . . presented to the Church of Christ in Northampton, if continuing in the congregational way." None of Cook's sons apprenticed in their father's shop or learned woodworking trades. His only known apprentice was his cousin Nathaniel, who remained in Windsor his entire life. Nathaniel apparently succeeded in his trade, carrying out town contracts to supply timber for the meetinghouse and performing unspecified carpentry work.[69]

Although primary documents shed little light on the longevity of the woodworking tradition associated with Aaron Cook, furniture attributed to his shop constitutes a considerable legacy. The distinctive structural and decorative traits that identify this work appear in late seventeenth- and early eighteenth-century furniture made by other craftsmen active in the upper Connecticut River Valley. How the conventions of Cook's shop propagated throughout the region is not known. He may have trained apprentices in each of the towns he lived in after leaving Windsor, or he may have influenced the region's craftsmen who worked with him on important building projects such as the Northampton meetinghouse.

Large in scale, constructed with riven oak floorboards, and decorated with carved ornament and applied molding, a chest with a history of ownership in Hatfield, Massachusetts (north of Northampton), appears to be the earliest surviving piece of furniture from the Cook shop (fig. 56). This object may represent an immigrant-generation or native first-generation interpretation of the tradition's range of structural and stylistic traits. It exhibits many of the hallmarks of a large group of case furniture that also includes low chests, chests with one or two drawers in both three- and four-panel configurations, and a cradle. Whereas these objects vary widely in their layout and decorative schemes, they relate in the uniformity of their construction, inclusion of select elements of ornament, and stock preparation.

Like other chests in the Cook shop group, this example is framed with pentagonal stiles. Two horizontally oriented, heavily chamfered yellow pine panels form the back of its upper case, and single yellow pine panels that extend below the level of the floor rail form its sides. An applied oak ogee profile molding covers the face of the front floor rail and extends across the yellow pine panels of the sides. As the lower side rails are framed to the stiles beneath the level of the façade floor rail, the applied side moldings are attached to boards fitted between the molding and the recessed panel, simulating side floor rails. The floor is composed of seven tapered, riven oak boards—three on each side of a central, shallow, V-shaped board. Each is cut

Figure 56 Chest attributed to Aaron Cook, Windsor, Connecticut, or Northampton, Massachusetts, ca. 1660. Oak with yellow pine. H. 28", W. 56½", D. 20". (Courtesy, Historic Deerfield, Inc.; photo, Gavin Ashworth.) The drawer is missing.

with a channel along its broad edge to receive the narrow edge of the adjacent board. These floorboards are set into grooves in the front rail, butted and nailed to the rear rail, and cut to conform to the stiles and chamfered side panels. Wide, shallow oak cleats are attached to the edges of the yellow pine lid. All of the interior and exterior surfaces of the framing members, panels, drawer components, and floorboards are well planed and smoothed.[70]

Furniture from the Cook shop tradition features one or more molding courses of three different types: a single or double course of half-inch-wide triple-groove molding usually run on the fronts of their drawers, on their front and side rails, and on the fronts and sides of their stiles; a one-and-one-quarter-inch-wide ogee molding flanked by quarter-inch-wide grooves, either alone or in multiple courses, run on their horizontal framing members, drawer fronts, and in a few instances on the front faces of the stiles; and fine step-fillet-groove molding usually run on the edges of their façade and side muntins and occasionally paired on the center section of their façade muntins. The ogee molding identified with products of the Cook shop tradition appears on the chest illustrated in figure 56 as a single horizontal course on the lower side rails and in a single vertical course on yellow pine plaques applied to the fronts of the stiles beneath the floor rail to bring the faces of the feet to a level on plane with the now-missing drawer front. Triple-groove moldings run on the sides of the stiles further identify this chest as a product of the Cook shop tradition.

Case furniture in the Cook shop tradition may also feature applied moldings, relief carving, paint decoration, and inlay. On the chest illustrated in figure 56, the carving consists of staggered rows of flutes on the upper front rail, stacked flutes on the muntins, and carved reserves on the front stiles. The large diamond-shaped reserves may have once held inlay.

Jonathan Morton (1684–1776) and Sarah Smith (1688–1760) of Hatfield first owned this chest. Born in Hadley to Chileab Smith (1636–1731) and Hannah Hitchcock (1645–1733), Sarah was the niece of Rebecca Foote Cook, the fourth wife of this shop tradition's probable progenitor, Aaron

Cook. The daughter of Nathaniel Foote (1593–1644), a founding settler of Wethersfield, Rebecca first married Sarah Smith's uncle, woodworker Phillip Smith (1632–1685), in Wethersfield in 1658. In 1688, three years after Phillip Smith died, Rebecca Foote married Aaron Cook. Although Sarah Smith's grandfathers and uncle were capable of producing joined furniture, the East Anglian traditions in which they probably had been trained suggest that their work would have differed from furniture that Cook constructed in a southwest country style.

The identity of the couple who owned the chest illustrated in figure 57 is unknown, but their joint initials were "MND." This object's attribution to Aaron Cook is based on the ogee moldings on the front and side rails of the façade. Unlike other case furniture associated with the Cook shop, this chest

Figure 57 Chest, Windsor, Connecticut, or Hampshire County, Massachusetts, ca. 1680. Oak with yellow pine. H. 30¼", W. 47", D. 18". (Courtesy, Pocumtuck Valley Memorial Association, gift of James A. Reed; photo, Gavin Ashworth.) The drawer is missing.

is enlivened by inlay that is stained a dark color to contrast with the natural oak of the chest. Inlaid into the upper and lower ends of each façade muntin are two diamonds, separated by a narrow rectangle flanked by two small circles. In their size and placement, these inlays echo the relief-carved reserves on the front stiles of the Morton chest (fig. 56). Four round inlays beneath the course of ogee molding on the floor rail alternate with each letter of the initials "MND." The letters are composed of multiple small round inlays that suggest nail heads. An inward-facing triangular plaque surrounded with a step-half-round mitered molding is applied to each edge of the central panel. Four smaller triangles edged with mitered moldings are set at the corners of the panel, creating a central, recessed X shape. Each of the two side panels features rectangular plaques edged with mitered molding set diagonally in the panels' corners and intersecting at the center. Primarily the domain of sophisticated urban shops, geometric plaques, mitered moldings, and contrasting inlay do not appear on any other Cook shop products. Their presence on this example was coeval with the appearance of turned half-spindles, contrasting wood inlay, applied geometric plaques, and mitered moldings in sophisticated tulip-and-leaf carved furniture made in Springfield, Massachusetts, woodworking shops at the end of the seventeenth century.[71]

David Hoyt (1651–1704), the original owner of two closely related joined chests with prominent ogee molding, moved from Windsor to Hadley in 1678 and finally settled in Deerfield in 1682 (figs. 58, 59). In 1690, following the death of his second wife, Mary Wilson (1651–1689), Hoyt married Abigail Cook (1659–1708), who probably brought the chests into the marriage. Recently widowed herself, Abigail and her first husband, woodworker Joshua Pomeroy (1646–1689), had come to Deerfield from Windsor in 1676. Abigail's father, Windsor woodworker Nathaniel Cook Sr., probably trained her first husband. Her father, in turn, probably learned his trade under the tutelage of his elder brother, Aaron Cook. Both chests could be

Figure 58 Chest, Windsor, Connecticut, or Hampshire County, Massachusetts, ca. 1680. Oak with yellow pine. H. 30¼", W. 47", D. 18". (Courtesy, Historic Deerfield, Inc.; photo, Gavin Ashworth.) The lid and lock are replacements.

Figure 59 Chest, Windsor, Connecticut, or Hampshire County, Massachusetts, ca. 1680. Oak with yellow pine. H. 26¼", W. 51", D. 20½". (Courtesy, Pocumtuck Valley Memorial Association, gift of Mary Wright Davis; photo, Gavin Ashworth.) The drawer is missing.

Figure 60 Chart pertinent to the chests illustrated in figs. 56, 58, and 59.

Marriage Date	Name	Dates	Birth location	Death location	Marriage location	Occupation/note
COOK-SMITH-HOYT						
COOK						
Generation 1						
	Aaron Cook	1585–?	Bridport, Devon, Eng.	Windsor, CT	Bridport, Devon, Eng.	
1610	Elizabeth Chard	1586–1643	Bridport, Devon, Eng.	Windsor, CT		
Generation 2						
Children of Aaron Cook 1585 and Elizabeth Chard						
	Aaron Cook	1614–1690	Bridport, Devon, Eng.	Hadley, MA	Windsor, CT	Woodworker
1637	Mary Ford	1612–1645	Bridport, Devon, Eng.	Hadley, MA		
1649	Johanna Denslow	1627–1676	Allington, Dorset, Eng.	Northampton, MA	Windsor, CT	
1676	Elizabeth Nash	1632–1687	Lancaster, Bedford, Eng.	Northampton, MA	Springfield, MA	
1688	Rebecca Foote	1635–1701	Wethersfield, CT	Hadley, MA	Hadley, MA	Aunt of the owner of the chest illustrated in fig. 56
	Nathaniel Cook	1625–1688	Bridport, Devon, Eng.	Windsor, CT	Windsor, CT	Woodworker
1649	Lydia Vore	1633–1698	Crewhaven, Somerset, Eng.	Windsor, CT		
Generation 3						
Children of Nathaniel Cook 1625 and Lydia Vore						
	Hannah Cook	1655–1702	Windsor, CT	Windsor, CT	Windsor, CT	
1691	John Loomis	1651–1732	Windsor, CT	Windsor, CT		Woodworker
	Nathaniel Cook	1658–1724	Windsor, CT	Windsor, CT		Woodworker
	Abigail Cook	1659–1708	Windsor, CT	Deerfield, MA		
1676	Joshua Pomeroy	1646–1689	Windsor, CT	Deerfield, MA	Northampton, MA	Woodworker
1690	David Hoyt	1651–1704	Windsor, CT	Deerfield, MA	Deerfield, MA	Owner of the chests illustrated in figs. 58, 59
HOYT						
Generation 1						
	Nicholas Hoyt	1622–1655	Upway, Dorset, Eng.	Windsor, CT	Windsor, CT	Owner of the chest illustrated in fig. 11
1646	Susannah Joyce	1622–1655	Dorchester, Dorset, Eng.	Windsor, CT		
Generation 2						
Children of Nicholas Hoyt and Susannah Joyce						
	David Hoyt	1651–1704	Windsor, CT	Deerfield, MA	Windsor, CT	Owner of the chests illustrated in figs. 58, 59
1673	Sarah Wells	1655–1676	Wethersfield, CT	Windsor, CT		
1676	Mary Wilson	1651–1689	Windsor, CT	Deerfield, MA	Windsor, CT	
1690	Abigail Cook	1659–1708	Windsor, CT	Deerfield, MA	Deerfield, MA	Daughter of Nathaniel Cook (1625–1688)

Generation 3						
Children of David Hoyt 1651 and Mary Wilson						
	Mary Hoyt	1684–?	Deerfield, MA	Deerfield, MA	Deerfield, MA	
1707	Judah Wright	1677–1737	Springfield, MA	Deerfield, MA		Later owner of the chest illustrated in fig. 59
SMITH						
Generation 1						
	Samuel Smith	1602–1681	Hadleigh, Suffolk, Eng.	Hadley, MA	Whatfield, Suffolk	
1624	Elizabeth Chileab	1602–1686	Whatfield, Suffolk, Eng.	Hadley, MA		
Generation 2						
Children of Samuel Smith 1602 and Elizabeth Chileab						
	Phillip Smith	1632–1685	Hadleigh, Suffolk, Eng.	Hadley, MA	Wethersfield, CT	
1658	Rebecca Foote	1635–1701	Wethersfield, CT	Hadley, MA		4th wife of Aaron Cook (1614–1690)
	Chileab Smith	1636–1731	Wethersfield, CT	Hadley, MA	Wethersfield, CT	
1661	Hannah Hitchcock	1645–1733	Hartford, CT	Hadley, MA		
Generation 3						
Children of Chileab Smith 1636 and Hannah Hitchcock						
	Sarah Smith	1688–1760	Hadley, MA	Hatfield, MA	Hatfield, MA	Owner of the chest illustrated in fig. 56
1710	Jonathan Morton	1684–1776	Hatfield, MA	Hatfield, MA		

the products of either Abigail Cook's father, uncle, first husband, or brother, Nathaniel Cook Jr. (1658–1724), all of whom were woodworkers likely trained in the Cook shop tradition (fig. 60). The nearly identical ground plan, framing configuration, ornament, and overall execution of these objects suggest that they were made by the same craftsman probably sometime after Abigail Cook's move to Deerfield.[72]

Aside from the structural changes made to accommodate a drawer, these two chests diverge in only one respect. The back of the chest with drawer is framed with two horizontal, deeply chamfered oak panels, whereas the back of the low chest is framed with one large yellow pine panel. The floors of both chests consist of three transverse yellow pine boards, lapped together and set into a groove in the front floor rails and butted and nailed against the rear floor rails. On the chest with drawer, the free-floating sides of the floorboards conform to the shape of the side panels. The sides of the floorboards on the low chest are nailed to the bottom of the side floor rails.

Practitioners of the Cook shop tradition embellished board chests with moldings similar to those they used on joined chests. Composed of mill-sawn yellow pine boards nailed together, the example illustrated in figure 61 has gouged notches on the edges of the lid and front, five continuous horizontal courses of ogee molding on the façade, and five vertical courses of the same molding on the sides. Like many seventeenth-century board chests, this example also has scrolled brackets. The brackets are integral with the front board, are unusually long and deep, and have contours from a sixth ogee molding (largely removed in the process of cutting the brackets) run on the lower edge of the front board. As on most Connecticut River Valley board chests, the side boards extend to the floor and have elaborate cutwork

Figure 61 Chest, Windsor, Connecticut, or Northampton, Massachusetts, ca. 1680. Yellow pine. Dimensions not recorded. (Courtesy, Antiquarian and Landmarks Society, Inc.; photo, Gavin Ashworth.)

voids separating the feet. On this example, the voids appear as triangles surmounting two rectangular steps. The tip of the void terminates in two intersecting cuts like the feet of board chests made farther up the Connecticut River Valley in Massachusetts.[73]

The Stoughton Shop

While Moore and Drake family woodworkers cultivated political connections within the town and colony and Aaron Cook assumed increasingly important leadership roles in local and regional militias, the Stoughtons leveraged their descent from the English nonconformist minister Reverend Thomas Stoughton Sr. (1557–1612), their inherited wealth, and their education to gain entry into elite social circles not traditionally open to woodworkers. They formed associations with merchants' and ministers' families in the Connecticut River Valley and eastern Massachusetts, marrying into their ranks, building their houses, and filling their commissions for expensive, status-bearing furniture.

Thomas Stoughton Jr. (1591–1661), his wife, Elizabeth Montpeson (1591–1676), and their children, together with the family of his brother Israel (1603–1644), immigrated with Reverend John Warham's congregation to Dorchester, Massachusetts, in 1630. Both brothers were outspoken nonconformists who modeled their religious beliefs after those of their father, a 1580 graduate of Queens College, Cambridge University, who served as vicar of Coggeshall Parish, Essex, from 1600 until 1606, when his dissenting views precipitated his dismissal. Two years after arriving in Dorchester, Thomas Jr. received a citation from the Massachusetts Bay Court for solemnizing a marriage. The court obviously felt that he had exceeded his authority as constable of the settlement.[74]

When Warham's group moved to Connecticut, Thomas Stoughton joined them. The latter received the third-largest land grant in the new settlement, totaling more than one hundred fifty acres and including twenty-five acres of prime tillage in the Great Meadow and a fifty-two-acre home lot. The size of this grant put him in the top 10 percent of land recipients. In 1645 he conveyed his home lot and land in the Great Meadow to his son Thomas III (1624–1689). The younger Stoughton had just reached the age of twenty-one and had presumably completed his apprenticeship with his father.[75]

This land grant made Thomas III one of the wealthiest men in Windsor. At the age of thirty-one, he married Mary Wadsworth (1632–1712), daughter of William Wadsworth (1594–1674), a wealthy Hartford merchant who had emigrated from Braintree, Essex, and Sarah Talcott (1600–1643), daughter of a Hartford and Wethersfield merchant. That same year, he became involved in Windsor's town government, serving first as the way warden and subsequently as constable (1657–1660), assessor (1660), ensign of the militia, and selectman (1667–1678). He and Mary raised five children, including woodworkers John (1657–1712), Thomas IV (1662–1748), Samuel (1665–1712), and Israel (1667–1736), all of whom Thomas III presumably trained. Together, he and his sons provided furniture, cooperage, and carpentry for extended-family members, neighbors, and patrons in Hartford, Wethersfield, and their satellite communities.[76]

Following a well-established pattern among Windsor's other woodworkers, several of Thomas and Mary Stoughton's children married into local woodworking families. John married Elizabeth Bissell, daughter of John Moore I's apprentice Thomas Bissell, and Samuel married Dorothy Bissell (1665–1713), daughter of John Drake's probable apprentice John Bissell. Israel Stoughton married Mary Birge (1677–1755), a member of a non-woodworking family, and remained in Windsor's original settlement on the west side of the river. He died in 1736, leaving an estate valued at more than £2,000 and property including "joiners tooles . . . creasing plains, match plains and stocks, a philister, and a bench with vice." Some of Thomas and Mary Stoughton's children married members of merchant families associated with their parents and grandparents, and others married members of ministerial families. In 1694 Rebecca Stoughton (1673–1704) married Atherton Mather (1663–1734), brother of Reverend Samuel Mather, and in 1699 Elizabeth Stoughton (1660–1724) married John Eliot (1669–1719), grandson of Reverend John Eliot, "Apostle to the Indians." Eliot had received the contract to oversee construction of the Windsor ironworks in 1699.[77]

Thomas Stoughton IV married Dorothy Talcott (1665–1696) in 1691. Her aunt Sarah Talcott was Thomas IV's grandmother. Through this union Thomas became linked to both the merchant and the ministerial elite. By 1680 Thomas had moved to Windsor's settlement on the east side of the Connecticut River (later the East Windsor Hill section of South Windsor), built a house, and joined the other members of that fledgling community in petitioning the Connecticut General Court for permission to establish Windsor's Second Congregational Church on their side of the river. While waiting for a decision, the group began to search for a minister and build a meetinghouse. In 1694, having not yet received official sanction from the General Court, the incipient congregation invited Reverend Timothy Edwards (1669–1758) to be their pastor. Thomas IV may have first encountered Edwards in 1692, when the minister's father, Richard (1647–1718), married Mary Talcott (1661–1733), his first wife's elder sister. Thomas's familiarity with the Edwards family and his prominence in the community may have prompted him to have Reverend Timothy Edwards, the latter's wife, Esther Stoddard (1672–1725), and the minister's sister Abigail Edwards stay as guests in his home until a house for their use could be built. Reverend Edwards conducted weekly religious services in the Stoughton home until the meetinghouse was completed. Three years later, following the death of Dorothy Talcott in 1696, Stoughton married Abigail Edwards. By 1698 the meetinghouse was finished, the General Court approved the church, and the congregation witnessed the ordination of Timothy Edwards as their minister.[78]

Through their connections to other woodworking families and to the ministerial elite, the Stoughtons were well positioned to provide joined and carved case furniture to wealthy patrons throughout the region. Evidence suggests that the construction techniques and carving motifs used by Thomas Stoughton III and other craftsmen from his shop tradition had a substantial influence on furniture styles in the central portion of the Connecticut River Valley. During the last quarter of the seventeenth century, the visual language of several shops merged to form a distinctive idiom. This new style is manifest most notably in the joined and foliate-carved chests and cupboards from the Wethersfield area. The chests with drawers illustrated in figures 62 and 63 illustrate the latter point. Both are from the Stoughton shop tradition and are similar in their construction and decoration. Their lids consist of two oak boards held together with heavy oak

Figure 62 Chest attributed to Thomas Stoughton III or Thomas Stoughton IV, Windsor, Connecticut, ca. 1680. Oak with yellow pine. H. 39½", W. 45¾", D. 19¾". (Courtesy, Connecticut Historical Society, gift of Thaddeus Mather; photo, Gavin Ashworth.)

Figure 63 Chest attributed to Thomas Stoughton III or Thomas Stoughton IV, Windsor, Connecticut, ca. 1680. Oak with yellow pine. H. 41", W. 48", D. 20". (Courtesy, Historic Deerfield, Inc.; photo, Gavin Ashworth.) The lid has been altered.

cleats. The bottoms of the chests are constructed of yellow pine boards attached with V-joints at their edges; set into a groove in the front floor rail, side rails, and all four stiles; and nailed to the back floor rail, a technique also used in joined chests in the foliate-carved style attributed to a Hartford County shop currently associated with Wethersfield woodworker Peter Blinn. The bottoms of the cases below the drawers are fitted with yellow pine dust boards nailed to the bottom rails. The backs are enclosed with undivided yellow pine panels that run the length of the case; the upper panel of each is set into grooves in all four framing members, and the lower panel behind the drawers is slotted into grooves in the stiles and nailed to the edge of each chest's dust board. The sides of the drawers are nailed into rabbets in the front and back, and their yellow pine bottom boards are set into a groove in the front and are nailed to the sides and back. All of the joints are double-pinned except those that join the front drawer rails to the stiles, the bottom side rails to the stiles, and the muntins to the sides' floor and bottom rails. These joints are all single-pinned.[79]

All of the applied moldings and corner plaques on the chests are made of oak. Relief-carved foliate motifs consisting of abstract meandering vines with leaves and flower heads with serrated edges suggesting multiple petals adorn the panels. These foliate designs are accented with punches and both incised and carved veining. Some of the other designs that the Stoughtons used on their furniture have parallels in furniture attributed to John Thurston (1607–1685), a woodworker who moved from Wrentham, Suffolk, to Dedham and Medfield, Massachusetts (fig. 64). Wrentham was only a short distance north of Southwold, Suffolk, the ancestral home of the

Figure 64 Chest attributed to John Thurston, Dedham or Medfield, Massachusetts, 1660–1685. Oak with pine. H. 31⅜", W. 47¾", D. 21". (Courtesy, Museum of Fine Arts, Boston.)

Moores and northeast of the inland town of Naughton, Suffolk, the ancestral home of the Stoughtons. It is possible that the immigrant-generation woodworkers from all three families were familiar with similar designs on Suffolk County carved woodwork and embroidered textiles. The chest with drawers illustrated in figure 63 has a history of ownership extending back to Sarah Chester (1707–1770), but it probably belonged to her parents, Hannah Talcott (1658–1741), daughter of a Hartford merchant, and John Chester (1656–1711), a wealthy Wethersfield merchant. John and Hannah married in 1686. They may have commissioned this chest from either Thomas Stoughton III or Thomas IV, each of whom married one of Hannah's cousins (fig. 65).[80]

Ordained as minister of Windsor's first church in 1684, Reverend Samuel Mather (1650–1728) originally owned the chest with drawers shown in figure 62. He probably commissioned this expensive object either from his brother-in-law Thomas Stoughton IV or the joiner's father. Reverend Mather's association with the elder Stoughton extended back several generations to the moment when Thomas III's brother Israel chose to remain in Dorchester, Massachusetts. After Reverend Warham left for Windsor in 1635, Israel probably helped settle Reverend Richard Mather (1596–1669) as Dorchester's second minister. Among Mather's more distinguished children were Reverend Eleazer Mather, minister of Northampton's First Church and husband to Abigail Warham, Reverend John Warham's daughter; Reverend Increase Mather, president of Harvard College; and Timothy Mather (1628–1684), who moved from Dorchester to Lyme, Connecticut, and married Elizabeth Atherton (1628–1678). In 1694 Atherton Mather, son of Timothy and Elizabeth Atherton Mather, married Thomas Stoughton III's daughter Rebecca. Through this union, Rebecca's brothers, the woodworkers Thomas Stoughton IV and Israel Stoughton, gained Reverend Samuel Mather as a brother-in-law.

Figure 65 Chart showing family genealogies pertinent to the furniture illustrated in figs. 62, 63, and 66.

EDWARDS BOX / TALCOTT-CHESTER CHEST

Marriage Date	Name	Dates	Birth location	Death location	Marriage location	Occupation/note
STOUGHTON						
Generation 1						
	Thomas Stoughton	1591–1661	Naughton, Suffolk, Eng.	Windsor, CT	Naughton, Suffolk, Eng.	
1612	Elizabeth Montpeson	1591–1676	Wilts, Eng.	Windsor, CT		
Generation 2						
Children of Thomas Stoughton 1591 and Elizabeth Montepeson						
	Thomas Stoughton	1624–1689	Naughton, Suffolk, Eng.	Windsor, CT	Windsor, CT	Woodworker
1655	Mary Wadsworth	1632–1712	Braintree Essex, Eng.	Hartford, CT		
Generation 3						
Children of Thomas Stoughton 1624 and Mary Wadsworth						
	John Stoughton	1657–1712	Windsor, CT	Windsor, CT	Windsor, CT	Woodworker
1682	Elizabeth Bissell	1666–1688	Windsor, CT	Windsor, CT		Owner of the box illustrated in fig. 49, daughter of Thomas Bissell (1628–1689)
1689	Sarah Fitch	1661–?	Windsor, CT	Windsor, CT	Windsor, CT	
	Thomas Stoughton	1662–1748	Windsor, CT	Windsor, CT	Hartford, CT	Woodworker
1691	Dorothy Talcott	1665–1696	Hartford, CT	Windsor, CT		
1697	Abigail Edwards	1672–1754	Hartford, CT	Windsor, CT	Windsor, CT	Sister of owner of the box illustrated in fig. 66
	Samuel Stoughton	1665–1712	Windsor, CT	Windsor, CT	Windsor, CT	Woodworker
1693	Dorothy Bissell	1665–1713	Windsor, CT	Windsor, CT		Daughter of John Bissell (1630–1693)
	Israel Stoughton	1667–1736	Windsor, CT	Windsor, CT		Woodworker
	Rebecca Stoughton	1673–1704	Windsor, CT	Suffield, CT	Windsor, CT	
1694	Atherton Mather	1663–1734	Dorchester, MA	Suffield, CT		Brother of owner of the chest illustrated in fig. 62
Generation 3						
Children of John Stoughton 1657 and Sarah Fitch						
	Elizabeth Stoughton	1692–1760	Windsor, CT	Windsor, CT	Windsor, CT	
1713	Joseph Mather	1689–1717	Windsor, CT	Windsor, CT		Son of owner of the chest illustrated in fig. 62
EDWARDS						
Generation 1						
	Richard Edwards	1647–1718	New Haven, CT	Windsor, CT	New Haven, CT	
1667	Elizabeth Tuttle	1645–1679	New Haven, CT	Windsor, CT		
1692	Mary Talcott	1661–1733	Hartford, CT	Hartford, CT	Hartford, CT	Sister-in-law of Thomas Stoughton (1662–1748)
Generation 2						
Children of Richard Edwards and Elizabeth Tuttle						
	Timothy Edwards	1669–1758	New Haven, CT	Windsor, CT	Northampton, MA	Owner of the box illustrated in fig. 66
1694	Esther Stoddard	1672–1725	Northampton, MA	Windsor, CT		
	Abigail Edwards	1672–1754	Hartford, CT	Windsor, CT	Windsor, CT	
1697	Thomas Stoughton	1662–1748	Windsor, CT	Windsor, CT		Woodworker
MATHER						
Generation 1						
	Timothy Mather	1628–1684	Liverpool, Lancs, Eng.	Dorchester, MA	Dorchester, MA	

1648	Elizabeth Atherton	1628–1678	Warwick, Lancs, Eng.			
Children of Timothy Mather 1628 and Elizabeth Atherton						
	Samuel Mather	1650–1728	Dorchester, MA	Windsor, CT	Milford, CT	Owner of the chest illustrated in fig. 62
1680	Hannah Treat	1660–1708	Milford, CT	Windsor, CT		
	Atherton Mather	1663–1734	Dorchester, MA	Suffield, CT	Windsor, CT	
1694	Rebecca Stoughton	1673–1704	Windsor, CT	Suffield, CT		Daughter of Thomas Stoughton (1624–1689)
Children of Samuel Mather 1650 and Hannah Treat						
	Joseph Mather	1689–1717	Windsor, CT		Windsor, CT	Windsor, CT
1713	Elizabeth Stoughton	1692–1760	Windsor, CT		Windsor, CT	Daughter of John Stoughton (1657–1712)
TALCOTT						
Generation 1						
	John Talcott	1562–1604	Colchester, Essex, Eng.	Braintree, Essex, Eng.	Braintree, Essex, Eng.	
1591	Anne Skinner	1574–1637	Braintree, Essex, Eng.	Braintree, Essex, Eng.		
Generation 2						
Children of John Talcott 1562 and Anne Skinner						
	John Talcott	1592–1660	Braintree, Essex, Eng.	Hartford, CT	Braintree, Essex, Eng.	
1630	Dorothy Mott		Colchester, Essex, Eng.	Hartford, CT		
	Sarah Talcott	1600–1643	Braintree, Essex, Eng.	Hartford, CT	Braintree, Essex, Eng.	
1625	William Wadsworth	1594–1674	Long Buckley, Northampton, Eng.	Hartford, CT		Father-in-law of Thomas Stoughton (1624–1689)
Generation 3						
Children of John Talcott 1592 and Dorothy Mott						
	John Talcott	1632–1688	Braintree, Essex, Eng.	Hartford, CT	Hartford, CT	
1650	Helena Wakeman	1632–1674	New Haven, CT	Hartford, CT		
	Samuel Talcott	1635–1691	Hartford, CT	Wethersfield, CT	Hartford, CT	
1661	Hannah Holyoke	1644–1678	Springfield, MA	Wethersfield, CT	Hartford, CT	
Generation 4						
Children of John Talcott 1632 and Helena Wakeman						
	Elizabeth Talcott	1656–1718	Hartford, CT	Hartford, CT	Hartford, CT	
1682	Joseph Wadsworth	1650–1729	Hartford, CT	Hartford, CT		Brother-in-law of Thomas Stoughton (1624–1689)
	Mary Talcott	1661–1723	Hartford, CT	Hartford, CT	Hartford, CT	
1692	Richard Edwards	1647–1718	New Haven, CT	Hartford, CT		Father of the owner of the box illustrated in fig. 66
	Dorothy Tallcott	1666–1696	Hartford, CT	Windsor, CT	Windsor, CT	
1691	Thomas Stoughton	1662–1748	Windsor, CT	Windsor, CT		Woodworker
Children of Samuel Talcott 1635 and Hannah Holyoke						
	Hannah Talcott	1658–1741	Wethersfield, CT	Wethersfield, CT	Wethersfield, CT	Traditional owner of the chest illustrated in fig. 63
1686	John Chester	1656–1711	Watertown, MA	Wethersfield, CT		
Generation 5						
Children of John Chester 1656 and Hannah Talcott						
	Sarah Chester	1707–1770	Wethersfield, CT	Wethersfield, CT	Hartford, CT	Owner of the chest illustrated in fig. 63
1731	Israel Williams	1709–1789	Hatfield, MA	Wethersfield, CT		

Figure 66 Box attributed to Thomas Stoughton IV, Windsor, Connecticut, ca. 1695. Oak and yellow pine with yellow pine. H. 7½", W. 29", D. 17½". (Private collection; photo, Gavin Ashworth.)

Figure 67 Detail showing the lid, cleats, and till of the box illustrated in fig. 66. (Photo, Gavin Ashworth.)

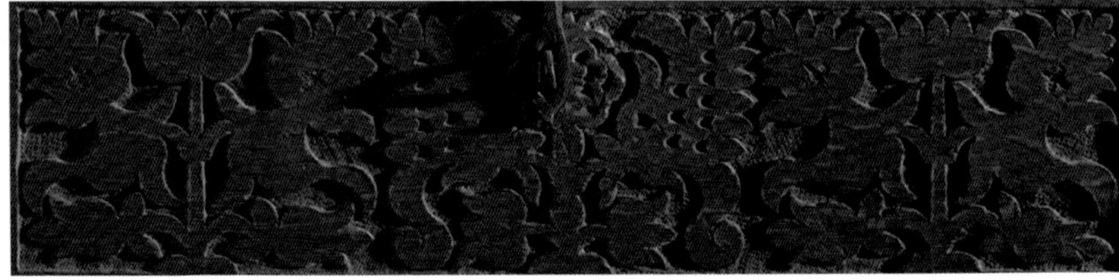

Figure 68 Detail of the carving on the box illustrated in fig. 66. (Photo, Gavin Ashworth.)

Thomas Stoughton IV may have made the box illustrated in figure 66 between 1695 and 1700 for Reverend Timothy Edwards, while the latter was residing in Thomas Stoughton IV's house. It may be the box described in the 1771 inventory of Timothy Edwards Jr. as a "Carv^d Box 1/ in the South Chamber." The front, sides, and backboard of the box are made of oak, and the lid, till, and bottom are yellow pine. Butted and nailed to the case, the bottom has an angular edge that projects from the case at the front and sides. Heavy oak cleats with molded sides secure the lid boards and extend beyond the case sides, terminating in an ogee bracket (fig. 67). The decoration on the façade (fig. 68) is laid out in a manner similar to that on the front panels of the chests with drawers mentioned above (figs. 62, 63). Divided by two scribed lines into three equal segments, the carving on the box features foliate motifs, accented with gouge cuts and serrations at their upper edges, that symmetrically flank a central rosette embellished with multiple tiers of gouge-accented petals (fig. 68). Variations of the box's rosette motif appear in the central panel of each chest, and versions of the box's flanking foliate forms adorn the symmetrical panels on both sides of each chest's central panel. A band of incised, intersecting lunettes ornaments the outer edge of the front board, each arc converging at a cruciform punch. The carved foliate forms with serrated edges and curved tips and the flower heads with horizontal veining incised with a parting tool are similar to the foliated, veined elements on other carved case furniture attributed to the Stoughton shop.[81]

The White Shop

A group of joined chests believed to have originated in Hatfield, Massachusetts, in the first decade of the eighteenth century documents the convergence of Windsor shop traditions in furniture made in the Connecticut River Valley of central Massachusetts. With its turned legs, foliate and vine decoration, and initials "MS," the chest illustrated in figure 69 illuminates the role that family connections played in the products of third- and fourth-generation woodworkers who decorated their furniture with carving that provided both visual delight and symbolic meaning. Incorporating motifs recalled from the past, the chest's ornament can be interpreted as a map of intertwined family histories and a bridge between culturally different communities approximately forty years apart.

Figure 69 Chest attributed to Daniel White Jr., probably Hatfield, Massachusetts, ca. 1710. Maple with yellow pine. H. 45¼", W. 43½", D. 19¾". (Courtesy, Wadsworth Atheneum, Wallace Nutting Collection, gift of J. Pierpont Morgan, by exchange and the Evelyn Bonar Storrs Trust Fund.)

Figure 70 Chart showing genealogies relevant to Daniel White, probable maker of the chest illustrated in fig. 69.

BISSELL						
Marriage Date	Name	Dates	Birth location	Death location	Marriage location	Occupation/note
Generation 1						
	John Bissell	1591–1677	Somerset, Eng.	Windsor, CT	Somerset, Eng.	
1627	Elizabeth Thompson	1596–1641	Somerset, Eng.	Windsor, CT		
Generation 2						
Children of John Bissell 1591 and Elizabeth Thompson						
	Mary Bissell	1627–1689	Somerset, Eng.	Windsor, CT	Windsor, CT	
1649	Jacob Drake	1621–1689	Wiscomb, Devon, Eng	Windsor, CT		Woodworker; possible maker of the box illustrated in fig. 49
	Thomas Bissell	1628–1689	Somerset, Eng.	Windsor, CT	Windsor, CT	Woodworker; probable apprentice of John Moore I (1614–1677)
1655	Abigail Moore	1639–1728	Windsor, CT	Windsor, CT		Daughter of John Moore I (1614–1677)
	John Bissell	1630–1693	Somerset, Eng.	Windsor, CT	Windsor, CT	Woodworker; possible apprentice of John Drake I (1592–1659) or John Drake II (1621–1688)
1658	Isabel Mason	1640–?	Saybrook, CT	Windsor, CT		
	Samuel Bissell	1635–1697	Somerset, Eng.	Windsor, CT	Windsor, CT	Woodworker; probable apprentice of Thomas Holcomb (1608–1657)
1658	Abigail Holcomb	1639–1688	Windsor, CT	Windsor, CT		Daughter of Thomas Holcomb (1608–1657)
	Nathaniel Bissell	1640–1713	Windsor, CT	Windsor, CT	Windsor, CT	Woodworker; probable apprentice of John Moore I (1614–1677)
1662	Mindwell Moore	1643–1682	Windsor, CT	Windsor, CT		Daughter of John Moore I (1614–1677)
	Joyce Bissell	1641–1690	Windsor, CT	Windsor, CT	Windsor, CT	
1665	Samuel Pinney	1635–1681	Dorchester, MA	Windsor, CT		Brother of Nathaniel Pinney (1641–1676)
Generation 3						
Children of Thomas Bissell 1628 and Abigail Moore						
	Thomas Bissell	1656–1738	Windsor, CT	Windsor, CT	Windsor, CT	
1678	Esther Strong	1661–1726	Northampton, MA	Windsor, CT		
	Abigail Bissell	1658–1723	Windsor, CT	Windsor, CT	Windsor, CT	
?	Nathaniel Gaylord	1656–1720	Windsor, CT	Windsor, CT		Woodworker; owner of the chest illustrated in fig. 43
	Joseph Bissell	1663–1689	Windsor, CT	Windsor, CT	Windsor, CT	Woodworker
1687	Sarah Strong	1666–1739	Northampton, MA	Windsor, CT		Daughter of Thomas Strong (1638–1689)
	Elizabeth Bissell	1666–1688	Windsor, CT	Windsor, CT	Windsor, CT	Owner of the box illustrated in fig. 49
1682	John Stoughton	1657–1712	Windsor, CT	Windsor, CT		Woodworker; son of Thomas Stoughton (1624–1689)
	Benjamin Bissell	1669–1698	Windsor, CT	Windsor, CT		Woodworker
	Sarah Bissell	1672–1703	Windsor, CT	Hatfield, MA	Hatfield, MA	
1696	Daniel White	1671–1726	Hatfield, MA	Windsor, CT		Woodworker; probable maker of the chest illustrated in fig. 69; husband of Ann Bissell (1675–1709)
Children of John Bissell 1630 and Isabel Mason						
	Mary Bissell	1658–1690	Windsor, CT	Windsor, CT	Windsor, CT	
1681	Daniel Owen	1658–1683	Windsor, CT	Windsor, CT		Son of John Owen (1624–1698)
1700	Hezekiah Porter	1658–?	Windsor, CT	Windsor, CT	Windsor, CT	

	John Bissell	1661–?	Windsor, CT	Lebanon, CT	Windsor, CT	
1689	Sarah White	1662–?	Hatfield, MA	Lebanon, CT		Sister of Daniel White (1671–1726)
	Daniel Bissell	1663–1738	Windsor, CT	Windsor, CT	Windsor, CT	
1692	Margaret Dewey	1674–1712	Westfield, MA	Windsor, CT		Daughter of Josiah Dewey (1641–1732)
	Dorothy Bissell	1665–1713	Windsor, CT	Windsor, CT	Windsor, CT	
1685	Nathaniel Watson	1663–1690	Windsor, CT	Windsor, CT		Woodworker
1693	Samuel Stoughton	1665–1712	Windsor, CT	Windsor, CT		Woodworker; son of Thomas Stoughton (1624–1689)
	Hezekiah Bissell	1673–1709	Windsor, CT	Windsor, CT		Woodworker
	Ann Bissell	1675–1709	Windsor, CT	Windsor, CT	Windsor, CT	
1704	Daniel White	1671–1726	Hatfield, MA	Windsor, CT		Woodworker; probable maker of the chest illustrated in fig. 69; husband of Sarah Bissell (1672–1703)
	Jeremiah Bissell	1677–1755	Windsor, CT			Woodworker
1705	Mehitable White	1683–?	Hatfield, MA	Windsor, CT		Sister of Daniel White (1671–1726)
Children of Nathaniel Bissell 1640 and Mindwell Moore						
	Hannah Bissell	1671–1708	Windsor, CT	Windsor, CT	Windsor, CT	
1698	Samuel Bancroft	1667–1742	Windsor, CT	Windsor, CT		Woodworker
	David Bissell	1681–1733	Windsor, CT	Windsor, CT		Woodworker
WHITE						
Generation 1						
	John White	1596–1665	Shalford, Essex, Eng.	Hartford, CT	Shalford, Essex, Eng.	
1622	Mary Levett	1601–1667	Shalford, Essex, Eng.	Hartford, CT		
Generation 2						
Children of John White 1596 and Mary Levett						
	John White	1623–1684	Shalford, Essex, Eng.	Hatfield, MA	Hartford, CT	Woodworker
1658	Sarah Bunce	1636–1676	Hartford, CT	Hatfield, MA		
	Mary White	1626–1650	Shalford, Essex, Eng.	Hartford, CT	Hartford, CT	
1646	Jonathan Gilbert	1627–1682	Beverly, York, Eng.	Hartford, CT		Woodworker; son of Thomas Gilbert (1589–1659)
	Sarah White	1635–1702	Hartford, CT	Hatfield, MA	Hartford, CT	
1656	Stephen Taylor	1644–1665	Windsor, CT	Hatfield, MA		Woodworker
1666	Barnabas Hinsdale	1639–1675	Dedham, MA	Deerfield, MA	Hatfield, MA	Woodworker
	Daniel White	1644–1713	Hartford, CT	Hatfield, MA	Hartford, CT	Woodworker
1661	Sarah Crow	1647–1719	Hartford, CT	Hatfield, MA		Daughter of John Crow (1605–1681)
Generation 3						
Children of John White 1623 and Sarah Bunce						
	Sarah White	1659–1741	Hatfield, MA	Deerfield, MA	Hatfield, MA	
1678	John Graves	1652–1730	Wethersfield, CT	Deerfield, MA		Woodworker
	John White	1663–1750	Hatfield, MA	Hardwick, MA	Hatfield, MA	Woodworker
1687	Hannah Wells	1668–1733	Hadley, MA	Hatfield, MA		Daughter of John Wells (1628–1692)
Children of Daniel White 1644 and Sarah Crow						
	Sarah White	1662–?	Hatfield, MA	Lebanon, CT	Hatfield, MA	
1680	Thomas Loomis	1653–1688	Windsor, CT	Windsor, CT		
1689	John Bissell	1661–?	Windsor, CT	Lebanon, CT	Windsor, CT	Son of John Bissell (1630–1693)
	Elizabeth White	1667–1736	Hatfield, MA	Windsor, CT	Windsor, CT	Probable maker of the sampler illustrated in fig. 10
1688	Samuel Loomis	1666–1754	Windsor, CT	Windsor, CT		Woodworker
	Esther White	1670–1766	Hatfield, MA	Windsor, CT	Windsor, CT	

1691	John Ellsworth	1671–1720	Windsor, CT	Windsor, CT		Brother of Jonathan Ellsworth (1664–1749)
	Daniel White	1671–1726	Hatfield, MA	Windsor, CT	Hatfield, MA	Woodworker; probable maker of the chest illustrated in fig. 69
1696	Sarah Bissell	1672–1703	Windsor, CT	Hatfield, MA		
1704	Ann Bissell	1675–1709	Windsor, CT	Windsor, CT	Windsor, CT	
1710	Elizabeth Bliss	1687–1757	Norwich, CT	Windsor, CT	Windsor, CT	
	Hannah White	1679–1756	Hatfield, MA	Hatfield, MA	Hatfield, MA	
1700	Nathaniel Dickinson	1672–1713	Hadley, MA	Hatfield, MA		Son of Nathaniel Dickinson (1643–1719)
	Mehitable White	1683–?	Hatfield, MA	Windsor, CT	Windsor, CT	
1705	Jeremiah Bissell	1677–1755	Windsor, CT	Windsor, CT		Woodworker; son of John Bissell (1630–1693)
Generation 4						
Children of John White 1663 and Hannah Wells						
	Jonathan White	1701–1748	Hatfield, MA	Hebron, CT	Hebron, CT	Probable owner of the chest illustrated in fig. 37
1728	Anna ?	1703–1747	Hebron, CT	Hebron, CT		
	Elizabeth White	1705–1770	Hatfield, MA	Bolton, CT	Hatfield, MA	
1726	Daniel White	1798–1786	Hatfield, MA	Hatfield, MA	Hatfield, MA	Woodworker; son of Daniel White (1671–1726)
Children of Daniel White 1671 and Sarah Bissell						
	Daniel White	1698–1786	Windsor, CT	Hatfield, MA	Hatfield, MA	Woodworker
1726	Elizabeth White	1705–1770	Windsor, CT	Hatfield, MA		

This chest's probable maker, Hatfield, Massachusetts, woodworker Daniel White Jr. (1671–1726), combined motifs indicative of the Moore, Drake, and Stoughton shop traditions. The squat flowers carved in the front flanking panels parallel those on furniture ascribed to the Moore shop. White was exposed to that tradition when he moved from Hatfield to Windsor in 1696 to marry Sarah Bissell (1672–1703), the youngest daughter of Thomas Bissell and Abigail Moore. For a short time after his move, Daniel's closest woodworking colleague was his brother-in-law Benjamin Bissell (1669–1698). Bissell presumably trained with his father, who passed on designs and work habits learned during his probable apprenticeship with his own father-in-law, John Moore I. Daniel White may also have associated with Nathaniel Gaylord who likely also trained with Thomas Bissell. Gaylord married Abigail Bissell, the sister of Daniel White Jr.'s wife, Sarah Bissell (fig. 70).

The vine-and-leaf motif on the stiles and rails below each drawer and the multitiered rosette with sawtooth petals in the central panel have antecedents in the carving on the front rails, stiles, and center panels of the two chests associated with the Stoughton shop (figs. 62, 63). White's inclusion of this central rosette, a subtle element that visually departs from the rest of the carving scheme, also relates to the similar placement of a flower head on the center panel of the Thankful Noble chest (fig. 54). Through his marriage into the Bissell family, White encountered the work of John Stoughton, who had married the former's sister-in-law Elizabeth Bissell. Moreover, in 1693 Stoughton's brother Samuel married Dorothy Bissell, Sarah Bissell White's cousin.

The asymmetrical leaves accented with gouge cuts and connected to modeled stems carved on the central panel of its façade and the shield-shaped reserve for the escutcheon are similar to the leaves and reserve carved on the EB box attributed to the Drake shop (fig. 49). One year after his first wife, Sarah, died in 1703, Daniel White married her cousin Ann Bissell (1675–1709), an act that introduced him to members of the Drake family. Ann's brothers Hezekiah (1673–1709) and Jeremiah (1677–1755) probably trained with their father, John, who most likely learned the woodworking trade from John Drake Sr. or Jacob Drake. In 1705 Daniel White's younger sister, Mehitable (b. 1683), married Jeremiah Bissell, Ann Bissell White's younger brother.

After Ann Bissell died in 1709, Daniel White returned to Hatfield. Three years later he married as his third wife, Elizabeth Bliss (1687–1757), daughter of Springfield woodworker Samuel Bliss (1657–1749) and the granddaughter of millwright John Elderkin and his wife Elizabeth Drake. Daniel and Elizabeth subsequently moved back to Windsor, where he continued to work until his death in 1726. As in his life, his work reflected a convergence of three distinctly different Windsor shop practices: that of the Stoughton, Drake, and Moore traditions.

Politics and Patronage: Windsor's Woodworkers in Hartford County and the Connecticut River Valley

Ten years after Thomas Cole depicted the Connecticut River Valley as an idealized pastoral landscape in *The Oxbow,* his student Frederic Edwin Church produced another idealized image of the Connecticut River Valley in his monumental painting *Hooker and Company Journeying through the Wilderness, from Plymouth to Hartford, in 1636.* This work depicts a group of Puritans following Reverend Thomas Hooker—Reverend John Warham's colleague and the leading minister in Hartford, Wethersfield, and Windsor—into wilderness leading to the banks of the Connecticut River (fig. 71). Fusing the genres of landscape and history painting, the twenty-year-old Church layered his canvas with religious and historical references, touching on such themes as the naturalized presence of English pioneers advancing through God's country and the Puritan pursuit of a supposed manifest destiny. The painting raises to mythic heights the notion that Hooker's Puritans were ushering in the dawn of a new, uniquely American identity—an idea that still pervades textbook histories of the early settlement of Connecticut's river towns. A similar outlook pervaded the sermon that Reverend Hooker delivered to representatives from Connecticut's three river towns at a meeting of the General Court in Hartford on May 31, 1638. He used the occasion to explain that "the foundation of authority is laid, firstly, in the free consent of the people," and that the democratic election of civil leaders follows from a social contract based "on the will and law of God." Taking Hooker's words to heart, lawyer and Windsor resident Roger Ludlow (1590–1666) drafted an outline for representative colonial government titled the "Fundamental Orders." On January 14, 1639, the Connecticut General Court ratified the "Fundamental

Figure 71 Frederic Edwin Church, *Hooker and Company Journeying through the Wilderness, from Plymouth to Hartford, in 1636,* 1846. Oil on canvas. 40¼" x 60³⁄₁₆". (Courtesy, Wadsworth Atheneum, Museum purchase.)

Orders," which many historians consider an important precursor to the United States Constitution. In this work, Ludlow proposed a structure of government thoroughly in accord with Puritan doctrine, but one that also hinted at a new order.[82]

Those who celebrate Connecticut River Valley furniture as uniquely American iterations join consensus historians who interpret Hooker's and Ludlow's framework for representative government as a milestone in the development of American democracy. Yet neither group has investigated the implications of the "Fundamental Orders" for the culture of the period. The government that Ludlow formalized in his "Fundamental Orders" was the product of the same religious values, political ideals, and social aspirations that motivated Windsor's settlers to relocate from Dorchester, Massachusetts, to Windsor and perhaps that guided, in subtle but significant ways, the hands of the woodworkers among Windsor's settlers, who, in their own way, also framed community as they fashioned furniture.

A native of Dorchester, England, Ludlow knew members of the Windsor community well, having grown up with many of them as a member of Reverend John White's church. The minister knew Ludlow, who was married to one of White's wife's cousins, and identified him as a promising recruit for his planned New England colony, signing him on in 1627 as an investor in the Dorchester Company. Ludlow threw himself into preparations for the colonial settlement. He became an assistant with the Massachusetts Bay Company, helped outfit the vessel *Mary and John* for its voyage to America, and joined the shipboard congregation under White's handpicked leader, Reverend John Warham. After the group arrived in Dorchester, Massachusetts, Warham, Ludlow, Israel and William Stoughton, and others established a community based on open-field farming in which the town's freemen collectively agreed on crops, determined planting and harvest times, shared labor, and worked together to maintain fences. They also ran for offices in local and colonial government, serving as selectmen, magistrates, and, in Ludlow's case, deputy governor in 1634.

Through the early years of the 1630s, however, this core community of southwest country settlers found themselves increasingly outnumbered by immigrants from East Anglia—newcomers who disagreed with their customs, politics, and, particularly, their practice of open-field farming. As historian Gloria Main explains, East Anglians had been enclosing their fields since the thirteenth century, much earlier than their southwest country counterparts, and had developed active real estate markets. From Dutch Protestant immigrants, they had learned progressive agricultural practices such as the draining of fields and cultivation of new crops and had invested heavily in wool production. Ambitious men, they wanted no part of a farming system that required negotiation, accommodation, "patience, courtesy, [and] listening respectfully," all the "traits that brought material rewards in open field agriculture." These East Anglians expressed their views by voting their more conservative southwest country counterparts out of office, defeating Ludlow in his bid for the governorship in 1635. According to Main, Ludlow and his fellow southwest country settlers "reacted negatively [to the East Anglian colonists] and many chose to leave rather than live with the obnoxious newcomers. West Country colonists led by John Warham left Dorchester and founded Windsor."[83]

At the outset of colonization, Ludlow negotiated with leaders of the Massachusetts Bay Colony to form a provisional Connecticut government. He was one of the commissioners appointed to carry out the Bay Colony's instructions and later served as a magistrate and deputy governor in Connecticut's government. Despite the loss of documentary records for the early years of Windsor's settlement, it is logical to assume that Ludlow also played a leading role in governing and modeled its open-field farming community on that of the Dorchester, Massachusetts, settlement. The Dorchester group's commitment to this type of farming may partly explain their vitriolic reaction to the Stiles group, for Francis Stiles and his woodworkers, including Thomas Barber Sr., had begun construction on what amounted to an enclosed private estate for their employer, Sir Richard Saltonstall. This exclusionary act would have served as a bitter reminder of events that had caused the Dorchester group to leave their original settlement. In addition, worries over the tenuous legal basis of their own land claims must have sharpened the Dorchester group's antagonism toward Stiles and his men, who were pursuing their own competing land claims in court. As historian Paul Lucas has noted, the Earl of Warwick had conferred on a small group of Englishmen his patent for land in Connecticut, encompassing the three river towns without providing for a civil government able to charter towns and to invest local officials with the authority to distribute land. As the chief commissioner, Ludlow had as his main objective in drafting the "Fundamental Orders" the establishment of a regional government in accordance with Puritan principles that would help shore up the Dorchester group's land claims. Acting without legal sanction, Hartford, Wethersfield, and Windsor adopted the "Fundamental Orders," not on the lofty principles of democracy but, rather, "as a desperate bid to create the appearance of legitimacy."[84]

Ludlow also drafted the "Fundamental Orders" to reject the policies and politics of the East Anglians who had displaced him and his southwest country colleagues in Dorchester, Massachusetts. To his contemporaries, this framework for government was as notable for what it was *not* as for what it *was*. In a departure from Massachusetts law, the "Fundamental Orders" espoused a franchise independent of church membership and avoided any reference to outside authority such as the Massachusetts Bay government or the king. For furniture historians, Ludlow's motives and his connections with members of Windsor's woodworking community raise the question: Did local artisans collectively attempt in the material realm what Ludlow accomplished in the political realm? Ludlow's rejection of East Anglians' politics raises the possibility that his supporters among Windsor's woodworking community followed suit and crafted furniture that was as important for what it was *not* as for what it *was*—that is, furniture that offered a deliberate counterpoint to the ambitious forms popular among the East Anglian elite of eastern Massachusetts. Furniture historian Robert Trent posits two phases of mannerist design in furniture, a carved style of ornament rooted in Renaissance classicism and a later style that relied on applied ornament for its decorative impact. Derived from architectural decoration and developed in Italy and Germany, the applied-ornament style had displaced the carved style in London by the turn of the seventeenth century and had arrived in Boston by the 1630s. Furniture decorated in this manner included large and ostentatious objects such as cupboards with multiple jetties, complex moldings, and classically inspired turnings that Trent attributes to the northern Essex County, Massachusetts, shop of Daniel Rindge Jr.[85]

In his "Fundamental Orders," Ludlow provided for a colonial government with limited authority to regulate affairs in the river towns while acknowledging freemen's rights. He anticipated the need to provide freemen the means not only to participate in government but also to check its power. In Windsor, Ludlow and his associates in town government seem to have welcomed the contribution of all freemen, and especially skilled craftsmen, to the community. They found reinforcement for such ideas in Reverend John White's own apology for colonization, *The Planter's Plea* (1630):

> [A mother country] must allow to her [colony] such a proportion of able men as may bee sufficient to make the frame of that new formed body: As good Governours, able Ministers, Physitians, Souldiers, Schoolemasters, Mariners, and Mechanicks of all sorts; who had therefore need to bee of

> the more sufficiency, because the first fashioning of a politicke body is a harder taske then the ordering of that which is already framed; as the first erecting of a house is ever more difficult than the future keeping of it in repaire.

This imagery must have resonated with Windsor's woodworkers, who were engaged in constructing houses and furniture and building a "politicke body" through service in town offices, and with Ludlow who chose "Mechanicks . . . of the more sufficiency" to participate in local government.[86]

Matthew Grant's diary of sermon notes suggests that local ministers continued using the house framing metaphor. On August 15, 1647, Reverend John Warham compared the covenanted church to both a body and a house: "There is no union in a body unlesse ye members be knit together by Ioynts and senewes. So in a house ye locking of timber together makes it a house." Shortly thereafter Grant noted that a visiting minister, Mr. Raynor, delivered a sermon based on I Corinthians 3:11: "a metaphor of a building [can be used to describe the church] . . . because as to a building ther goes first ye fondation, then stones, then builders, to make up. Euen so to ye church of Chrst, there is required, first a foundation to build soules on, that's none other but Christ, & stones, liuing stones yt is ye people of God, and builders, yt is ye minestres of God. . . . Christ is the foundation, joins crosswalls together, supports weight of walls, roof." This imagery invested woodworking and public service with rich symbolic meaning. In the minds of Windsor residents, woodworkers were essential to the church and town, the main components of the "politicke body" in colonial New England.[87]

Windsor's early leaders appear to have favored craftsmen in the areas of land distribution, access to resources on the town commons, and participation in local government to a greater extent than did leaders in other river towns. With their natural harbors on the Connecticut River, Hartford, Middletown, and Wethersfield had, by 1640, attracted a significant contingent of elite East Anglian families with mercantile ties to New England coastal ports, England, and the Caribbean. Hartford merchants John Talcott (1592–1660) from Braintree, Essex; his brother-in-law William Wadsworth from Long Buckley, Northampton; Balthazaar DeWolfe (1621–1696) from London; and Peter Bulkeley (1582–1659) from Odell, Bedfordshire, benefited the most in distributions of house lots, uplands, woodlots, fields, wastes, and attendant rights of commonage, leaving little land for the town's craftsmen. Historian Frank Thistlethwaite observed that in Windsor, by contrast, "a few key people" distributed 16,600 acres of land to the town's inhabitants between 1636 and 1641. Among those responsible were Roger Ludlow and George Phelps, Windsor's commissioners in Connecticut's provisional government, the minister, church elders, and the constable. According to Thistlethwaite, most home lots ranged between 10 and 13 acres. Ludlow, however, granted himself a home lot of 122 acres and approved grants of 30 acres to woodworker Edward Griswold, 52 acres to Thomas Stoughton, and 45 acres (along with an additional 360 acres on the east side of the Connecticut River) to Francis Stiles. Allotments of other types of land—meadow and upland for corn and hay, marsh for pasture, and woodlots—varied widely. The top 10 percent of families received 37 percent of the total allotted land, and the top 25 percent of families received 57½ percent of the total allotted land. The bottom quarter consisted of nineteen families who received less than 5 percent of the town's land, averaging 42 acres each. Most of Windsor's woodworkers were in the top 50 percent wealth bracket and received relatively generous land grants. Many of these craftsmen also received subsequent grants from the town in compensation for work contracts.[88]

Windsor's first tax, taken in 1663, indicates that the town's woodworkers attained financial success disproportionate to that of most residents. Twenty-four percent (36) of the 150 assessed estates belonged to woodworkers, yet these same estates represented 32 percent of the town's total wealth. This trend continued in subsequent taxes. In 1676 woodworkers' estates accounted for 31 percent (58) of those assessed and 42 percent of the town's total wealth. Through land-ownership, town contracts, and the skillful practice of their trade, Windsor's craftsmen amassed enough wealth to equip and sustain their shops, employ apprentices and journeymen, and establish profitable relationships in the public and private arenas. This geographic and economic stability set the town's immigrant-generation woodworkers apart from most of their peers in Hartford, Wethersfield, and Middletown and ensured the survival of multigenerational shop traditions.

When Ludlow helped establish Windsor's government, he must have recalled the importance of the woodworkers in leading the original Dorchester group and building its settlement. He clearly considered artisans like John Moore I, Benjamin Newberry, William Gaylord, George Phelps, John Drake, Thomas Stoughton, and Matthew Grant as "Mechanicks . . . of the more sufficiency" and endeavored to secure a place for them in town government. Ludlow may also have derived satisfaction from the knowledge that such inclusive policies set Windsor apart from communities dominated by East Anglians. Whereas members of the merchant elite controlled town government in Hartford, a mix of merchant-landowners, yeomen, and craftsmen governed Windsor. Between 1640 and 1655 seventeen (42 percent) of the thirty-six men elected to town office in Windsor were woodworkers; between 1655 and 1670, that percentage increased to 55 percent (thirty-one of fifty-five); and between 1670 and 1685, the percentage totaled 61 (forty-four of seventy-two). Of the twenty men elected as selectmen between 1655 and 1670, eleven out of twenty (55 percent) were woodworkers, a number that jumped to fourteen out of twenty (70 percent) between 1671 and 1685. Serving concurrent two-year terms of office as the town's governing committee, the five biannually elected selectmen who took office between 1650 and 1680 included eighteen woodworkers, seven of whom served between four and fourteen terms of office. These seven repeat selectmen—woodworkers Matthew Grant, William Gaylord, Edward Griswold, John Moore I, Benjamin Newberry, Jacob Drake, and Thomas Stoughton—were involved in the community on several fronts. They served in the church and military and were kin to, as well as masters of, numerous other woodworkers. Their service as selectmen confirmed and advanced their status as craftsmen, enabling them to wield both political and artistic influence that reached far beyond the town's borders.

Windsor's townspeople obviously valued the expertise that woodworking selectmen brought to bear on public building projects such as construction of the meetinghouse in the 1660s. At the same time, these selectmen profited from overseeing the distribution of land, awarding town construction and repair contracts, and formulating policies regarding access to and use of land and timber on the town commons. In his service as a selectman from 1653 until 1674 and as moderator of the selectmen from 1660 to 1674, John Moore I exemplified the woodworker-as-officeholder. During his tenure, he received numerous town contracts and land grants awarded by the governing board of which he was the elected leader.

Comparison of timber regulation in Hartford and Windsor illustrates differences between the woodworking trades in the two communities and illuminates the moderating influence that woodworking selectmen in the latter town exerted on its social economy. On December 31, 1661, the selectmen of Windsor passed an act for preserving the "Timber and candelwod in our Comones wherein we have been Injured by some of Hartford by pillaging our commons." They agreed to fine anyone who crossed the town's border to take timber and empowered four men—all woodworkers—to detain and prosecute thieves, but imposed no limit on the amount or type of wood Windsor artisans could take from the town commons.[89]

In contrast, Hartford, Wethersfield, and Middletown merchants depended on access to timber to carry out their trading activities, including the shipping of unassembled white oak staves to the Caribbean for barreling rum and to Portugal and Spain for producing and casking Madeira. Those involved in the textile trade required barrels in which to pack raw wool and timber to construct the pale-and-five-rail fences needed to enclose their flocks. Serving the interests of the merchants, the selectmen of Hartford, Wethersfield, and Middletown restricted the use of white oak to cooperage and fencing. These officials were obviously more concerned with wood use by local inhabitants than with outside timber poachers. On February 6, 1654, the selectmen of Middletown ordered that "no man Should fell any timber within the bounds of the plantation for his own use except those who shall ffully work up such timber they got into Casks or pales or such like." As oak began to disappear from the commons and woodlots of Hartford, Wethersfield, and Middletown, woodworkers from those towns started to encroach on Windsor's woodlands. Starting in the 1660s Windsor's selectmen reacted with yearly regulations aimed at curbing timber theft.[90]

With little land of their own and no authority to control the allocation of timber, woodworkers in Hartford, Middletown, and Wethersfield resorted to desperate actions to procure resources for their trade. On January 1, 1660, Hartford woodworker Robert Sanford (1615–1676) petitioned the townsmen of Windsor to gather timber for two hundred rails and attendant pales for fencing. In exchange, he offered to identify and detain any of his fellow Hartford woodworkers who trespassed Windsor's bounds in search of timber. As Sanford's appeal suggests, the lives and careers of woodworkers in Hartford, Middletown, and Wethersfield differed significantly from those of their counterparts in Windsor. Hartford woodworker William Clark (1609–1681), who hailed from Great Bromley, Essex, received a contract to construct pillars and pews for the town meetinghouse in March 1650 and later did work that required considerable sophistication and skill; however, he achieved less financial success than Windsor woodworkers engaged in similar work. Clark's fulfillment of these contracts apparently did little to elevate his position in the community, and for several years he and his family had to rely on the town dole to subsist.[91]

Reverend White's careful recruitment of "Mechanicks . . . of the more sufficiency," Windsor's land distribution policies, and the town's willingness to give artisans a role in local government encouraged many of the community's twenty-seven immigrant-generation woodworkers to establish shops and lay the groundwork for craft traditions that would endure for decades. The longevity of each tradition was largely determined by practitioners' participation in the town's religious, military, and civil affairs and intermarriage with members of other woodworking families. Windsor residents witnessed the early disappearance of shop traditions established by such craftsmen as Thomas Barber Sr. and William Buell, neither of whom was involved in town affairs to any significant degree. The children of these two craftsmen moved to newly established settlements and became involved in building the infrastructure of their communities, yet prevailing tastes and social economies impelled them to adopt styles different from those they had learned from their fathers. As woodworkers such as John Moore I, the Drake brothers, and Thomas Stoughton became embedded in their communities, they solidified their positions as style brokers within a region-wide metacommunity of interrelated woodworkers.

Intermarriage provided woodworkers with a web of advantageous connections. It enabled them to gain political allies, secure land and timber resources, share town contracts, and create a network of support that helped them better adjudicate disputes and work toward resolution of court cases in which they were litigants. Eventually, nearly all of Windsor's early woodworkers became kin: nearly half (96 out of 205) married either the sister or daughter of another woodworker; and 71 percent of the sons of first-generation woodworkers married daughters of woodworkers.

As exemplified by Daniel White, later generations of Windsor woodworkers appear to have used motifs emblematic of family identity and, perhaps more significant for their generation, family history in the Connecticut River Valley. He and other woodworkers active at the turn of the eighteenth century made furniture in an older style redolent of nostalgia for a bygone era that was marked, above all, by Puritan religious conviction. Perhaps it was strains of this same nostalgia that carried over into Timothy Dwight's idyllic assessment of the Connecticut River Valley, its inhabitants, their houses and furniture, and what he interpreted as their pious, democratic politics that the region's woodworkers had helped to develop more than a century before.

1. A Dutch trading post known as the House of Good Hope was established in the early 1620s. Native Americans on the east side of the Connecticut River included the Podunks and on the west side the Poquonocks, Saukiogs, Tunxis (see www.members.tripod.com/SCPickens/windsor.html). Henry Stiles, *The History and Genealogies of Ancient Windsor, Connecticut,* 2 vols. (Hartford, Conn.: Case, Lockwood and Brainard Co., 1891), 1: 103–21. Timothy Dwight, *Travels in New England and New York* (1821–22; reprint, Cambridge, Mass.: Belknap Press, Harvard University Press, 1969). Robert Blair St. George, "Artifacts of Regional Consciousness in the Connecticut River Valley, 1700–1780," in *The Great River: Art and Society of the Connecticut River Valley, 1635–1820,* edited by Gerald W. R. Ward and William N. Hosley (Hartford, Conn.: Wadsworth Atheneum, 1985), p. 37. In an essay entitled "Timothy Dwight: Classroom Issues and Strategies," Carla Mulford observed that Dwight "attempted to find a way to model or represent a civic culture that the populace could only pretend to imitate" (www.georgetown.edu/faculty/bassr/heath/syllabuild/iguide/dwight.html). Historian Kevin Sweeney noted that "the diversity, the turbulence, and the special character of the early history of the Connecticut River Valley are often overlooked," in "From Wilderness to Arcadian Vale: Material Life in the Connecticut River Valley, 1635–1760," in *The Great River,* pp. 17, 19, 21. According to Sweeney, 70–80 percent of residents in most towns were offspring of original settlers.

2. St. George, "Artifacts of Regional Consciousness," pp. 29–39.

3. Patricia E. Kane, "The Seventeenth-Century Furniture of the Connecticut River Valley: The Hadley Chest Reappraised," in *Arts of the Anglo-American Community in the Seventeenth Century,* edited by Ian M. G. Quimby (Charlottesville: University Press of Virginia, 1975); Patricia E. Kane, "The Joiners of Seventeenth Century Hartford County," *Connecticut Historical Society Bulletin* 35, no. 3 (July 1970); Philip Zea, "The Fruits of Oligarchy: Patronage and the Hadley Chest Tradition in Western Massachusetts," in *New England Furniture: Essays in Memory of Benno M. Forman* (Boston: Society for the Preservation of New England Antiquities, 1987); Philip Zea and Susan L. Flynt, *Hadley Chests* (Deerfield, Mass.: Pocumtuck Valley Memorial Association, 1992); Susan Prendergast Schoelwer, "Connecticut Sunflower Furniture: A Familiar Form Reconsidered," *Yale University Art Gallery Bulletin* (Spring 1989); and Kevin M. Sweeney, "Furniture and the Domestic Environment in Wethersfield, Connecticut, 1639–1800," in *Material Life in America, 1600–1860,* edited by Robert Blair St. George (Boston: Northeastern University Press, 1988).

4. Edward S. Cooke Jr., *Making Furniture in Preindustrial America* (Baltimore: Johns Hopkins University Press, 1996).

5. Roger Clap, *Roger Clap's Memoirs, With an Account of the Voyage of the Mary and John, 1630* (1731; reprint, Seattle; Pigott-Washington Printing Co., 1929); Frank Thistlethwaite, *Dorset Pilgrims: The Story of West County Pilgrims Who Went to New England in the Seventeenth Century* (Interlaken, N.Y.: Heart of the Lakes Publishing, 1993), pp. 55–56. Reverend White recruited from his own family, including Roger Ludlow, a lawyer, member of the minor gentry, and cousin of White's wife, Mary Cogan; children of his brother-in-law Reverend John Terry (rector of Stockton, Wiltshire); and the son and nephew of another brother-in-law, Reverend William Cooke, vicar of Crediton, Devonshire. White also turned to former Oxford classmates and fellow ministers. Reverend William Gillet, rector of nearby Chafcombe, sent two of his sons; and Reverend Edward Clarke, vicar of Taunton, sent a relative, Reverend Walter Newburgh, rector of Simonsbury, and Reverend John Stoughton, rector of St. Mary, Aldermanbury, London, who married Newburgh's widow. Reverend Stoughton convinced his two sons, Israel Stoughton and William Stoughton, to join the group immigrating to Massachusetts.

6. Thistlethwaite, *Dorset Pilgrims,* p. 94. Thirty families and twenty bachelors totaling 140 men, women, and children sailed on the *Mary and John*. They changed the name of their settlement to Dorchester in honor of "the patriarch of Dorchester," Reverend White.

7. Members of the Plymouth group formally complained first to Plymouth officials then to leaders of the Massachusetts Bay Colony, of the many "injuries offered them . . . by those of Dorchester, in taking away their land" (*The Journal of John Winthrop, 1630–1649,* edited by Richard S. Dunn, James Savage, and Laetitia Yeandle [Cambridge, Mass.: Belknap Press, 1996], pp. 35–37).

8. Hartford County Probate Records (hereafter HCPR), vol. 5, pp. 227–30, Connecticut State Library (hereafter CSL), History and Genealogy Unit (hereafter HGU), Hartford. Stiles, *History and Genealogies of Ancient Windsor,* 2: 29.

9. Randle Holme, *The Academy of Armory, or, A Storehouse of Armory and Blazon* (Chester,

Eng.: By the author, 1688), pp. 86, 127. Holme noted that crowns of oak leaves were "given to them who had well deserved of the publick Estate, and managed Matters well for the conservations of their civil Affairs." King Charles I reinforced these cultural associations when he hid from Oliver Cromwell in an oak tree, famously dubbed the "royal oak," after the latter defeated him in the Battle of Worcester in 1651. At a local level, these associations were reinforced at a meeting in Hartford between Sir Edmund Andros, whom King Charles II had appointed governor of New England and New York, and outgoing Connecticut governor Robert Treat. Treat and other officials were expected to surrender Connecticut's colonial charter, but Captain Joseph Wadsworth removed the document and reputedly hid it in a nearby oak tree, thereafter known as the "charter oak." Matthew Grant Diary (hereafter MGD), typescript transcription by Jessie A. Parsons, p. 29, CSL, HGU. Hooker based his sermon on one that English Puritan divine Richard Sibbes (1577–1635) included in his 1630 religious tract, *The Bruised Reed and Smoking Flax*.

10. Philip Ayres, *Mythologia ethica, or, Three centuries of Æsopian fables in English* (London: Printed for Thomas Hawkins, 1689).

11. Robert F. Trent, "The Concept of Mannerism," in *New England Begins,* edited by Jonathan Fairbanks and Robert F. Trent, 3 vols. (Boston: Museum of Fine Arts, 1982), 3: 368–79. Arthur Lotz, *Bibliographie der Modelbücher: beschreibendes Verzeichnis der Stick- und Spitzenmusterbücher des 16. und 17. Jahrhunderts* (Stuttgart: A. Hiersemann, 1963). Laurel Thatcher Ulrich, "Furniture as Social Property: Gender, Property, and Memory in the Decorative Arts," in *American Furniture,* edited by Luke Beckerdite and William N. Hosley (Hanover, N.H.: University Press of New England for the Chipstone Foundation, 1995), pp. 39–69.

12. Windsor settler Nicholas Hoyt is believed to have passed this chest to his son David (1651–1704), who brought it with him and his family to Deerfield, Massachusetts. David was killed in the 1704, when a coalition of Native Americans and their French allies from Canada raided the town, burned much of the settlement, and took captives. The chest survived and continued to descend in the Hoyt family until Catherine W. Hoyt donated it to Memorial Hall, Pocumtuck Valley Memorial Association, in 1886. Suzanne L. Flynt, Susan McGowan, and Amelia F. Miller, *Gathered and Preserved, Memorial Hall, Deerfield, Massachusetts* (Deerfield, Mass.: Pocumtuck Valley Memorial Association, 1991), p. 22, cat. no. 26.

13. One of two related chests is in the Wallace Nutting collection at the Wadsworth Atheneum (see Wallace Nutting, *Furniture Treasury,* 2 vols. [Framingham, Mass.: Old America Co., 1928], 1: fig. 7). Its structure is consistent with that of the Hoyt and Phelps chests, and its decoration features several motifs present on the Hoyt chest. The Atheneum example appears to be from the second generation of this shop tradition. Its carving is less detailed and less elaborate than that on the Hoyt chest, and the trefoil design on the face of the front stiles is simplified like that on the Phelps chest. The top rail of the Atheneum chest has gouge-cut arcades, like that on the Hoyt chest; however, the carved design on the former chest lacks the angled convex rectangles present on the latter. A nearly identical chain motif is carved on the face of the façade muntins of both chests. Fine courses of step-groove-half-round molding are on the inner edges of the front stiles, the lower edge of the top front rail, and the sides of the front muntins of the Atheneum chest. This same molding appears on the side rails and till lid of the Phelps chest. The other related chest, which belonged to William G. Irving, of Washington, D.C. (ibid., fig. 15), appears to be the latest example. Its carving is simplified and schematized.

14. The men employed by Stiles are identified on a March 16, 1635, passenger list for the party's ship, the *Christian de London,* in the Augmentation Office of the Rolls Court in Westminster Hall: Thomas Basset, Thomas Stiles, Thomas Barber, John Dyer, John Harris, James Horwood, John Reeves, Thomas Soulfoot, James Busket, Thomas Cooper, Edward Preston, John Cribb, George Chappell, Robert Robinson, Edward Patteson, Francis Marshell, Rich Heyley, Thomas Halford, Thomas Haukseworth, John Stiles, Henry Stiles, Jane Worden, Joan Stiles, Henry Stiles (child), John Stiles (child), and Rachell Stiles (James Savage, "Gleanings for New England History," *Collection of the Massachusetts Historical Society* [Boston: Massachusetts Historical Society, 1843], 8: 252), February 28, 1639, Windsor Land Records (hereafter WLR), 1: 90, Office of the Town Clerk (hereafter OTC), Windsor Town Hall (hereafter WTH), Windsor, Conn. Sir Richard Saltonstall to John Winthrop Jr., February 27, 1635/36: "Good mr. Winthrop, being credibly informed that there has bene some abuse and Injury done me by Mr. Ludlow and others of Dorchester who would not suffer Francis Styles and his men to Impayle grounds wheare I Appoynt them at Connecticute, although both by

patent which I took above 4 yeares since and prepossion. Dorchester men, being then unsettled and seeking up river above the falls for a place to plant upon but finding none better to their liking, they speedily came back againe and discharged my worke men, Casting lots upon the place where he was purposed to begin his worke, notwithstanding he often told them what great charge I had bene at In sending him and soe many men to prepare a house against my coming, and inclose grounds for my cattle, and how the damage would fall heavy upon thos that thus hindered me, whom Francis Styles Conceived to have best right to make choice of any place there. Notwithstanding, they resisted him, slighting me with many unbeseeming words such as he was not willing to relate to me, but Justifie upon my oath before authority when called to itt" (*Saltonstall Papers, 1607–1815: Selected and Edited and with Biographies of Ten Members of the Saltonstall Family in Six Generations,* edited by Robert E. Moody, 2 vols. [Boston: Massachusetts Historical Society, 1972–1974], 1: 124–25).

15. On March 28, 1637, the newly formed Connecticut General Court ordered that "mr ffraunces Stiles shall teach Geo. ~~Reeves~~ Chapple Tho: Coopr Tho: barber his servants in the trade of a Carpenter accordinge to his *p*mise for there service of their terme behinde 4 dayes in a weeke onelie to sawe & slitt their owne worke & that they are to frame themselves w^{t}h their owne hands to gether w^{t}h himselfe or some othe mr workman the tyme to begin for *p*formance of this order 14 dayes hence w^{t}hout faile." Public Records of the Colony of Connecticut (hereafter PRCC), 1: 4 (March 28, 1637), 6 (Nov. 1, 1636), 33 (Sept. 5, 1639), 66 (Sept. 2, 1641), 76 (Dec. 9, 1641), 71 (May 11, 1642), CSL, HGU. Records of the Particular Court (hereafter RPC), 1: 5 (Oct. 3, 1639 and Sept. 5, 1641), 41 (June 29, 1646), 47 (May 29, 1647), CSL, HGU.

16. In late March 1637 Thomas Stiles, Thomas Barber Sr., John Dyer, and Edward Preston were members of troops that Captain John Mason led in an attack on the Pequots at Fort Mystic (John Mason, *A Brief History of the Pequot War* [New York: Readex Microprint Corporation, 1966], pp. 8, 22). Between 1635 and 1642 Thomas Cooper was tried in twelve separate misdemeanor cases, lost each, and received monetary fines. In 1643 he accepted a land grant in Springfield, and in 1645 he received the contract as head carpenter to build that town's meetinghouse (PRCC, 1: 102, 127, 130, 133; 2: 14, 15, 523. Springfield Town Records, 1: 3, 37; City Clerk's Office; Springfield City Hall, Springfield, Mass. WLR, 1: 47). In 1643 Thomas Basset lost a protracted three-year court battle with his neighbor over property boundaries and moved to Saybrook, Connecticut (RPC, 1: 25). Two years later Edward Preston moved to New London after losing a series of nuisance lawsuits brought by his neighbors (PRCC, 1: 102, 133; RPC, 1: 25). In 1647 Francis Stiles moved to Stratford, Connecticut, while bringing suits and countersuits against Saltonstall's agents, the Massachusetts Bay Colony, and the Connecticut Colony (RPC, 1: 47, May 24, 1647). Before 1648 Thomas Stiles moved to Long Island. John Stiles died in 1648. George Chappel, also subject to heavy fines resulting from nuisance lawsuits, was listed as one of New London's freemen in 1669 (RPC, 1: 25, 36, 38, 39, 42, 43, 44, 47, 48, 50, 51, 52, 54, 58, 62, 63, 71, 82, 121, 130, 145, 166; 2: 29; PRCC 2: 523). In 1649 Henry Stiles was "accidentally" shot and died two years later (RPC, 2: 29). John Dyer moved to New London in 1651 (PRCC, 1: 218).

17. "6th: Decemb^{r}: *1649* S^{r}geant Barber for his disorderly Striking Leiftenant Cooke is Aiudged to Lay downe his place And is fined to the Country *5£* A Perticular Courte in Hartford 28th of march *1650*. This Courte frees Tho: Barber from hi fyne of *5£* it appearing to them that hee is affected with his great Evill and rash passionate Carriage in striking the Lieftennant" (RPC, 1: 210; 2: 5). John Pynchon Account Books, 1652–1702 (hereafter JPAB), 2: 38, 126, Connecticut Valley Historical Museum (hereafter CVHM), Springfield, Mass. William Pynchon Account Book (hereafter WPAB), 1: 26, 106, CVHM. *Northampton Town Records* (hereafter NTR), 1: 26, City Hall, Office of the City Clerk, Northampton, Mass. RPC, 2: 184.

18. RPC, 2: 187–88.

19. Simsbury Town Record (hereafter SimTR), bk. 1, pp. 3, 14, 15, 27; bk. 2½, pp. 5, 7, 8, 178, Office of Town Clerk, Simsbury Town Hall, Simsbury, Conn. PRCC, 4: 25, HCPR, p. 469.

20. HCPR, p. 469.

21. The authors thank textile historian Edward Maeder for information on the use of waxed linen.

22. HCPR, 1712.

23. Dr. Wales Buel, a direct descendant of William Buell, donated this box to the Oneida County Historical Society, Oneida, New York. The two related boxes are in the collections of the Metropolitan Museum of Art and the Yale University Art Gallery.

24. Albert Welles, *History of the Buell Family in England, from the Remotest Times Ascertainable from Our Ancient Histories, and in America, from Town, Parish, Church and Family Records* (New York: Society Library, 1881), pp. 20–21; Windsor Town Acts (hereafter WTA), 1: 8, 43; 2: 1, 4, 18, OTC, WTH. Buell received work from the town between 1652 and 1679. Windsor Grand List (hereafter WGL), pp. 52, 58, OTC, WTH. Samuel worked with his father on the Springfield meetinghouse, receiving credit in John Pynchon's account books for helping "Old Goodman Buell" with "work about the galleries" and other tasks. JPAB, 2: 38, 126, 74, 365.

25. See, for example, JPAB, June 25, 1659, 2: 38. RPC, 1: 76.

26. HCPR, reel no. 483.

27. SimTR, bk. 2½, p. 85.

28. Nutting, *Furniture Treasury*, 1: fig. 158. Luke Vincent Lockwood, *Colonial Furniture in America*, 2 vols. (New York: Castle Books, 1921), 1: 27, fig. 10.

29. The top rail features bilaterally symmetric lunettes containing opposing, angled, convex, ovoid forms. Unlike the rosettes, this motif is not unique to the Buell shop. Joined chests produced by Braintree, Massachusetts, woodworker William Savell, who worked in a Saffron-Waldon, County Essex, tradition, have motifs of similar design and execution on their top rails. See Peter Follansbee and John D. Alexander, "Seventeenth-Century Joinery from Braintree, Massachusetts: The Savell Shop Tradition," in *American Furniture*, edited by Luke Beckerdite (Hanover, N.H.: University Press of New England for the Chipstone Foundation, 1996), pp. 81–105.

30. Family tradition maintained that Windsor resident Anne Millington, daughter of Thomas Millington and Anne Russell, first owned this chest and brought it to Fairfield, Connecticut, when she married Gershom Lockwood (1643–1719) (Lockwood, *Colonial Furniture in America*, 1: 26–27, fig. 10; Frederic Augustus Holden and E. Dunbar Lockwood, *Descendants of Robert Lockwood: Colonial and Revolutionary History of the Lockwood Family in America from A.D. 1630* [Philadelphia: By the family, 1889], p. 16). On May 11, 1668, Anne Millington's brother John received a contract from the town of Windsor to maintain the ferry over the Connecticut River (WTA, 2: 17–18).

31. Thistlethwaite, *Dorset Pilgrims*, p. 49. Stiles, *The History and Genealogies of Ancient Windsor*, 1: 165, 2: 647–48. Henry Ensign Rockwell, *The Rockwell Family in America* (Boston: Rockwell & Church, 1873), p. 244. HCPR, p. 596. John Rockwell I and William Phelps appear to have been the only coopers active in Windsor between 1635 and 1645. Seven coopers worked there between 1646 and 1655, eleven between 1656 and 1665, and twenty-one between 1666 and 1675.

32. William Rockwell's daughter Ruth (1633–1683) married Christopher Huntington (b. 1624), brother of Windsor woodworker Thomas Huntington (1626–1685). He moved to eastern Connecticut by 1660 (WTA, 1: 35).

33. Thistlethwaite, *Dorset Pilgrims*, pp. 147, 167.

34. John Rockwell II served the town as perambulator (maintained boundaries) for one term. Inventory of John Rockwell II, HCPR, 1673: "In copres [cooper's] timber, in copres tooles of several kinds." Inventory of John Rockwell III, HCPR, 1746.

35. Windsor's five selectmen often asked Rockwell to provide rope for use in the town's gates and ferryboat and to perform minor carpentry work. On October 31, 1668, he received a credit of 13s.9p. for making a rope for the Connecticut River ferryboat, run by John Bissell (WTA, 2: 12). Three months later, the selectmen, represented by Matthew Grant, requested that Samuel Sr. repair the boat (ibid., p. 14). Matthew Grant, Church Record (hereafter MGCR), p. 3, Connecticut Historical Society (hereafter CHS), Hartford. Samuel Rockwell Sr. served as way warden in 1671 and 1695, fence viewer in 1674, bounds goer in 1676, and assessor in 1700. Assessed at £74 in 1676, Samuel Rockwell's personal wealth was only slightly above the £70 mean held by Windsor's 187 taxable inhabitants (WGL, pp. 39–41).

36. Samuel Rockwell Account Book (hereafter SRAB), CHS.

37. Ibid., pp. 23, 47, 56, 102. Rockwell paid Grant £3.12 for felling and hewing timber, six and a half days labor constructing the house frame, and one day erecting it. Six additional days were dedicated to finish work including shaping and applying exterior brackets, shingling, and the fabrication and installation of flooring and doors (pp. 19, 56). In 1696 John Moore III sold Rockwell three taps and faucets for five pence each. Three years later John Moore III bought nine feet of oak plank from Rockwell for nine shillings. In 1705 Rockwell applied rims to nine wheels made by John Moore II On January 21, 1697, Rockwell credited John Moore II 5s.6p. for two chairs (p. 73).

38. Ibid., pp. 50, 6. Loomis was the brother-in-law of Rockwell's sister Mary (1662–1738),

and Ellsworth was the brother-in-law of Rockwell's sister-in-law Martha Gaylord (1659–1721). Ibid., pp. 11, 47, 80, 121. An example of Rockwell's later production is the bedstead he made for Jonathan Bissell (p. 102).

39. Rockwell's purchase of Grant's share is recorded in ibid., p. 5. In November 1700 Samuel Grant Jr. paid Rockwell sixteen shillings for 450 feet of boards. That same month, Thomas Ellsworth paid Rockwell sixteen shillings for 200 feet of slitwork (ibid., p. 55). HCPR, 1725. Stiles, *History and Genealogies of Ancient Windsor,* 1: 578, 873; 2: 649, 647–48.

40. Irving W. Lyon, "Notebook," 1: 92, Winterthur Library, Winterthur Museum, Winterthur, Delaware. Hartford County Vital Records, CSL, HGU.

41. Windsor woodworkers who probably were trained in the Moore shop tradition include Samuel Bancroft (1667–1742), Josiah Barber (1653–1729), Benjamin Bissell (1669–1698), David Bissell (1681–1733), Ebenezer Bissell (1685–1750), Joseph Bissell (1663–1689), Joseph Bissell (1663–1713), Nathaniel Bissell (1640–1713), Thomas Bissell (1628–1689), Nathaniel Gaylord (1656–1720), Anthony Hoskins (1633–1706), Daniel Loomis (1656–1740), Daniel Loomis (1682–1754), David Loomis (1694–1752), Nathaniel Loomis Jr. (1656–1733), Andrew Moore (1649–1719), John Moore II (1645–1718), John Moore III (1665–1752), John Moore (1694–1787), Josiah Moore (1679–1751), Thomas Moore (1667–1735), and Thomas Moore (1678–1754). A chest made and owned by third-generation Moore shop woodworker Nathaniel Gaylord has a drawer with one, large half-dovetail joining each of the sides to the front. The drawer runs on its bottom. The drawer of another Moore shop chest that probably predates the Gaylord example runs on supports set into grooves cut in the drawer sides. The sides of this drawer are nailed into rabbets in the edges of the drawer front.

42. Variations in the size and shape of these punches serve as further evidence of diverse tool kits used by multiple craftsmen in executing the ornament of these objects.

43. The Drake shop box initialed "EB" (see fig. 49) also features a similar, though smaller, notch cut in the upper left interior corner of its backboard.

44. In the early seventeenth century, a fleet of fifteen to twenty fishing barques sailed from Southwold's harbor annually to take part in the Icelandic fishing industry (Evan T. Jones, "England's Icelandic Fishery in the Early Modern Period," in *England's Sea Fisheries: The Commercial Fisheries of England and Wales since 1300,* edited by David Starkey et al. [London: Chatham Publishing, 2003], pp. 105–10). John Moore received an initial land grant in Windsor of six acres and thirty rods "bounded north by Thomas moore" (WLR, 1: 84). Family tradition and genealogy indicate that John Moore immigrated with his father, Thomas, who died in 1645 (Stiles, *History and Genealogies of Ancient Windsor,* 2: 501). Thomas Moore and his children may have been related to Thomas Moore Sr. (ca. 1580–1636). The elder Moore was associated with the nonconformist ministry of Reverend John Youngs in Southwold. He emigrated with his family to Salem, Massachusetts, in the 1630s (*The Journal of John Winthrop,* p. 1). Situated next to the lot of John Brancor, Windsor's schoolmaster, Thomas Moore's home lot consisted of a six-acre thirty-rod parcel (WLR, 1: 83).

45. Thistlethwaite, *Dorset Pilgrims,* p. 138. February 24, 1640, WLR, 1: 84. In 1665 Matthew Grant recorded John Moore as one of only nineteen fully covenanted members of the Dorchester Church still living in Windsor: "A List of those members of the church that were so in Dorchester and came up here with Mr. Wharam and still are of us. of men John Moor" (MGCR, p. 9).

46. At least two other woodworking traditions with roots in Suffolk County, England, were active in seventeenth-century New England; John Thurston (1607–1685) practiced a Wrentham, Suffolk, tradition in Dedham and Medfield, Massachusetts, and Thomas Mulliner (d. after 1658) worked in an Ipswich, Suffolk, tradition in New Haven, Connecticut, and Southold, Long Island. Furniture attributed to both men features a shallow, foliate carving style similar in form and execution to that associated with John Moore. A chest that descended in the Fairbanks family of Dedham (Fairbanks House Museum) probably represents the work of Thurston's principal apprentice, John Houghton (1624–1684). It has a center panel with abstract, tulip-form flower heads linked with a flowing vine. The central panels of a chest with drawer attributed to Mulliner have relief carving featuring a central vertical stem surmounted by a large flower head and abstract foliate forms extending from the sides. Thomas Osborne reputedly brought the chest from New Haven to Easthampton, Long Island, before 1650 (Patricia Kane, *Furniture of the New Haven Colony: The Seventeenth-Century Style* [New Haven, Conn.: New Haven Colony Historical Society, 1973], pp. 10–11, fig. 1). All of the aforementioned work demonstrates a Suffolk predilection toward abstract vegetal and foliate relief carving.

47. In 1666 Matthew Grant recorded that John Moore's wife was one of seven fully covenanted female members of John Warham's church in Dorchester who continued in Windsor (MGCR, p. 9). Abigail's mother, Mary Hull, was the sister of Josiah Hull, who was married to Joseph Loomis's daughter Elizabeth. Mary's sister married Samuel Gaylord, brother of William Gaylord. In subsequent years, members of both the Gaylord and Loomis families became active members of John Moore's shop tradition. In 1669 Moore and Newberry received eighteen pounds from the town for framing and raising a house for Job Drake (WTA, 2: 9). In his capacity as townsman, Newberry was empowered to negotiate with Moore for the contract to build the third ferryboat in 1674. Newberry apparently had to "grease the wheel" to make the contract go. On February 11, 1674, he paid 10s."for liquer what was used to agree about ye fery boote" (WTA, 2: 28). Moore's contract for the hafts and pikes is in WTA, 2: 9 (March 15, 1667), 39 (July 13, 1676).

48. The range of Moore's documented work is suggested in WTA, 2: 5 (March 15, 1667), 7 (July 3, 1667), 8 (September 8 and 30, 1667), 9 (July 1667), 15 (Feb. 15, 1669), 28 (Feb. 11, 1674), 32 (March 27, 1674); and WGL, p. 20 (Jan. 23, 1675). In 1669 Moore received 2s.6p. for making three oars (WTA, 2: 15). In 1667 he contracted to build a second ferryboat for the town: "Also the day above said the townes men have agreed with deacon moore to make a new fery boat for the fery of good chestnut timber if it can be got to be fitted for calking by the middle of febuery nixt and he is to be paid in paye out of the towne rat it must be as much as to bigness in lenght and breadth as the ould" (WTA, 2: 7). That same year, he received £6.4 for building and raising a schoolhouse frame (with his sons) for John Witchfield (WTA, 2: 6). Moore's work on the meetinghouse is in WTA, 2: 2. Moore received £10.3 for overseeing construction of a third ferryboat. His second son Andrew and brother-in-law Nathaniel Pinney performed the work (WGL, p. 20). Evidence of Moore's monopolies can be found in WTA, 2: 6, 8, 9, 10. In 1675 Hartford merchant John Talcott paid Moore six shillings for a spinning wheel, eight shillings for a pair of cart wheels, and £1.6 for a cradle. This reference to a cradle, near the end of Moore's life, is the only documentary evidence of his furniture production ("The Account Book of John Talcott, 1672–1712" [hereafter ABJT], p. 42c, CSL, HGU).

49. Early Windsor Records, p. 110, CHS. References to Moore's reelection as townsman are in WTA, 1: 1, 17, 21, 48; 2: 28, 44, 77. For Newberry's election and reelection, see WTA, 1: 1, 17, 21, 48; 2: 28, 44, 77. For more on Moore's church service, see MGCR, pp. 10, 96–97. Moore died in September 1677.

50. WTA, 2: 14. PRCC, Early General Records (hereafter EGR), 2: 97, 168, 185. For the quote pertaining to John Moore I's and Newberry's duties, see PRCC, 2: 168 (May 9, 1672). On October 8, 1668, both men and Simon Wolcott petitioned the court to establish a separate and distinct plantation at Massaco. Moore and Newberry were appointed to survey and lay out Job Drake's lands in Massaco in 1669 (PRCC, 2: 97), WTA, 2: 15.

51. Although no documentation conclusively identifies John Bissell as a woodworker, family connections strongly suggest that he trained with John Drake Sr. In seventeenth-century New England, fourteen was the customary age for a boy to begin his woodworking apprenticeship. HCPR, p. 469.

52. WLR, 1: 107 (Dec. 8, 1669); SimTR, 1: 5 (Jan. 28, 1674); WTA, 2: 57 (Dec. 30, 1687). After 1668 Windsor residents obtained most of their sawn timber from the sawmill on the east side of the river. Before that, they relied on pit-sawing. As late as 1664 Samuel Buell and John Maudsley received payment for "carting of tember out of ye woods and to ye pit and from the pit to ye mettinghowse" (WTA, 2: 2 [Dec. 8, 1664]).

53. John Moore I's two sons occupied subordinate positions in their father's shop during his lifetime. On April 1, 1667, the elder Moore received 8s.7p. for work done by them (WTA, 2: 6), and on March 13, 1669, John Moore I received £5.4 for his sons' labor in finishing John Witchfield's house (WTA, 2: 9). John I and Benjamin Newberry had framed and raised Witchfield's house (ibid.). Like their father, the Moore brothers were ship carpenters. In 1674 Andrew Moore and his uncle Nathaniel Pinney each received £3.10.8 for constructing Windsor's third ferryboat. John Moore I received £10.0.3 for supervising the project (WGL, p. 20). The Moore family appears to have had a monopoly on the construction, maintenance, and outfitting of the town's ferryboats. On November 23, 1679, John Moore II received seven shillings for repairs to the ferryboat (WGL, p. 99). John II also worked independently as a house carpenter. On January 25, 1676, he received 15s.7p. for eight days' work making repairs and improvements to the meetinghouse (WGL, p. 49). From his father, John Moore II acquired the skills and tools of a turner and wheelwright. On two occasions, the younger

Moore made sets of cart wheels for Hartford merchant John Talcott. The first set cost £1.8 and the second £1.14 (ABJT, p. 42c). For the inventory of John Moore III, see HCPR, p. 561; SRAB, p. 73. Other artisans from the Moore shop tradition made tables. The inventory of Thomas Bissell listed "Table frames unfinished" (HCPR, 1688). Like his ancestors, John Moore III also produced cart wheels and spinning wheels. Samuel Rockwell Jr. paid him 7s.6p. for a cart wheel before January 1697 and 6s.4p. for a great wheel in 1709 (SRAB, p. 73).

54. HCPR, 1706. WGL, p. 28. On July 3, 1667, John Moore paid tax on behalf of "his man: Anthony Hoskens" (WTA, 2: 7). For Barber's apprenticeship, see RPC, 1: 55, 56, 2: 187–88; WGL, p. 52. Like Thomas Bissell and John Moore II, Josiah Barber acquired the skills of a wheelwright during his apprenticeship with John Moore I. In 1682 John Talcott purchased a set of cart wheels valued at £1.11 from Barber (ABJT, p. 74c).

55. For the sawmills, see WLR, 2: 293 (Jan. 31, 1689), 362 (Feb. 17, 1696); and WTA, 2: 71 (Jan. 9, 1696). SRAB, 50.

56. For Thomas Moore's inventory, see HCPR, p. 561. Genealogical information on the Barber and Loomis families was gleaned from Donald S. Barber, *The Connecticut Barbers* (Middlefield, Conn.: McDowell Publications, 1992); and Elias Loomis, *The Descendants of Joseph Loomis* (New Haven, Conn.: Tuttle, Morehouse and Taylor, 1875). www.holcombeGenealogy.com/data/p99.htm. The authors thank Frances Gruber Safford for calling this provenance to their attention. A handwritten note on the inside of the lid of the box illustrated in figure 47 is inscribed: "This chest brought from England 1638 by Joseph Loomis who settled, lived and died at Windsor. Conn. He was an ancestor of D. P. Loomis of Unadilla to whom this chest now belongs."

57. WLR, 1: 24.

58. William Gaylord's estate was valued at £473 and was the second largest amassed by an immigrant-generation woodworker in Windsor (RPC, 2: 108). MGCR, p. 9.

59. Elderkin came to New England with the Winthrop fleet and settled in Essex, Massachusetts, by 1630. He moved to Dedham, Massachusetts, by 1641, to New London, Connecticut, by 1652, and to Norwich, Connecticut, by 1662. Elderkin's skills as a millwright and housewright were in constant demand throughout southern New England. Elderkin built a meetinghouse in New London in 1652 (Robert C. Winthrop Collection, vol. 3, doc. 258, CSL). He was working for John Winthrop in Saybrook in 1654 (*Winthrop Papers, 1498–1649,* edited by Francis J. Bremer, 6 vols. [Boston: Massachusetts Historical Society, 1929], 6: 132). Elderkin built a mill in Norwich before 1662 (PRCC, EGR, 1: 288), another mill in Hartford in 1663 (PRCC, EGR, 2: 189), and a third in Killingworth in 1671 (PRCC, EGR, 3: 30). Dated June 24, 1662, the contract transferring ownership of the mill Elderkin built with Jacob and John Drake is in PRCC, EGR, 1: 288.

60. WTA, 1: 15; HCPR, 1659. Of all the immigrant-generation woodworkers active in Windsor, Falstead, Essex, tradesman John Porter (1622–1688) amassed the largest estate (£673.2.4). Much of his wealth derived from mercantile pursuits and land speculation. In comparison, William Gaylord's estate was valued at £473, Benjamin Newberry's at £437, and John Moore I's at £295 (RPC, 2: 108; HCPR, 1688, 1677). Land values increased after conflicts with Native Americans in the region ended. Between 1663 and 1686 the average value of rated estates in Windsor jumped £32, to £98. Drake's estate was appraised before this increase.

61. For the General Court directives, see PRCC, EGR, 1: 397, 2: 97. The grants to John and Job Drake are recorded in SimTR, bk. 2½, p. 178. For Moore and Newberry's survey, see WTA, 2: 10, 15. The contract for Job Drake's house is in WTA, 2: 9.

62. The contract for the stocks is in WGL, p. 99. Job and John Drake's estates were valued at £71 and £45 respectively in 1663 (Windsor Town Rate 1663, WTA, 2: n.p.). After the Simsbury land grant in 1676, the same estates were valued at £238 and £214 (WGL, pp. 43–45). The inventories of John Drake Jr., Jacob Drake, and Job Drake are in HCPR, 1688 and 1689 (Jacob and Job).

63. John III's contract for coffins is in SimTR, 3: 19. For John Drake III's inventory, see HCPR, 1724, and SimTR, bk. 2½, p. 178: "Shop toules as followeth: beetle and wedges 4-6 a narrow ax 3, broad ax 10, hatchet 4, 2 broad chisels 4, 2 gouges 3, a great aguor 3, a tenant saw 6, hand jointer with a iron in it 3-6, joiners plow 3, round plain 1-6, stock for a brass wimbol 1, 2 drills 2, drawng knife 9, small chizel 1-6, pair of compases 1-4, iron from [illegible] saw 1-6, pair of plyers 2, 2 small fills 1, irons for a layor 6, pound of wior 5, crooked knife 1, saw 4, old broad ax 3, ads 4, narrow chizzols 3, one hamor 1-6, small tapor agur 2-6, a square 5, 2 plains 4s, a hand jointor 2-6, 5 wimbols and bits 5, 4 other bits, small gouge 1, another drawing knife 2, gouge 2-6, spook shave 2, pair of nipers 16, rasp & file 16, vice 15, grindston with a iron winch

6, a small screw 1-6, a small chest not finishts, 300 and 60 foot of boards 14-6." Evidence that Job and Joseph were woodworkers can be found in their inventories (HCPR, 1730, 1733) and SRAB, p. 94. John Higley's sons were John III (1673–1741), Brewster (1675–1760), and Samuel Higley (1687–1737). The inventories of the younger Higleys are in SimTR, bk. 2½, pp. 166, 169. Joseph Loomis III and his brother James were referred to as "carpenters" in WTA, 2: 61, 87. Job Drake Jr. and woodworker Samuel Cross (1641–1707) established a gristmill in Windsor in March 1703 (WTA, 2: 87).

64. See Victor Chinnery, *Oak Furniture: The British Tradition* (Woodbridge, Suffolk, Eng.: Baron Publishing, 1979), p. 333, pl. 11; and John T. Kirk, *American Furniture and the British Tradition to 1830* (New York: Knopf, 1982), pp. 44–82.

65. Oral tradition regarding the box indicates that it was originally made for Elizabeth Bissell. The earliest owner that can be documented with certainty was Sybil Montague (b. 1780), who married Eleazer Coles (1784–1849) in 1810 in Amherst, Massachusetts. Sybil's lineage can be traced back to Elizabeth Bissell. *A Place for Everything: Chests and Boxes in Early Colonial America* (Winterthur, Del.: Winterthur Museum, 1986), pp. 9–13, cat. no. 1. For a shop-based inquiry of Dennis's woodworking practices, see Robert Tarule, *The Artisan of Ipswich: Craftsmanship and Community in Colonial New England* (Baltimore: John Hopkins University Press, 2004).

66. Ford's land grants included a sixteen-acre home lot and two hundred acres of rich planting ground in Pine Meadow (WLR, 1: 3, 27). The relation between Mary Ford and Thomas Ford is unclear. Mary may have been Thomas's daughter and therefore Cook's stepsister. Cook moved his household to the home lot located outside the protected walls of the palisade when they married.

67. For court cases involving Cook, see RPC, EGR, 1: 55, 56, 159, 169, 170; 2: 15–17, 24, 27, 39, 43, 56, 77, 86, 110, 112, 127, 129, 131, 132, 136–39. Although the document recording Cook's commission does not survive, Windsor town records refer to him as "Lieutenant" by 1653 (WTA, 1: 15). PRCC, 2: 35. Cook received 87 of 106 votes on May 28, 1665 (WTA, 1: 24).

68. Cook received fifty acres of a larger grant given to Thomas Ford: "Lieutenant Cooke is allowed fifty acres of meadow in Massacoe this Lt Cooke owns to be his father Fords improvement." The grant specified that Ford had to settle on the land to gain title. Aaron Cooke served as his stepfather's proxy in settling on the fifty-acre parcel. When Ford failed to take up his grant, the court issued two directives: "Capt Cook is required to desist in any further Labour on the lower ffarme at Mussaco"; and "Respecting Capt Aaron Cooks grant at Mussaco This Court doth judge the grant is not in force" (PRCC, HGU, 2: 40, 141, 144). Northampton Church Records, p. 1, First Congregational Church of Northampton, Northampton, Mass. NTR, 1: 45. Miscellaneous Records of Early Westfield, p. 22, Office of the Town Clerk, Westfield Town Hall. A twentieth-century flood destroyed most of the seventeenth-century records. Miscellaneous surviving documents from multiple sources were bound together in a single volume. Although no document recording Aaron Cook's appointment is known, he was referred to as "Captain" by 1660 (NTR, 1: 19). Stiles, *The History and Genealogies of Ancient Windsor,* 2: 160.

69. Linda Auwers Bissell, "Family, Friends and Neighbors: Social Interaction in Seventeenth-Century Windsor, Connecticut" (Ph.D. diss., Brandeis University, 1973), pp. 59–65. Hampshire County Probate Records, 1690, Office of the County Clerk, Hampshire County Courthouse, Northampton, Mass. In 1668 Northampton's minister, Reverend Eleazer Mather, lay near death and members of the church drafted a church covenant that allowed for the baptism of church members' unconverted children (the doctrine known as the Halfway Covenant). Cook moved to Westfield that year, perhaps in protest of the church's softening policy on membership. In 1669 Reverend Solomon Stoddard was invited to become minister. Influenced by Scottish Presbyterian theology, Stoddard developed policies that further relaxed qualification for church membership and opened participation in ordinances such as communion to the community. In so doing, Stoddard downplayed the role of members in overseeing affairs of the church—breaching congregational conventions. The stipulations in Cook's will represent his opposition to Stoddard's position. Although the bowl was melted down in the eighteenth century, a silver cann made from the same silver is inscribed "The Gift of Maj. Aaron Cooke to the / Church of Christ in Northampton" (on loan from Northampton's Congregational Church to Historic Deerfield). This suggests that the church continued "in the congregational way," to the approval of Cook's heirs. WGL, p. 48.

70. One inch of the radial cross section of each floorboard is sapwood. These boards were probably scrap produced from riving larger, heartwood stock. The sapwood made the boards unsuitable for panels.

71. Ward and Hosley, eds., *The Great River,* pp. 202–3, cat. no. 81.

72. In subsequent years, both chests passed to the children of David Hoyt and Mary Wilson. The low chest descended through successive generations of the Hoyt family from David's son Jonathan (1688–1779). The chest with drawer (missing) was owned in the Wright family, after Judah Wright (1677–1737) married David Hoyt's eldest daughter, Mary (b. 1684), in 1707.

73. Cutwork voids terminating with intersecting saw cuts occur on board case furniture with histories of ownership or recovery in the upper Connecticut River Valley but are rare on examples found in Hartford County.

74. Stiles, *The History and Genealogies of Ancient Windsor,* 2: 721–24. In England, other members of the Stoughton family were ministers or were linked by marriage to ministers. Thomas and Israel Stoughton's sister Elizabeth (b. ca. 1590) married the "pastor of the Parish of Stroud" in 1627. He was her second husband. Their brother John Stoughton (d. 1639) was appointed curate of Aldermansbury Parish, London, in 1632. His two wives were the widows of clerics.

75. WLR, 1: 16, 17.

76. WTA, 1: 34, 48; 2: 8, 9, 11, 13, 14, 17, 19–23, 26–29, 31–35, 40, 43, 46, 49, 51, 55, 57, 59, 60–77. PRCC, EGR, 3: 186.

77. For Israel Stoughton's will, see HCPR, 1736. The contract for the ironworks is in WTA, 2: 80.

78. Connecticut Archive: Ecclestiastica 1, 2: 103, CSL, HGU. Stiles, *The History and Genealogies of Ancient Windsor,* 1: 553–57. PRCC, 4: 255.

79. Since 1958 furniture historians have attributed this group of objects to the shop of woodworker Peter Blinn. Houghton Bulkley, "A Discovery on the Connecticut Chest," *Connecticut Historical Society Bulletin* 23 (January 1958): 17–19.

80. See Robert Blair St. George, *The Wrought Covenant: Source Material for the Study of Craftsmen and Community in Southeastern New England, 1620–1700* (Brockton, Mass.: Brockton Art Center, Fuller Memorial, 1979), pp. 56–59, figs. 61–67. Hannah Talcott's cousin Mary Wadsworth, daughter of her aunt Sarah Talcott Wadsworth and uncle William Wadsworth, married Thomas Stoughton III in 1655. Her cousin Dorothy Talcott, daughter of her uncle John Talcott and aunt Helena Wakeman Talcott, married Thomas Stoughton IV in 1691.

81. For the inventory of Timothy Edwards, see HCPR, 1771.

82. Only notes of the sermon survive. They were recorded by twenty-six-year-old Windsor resident Henry Wolcott, brother-in-law to woodworker Job Drake.

83. Gloria L. Main, *Peoples of a Spacious Land: Families and Cultures in Colonial New England* (Cambridge, Mass.: Harvard University Press, 2001), p. 45. Ludlow's "great disappointment in not being elected governor in 1635 caused him to protest the election of Winthrop [John Haynes defeated Ludlow]; and this so offended the freemen [of Dorchester] that they left him entirely out of the magistracy. This was more than his proud nature could endure, so he joined the party which emigrated to Windsor, Connecticut, later in that year" (William Dana Orcutt, *Good Old Dorchester: A Narrative History of the Town, 1630–1893* [Cambridge, Mass.: University Press, 1908], quoted in www.dorchesteratheneum.org/page.php?id=108.

84. Thistlethwaite, *Dorset Pilgrims,* p. 113. In appreciation, the inhabitants named their settlement Windsor, probably to honor Ludlow by commemorating his paternal grandmother, Edith Windsor, daughter of Sir Andrew Windsor and Elizabeth Blount. Main, *Peoples of a Spacious Land,* pp. 42–43. Paul R. Lucas, *Valley of Discord: Church and Society along the Connecticut River, 1636–1725* (Hanover, N.H.: University Press of New England, 1976), p. 9. In 1635 six of the grantees entered into an agreement with John Winthrop Jr. to form Connecticut colony, with him serving as governor. Winthrop negotiated with representatives from Connecticut River Valley towns to stike a bargain with Warwick's grantees: the grantees would recognize the validity of Connecticut's settlements and allow Winthrop to be governor, and Connecticut would acknowledge the legitimacy of their claims.

85. Trent, "The Concept of Mannerism." Robert F. Trent, Peter Follansbee, and Alan Miller, "First Flowers of the Wilderness: Mannerist Furniture from a Northern Essex County, Massachusetts, Shop," in *American Furniture,* edited by Luke Beckerdite (Hanover, N.H.: University Press of New England for the Chipstone Foundation, 2001), pp. 52–53. According to Trent, no seventeenth-century Boston case furniture is ornamented with carving. A seventeenth-century Boston table with carved brackets (Chipstone Foundation) and a fireback cast from a pattern with simple relief carving have survived.

86. John White, *The Planters Plea or The Grounds of Plantations Examined, and Usuall Objections Answered* (1630; reprint, New York: Theatrum OrbisTerrarum and Da Capo Press, 1968), p. 34.

87. MGD, pp. 29, 39.

88. Thistlethwaite, *Dorset Pilgrims,* p. 137. Thistlethwaite noted, "however well-to-do the family, size of homelot was designed to be comparable. The pattern of settlement, like that of Dorchester, was an oligarchy with a strong egalitarian base."

89. WTA, 1: 50.

90. For timber restrictions, see Middletown Town Records, February 6, 1653, OTC, Middletown Town Hall, Middletown, Conn., 1: 7. On February 1, 1641, the General Court at Hartford, led at the time by Magistrates John Talcott and William Wadsworth, declared that "for the better Presearveing of Tymbr that the Country may have pvisions of Pipe Staves for the furthering the said Trade of Cotton Wool, It is Ordered that no Timber shall be felld fro wthout the bownds of these Plantations wthout Lycence fro the Court." This declaration went on to impose fines for default on any violator (PRCC, 1: 57).

91. For Sanford's petition, see WTA, 1: 41. Clark's contract is mentioned in Hartford Town Votes, 1: 43, Hartford City Hall, Hartford, Conn. "Considering the low Estate of Willm Clark & his family do order to pay to him from ye public Treasurey 40s p yeare foure yeares" (PRCC, 2: 59, Feb. 23, 1660).

Book Reviews

Thomas P. Kugelman and Alice K. Kugelman, with Robert Lionetti et al. *Connecticut Valley Furniture: Eliphalet Chapin and His Contemporaries, 1750–1800*. Edited by Susan Schoelwer. Hartford: Connecticut Historical Society, 2005. 540 pp.; 445 color & bw illus., maps, glossary, bibliography. Distributed by University Press of New England, Hanover and London. $75.00.

The study of American furniture has rarely produced such an exhaustive and revealing analysis as Thomas and Alice Kugelman's *Connecticut Valley Furniture: Eliphalet Chapin and His Contemporaries, 1750–1800*. It brings us closer than ever to an understanding of the cultural, artistic, and technological matrix of a body of regional art and therefore closer to the creative process in early America. The ability to plumb such depths reveals what students of American furniture have long known. Furniture is deep and offers profound insights into people, places, and things. In the traditional orthodoxy of art history, the "minor arts" are presumed to add only a minor dimension to the story of art. But here we see, at least in the not quite rural, not quite urban, backcountry commonwealth of Connecticut, that furniture is revealing in ways that not only provide immense aesthetic pleasure, but also take us places other paths through history cannot.

As art, furniture has been damned by its utility. None of the artisans involved in producing the work shown here ever thought of themselves as "artists." Although pride and competitiveness are apparent, America's eighteenth-century furniture makers, especially in backcountry locales like the Connecticut River Valley, did not have the sense of self that we associate with modern artists. Eliphalet Chapin himself would, no doubt, be startled to imagine his name in lights two centuries past his time. What the Kugelmans and their partner and associate Robert Lionetti have shown so vividly is a meandering path of creative expression that, fully contextualized, offers an astonishing platform for adaptation and invention. What better outlet was there for gifted creative mechanical minds in eighteenth-century America? One hundred years of scholarship have repeatedly found allure in the furniture of the Connecticut River Valley. But circumstances never brought together the time and talent needed to rise to the challenge of sorting it all out, a challenge involving analysis, painstaking observation, and almost obsessive detective work. Kugelman and company's fifteen-year odyssey is an epic achievement, resulting in this book, an exhibition, and an array of accompanying programs that will shape the field of American furniture studies for years to come.

The book is composed of a methodological overview and some historiography followed by extensive catalogue entries that zero in on the best of what the Hartford Case Furniture Survey (HCFS) found. Inasmuch as it weighs in at seven pounds and contains 550 pages, as a reader I might have preferred if the book contained a compact disc illustrating about half the items published as bonus entries. I am sure that cutting the list would have been painful, but wading through so much visual evidence can diminish the eye-popping sense of wonder that the delicious and abbreviated companion exhibition at the Connecticut Historical Society Museum actually provides. The catalogue is followed by a series of probing and evocative essays by some of the best minds in American furniture studies. This crisscrossing of evidence and analysis with interpretation produces some revealing moments and a book of enduring value and beauty.

Having led a team that conducted a survey of Connecticut River Valley furniture and material culture twenty years ago, I am familiar with the subject matter, including renowned master works that have long eluded proper characterization. Despite the Kugelmans' characterization of Wethersfield, Colchester, and Eliphalet Chapin's East Windsor as "major style centers," even these communities produced nothing like the volume of work that came out of Boston, Philadelphia, and Newport. None of the Connecticut River Valley furniture makers was truly prolific. Indeed, most worked at furniture making part-time. The patronage base simply was not there and, at least prior to the Revolution, it does not appear that the export trade was much of a factor. The authors have identified and classified a few dominant stylistic types and numerous discordant variations that have been brilliantly incorporated into an understanding of the region's output—a task made especially difficult when you realize that some of the variations exist in groupings as small as three. These variants were revealed because the HCFS team was relentless in searching out literally hundreds of unpublished objects to review and compare.

Perhaps novelty factors into it, but to my eye, some of the most remarkable, inventive, and aesthetically pleasing objects are in these obscure groups, some of which have never been published before and others never documented or attributed to a shop or locale. Especially noteworthy is the analysis and documentation of the japanned and spool-foot group of chests produced in East Windsor and Windsor during the 1730s and 1740s, the region's earliest foray into the new technology of cabinetwork. This is highly novel design that, once observed, is hard to forget. The Kugelmans have also settled some long-standing confusion about the work of Isaac Tryon of Glastonbury, Connecticut, and that town's iconoclastic role in the region's aesthetic oeuvre. Suffield, Connecticut, furniture makers also produced a stand-alone style that bespeaks ingenuity, while a newly discovered cluster of case pieces associated with Wallingford, Connecticut (which the authors dub the "Silas Rice group"), has a kind of over-the-top boldness of design that suggests why we are drawn to this stuff in the first place.

Despite creating a star turn for one Eliphalet Chapin and the attribution to specific furniture makers here and there, one of the substantial contributions of this book is to bury, with luck forever, the false preoccupation with attaching objects to specific makers. Although many, perhaps most, of the objects illustrated were made by individuals, individuality is almost never the dominant force in shaping design. Connecticut River Valley furniture is not quite "made by committee" and communal stylistic preferences are not particularly tyrannical in forcing conformity among furniture makers of a particular town. Nonetheless, the Kugelmans' scholarship verifies the operating force of shop tradition. Innovation begets emulation begets dissemination to create stylistic patterns that are almost pointless to untangle. The Kugelmans have deftly used artisan and patron genealogy, among other research tools, to establish a kind of genealogy of style. Indeed, never before in American furniture studies have the art and science of family genealogy proven more indispensable or been utilized with such conviction and precision. At the outset, they believed it would be necessary to use computers to sort and analyze their data. In the end, close observation and the inherently speculative effort to reconstruct lines of descent and original ownership combined to create something much more interesting.

Among the many fascinating examples of documentation through reconstructive provenance is the East Windsor japanned high chest at Winterthur (cat. no. 1). They assert that the chest "was made for the June 1736 marriage of Gershom Loomis to Mary Grant" and note that the chest was listed "at the extraordinary value of £5.10.0" in Loomis's estate inventory just two years later, making it "one of the first high chests mentioned in the probate records of Hartford County." They then track its descent through various family members to a South Windsor farmer who sold it to Henry Francis du Pont in 1946. It doesn't get much better than this.

More speculative, but not less convincing, is the discussion of a high chest attributed to Eliphalet Chapin (cat. no. 61) that was auctioned in the estate of Richard Mather in 1930. It took the Kugelmans' sleuthing to determine that Mather, born in 1856, was "a bachelor who had lived in the family homestead in Windsor for seventy-four years" and that the most likely original owners were his maternal great-grandparents, Anna Palmer and Eliakim Marshall, who married in 1785, "a date in keeping with the features of the high chest."

If this kind of creative reconstructive provenance popped up occasionally it would be cause for celebration, given that the vast majority of American antiques have been divorced from their contexts and history. But here, most of the 191 objects catalogued are published with a probable assertion of original ownership, a feat rarely attempted and never before achieved in a publishing effort like this.

Years ago, when I was hot on the trail of Connecticut furniture and obsessing about the importance of provenance, a prominent American furniture dealer counseled me that whatever such details might mean to museum curators, in the trade "50 cents and a provenance won't buy a cup of coffee." That did not make sense then, and it does not make sense now. With the publication of this extraordinary work we can bury forever any sense that an object's history is not pertinent to its value as a work of art.

Value is arbitrary and will inevitably hinge on a variety of connecting factors, not the least of which is a publication like this that explicates, glorifies, contextualizes, illustrates, and reveals connections between objects.

A major contribution of the book is to prove that the classic, spare, cabriole-legged case furniture associated with Wethersfield and elsewhere, while it clearly predates the work of the Chapin school and Colchester, is also contemporaneous and continued to be preferred in some communities (Wethersfield, Middletown, and Windsor, for example) well into the 1790s and right up to the end of the Chapin era.

The book further proves that Eliphalet Chapin, while clearly a maverick and innovator, was widely imitated and that much of the best work formerly attributed to him was made by cabinetmakers in the Massachusetts towns of Northampton and Springfield and possibly as far away as Worcester County. Chapin himself rarely sold anything outside the immediate vicinity of his East Windsor home. The fact that his style was popular farther afield is because he trained apprentices who migrated elsewhere and made a success of it.

Finally, though I would not have thought a study of Colchester furniture, traditionally associated with the area in eastern Connecticut around Norwich and New London, made sense in the context of a book focusing on the Connecticut River Valley, the authors make sense of it by explaining Colchester's many connections with Hartford. Colchester furniture, which the authors say "brims with originality and dynamism," has long fascinated students of American furniture for its exuberance, innovation, and voluptuous ornament, almost the mirror opposite of the delicate and restrained formalism produced in nearby Wethersfield. But the Colchester cabinetmakers did, occasionally, adopt "Chapinisms" into their ornamental vocabulary and made their presence known in the Connecticut River Valley by their work in the lower valley and by their influence on the unidentified furniture maker(s) responsible for the Glastonbury style, which is a hybrid with a strong Colchester-based feel.

Middletown, which was the largest and richest trade port on the Connecticut River in 1760, still feels like a puzzle. The authors assert that Hartford and Middletown played a secondary and subordinate role in the development of regional furniture styles. The implication is not just that the furniture makers in those towns were less prone to innovate, but that there were fewer of them, an assertion yet to be fully proved. It was certainly not for their lack of money that we do not have more evidence and insight into Middletown's furniture history. Clearly, the Kugelmans' analysis has taken the study of Middletown further than it has ever gone. But there is still a need for a comprehensive, multimedia, material-cultural study of this fascinating place. In the meantime, don't bet long on their Middletown attribution of the Ford Museum's iconic masterpiece desk-and-bookcase (cat. no. 56), one of the most alluring designs in American furniture. There's more evidence to uncover. Of the handful of Middletown furniture makers the authors cite, no mention is made of Samuel Hall or Captain William Sage, or of the amazing desk-and-bookcase at Middlesex County Historical

Society, Middletown (see *Antiques* 20 , no. 3 [March 1991]: 597) associated with him. This desk might not matter except that it is arguably the best piece in one of the smallest, but most interesting, subgroups of furniture they associate with Middletown and might have influenced their interpretation.

The catalogue section of this book displays a mastery of furniture taxonomy and description. A language of description that is both consistent and compelling has taken generations to create. Fylfots, pinwheels, and "cyma curved front aprons" are not words that come tripping off the tongue of even the most seasoned furniture aficionados. This devotion to precision strikes me as overdrawn when they substitute the jargony notion of "index features" for the simpler notion of "characteristics." But I like fylfots and appreciate the achievement of conquering a language that can be off-putting and obscure.

Six interpretative essays, a glossary, and a compendium of cabinetmaker biographies follow the catalogue.

The opening essay, by Robert F. Trent, titled "The European Origins of Eighteenth-Century New England Case Pieces," strikes me as the least necessary and, while interesting, exhibits a familiar weakness of art history: confusing cause and effect by assuming that if something looks like something else, or one thing followed another, that it must necessarily have been derivative when, in fact, the world is filled with evidence of creativity and invention that are nonlinear in derivation. The presence of an idea in one place does not preclude another place from inventing the same solution independently. The idea that "what provincial New Englanders of the eighteenth century thought and felt about their furniture" was somehow shaped by European court practices of a century or two before strikes me as a stretch.

The second essay, "Connecticut River Valley Woodworking Dynasties," also by Trent, is far more relevant. When he first began publishing the fruits of this important body of research in the early 1990s, it was revolutionary. Although others had dabbled in furniture-maker genealogies before, no one ever connected so many dots and took it far enough to reveal, emphatically, the almost guildlike structure of these family networks. It makes Chapin's contribution seem all the more impressive to realize that he broke into the trade without connections and nevertheless achieved dominance in it. Trent demonstrates how fluidly shop traditions moved up and down the valley and asserts, significantly, that "only when the family networks have been established, amplified with data from probate records and account books, and collated with surviving objects, can the entire body of data be organized in a meaningful way." This is pretty much the assignment going forward for any young scholar looking to advance knowledge about craft traditions in any particular place at any given time. Alas, when the essay debunks the notion of "individual creativity" and sneers at the notion of "regional mystique," it risks dismissing qualities that give this work meaning. Places have a right to claim and celebrate their material culture. Individuality of style is, to be sure, one of the characteristics that have drawn attention to Connecticut River Valley furniture for so long. Why some art historians seem almost unwilling to accept the mystery of creative thought is beyond me. But it is equally clear that to call the Colchester work or even Chapin's contributions a mere "reflection of... diverse sources" belies the possibility of individual ingenuity and invention which I find so apparent and inspiring in this work.

Susan Schoelwer provides a colorful historiography of Eliphalet Chapin scholarship in "Writings on Eliphalet Chapin," beginning with the fact that his reputation survived in oral tradition among the region's furniture makers so that it first became known to Hartford's nineteenth-century antiquarians and collectors through the region's early antique dealers, cabinetmakers, and restorers. Schoelwer provides a fascinating account of the generation-long conflict between Luke Vincent Lockwood, who thought the absence of documented work made Eliphalet Chapin's reputation overblown, and Wallace Nutting and Homer Eaton Keyes, the latter the founder of *Antiques* magazine, who were more willing to speculate based on visual evidence. Clearly, this book ends the debate, making Nutting appear remarkably prescient for devoting so much attention to a figure only now being more thoroughly understood. As Keyes put it, "the curvature of the front legs and the shape of the feet are so specific as almost to qualify as the maker's signature." John T. Kirk, famous for relying on keen visual analysis and foregoing documentation or even the more painstaking nuances of construction, nonetheless determined that Chapin had "arrived at something that can be considered wholly new," thus fostering the myth of Chapin as a "creative genius." Although the Kugelmans never quite come out and say it, all evidence suggests that they would agree with Kirk's conclusions. Let me say it for them. Eliphalet Chapin was a creative genius, and we should all be grateful to Kirk and Nutting for calling him what he was early enough to keep his important legacy in the public eye.

In "New Evidence on Eliphalet Chapin," Schoelwer and Dawn Bobryk provide a masterful reconstruction of a life and career based on what remains an incredibly thin paper trail. Eliphalet Chapin grew up surrounded by a veritable "hive of Chapins" in Enfield, Connecticut, a daughter town that borders Springfield, Massachusetts, where his ancestors were among the most prominent founding families. Indeed, a statue of his paternal ancestor Samuel Chapin by Augustus Saint-Gaudens is a beloved Springfield landmark. The paternity suit that prompted Chapin to hightail it to Philadelphia turns out to be not just a momentary blip in his life but a stain that never quite goes away. His decision to return to East Windsor, the scene of the crime, and make a go of furniture making, when setting up almost anywhere else—Middletown or Hartford, for example—might have proved more beneficial, says something about his character and ability to function or perhaps even thrive in the face of adversity. The essay also proves that, unlike most of his contemporary furniture makers in the Connecticut River Valley, Chapin seeks, and apparently succeeds, in making furniture making a full-time occupation, living on a half-acre lot with "an attention-getting brick house," at a time when there probably was not another brick house in town, brick being associated with, if anything, urban living.

One important thing missing here—a puzzling omission for a book that covers so many other bases and interpretive perspectives—is an attempt to explain the economy of furniture making, both for Chapin's shop in particular and in general practice in the region at the time. When Schoelwer and Bobryk note that "If he was like most woodworkers of the period, his business undoubtedly included a great deal of repair work and utilitarian goods in addition to high-style case pieces and upholstered chairs," one is puzzled why the authors, having turned over so many other stones successfully, left readers to guess about this. Indeed, evidence suggests that there was little division of labor between furniture makers and housewrights, or between those who made things and those who did repair work, anywhere in rural New England before the Revolution and almost as rare right up to 1800. The Dunlaps of New Hampshire and the Connecticut River Valley's Timothy Loomis, both exceptionally well-documented woodworkers in eighteenth-century interior New England, demonstrated extraordinary fluidity in following the market wherever there was opportunity. In the case of Loomis, that meant installing flooring in a pigpen one day and crafting a high chest the next. If Chapin was, as Schoelwer and Bobryk suggest, "moving away from a traditional, family based, artisan shop to a more modern showroom-warehouse, offering a wider variety of products and services at the same location," then Chapin deserves credit not only as an innovator in design but as someone who anticipated impending transformations and was the first in the Connecticut River Valley to adapt to them.

I suspect this omission has to do with research methodology and the priority given to object analysis and genealogy rather than account book evidence. Although the single most important document associated with Chapin is the Grant-Marsh marriage commission recorded in Ebenezer Grant's ledger, the Kugelmans do not appear to have analyzed even the account books belonging to Connecticut River Valley furniture makers (of which there are very few), much less the oftentimes incredibly revealing information contained in the trade credits of other ledger keepers, accounts that document furniture makers' practices because they document real, day-to-day transactions. A tasty example they appear to have overlooked is a magnificent ledger kept by a member of the Wolcott family of Windsor or East Windsor and now in the collections of the Pocumtuck Valley Historical Society in Deerfield. Eliphalet Chapin's account includes about a dozen transactions over a number of years, including payment for making a spinning wheel and some repair work, not activities this book associates with him. The account, which was closed out for some reason, also includes Chapin's signature, which might have been worth illustrating in a once-in-a-lifetime publication like this.

Next is Philip Zimmerman's "Method in Early American Furniture Identification," an essay that deepens the case attributing individual works to specific makers by highlighting the egregious traditions of dealers and collectors desperate to attach a maker's name to everything and anything, despite overwhelming evidence that doing so makes no sense. Zimmerman makes this point by critiquing one of the underlying assumptions of this entire scholarly effort and one of the sacred cows of furniture scholarship going back to Charles F. Montgomery's deservedly famous book *American Furniture: The Federal Period* (1966), which is the assumption that furniture makers, in a rotelike way, systematized their production, particularly with construction features that did not bear heavily on form, function, or style. If furniture makers do not behave predictably it makes attribution all that much harder. Zimmerman notes, "Pervasive consistency may be a hallmark of certain individuals, shops, or communities, but does not necessarily apply broadly throughout the furniture trade in early America." He cites several key studies that refute conventional wisdom, including an extensive analysis of the documented work of John Shaw of Annapolis, in which "no shop traits . . . emerged," and a similar study of Benjamin Frothingham of Boston, which was "unable to identify signature features that identify the maker's work."

The final essay is Schoelwer's "Beyond Regionalism: Town History and Connecticut Furniture," which asserts that stylistic preferences between towns were more pronounced than hitherto recognized and that the notion of a stylistic region should be supplanted by a model that is multicentered and more diverse. Her analysis of the "persistent localism that remains evident today" throughout Connecticut is compelling. She lists the "oasis like quality of settlements" and "relative isolation" even 150 years after settlement and the absence of a major cultural or economic center as characteristics that made the Connecticut River Valley different from other American settlement regions, but that did not make the region internally homogenous. This and the demographic persistence of founding families in particular towns encouraged what Schoelwer describes as a "closed shop mentality" in the woodworking trades, a phenomenon exhaustively and convincingly explored in last year's path-breaking *The Woodworkers of Windsor: A Connecticut Community of Craftsmen and Their World, 1635–1715* by Joshua Lane and Donald White.

The arts of the Connecticut River Valley cast a lengthening shadow on the American imagination. Epitomizing the spare lines and creative elegance of the colonial experience, this work suggests a kind of premonition of independence. Because the region remained agricultural longer than most American cultural centers, a lot of stuff retained its contexts and connections into the twentieth century, when the pioneer collectors and dealers had a field day scouting up treasures that were still relatively abundant.

In her rather somber foreword to the book, Patricia E. Kane lauds the authors' achievement in producing such a monumental study, but laments that "few museums . . . have the resources to . . . run large research projects." This is nothing new. Independent scholar-collectors, from Irving Lyon, Luke Lockwood, the Reverend Clare Luther, and Houghton Bulkeley, have generated the bulk of the scholarship over the years. The more the merrier. In this remarkable achievement the Kugelmans and Robert Lionetti have added the biggest and most complete brick to the pile yet. Regardless of interpretation and attribution, the visual power and sheer magnitude of evidence shown here is overwhelming and cannot fail to leave the reader with an impression that the Connecticut Valley produced some of the most inspiring art in America, art that reflects minds at work, solving problems on the ground through a combination of resourcefulness and ingenuity that is hard not to love.

William Hosley
Hartford, Connecticut

Morrison H. Heckscher, with the assistance of Lori Zabar. *John Townsend: Newport Cabinetmaker*. New Haven: Yale University Press; New York: Metropolitan Museum of Art, 2005. xii + 224 pp.; numerous color and bw illus., appendixes, bibliographies, index. $75.00.

The "great artist" approach is a genre of the history of art well suited for the study of painters, as witnessed in the American field, for example, by recent works on Copley, Stuart, Sargent, Homer, and many others. Over time, it has been applied to studies of furniture makers as well, even though chair makers and cabinetmakers, especially urban ones, tended to work in large shops replete with apprentices, journeymen, and specialists, and their products are often (to coin a phrase) "the work of many hands." Functional works of art, moreover, usually need to respond to the demands and requirements of patrons and the marketplace in ways that do not ordinarily inhibit the more idiosyncratic creations of painters. Thus, furniture and other objects are often more revealing of preconceptions, attitudes, and values among consumers, providing evidence that flows outward from the object to society at large, rather than spiraling downward into the psyche of an individual. Nevertheless, the "great man" approach is apropos for the study of John Townsend (1733–1809) of Newport, Rhode Island, who manufactured a largely homogenous body of outstanding material in a small community and who took the time and trouble to label or otherwise identify much of his furniture as the product of his own eye, hand, and mind.

Regular readers of *American Furniture* will need no urging to consult this exemplary monograph on Townsend—hardly an unknown figure in the annals of American cabinetmaking and arguably one of the most important—given the organizing institution behind the publication and the impeccable reputation of Morrison Heckscher, its principal author. Nor will they be disappointed. *John Townsend* manages to bring together nearly all that has been previously written about him, while simultaneously adding substantially to the record. The results are all presented in a compact, beautifully illustrated, clearly written volume. It begins with five contextual chapters on Newport and Townsend, moves to a lengthy catalogue section detailing some forty-eight examples of his work, and concludes with various appendixes that set forth a detailed genealogical and documentary record.

The volume starts by putting Townsend into context, first within the historiography of Newport as a whole and Newport furniture in particular, and then by identifying his furniture's relationship to that of other American centers, principally Boston, Massachusetts. A chapter on the Townsend family as a whole is extremely helpful in identifying and separating the work of several generations of Townsends, including those who worked in both the "Job Townsend shop tradition" and the "Christopher Townsend shop tradition" (of which John was a part). The identities of individual members of the intertwined Townsend-Goddard families can be difficult to separate in one's mind, and this chapter does an excellent job of establishing the family and working relations in a clear and concise manner.

The last introductory chapter will be of most interest to collectors and connoisseurs, inasmuch as it describes in detail the diagnostic features that, when present, allow for an attribution of an unsigned object to Townsend's shop. In addition to sections on his signatures and labels, use of woods, and choice of hardware, the authors present their conclusions concerning several details of construction that in and of themselves are "tantamount to a signature." These include "the use of unusually small bore (¼–⅓ inch), perfectly round wooden pins to secure the components" of mortise-and-tenon joints (p. 68); the common use of tulip poplar for drawer sides in conjunction with thick mahogany drawer fronts; standardized chestnut glue blocks; and a unique framing system for tables, featuring a web of cross braces; and so forth. Additional features are identified for Townsend's case furniture. In all, because of the consistency of Townsend and his high degree of technical skill in joinery and carving, these characteristics are extremely useful indicators of origin.

The catalogue section, divided into four largely chronological groups—cabriole furniture; case furniture (block and shell and flat front); stop-fluted furniture; and federal furniture—intensifies the points made in the opening chapters through a detailed written description and visual look at nearly fifty examples of Townsend's work. Excellent use is made of supplementary images here, showing many details of construction and ornament as well as some pieces upside down and from the back. (The points made here are amplified by Appendix 1, "Pictorial Parallels: The Furniture of John Townsend and His Contemporaries," a series of detailed visual comparisons.)

Several points of various magnitude stand out from a reading of this volume. One is Townsend's ability as a carver, which is emphasized time and again. It is the almost machinelike regularity and repetition of his carved shells and knees that allow for the identification of much of his work. Heckscher likens Townsend's wielding of the chisel to a painter's use of the brush (p. 185), and his skill at this task elevates his furniture to the highest realm of American artistic expression in the eighteenth century.

A second point is the reaffirmation of the Newport block-and-shell design as a major development in the history of furniture. Its creation resulted in "a perfectly integrated, and uniquely American, design—an example of the ability of the Newport joiners to demonstrate their independence of thought from the rest of New England" (p. 18). It is "a triumph of American design" with "no precise analogy elsewhere" (p. 18), although John T. Kirk and others have suggested German and other prototypes not only for block-front façades but for block-and-shell designs as well. (A fascinating observation—that the ancestral Townshend family coat of arms of "Three escallops argent" [three silver scallop shells] might have been a source of inspiration for the Newport shell—is tantalizingly noted on page 35 but not elaborated on in any detail.) Another point that is noted, but not necessarily addressed, is the absence of case furniture by Townsend in the federal style, as well as other forms common to Newport (see p. 57). What does the lack of these forms say about specialization or the nature of regional preferences, or are there additional attributions to be made for objects of this type?

What is perhaps most interesting about this work to me personally, however, is the assertion of Townsend's intentionality in his labeling of furniture. At least thirty-four pieces are known at the moment bearing Townsend's name, and probably a few more will emerge in the years ahead. Rather than seeing this as evidence of a type of proto-advertising, the authors see it as Townsend's attempt to secure his place in history and document his legacy. These objects are "the statement that he made for posterity and by which he must be judged. It is the *altogether self-conscious record* of a supremely accomplished master craftsman" (p. 51, emphasis added). This viewpoint makes Townsend's ego, while perhaps not on the level of a Cellini, seem almost on a par with that of John Singleton Copley, who felt very much unappreciated by the citizens of Boston and who wanted desperately to establish his own reputation for posterity. To find a preindustrial artisan in early America also striving to achieve an artistic legacy in an overt manner—not only in his own day but perhaps for generations to come—is revealing. It reminds us that the nature and degree of creativity and innovation always need to be addressed in studies of furniture—a sturdy, old-fashioned notion to some extent perhaps, but one that nevertheless needs to survive in the face of approaches that downplay the importance of aesthetics and artistic vision in the study of decorative arts.

Finally, the figure of John Goddard (1724–1785) manages to emerge from these pages as an artist worthy of consideration in the same breath as Townsend. Noted for his "ambition and exceptional talent" (p. 43), he also developed "a distinctive personal style" by the mid-1750s and became "a consummate craftsman" (p. 47) supported by significant patronage from the Brown family of Providence. He, too, was a superb carver, perhaps more talented than Townsend, and notable for the grace, realism, articulation, and modeling of his ornaments. This is all familiar territory, given the attention that Goddard has also received for the past century or so, but it made this reader hope that Heckscher and his colleague Lori Zabar will utilize their considerable talents to tackle Goddard next.

Gerald W. R. Ward
Museum of Fine Arts, Boston

Robert Tarule. *The Artisan of Ipswich: Craftsmanship and Continuity in Colonial New England.* Baltimore: Johns Hopkins University Press, 2004. xi + 155 pp.; 9 bw illus., 27 line drawings, index. $42.00.

The Artisan of Ipswich is the outgrowth of the author's dissertation, for which he was allowed "to make, as the centerpiece . . . , a piece of furniture and to let the process of making drive the research" (p. ix). The centerpiece of the study is a seventeenth-century chest owned by the Ipswich Historical Society. Robert Tarule reproduced the chest using the same tools, techniques, and materials that he believes Thomas Dennis (1638–1706) of Ipswich, Massachusetts, employed to make the original object. In his introduction, Tarule describes the chest in detail and wonders what it can tell us about the man who made it. "When you look the chest all over, you see equally the hand of the artisan and the hand of nature," he writes, and this insight provided the inspiration for this book. It is a journey into the mind of the chest's maker through the experience of reproducing his every action, his selection of every piece of wood, and his every stroke with a gouge. Tarule concludes his introduction by stating, "This joined chest, because of the direct processing of local materials and the highly visible craft of the joiner, can illuminate the local landscape, the community in which it was made, and the artisan who made it in his shop" (p. 6).

The preface, "Things I Should Have Learned as a Boy," explains how Tarule first discovered woodworking while teaching medieval comparative literature at a small college in Vermont. His first lessons came from an elderly neighbor, but for the most part Tarule learned by close observation and by trial and error. Shortly after he built his own timber-frame house, Tarule was laid off from his teaching position and was able to secure the position of Curator of Mechanick Arts at Plimoth Plantation. In this new role he was responsible for creating furniture replicas for the homes of the re-created Pilgrim village. By closely studying the objects, he found himself "figuring out some of the lost secrets of the seventeenth-century woodworker," and he realized that the people whose work he was re-creating were "not far removed from the social world of their medieval ancestors" (p. ix). The experience of working with others who shared his passion, on such projects as raising a replica of the 1636 Fairbanks House of Dedham on the Boston Common, fueled his desire to return to graduate school to complete his doctorate.

The first chapter is a review of the history of the settlement of Ipswich and the development of the Massachusetts Bay Colony that includes a brief introduction to the life and work of Thomas Dennis. Chapter 2 is a detailed discussion of the properties of oak, the characteristics of the forests and woods of England and New England, and patterns of wood harvesting and the regulations governing them with special attention to documents that specifically reveal practices in Ipswich. This is followed by a chapter that takes Thomas Dennis into the Ipswich woods and imagines the process by which he chose and felled the trees that he made into furniture. Chapter 4 is a review of all the different types of woodworkers who resided in Ipswich, from coopers and carpenters to joiners, turners, and wheelwrights. Tarule provides short biographies of each of the known artisans in these trades. Although these biographies help us to imagine the community, I was disappointed when the chapter ended without a discussion, or perhaps just an example taken from the documents, of how these artisans interacted with one another, or a discussion of whether or not woodworkers in one branch of the trade apprenticed their sons to another woodworking trade in an effort to diversify the family's business or create allies in allied trades. It seems particularly surprising that Tarule does not include the scholarship linking the works of Thomas Dennis to those of William Searle (1634–1667). Dennis married Searle's widow, Grace, and inherited the contents of Searle's shop, and although the two men undoubtedly came out of the same Devonshire woodworking tradition, significant similarities and differences in their works have been identified.

In Chapter 5, Tarule takes us through the process by which the maker of the chest planned and built it. This chapter is written in the present tense, as if the reader is looking over Dennis' shoulder, and Tarule is successful in creating this illusion. However, a reader without detailed knowledge of woodworking is often at a loss to follow the particulars of the discussion because Tarule uses specialized terms that are not defined in the book. A glossary and several fully labeled diagrams would have been enormously helpful, and would expand the readership for the book beyond the world of contemporary craftsmen, preservation timber-framers, and furniture curators to scholars with a more general interest in the social and cultural world of the preindustrial artisan. I had hoped, for example, that this chapter would be one I could assign to the students in my material culture course. Had Tarule explained how the irregularities that he sees in the wood used in the chest reveal to him the process that the artisan went through in choosing the pieces of wood from his stock, it would be a model of how to do close analysis of an object to determine the working methods of its maker, but this analysis is lacking. Instead, the reader is left to make the connections, or to read the narrative with faith that Tarule has evidence for each of the actions he ascribes to Dennis.

If the essential thesis of the book is that we can learn more about artisans by doing the same work that they did, then Tarule's defense of that thesis should have described more clearly how the process informed his research. Yes, Tarule tells us about Ipswich, and about the materials and techniques used by Thomas Dennis and his fellow woodworkers. But he could have made the connection between this information and the process of making the replica more explicit by tying each step in the process, each observation of the characteristics of the wood in the chest, or of tool marks or scribe lines, to his wider questions and avenues of research.

The final section of the book is particularly disappointing. Johns Hopkins University Press failed Tarule, and failed the readers of the book, by not including detailed notes and an extensive bibliography. This I find inexplicable in a university press book. The notes, which take up exactly two pages, completely ignore secondary works and include no information about the place of this particular study in the enormous body of scholarly work on seventeenth-century New England joinery and early woodworking artisans in general, and Thomas Dennis and his predecessor William Searle in particular. There is no mention of previous historians' work on Ipswich or other New England towns, the timber trade, the ecology of New England before settlement, or on wood harvesting and production in New England

and Old England. There is also no acknowledgment of the work of other traditional woodworkers who have studied and revived the technology of green-wood joinery, nor of dozens of other scholars who have worked to rediscover the designs and carving techniques of early New England craftsmen. The "Essay on Methods and Sources" is more notable for what it omits or downplays than for what it includes. I was amazed to find no reference to the work of Benno M. Forman on seventeenth-century New England furniture and only passing references to Robert Trent, Jonathan Fairbanks, and Robert Blair St. George, all of whom have made enormous contributions to our understanding of the artisans of this period. One would think that Tarule would at least pay homage to Irving Lyon, the writer who first identified Dennis's work in groundbreaking articles published in *Antiques* in the 1930s. More important, Tarule does not justify the attribution of the Ipswich Historical Society chest to Thomas Dennis, rather than to William Searle as suggested by Trent in *New England Begins: The Seventeenth Century* (Boston: Museum of Fine Arts, 1982).

In the final analysis, *The Artisan of Ipswich* should not be read in isolation, nor should it be considered a definitive study of Thomas Dennis or his furniture. It is, however, an illuminating journey into the mind of the seventeenth-century joiner that includes interesting information about the nature of harvesting and working wood in the preindustrial world.

Barbara McLean Ward
Moffatt-Ladd House and Garden
Faculty in Museum Studies, Tufts University

Robert D. Mussey Jr. *The Furniture Masterworks of John and Thomas Seymour.* Salem, Mass.: Peabody Essex Museum, 2003. xiv + 462 pp., 174 color and 77 bw illus., catalogue. Distributed by University Press of New England, Hanover and London. $65.00.

The Seymours—father and son—and their cabinetmaking wizardry have been known for generations, largely thanks to the work of Vernon Stoneman who published *John and Thomas Seymour: Cabinetmakers in Boston, 1794–1816* (1959) and *A Supplement* six years later. Enthusiasm for the Seymours' aggressive designs has deeper roots, however, in the 1920s during the first wave of excitement for antique neoclassical furniture in America. Then as now, a craftsman's label on an object of great beauty and technical execution enlivens the marketplace. The Seymour label, identifying their location in "Creek Square, Boston," was found eighty years ago on two lady's tambour secretaries (cat. nos. 3 and 5 in the publication under review), including the satinwood gem now owned by the Museum of Fine Arts, Boston. The early collector George Alfred Cluett (1873–1955), a pioneer in neoclassical furniture-gathering, purchased it from Francis Hill Bigelow in Boston in 1925.

The Seymours used the "Creek Square" label from the date of their arrival from Maine in 1793 for three years or so. This early documentation clearly places the Seymours in the vanguard of moving stodgy Bostonians away from the furniture designs that had comforted them for three generations. How was that possible? The Seymours were from a place even more exotic than Maine: Axminster, Devonshire, England, which was near the place where John had been born in 1738 and where he left in 1784 with his large family for Falmouth (now Portland), Maine. In other words, noting that an expert is anyone from farther away than fifty miles, the Seymours through their drop-dead gorgeous furniture offered their new patrons both modernism and a republican zeal for design ideas loosely inspired by ancient precedent. The sheer volume of Seymour-like furniture that Stoneman later catalogued (as well as collected)—even though the Seymours did not make all that was attributed to them—nevertheless demonstrates that the father and son were major players in introducing British neoclassicism, not just to Boston or before that to Maine, but indeed to America during the 1780s and 1790s.

Here the story gathered dust for decades because the Seymours, despite their visibility, were obscure people whose shadowy record begged the difficult historical question: What is the significance of the fact that we do not seem to know who they were? Then, a dozen years ago, Robert Mussey, along with inveterate researchers Anne Rogers and Johanna McBrien, took up the question. Led by Mussey, their exhaustive examination of the Seymours' furniture and the difficult paper trail they left became the foundation of this influential book, which will be found on the shelves of students of American craftsmanship for generations. Considerable additional value is provided by another dedicated researcher with a deep devotion to Maine, Laura Fecych Sprague, who wrote chapter two and unraveled what can be known about the Seymour family's nine years by Casco Bay.

This reviewer's only substantive criticism of the book stems from its title, *The Furniture Masterworks of John and Thomas Seymour,* only because it sells the book short. To be sure, the great photographs of veneered "eye-candy," mostly by Gavin Ashworth and David Bohl, are heart-stopping reminders of what a masterwork should look like. Similarly, the deep empirical analysis of the furniture by conservator-cabinetmaker Mussey in chapter five, "Identification of the Works of John and Thomas Seymour," and in the lengthy catalogue section of 156 objects that follows leaves the reader trampled by relentless quality. In fact, from the viewpoint of object analysis, this reader found chapter five more useful than the catalogue itself, which is primarily descriptive with sporadic interpretation and no secondary photography. While the typologists among us, seeking clusters of sideboards or washstands without necessarily having to read the book, might curse Mussey, his storyline would be made crystal clear if these objects had been treated in chronological sequence regardless of form and, better yet, built into the text. That remains an inherent stumbling block of exhibition catalogues, even ones like Mussey's, which ambitiously try to elevate an interpretative thesis or hypothesis to its highest attainable level.

In this case, Mussey's book is really not about great English cabinetwork on American soil. It is about the interrelationships and influence of several British immigrant craftsmen, not just the vanguard of Seymours, on the evolution of the business of cabinetmaking in federal-period Boston's international economy. Although such subject matter might risk a deadly title in its own right, this book, while scholarly, is not academic and, while clearly about identifiable craftsmanship, still works hard (unlike many such "catalogues") to place the artifacts in context so that they can be better understood—the most important and still most overlooked tenet of connoisseurship.

Having lauded the book's important commitment to teaching both history and art as equal partners, there are weak elements. The discussion of the Seymours' competitors without illustrating their work constricts our understanding of the topic actually at hand—how the furniture trades and their wares reflect Boston's economy at the time—and compromises the argument that, technically if not financially, John and Thomas were ahead of the pack. There are also interpretative leaps of faith that fall short, such as the reference to the supposed conservatism and "Spartan simplicity of seventeenth-century Puritan settlers" (p. 28) whose actual complexity and hyperconsumerism are well documented; or the belief that Boston craftsmen advertised for apprentices "from the Country" because these boys were probably better disciplined and less assertive than city kids when in fact they probably came with fewer financial demands to their new masters (p. 33); or the assumption that because Thomas, the son, signed the Seymours' copy of Sheraton's *The Cabinet-Maker and Upholsterer's Drawing-Book* in ink with more authority than his dad he may have been more forward-looking than father John (p. 34). On the practical side, it is problematic that an index to the book was not included.

This sort of criticism aside, the discussion of the dominant roles of public auctions in selling stock-in-trade furniture to consumers and of cabinet warehouses as early-day, one-stop shopping for interior design makes for interesting reading. Other passages in the book are brilliant, such as Mussey's analysis of neoclassical veneer work as two-dimensional sculpture (p. 83) or many sections from chapter five, especially on the Seymours' veneer work, which was their signature skill that placed them above their peers (pp. 87–100), and on hardware and ivory work (pp. 109–14). These drive home the point that almost never sticks: that these objects—great and small—are the products of an economy more than the misconception that they are somehow the wares of a single craftsman. The first two chapters, about the Seymours in England and then in Maine, hold fresh, interesting material that is well presented. Although Portland may seem like an odd first stop to the reader who has never been there (it is considerably closer to England), Laura Sprague does an excellent job of explaining the character and needs of that small city, devastated and rebuilding after the American Revolution, and the role of a network of contacts and leads that any successful immigrant must have in place to make a success of it. Instead of doing Portland solo, the Seymours were part of a large contingent of transplants from the southwest of England to settle in Maine over a long period of time.

In the end, what makes Mussey's book worth having is twofold. First, the well-designed volume dramatically updates our knowledge of one of the more influential shop traditions in American material culture both aesthetically and commercially. Second, Mussey throws aside the protective umbrella of a traditional decorative arts catalogue to actually teach history with both objects and documents. He tells the often-told, but here surprising, American story of immigration, adaptation, collaboration, success, and utter failure despite the valid opportunities that drew John and Thomas Seymour, and countless others, to America, and despite their considerable reputation that has endured to this day. In the end, the Seymours fell on the thorny issue of poor business acumen and bad timing with Jefferson's embargo and the War of 1812. Their problems were with capital, overhead, and market share, not with sculptural veneers and gluepots. Ironically, it was the financial burden, not the drudgery, that the Seymours failed to outrun. This most basic irony, which dogs success in America to this day, comes clear in Robert Mussey's story of both craftsmanship and labor history. Only in this land of opportunity can one succeed and fail at the same time, or, more poignantly, only in America can your spectacular furniture command scholarship and bring millions on the auction block 150 years after your death in an almshouse. Understanding how that happened is a lesson well learned and certainly one that puts connoisseurship to the test.

Philip Zea
Historic Deerfield, Inc.

Neil Kamil. *Fortress of the Soul: Violence, Metaphysics, and Material Life in the Huguenots' New World, 1517–1751.* Baltimore and London: John Hopkins University Press, 2005. xxiv + 1,058 pp.; numerous bw illus., maps, line drawings, index. $75.00.

This long-awaited, immense book, based on twenty-five years of research in Europe and America, is not so much an artifact study (despite the title) as an investigation of how natural history and alchemical texts were read and interpreted by quasi-literate or "liminal" artisans in Europe and the New World. In pushing the interpretative possibilities of this approach to their limits, Neil Kamil has produced an extraordinary book. However, much of the decorative arts interpretation is, unfortunately, questionable.

Unlike most narratives about the Huguenots, Kamil's version begins by investigating mystic aspects of the most famous of the Huguenot writers, the extraordinary and turbulent potter Bernard Palissy (1510–1590), whose wares featuring aquatic creatures cast from live specimens have always been considered masterpieces of their genre. Kamil's method in explicating Palissy's mind and experience owes a conceptual debt to Carlo Ginzburg's famous *The Cheese and the Worms: The Cosmos of a Sixteenth-Century Miller* (1980), which analyzes the testimony of a similar autodidact artisan in a heresy trial. However, the artifacts to be studied in Palissy's case, other than his ceramic production, were not court documents but his two principal published works, *Recepte véritable* (1563) and *Discours admirables* (1580). In these, as well as Palissy's biography, Kamil has uncovered evidence for Palissy's interest in arcane literature of natural history, the occult, and alchemy, particularly the influence of the famous Philippus Aureolus Theophrastus Bombastus von Hohenheim (1493?–1541), otherwise known as Paracelsus. By examining the imagery employed in Palissy's ceramics and published works in the light of a broad range of texts, Kamil has produced an extremely useful compendium of conceptual frameworks for iconographic interpretation, particularly as regards the many allegorical prints used to illustrate this literature.

Palissy himself was a fascinating man. He was trained as a glass painter, and his curiosity about glaze chemistry, combined with a willful and searching personality, led him to experiment with glazes among the potters of Saintonge in southwest France, near the great Huguenot fortress and port of La Rochelle. There, presumably, he pursued a number of interests, including the formulation of his trademark pottery style and glazing, underground Protestant activity, and reading in a variety of texts. It is natural that he might have gravitated to reading Paracelsus and other mystics, for they were renowned as scientists in an age when the borders between natural history, chemistry, and alchemy were permeable. At the same time, Palissy recovered from deep depression over the state of the Protestant cause by taking long nature walks in tidal estuaries, undoubtedly where he contrived his style of pottery but also his theories regarding geology, astrology, and the need for Protestants either to find methods of concealment or to flee to colonial refuges.

Here is not the place to present all of Kamil's interpretation of Palissy, but it is worth noting that this ostensibly humble potter had other aspects to his personality, some of which were not appealing. By cultivating aristocratic patrons who were disposed to ignore his religious heterodoxy, Palissy found employment with the powerful Montmorency family and later was brought to Paris in the 1560s by none other than the queen mother, Catherine de Médicis, who commissioned a ceramic grotto for the Tuileries. Here Palissy was not only tolerated but enjoyed a reputation as a sort of rustic savante among the courtiers and the bourgeoisie. He was warned about the St. Bartholomew's Day massacre in 1572 and was protected until the 1580s, when his activities and behavior became too extreme and he was imprisoned.

Although Kamil presents Palissy as a clever and manipulative individual, others have noted rather vile behavior on his part. He referred to his wife as "my second persecution." He openly quarreled with all his patrons and with both Catholic and Protestant authorities. He even screamed at Philibert de l'Orme, the great French court architect, because de l'Orme was asked to contribute designs for a fountain in Palissy's grotto. In other words, Palissy did not always comport himself in an altogether sane manner, particularly given the volatility of the French court and the sectarian violence taking place all around him.

Yet one other decorative arts detail that is noteworthy is the possible relationship between Palissy and the makers of what are now called "Saint-Porchaire" wares. These extraordinary mannerist vessels are made of white kaolinitic clays and emulated courtly silver vessels. They also featured elaborate modeled figures and black clay inlays in the manner of book covers and damascene work. Fragments of these wares with Palissy-style cast creatures have been found in the Louvre courtyard near fragments of Palissy ware, and the possibility exists that Palissy worked with the shop that produced Saint-Porchaire wares for certain commissions. He thus would have been aware of the highest levels of mannerist design. Another suggestive possibility is that Catherine de Médicis also found Palissy useful because she may have wanted him to research the formula for true porcelain and for glazes that could withstand high firing temperatures. It is difficult to see how she could have tolerated him only for his own style of ceramics, even though it was perfect for a grotto.

In his pursuit of how Palissy's approach may have influenced other Protestants, Kamil explores the alchemical interests of John Winthrop Jr., whose medical, alchemical, and mystic researches can be explored through his correspondence and some of his library, which survives. Winthrop eagerly read the controversial literature on alchemy, particularly the writings of Robert Fludd and Jakob Böhme, and he conducted experiments near his headquarters in New London. Among Kamil's explications of this activity is an extraordinary analysis of the Winthrop wainscot armchair at the Connecticut Historical Society. Kamil asserts, with little justification, that the chair must have been made by John Elderkin in New London, because of a superficial resemblance between the arms and turned ornament of the Winthrop chair and those of the three-posted chair attributed to Elderkin, now in the collection of the Chipstone Foundation. He bases this on an interpretation of the chair's carved back panel as a solar system, after a print of the Copernican system, *The Circle of Urinary Colours,* in Fludd's *Integrum morborum mysterium* (1631), a book Winthrop owned. Although Winthrop's use of the print source for his chair is not implausible, an attribution to Elderkin is, and further, there is reason to think that the Winthrop chair was made in Dutch New York, as may be the case with the equally famous Allyn family draw table and Foote family turned great chair, also at the Connecticut Historical Society.

Another aspect of Winthrop's life was his presence at the siege of La Rochelle in 1628, when Louis XIII's armies effectively reduced the Huguenot citadel despite military support from an English expeditionary force on the Île de Ré outside the harbor. As Kamil suggests, the fall of this stronghold was regarded as a disaster for international Protestantism and influenced many English Calvinists to consider immigrating to the New World. La Rochelle also provides the occasion for Kamil's extended discussion of the interaction of English Protestantism and alchemical literature. It also leads to his intriguing discussion of the experience of Huguenot refugees in London between 1560 and 1740, where they, like the Palatine Germans, were simultaneously hailed as Protestant heroes and reviled as competitors for English tradesmen. Here Kamil suggests that Huguenots continued Palissy's tradition of "dissimulation," wherein they placated the British while systematically exploiting them by positioning themselves as mediators between English consumers and the Parisian luxury trades. The period covered by this interpretation is extremely broad, and Kamil at times seems not to recognize that many influential French Catholic artisans went to England as diplomatic courtesies of the French crown. Be that as it may, his treatment of the relationships between Huguenot artists and William Hogarth is extremely perceptive and amplifies existing treatments of Hogarth's development.

In further suggesting transatlantic implications of refugee thought, Kamil places great emphasis on a Johann Theodore de Bry engraving, *Theatrum orbi,* which appeared in Fludd's *Utriusque cosmi* of 1617, a book current among physicians, alchemists, and those interested in emblems and the occult. This "theater of the world" is depicted as a fortress with Renaissance detailing in the form of arches and an oriel, which Kamil relates to Rosicrucian imagery and to the *hôtel de ville* in La Rochelle or the small fort at Brouage nearby. From this concept he moves on to less useful comparisons with New England court cupboards, which he interprets as theaters of memory, with similar architectural features and smaller objects displayed on the shelves as tokens of origins and religious experience. Why this somewhat extreme conceit renders previous interpretations of these cupboards based on decades of careful antiquarian research "superficial and unsatisfying" (p. 652) is unclear.

In another instance, Kamil employs panels from Wethersfield chests as the headpiece of all the chapters but never addresses fundamental problems of "antiquarian" fact surrounding the maker to whom the chests and cupboards traditionally were ascribed, Peter Blin (1640?–1725). Kamil twice asserts that Blin was a Huguenot, when no proof for this has ever been found. All we know is that he was Francophonic. Also, recent studies of the woodworkers of Windsor, one of which is presented in this issue of *American Furniture,* demonstrate that the Blin style originated with English joiners in Windsor and is not to be regarded as French or Huguenot. All the elaborate iconographic analysis Kamil presents about the chests, to the effect that the motifs are cleverly disguised Huguenot emblems, is therefore cast into doubt.

The final chapters, where Kamil presents his thesis regarding Huguenot furniture-making in New York, is probably the weakest part of the entire book, although it is also obviously key to his arguments regarding the transmission of a Palissy-style, highly involved mystic culture to the New World. Once more, Kamil represents the Huguenot artisans of the colony as practicing "dissimulation" toward Anglo tastemakers in Boston, especially in his chapter "Hidden in Plain Sight," reprinted with little change from his 1995 article in *American Furniture.* In so doing, Kamil refuses to acknowledge the important article on Boston William and Mary leather chairs by Roger Gonzales and Daniel Putnam Brown Jr. in the 1996 issue of *American Furniture,* as well as the equally important article on Dutch New York seating by Erik Gronning in the 2001 issue of *American Furniture.* Gonzales and Brown present a fundamentally convincing case that several of the leather chairs attributed by Kamil to New York are in fact Boston products. It is true that some of the leather chairs (notably figures 15.22–15.26 in Kamil's book) might well be New York products, perhaps made by the Huguenot carver Jean Le Chevalier. Still, the gist of his elaborate argument is overthrown, as are comparisons to turned elements in buildings in Saintonge in southwestern France which he presents as sources. On the face of the illustrations, notably figures 15.28, 15.32, and 16.6, these French turnings are hardly even cognates, let alone direct sources, for the New York objects with which they are compared. A strained argument that the turnings and structure of New York oval-leaf tables of the New York and Kingston variants reflect French prototypes is completely unconvincing. Especially odd is the presentation of a French design for a draw-leaf table as a precedent for the lopers with track boards seen on New York leaf tables, an entirely different structure.

A final chapter aptly entitled "Fragments of Huguenot-Quaker Convergence" investigates the many genealogical and trade ties between Huguenot tradesmen and the Quaker communities on Long Island, which are a staple of New York genealogy and have long intrigued those searching for the origins of Newport block-and-shell furniture. Many of the objects here are almost throwaway inclusions, with no concrete ties to either the Huguenots or the Quakers, but are included simply because they were found in the area. Many of the comparisons between objects, noting the similarity of one detail to another, are implausible. Perhaps the only convincing point is the connection between the elaborate script inscription on the Samuel Clement high chest of drawers at Winterthur and penmanship manuals.

Ultimately it remains to be seen how far Kamil was justified in basing his book on the idea that the "Paracelsian tradition of natural-philosophical and alchemical discourse" was of widespread influence in the New York Huguenot community (p. 902). The psychological model of "dissimulation" seems far more pertinent to the history of eighteenth- and nineteenth-century eastern European Jewry than to French Protestants, who, whatever their difficulties, seem to have otherwise merged quite successfully with the prevailing Dutch culture in New York and New Jersey. In addition, although the Paracelsian tradition might yield important new iconographic results in the interpretation of provincial carving and painting, it can do so only when applied with extreme care. The loose and often inaccurate, use of artifacts in Kamil's book suggests two things. First, with the exception of the Palissy pottery and the many wonderful graphic sources presented, the book could just as easily have been written without any reference to objects at all. Second, one concludes from several careful readings of this huge book that it should have been broken into several related books. Kamil seems to have saved almost all of his research for more than twenty-five years, and during that time a great number of decorative arts researchers published monographs about pertinent material that this book fails to address.

Robert F. Trent
Wilmington, Delaware

Compiled by
Gerald W. R. Ward

Recent Writing on American Furniture: A Bibliography

▼ THIS YEAR'S LIST includes works published in 2004 and roughly through September 2005. As always, a few earlier publications that had escaped notice are also included. The short title *American Furniture 2004* is used in citations for articles and reviews published in last year's edition of this journal, which is also cited in full under Luke Beckerdite's name.

For their assistance in various ways, I am grateful to Jonathan L. Fairbanks, Luke Beckerdite, Tracey Albainy, Gary Albert, Nonie Gadsden, Kelly L'Ecuyer, Darcy Kuronen, Steven M. Lash, Johanna McBrien, and Robert F. Trent, as well as to those scholars who have prepared reviews for this issue.

I would be glad to receive citations for titles that have been inadvertently omitted from this or previous lists, as well as information about new publications. Review copies of significant works would also be much appreciated.

Abercrombie, Stanley. *A Century of Interior Design, 1900–2000: A Timetable of the Design, the Designers, the Products, and the Profession.* New York: Rizzoli, 2003. 240 pp.; 100 color and 300 bw illus., index.

Adams, Peter. "Should Life Influence Art?" *Turning Points* 17, no. 2 (winter 2005): 26–29. 3 bw illus.

Adamson, Glenn. "Unveiling the Renwick's Riches" (exhibition review). In *Furniture Studio 3: Furniture Makers Exploring Digital Technologies,* edited by John Kelsey, 125–26. Asheville, N.C.: The Furniture Society, 2005. Color illus.

———. Review of Robert D. Mussey Jr., *The Furniture Masterworks of John and Thomas Seymour.* In *Studies in the Decorative Arts* 12, no. 1 (fall/winter 2004–2005): 130–33.

Albers, Marjorie, and Peter Hoehnle. *Amana Style: Furniture, Arts, Crafts, Architecture, and Gardens.* Iowa City, Iowa: Penfield Press, 2005. 160 pp.; illus.

Albertson, Andrew. "A Stately Chest Befitting Its Owner: Jacob Kniskern's Schoharie County Chest." *Folk Art* 30, no. 3 (fall 2005): 46–50. 4 color illus.

American Period Furniture 4 (September 2004): 1–63. Numerous bw illus. (Journal of the Society of American Period Furniture Makers.)

Ames, Kenneth L. Review of Jennifer L. Howe, ed., *Cincinnati Art-Carved Furniture and Interiors.* In *American Furniture 2004,* 265–73.

Anderson, Christina. "A Great Exhibition Sideboard by Matthew Bland of Halifax." *Furniture History Society Newsletter,* no. 158 (May 2005): 5–6. 2 bw illus.

Andrews, John. *Arts and Crafts Furniture.* Woodbridge, Eng.: Antique Collectors' Club, 2005. 279 pp.; 275 color illus.

Arthur, Catherine Rogers. "The Work of Gilbert Bigger: Baltimore Clock and Watchmaker and a New Attribution to Levin Tarr." *The Catalogue of Antiques and Fine Art* 5, no. 4 (autumn 2004): 196–98. 4 color illus.

Arthur, Catherine Rogers, and Cindy Kelly. *Homewood House.* Baltimore: Johns Hopkins University Press, 2004. 174 pp.; illus.

[Auraden Collection]. *Americana: The Collection of the Late J. John Auraden of Hamilton, Ohio.* Cincinnati: Cowan's Auctions, October 21–22, 2004. 172 pp.; numerous color illus. (See esp. lots 750–64, furniture from nineteenth-century Germanic settlement in Oldenburg, Indiana.)

Bach, Debra Schmidt. "Witness to History: Furniture and Historic Relics" [in the New-York Historical Society]. *Antiques* 167, no. 1 (January 2005): 162–67. 11 color illus.

Baizerman, Suzanne, and Oscar P. FitzGerald. "Curv-iture." In *Furniture Studio 3: Furniture Makers Exploring Digital Technologies,* edited by John Kelsey, 72–85. Asheville, N.C.: The Furniture Society, 2005. Color illus.

Baker, Donna S., ed. *Danish Modern and Beyond: Scandinavian Inspired Furniture from Heywood-Wakefield.* Atglen, Pa.: Schiffer, 2005. 176 pp.; illus.

Baldon, Russell. "Emerging Artists Confront Traditional Notions about Function and Craft." In *Furniture Studio 3: Furniture Makers Exploring Digital Technologies,* edited by John Kelsey, 48–59. Asheville, N.C.: The Furniture Society, 2005. Color illus.

Balla, Wesley G. "Treasures of New Hampshire: Decorative Arts from the Collections of the New Hampshire Historical Society." *The Catalogue of Antiques and Fine Art* 6, no. 3 (late summer 2005): 162–65. 6 color illus.

Banks, William Nathaniel. "Living with Antiques: The Mary and Robert Raley Collection." *Antiques* 168, no. 4 (October 2005): 128–37. 13 color illus.

Bassett, Lynne Zacek. "Inspired Fantasy: Design Sources for New England's Whole-Cloth Wool Quilts." *Antiques* 168, no. 3 (September 2005): 120–27. 16 color and 4 bw illus.

Bates, Elizabeth. "The [John Townsend] Symposium." *Maine Antique Digest* 33, no. 7 (July 2005): 21A.

Baxter, Paula A. "The Regency Style's Debt to Napoleon." *Antiques* 166, no. 4 (October 2004): 152–61. 10 color and 1 bw illus.

Beach, Laura. *The Art of Stephen Hunek.* New York: Harry N. Abrams, 2004. 224 pp.; numerous color illus.

———. "Connecticut Valley Furniture: Eliphalet Chapin and His Contemporaries, 1750–1800." *Antiques and the Arts Weekly* (April 29, 2005): 1, 50–52. 20 bw illus.

———. "John Townsend, Newport Cabinetmaker." *Antiques and the Arts Weekly* (July 8, 2005): 1, 40–43. 18 bw illus.

———. "Living with Antiques: The Marc and Tracy Whitehead Collection." *Antiques* 168, no. 3 (September 2005): 110–19. 14 color illus.

———. "'Our Young Nation': American Federal Furniture and Decorative Arts from the Watson Collection" (book and exhibition review). *Antiques and the Arts Weekly* (September 24, 2004): 1, 50–51. 14 bw illus.

———. "The Past Is Present in Newport." *The Catalogue of Antiques and Fine Art* 6, no. 2 (summer 2005): 114–25. Color illus.

Beam, Michael J. *Wendell Castle: What Pluck!* Niagara, N.Y.: Castellani Art Museum of Niagara University, 2005. 4 pp.; color illus.

Beckerdite, Luke, ed. *American Furniture 2004*. Milwaukee, Wis.: Chipstone Foundation, 2004. vii + 301 pp.; numerous color and bw illus., index. Distributed by University Press of New England, Hanover and London.

Beckerdite, Luke, and Alan Miller. "A Table's Tale: Craft, Art, and Opportunity in Eighteenth-Century Philadelphia." In *American Furniture 2004,* 2–45. 76 color and bw illus.

[Bennett, Garry Knox]. "Furniture Exhibition in Oakland, Calif., Presents Chairs by Garry Knox Bennett." *Antiques and the Arts Weekly* (February 11, 2005): 54. 2 bw illus.

Benson, Jonathan. "The Commission: A Collaborative Process." In *Furniture Studio 3: Furniture Makers Exploring Digital Technologies*, edited by John Kelsey, 34–40. Asheville, N.C.: The Furniture Society, 2005. Color illus.

Berry, John D. *Herman Miller: The Purpose of Design*. New York: Rizzoli, 2004. 272 pp.; illus.

Binzen, Jonathan. "A Conversation with Furnituremaker Judy Kenlsey McKie." *Woodwork*, no. 95 (October 2005): 24–30. Color illus.

———. "The Marriage of Decorative and Fine Art." In *Furniture Studio 3: Furniture Makers Exploring Digital Technologies,* edited by John Kelsey, 115–18. Asheville, N.C.: The Furniture Society, 2005. Color illus.

Bony, Anne. *Furniture and Interiors of the 1960s*. Paris: Flammarion, 2004. 224 pp.; 216 color and 94 bw illus., bibliography, index. Distributed by Rizzoli, New York.

Boram-Hays, Carol. *Bringing Modernism Home: Ohio Decorative Arts, 1890–1960, Including Ceramics, Furniture, Glass, and Metalwork*. Athens: Ohio University Press in association with the Columbus Museum of Art, 2005. ix + 241 pp.; numerous color and bw illus., appendixes, bibliography, index.

Bowett, Adam. "Tea Tables and India Backs: Some Chinese Influences in Early Georgian Furniture." *The Catalogue of Antiques and Fine Art* 5, no. 5 (2004): 242–47. 10 color and bw illus.

Breed, Allan. "Creating a Newport Shell." *The Catalogue of Antiques and Fine Art* 6, no. 2 (summer 2005): 148–49. 11 color illus.

Breitner, Susan. "Pursuing Art for Three Generations." *The Catalogue of Antiques and Fine Art* 6, no. 4 (autumn/winter 2005): 156–67. Color illus.

Brooks, Bradley C. Review of Jennifer L. Howe, ed., *Cincinnati Art-Carved Furniture and Interiors*. In *Winterthur Portfolio* 39, no. 4 (winter 2004): 288–92.

Brown, Johanna. "Lewis Bond's Neoclassical Desk." *The Luminary* 26, no. 1 (spring 2005): 1, 7. 1 bw illus.

———. "MESDA and the Study of Early Southern Decorative Arts." *Antiques* 167, no. 3 (March 2005): 92–101. 15 color and 1 bw illus.

———, comp. "New to the Collections." *The Luminary* 25, no. 2 (autumn 2004): 6–7. (Includes bed, ca. 1810–1840, from Salem, North Carolina.)

Brown, Sandy, and Maya Kumar Mitchell, eds. *The Beauty of Craft: A Resurgence*. White River Junction, Vt.: Chelsea Green, 2005. 192 pp.; illus.

Burman, Bruce. "Alive and Kicking. . . ." In *Furniture Studio 3: Furniture Makers Exploring Digital Technologies,* edited by John Kelsey, 60–71. Asheville, N.C.: The Furniture Society, 2005. Color illus.

Busch, Jason T. "Lifestyle: Americana in Minnesota." *The Catalogue of Antiques and Fine Art* 6, no. 4 (autumn/winter 2005): 174–85. Color illus.

[Byers, John Eric]. *John Eric Byers: A Mid-Career Retrospective, Fuller Craft Museum, October 11, 2004–January 2, 2005, and John Eric Byers: New Work, Gallery NAGA, October 8–November 6, 2004, in Collaboration with Clark Gallery.* N.p.: n.p., 2004. 24 pp.; color illus. (Includes essay by Deborah Weisgall.)

Byrdcliffe 2005: The Property of Jill and Mark Willcox, with No Additions. Rose Valley, Pa.: James R. Bakker, auctioneer, in association with Robert Edwards, October 27, 2005. Unpaged; color illus.

[Cape Cod Museum of Art]. "Furniture as Sculpture at Cape Cod Museum of Art." *Antiques and the Arts Weekly* (July 15, 2005): 64. 1 bw illus. (Re contemporary studio furniture at museum in Dennis, Massachusetts.)

Carnot, Brooke. "Manufactured Taste or True Desire: How Commission Artists Learn to 'Read' the Client." In *Furniture Studio 3: Furniture Makers Exploring Digital Technologies,* edited by John Kelsey, 41–47. Asheville, N.C.: The Furniture Society, 2005. Color illus.

Carr, Dennis Andrew. "The Account Book of Benjamin Baker." In *American Furniture 2004,* 46–89. 14 color and bw illus., appendix.

Castle,Wendell. "Ruhlmann." *American Craft* 65, no. 1 (February–March 2005): 56–59. Color illus.

Chicirda, Tara Gleason. Review of Robert D. Mussey Jr., *The Furniture Masterworks of John and Thomas Seymour.* In *Winterthur Portfolio* 39, no. 4 (winter 2004): 281–84.

Cogdell, Christina. *Eugenic Design: Streamlining America in the 1930s.* Philadelphia: University of Pennsylvania Press, 2004. xvii + 328

pp.; bw illus., bibliography, index.
"Colonial Comfort: Trading in Furniture with the West Indies." *Furniture History Society Newsletter,* no. 159 (August 2005): 18–22. (Synopses of talks, written by the authors, from annual symposium held February 26, 2005).
Conforth, John. *Early Georgian Interiors.* New Haven: Yale University Press, 2004. 360 pp.; numerous color and bw illus., bibliography, index.
Convergence: Crossing the Divide; The Studio Furniture of Tasmania and America. Oceanside, Calif.: Oceanside Museum of Art, 2005. Unpaged; color illus.
Cooke, Edward S., Jr. "Refined Vernacular: The Work of Kenneth Fisher." *Woodwork,* no. 91 (February 2005): 53–59. Color and bw illus.
Cranz, Galen. "Reinterpreting the Windsor Chair." In *Furniture Studio 3: Furniture Makers Exploring Digital Technologies,* edited by John Kelsey, 86–91. Asheville, N.C.: The Furniture Society, 2005. Color illus.
Cross, John. "Ralph, Cuthbert and Thomas Turnbull: A Nineteenth-Century Jamaican Cabinet-Making Family." *Furniture History* 39 (2003): 109–20. 9 color and bw illus.
Curley, John J. "The Albatross of Functionality" (book review). In *Furniture Studio 3: Furniture Makers Exploring Digital Technologies,* edited by John Kelsey, 118–24. Asheville, N.C.: The Furniture Society, 2005. Color illus.
[Currier Museum]. "Currier Museum to Host New Hampshire Furniture Masters' Exhibit, Opens July 15." *Antiques and the Arts Weekly* (July 8, 2005): 51. 2 bw illus.
D'Ambrosio, Anna Tobin. "American Art Brass." *Antiques* 168, no. 4 (October 2005): 100–109. 17 color illus.
D'Ambrosio, Anna Tobin, with contributions by Nina Gray, Katherine A. Holbrow, and Gerri Strickler. *A Brass Menagerie: Metalwork of the Aesthetic Movement.* Utica, N.Y.: Munson-Williams-Proctor Arts Institute, 2005. 96 pp.; numerous color and bw illus., catalogue of the exhibition, bibliography, index.
Denenberg, Thomas A. Review of Mira Nakashima, *Nature, Form, and Spirit: The Life and Legacy of George Nakashima.* In *American Furniture 2004,* 277–84.
Dervan, Andrew H. "Waltham Clock Company: History and Clock Production." *NAWCC Bulletin* 47, no. 2 (April 2005): 193–207. 22 bw illus.
"Discoveries: Document Box." *The Catalogue of Antiques and Fine Art* 5, no. 4 (autumn 2004): 38. 1 color illus. (Re pine box of ca. 1690–1720 from the Connecticut River Valley, acquired by the Wadsworth Atheneum, Hartford.)
"Discoveries: Tall Case Clock." *The Catalogue of Antiques and Fine Art* 5, no. 4 (autumn 2004): 36. 2 color illus. (Re example by Simon Willard, ca. 1790.)
Disviscour, Jeannine. "Furniture in Maryland Life." *The Catalogue of Antiques and Fine Art* 6, no. 1 (spring 2005): 158–61. 6 color illus.
Douglas, Andrew. "A Jeffersonian Ideal: Selections from the Dr. and Mrs. Henry C. Landon III Collection." *The Catalogue of Antiques and Fine Art* 6, no. 4 (autumn/winter 2005): 192–98. Color illus.
Dunlop, Hank. "Living with Antiques: The Brune-Reutlinger House, San Francisco." *Antiques* 168, no. 2 (August 2005): 82–89.
Eco, Umberto, ed. *History of Beauty.* Trans. Alastair McEwen. New York: Rizzoli, 2004. 438 pp.; numerous color and bw illus., bibliography, indexes.
Edwards, Clive. *Turning Houses into Homes: A History of the Retailing and Consumption of Domestic Furnishings.* Aldershot, Eng., and Burlington, Vt.: Ashgate, 2005. 304 pp.; illus.
Eerdmans, Emily. "German Cabinet-Makers in New York, *c.* 1825–*c.* 1850." *Furniture History* 40 (2004): 99–112. 7 bw illus.
Esler, Jennifer. "Curator's Choice: A Collection of the Valley." *The Catalogue of Antiques and Fine Art* 6, no. 1 (spring 2005): 164–65. 4 color illus.
Evans, Nancy Goyne. "The Classical Impulse in American Vernacular Chairs." *The Catalogue of Antiques and Fine Art* 5, no. 4 (autumn 2004): 209–13. 8 color illus., line drawing.
Falino, Jeannine. "John Eric Byers." *American Craft* 65, no. 2 (April–May 2005): 44–47. 5 color illus.
Fariello, M. Anna, and Paula Owen, eds. *Objects and Meaning: New Perspectives on Art and Craft.* Lanham, Md.: Scarecrow Press, 2004. 235 pp.; illus.
Fayen, Sarah. "Tea Tables and Coffee Tables." *The Catalogue of Antiques and Fine Art* 6, no. 1 (spring 2005): 143–47. 6 color illus.
FitzGerald, Dennis. "New Chips off Old Blocks: Furniture Professors Choose Their Best Student Work." In *Furniture Studio 3: Furniture Makers Exploring Digital Technologies,* edited by John Kelsey, 20–33. Asheville, N.C.: The Furniture Society, 2005. Color illus.
Fitzgerald, Oscar P. "Who Makes Studio Furniture? Interviews with 109 Well-Known Artists." In *Furniture Studio 3: Furniture Makers Exploring Digital Technologies,* edited by John Kelsey, 92–105. Asheville, N.C.: The Furniture Society, 2005. Color illus.
Flanders, Judith. *Inside the Victorian Home: A Portrait of Domestic Life in Victorian England.* New York: W. W. Norton, 2003. xxviii + 499 pp.; numerous color and bw illus., line drawings, bibliography, index.
Fleming, John, and Michael Rowan. *Folk Furniture of Canada's Doukhobors, Hutterites, Mennonites, and Ukrainians.* Edmonton: University of Alberta Press, 2004. 176 pp.; 100+ color illus., bibliography, index.
Fogarty, Kate. "Design Takes Flight." *Modernism* 8, no. 2 (summer 2005): 132. 3 color illus.
Follansbee, Peter. "Hand Tools,

Green Wood." *Woodwork,* no. 93 (June 2005): 30–31. Color illus.
Forti, John, Elisabeth Garrett, and Carolyn Roy. "A Neighborhood through Time: Strawbery Banke Museum in Portsmouth, New Hampshire." *The Catalogue of Antiques and Fine Art* 6, no. 3 (late summer 2005): 148–55. 18 color illus.
Furniture Matters (A Periodic Forum of The Furniture Society) (October 2004): 1–12. bw illus.
Furniture Matters (A Periodic Forum of The Furniture Society) (March 2005): 1–12. bw illus.
Furniture Society, The. *Furniture 2005: The Other Side / A Tradition of Alternatives.* Asheville, N.C.: The Furniture Society, 2005. 224 pp.; numerous color and bw illus., index. (Includes program for ninth annual Furniture Society program and a makers' portfolio of new work.)
Galinou, Mireille, ed. *City Merchants and the Arts, 1670–1720.* London: Oblong Creative for the Corporation of London, 2004. xii + 216 pp.; 129 color and bw illus., biographies, bibliography, index.
"Gallery." *Woodwork,* no. 90 (December 2004): 52–57. Color illus.
"Gallery." *Woodwork,* no. 91 (February 2005): 46–52. Color illus.
"Gallery." *Woodwork,* no. 92 (April 2005): 44–48. Color illus.
"Gallery." *Woodwork,* no. 93 (June 2005): 49–55. Color illus.
"Gallery." *Woodwork,* no. 94 (August 2005): 45–51. Color illus.
"Gallery." *Woodwork,* no. 95 (October 2005): 44–51. Color illus.
"Gallery." *Woodwork,* no. 96 (December 2005): 38–45. Color illus.
Garfield, Davies. "The English Overmantel Looking Glass." *Antiques* 168, no. 4 (October 2005): 150–55. 7 color illus.
Garrett, Wendell. "Making a Name." *Sotheby's Preview* (September–October 2004): 52–59. Color and bw illus. (Re Jeffords collection.)
Gibson, Scott. "The Furniture Masters of New Hampshire." *Woodwork,* no. 93 (June 2005): 64–71. Color illus.
Gladwell, Malcolm. *Blink: The Power of Thinking without Thinking.* New York and Boston: Little, Brown, 2005. 277 pp.; index.
Glasgow, Andrew, et al. *Studio Furniture: Expression and Function.* Emory, Va.: Emory & Henry College, 2004. 40 pp.; color illus.
———. *Studio Furniture: Expression and Function: Addendum.* Emory, Va.: Emory & Henry College, 2005. 28 pp.; color illus.
Goloboy, Joan. "Treasures from the Marblehead Museum Collection." *The Catalogue of Antiques and Fine Art* 6, no. 4 (autumn/winter 2005): 206–8. 6 color illus.
Goodison, Nicholas. *Furniture History: Forty Years On.* London: Furniture History Society, 2004. 44 pp. ("Lecture delivered to the Furniture History Society on the occasion of its fortieth anniversary, on 4 October 2004, at the Meeting Room of the Society of Antiquaries, Burlington House, Piccadilly"; includes list of officers of the society; list of articles published in the society's journal; list of annual lectures, 1967–2004; and list of annual symposia, 1974–2004.)
Goodwillie, Christian. "Coloring the Past: Shaker Painted Interiors." *Antiques* 168, no. 3 (September 2005): 80–87. 12 color illus.
Gronning, Erik. "Period Pieces." *Sotheby's Preview* (January–February 2005): 82. 1 color illus.
Green, Nancy E. "Byrdcliffe and the 'Dream of Somewhere.'" *Decorative Arts Society 1850 to the Present* 28 (2004): 56–81. 26 color and bw illus.
Gustafson, Eleanor H. "Museum Accessions." *Antiques* 167, no. 3 (March 2005): 28. 4 color illus. (Includes three-part dining table, Middle Atlantic States, ca. 1795, acquired by Mount Vernon.)
———. "Museum Accessions." *Antiques* 167, no. 5 (May 2005): 32, 34. 5 color illus. (Re tall clock with works by Peter Stretch of Philadelphia, 1735–1746, acquired by Winterthur; Boston armchair of 1863 acquired by Historic New England; desk, York, Maine, ca. 1735–1745, acquired by Strawbery Banke Museum; tea table, Virginia, 1745–1750, acquired by Colonial Williamsburg; clothespress, eastern shore of Virginia, ca. 1800, acquired by Jamestown-Yorktown Foundation.)
———, ed. "Collectors' Notes: Nathan Starkey Redivivus." *Antiques* 168, no. 4 (October 2005): 68–72. 5 color illus.
Habegger, Jerryll, and Joseph H. Osman. *Sourcebook of Modern Furniture.* 3rd ed. New York: W. W. Norton, 2005. 788 pp.; numerous color and bw illus.
Hagen, Susan. "Woodworking Savoir-Faire: The Furniture, Vessels, and Sculpture of Mark Sfirri." *Woodwork,* no. 94 (August 2005): 26–32. Color illus.
Hanks, David A., and Anne Hoy. "Streamlining and Art Deco in American Industrial Design." *Antiques* 166, no. 4 (October 2004): 114–23. 12 color and 5 bw illus.
Heckscher, Morrison H. "Newport and the Townsend Inheritance." *Antiques* 167, no. 5 (May 2005): 100–105. 8 color and 1 bw illus.
———. "Newport in New York." *The Catalogue of Antiques and Fine Art* 6, no. 2 (summer 2005): 134–41. 9 color and bw illus.
Heckscher, Morrison H., with the assistance of Lori Zabar. *John Townsend: Newport Cabinetmaker.* New Haven: Yale University Press; New York: Metropolitan Museum of Art, 2005. xii + 224 pp.; numerous color and bw illus., appendixes, bibliographies, index.
Henderson, Michael. "Samuel Shourds and the Philadelphia Influence." *NAWCC Bulletin* 46, no. 5 (October 2004): 631–36. 6 bw illus.
"Highlights: Florence Knoll Bassett, Defining Modern." *The Catalogue of Antiques and Fine Art* 5, no. 4

(autumn 2004): 54. 2 color illus. (Re exhibition at Philadelphia Museum of Art.)

"Highlights: Quebec Country Furniture." *The Catalogue of Antiques and Fine Art* 6, no. 2 (summer 2005): 96. 2 color illus.

Hill, May Brawley. "Living with Antiques: New England and European Antiques at Home in Connecticut." *Antiques* 168, no. 1 (July 2005): 90–99. 16 color illus.

Hogbin, Stephen. "Broadening Experience." *Turning Points* 17, no. 2 (winter 2005): 6–7. 2 bw illus.

Holcomb, Grant. *Wendell Castle in Rochester.* Rochester, N.Y.: Memorial Art Gallery of the University of Rochester, 2005. 12 pp.; color illus.

Hughes, Robert. "Claw Daddy." *New York Times Magazine,* May 29, 2005, 50–53. Color illus. (Re John Townsend.)

Jannasch, Emanuel. "Like Seashells: The Work of John McNabb." *Woodwork,* no. 90 (December 2004): 26–37. Color illus.

Jayne, Thomas. "Designing for the 21st Century: Collecting Upholstered Furniture." *The Catalogue of Antiques and Fine Art* 6, no. 2 (summer 2005): 98–99. 3 color illus.

Johnson, Thomas B. "Maine Furniture Production from 1630 to 1830: Recent Research and Discoveries." In *Piscataqua Decorative Arts Society: Volume 1, 2002–2003 Lecture Series,* 22–29. Portsmouth, N.H.: Piscataqua Decorative Arts Society, 2004. 11 bw illus.

Julier, Guy. *The Thames & Hudson Dictionary of Design since 1900.* New York and London: Thames and Hudson, 2005. 224 pp.; 245 bw illus., chronology, bibliography. Distributed by W. W. Norton, New York.

Kagan, Vladimir. *The Complete Kagan: A Lifetime of Avant-Garde Design.* New York: Pointed Leaf Press, 2004. 272 pp.; numerous color and bw illus., bibliography, chronology, index.

Kamil, Neil. *Fortress of the Soul: Violence, Metaphysics, and Material Life in the Huguenots' New World, 1517–1751.* Baltimore: Johns Hopkins University Press, 2005. xxiv + 1058 pp.; numerous bw illus., maps, line drawings, index.

Kaplan, Wendy, et al. *The Arts and Crafts Movement in Europe and America: Design for the Modern World.* New York: Thames and Hudson in association with the Los Angeles County Museum of Art, 2004. 328 pp.; 256 color and 58 bw illus., checklist, index. Distributed by W. W. Norton, New York.

[Kelly Collection]. *Important New York Furniture and Decorative Arts: The Richard and Beverly Kelly Collection.* Portsmouth, N.H.: Northeast Auctions, April 3, 2005. 84 pp.; numerous color illus. (See also articles by Thomas Gordon Smith and Philip D. Zimmerman cited below.)

Kelsey, John, ed. *Furniture Studio 3: Furniture Makers Exploring Digital Technologies.* Asheville, N.C.: The Furniture Society, 2005. 128 pp.; numerous color illus., index.

Kenny, Peter M. "Opulence Abroad: Honoré Lannuier's Gilded Furniture in Trinidad de Cuba." In *American Furniture 2004,* 239–64. 29 color and bw illus.

Keno, Leslie. "Lines of Beauty and Grace." *Sotheby's Preview* (January–February 2005): 80–81. 4 color illus.

Kiesler, Frederick, ed. *Friedrich Kiesler: Designer, Seating Furniture of the '30s amd '40s.* Ostfildern, Germany: Hatje Cantz Verlag, 2005. 128 pp.; illus.

Kirtley, Alexandra Alevizatos. *The 1772 Philadelphia Furniture Price Book: A Facsimile.* Philadelphia: Philadelphia Museum of Art and Antique Collectors' Club, 2005. 96 pp.; 12 bw illus.

———. "The 1772 Philadelphia Furniture Price Book Rediscovered." *Antiques* 167, no. 5 (May 2005): 142–45. 4 color and 1 bw illus.

Koon, Larry. *Stickley Brothers Furniture: Identification and Value Guide.* Paducah, Ken.: Collector Books, 2004. 240 pp.; illus.

Kugelman, Alice, and Thomas P. Kugelman. "Case Furniture of the Chapin School, 1775–1800." *Antiques* 167, no. 2 (February 2005): 58–65. 18 color illus.

———. "Connecticut Valley Furniture, 1750–1800." *The Catalogue of Antiques and Fine Art* 5, no. 5 (2004): 236–41. 9 color and bw illus.

Kugelman, Thomas P., and Alice K. Kugelman. "Furniture in the Colchester, Connecticut, Style." *Antiques* 168, no. 3 (September 2005): 96–103. 12 color and 1 bw illus.

Kugelman, Thomas P., and Alice K. Kugelman, with Robert Lionetti. *Connecticut Valley Furniture: Eliphalet Chapin and His Contemporaries, 1750–1800.* Edited by Susan Schoelwer. Hartford: Connecticut Historical Society, 2005. 540 pp.; numerous illus., maps, glossary, bibliography. Distributed by University Press of New England, Hanover and London.

Kuronen, Darcy. "An Organized Piano by Alpheus Babcock." In *Organ Restoration Reconsidered: Proceedings of a Colloquium,* edited by John R. Watson, 159–69.Warren, Mich.: Harmonie Park Press, 2005. 11 bw illus.

Lambourne, Lionel. *Japonisme: Cultural Crossings between Japan and the West.* New York: Phaidon, 2004. 240 pp.; 220 color and 30 bw illus.

Lane, Joshua W. "A Tale of Two Craftsmen: Connecticut River Valley Neoclassical Furniture." *The Catalogue of Antiques and Fine Art* 5, no. 4 (autumn 2004): 194–95. 2 color illus.

———. "What's New at Historic Deerfield, Inc.? Recent Museum Acquisitions." *Antiques and the Arts Weekly* (September 30, 2005): 40–41. 7 bw illus.

Latta, Stephen. "Line and Berry Inlaid Spice Box: Hands-On." *The Catalogue of Antiques and Fine Art* 6, no. 1 (spring 2005): 176–77. 11 color illus.

Ledes, Allison Eckardt. "Current and Coming: Gothic Revival in Philadelphia." *Antiques* 167, no. 4 (April 2005): 18. 3 color illus. (Re exhibition at Philadelphia Antiques Show.)

———. "Current and Coming: More about Painted Finishes." *Antiques* 168, no. 3 (September 2005): 16. 1 color illus.

———. "Current and Coming: Tiffany, Virtuoso Designer." *Antiques* 168, no. 4 (October 2005): 18–20. 2 color illus.

Livingstone, Karen, and Linda Parry, eds. *International Arts and Crafts*. London: V&A Publications, 2005. 367 pp.; numerous color and bw illus., bibliography, indexes.

Locklair, Paula W. "The Museum of Early Southern Decorative Arts: Forty Wonderful Years." *The Catalogue of Antiques and Fine Art* 6, no. 1 (spring 2005): 170–75. Color illus.

———, et al. *Southern Perspective: A Sampling from the Museum of Early Southern Decorative Arts*. Winston-Salem, N.C.: Old Salem, Inc., Museum of Early Southern Decorative Arts, 2005. ix + 86 pp.; numerous color illus.

Logan, William Bryant. *Oak: The Frame of Civilization*. New York: W. W. Norton, 2005. 320 pp.; illus.

Long, Robert. "Brian Newell." *American Craft* 64, no. 5 (October–November 2004): 66–69. 5 color illus.

———. "Tommy Simpson: Tapping into Universal Memory." *American Craft* 65, no. 5 (October–November 2005): 60–63. 6 color illus.

Loring. John. *Tiffany Timepieces*. New York: Harry N. Abrams, 2004. 304 pp.; numerous color and bw illus., glossary, index.

Lowe, Philip C. "Hands On: Klismos Armchairs." *The Catalogue of Antiques and Fine Art* 6, no. 4 (autumn/winter 2005): 222–23. 12 color illus.

Mascolo, Frances McQueeny-Jones. "Arts and Crafts Movement Explored at LACMA." *Antiques and the Arts Weekly* (January 21, 2005): 1, 40–41. 13 bw illus.

———. "'Florence Knoll Basset: Defining Modern' at the Philadelphia Museum of Art." *Antiques and the Arts Weekly* (December 17, 2004): 1, 40–41. 11 bw illus.

———. "'A Jeffersonian Ideal.'" *Antiques and the Arts Weekly* (September 2, 2005): 1, 40–41. 13 bw illus. (Re exhibition at University of Virginia Art Museum of the Dr. and Mrs. Henry C. Landon collection.)

———. "A New Museum to Celebrate the Shenandoah Valley." *Antiques and the Arts Weekly* (April 22, 2005): 1, 40–41. 14 bw illus.

Mass, Jennifer L., Catherine R. Matsen, and Janice H. Carlson. "Materials of the Pennsylvania German Fraktur Artist." *Antiques* 168, no. 3 (September 2005): 128–35. 10 color illus.

[Mattia, Alphonse]. "Fellow: Alphonse Mattia." *American Craft* 65, no. 5 (October–November 2005): 53. 3 color illus.

McBrien, Johanna. "Harmonious Arrangements: A Collection of Folk and Contemporary Art." *The Catalogue of Antiques and Fine Art* 6, no. 3 (late summer 2005): 128–39. Color illus.

———. "Striking the Perfect Balance." *The Catalogue of Antiques and Fine Art* 6, no. 2 (summer 2005): 100–111. Numerous color illus.

———. "A Summer Estate Preserved." *The Catalogue of Antiques and Fine Art* 6, no. 3 (late summer 2005): 116–27. Color illus. (Re Stillington Hall, Gloucester, Massachusetts.)

McKie, Judy Kensley. "Judy Kensley McKie on Drawing." *Woodwork*, no. 95 (October 2005): 31. 1 line drawing.

McKinstry, E. Richard. "Scrapbook Houses." *Newsletter of the Decorative Arts Society* 13, no. 1 (spring 2005): 12–13. 3 bw illus.

[Memorial Art Gallery, Rochester, New York]. "Wendell Castle at Memorial Art Gallery." *Antiques and the Arts Weekly* (December 17, 2004): 56. 2 bw illus.

[Michalik, Daniel]. "Portfolio: Daniel Michalik." *American Craft* 65, no. 1 (February–March 2005): 61. 1 color illus.

Michels, Eileen Manning. *Reconfiguring Harvey Ellis*. Edina, Minn.: Beaver's Pond Press, 2004. ix + 364 pp.; numerous color and bw illus., appendixes, index.

Miller, Judith, ed. *Furniture*. New York: DK Publishing, 2005. 560 pp.; 3,500+ color illus., appendixes, glossary, bibliography, index.

Muller, Charles. "Soap Hollow and Jacob Knagy: Differences and Similarities." *Maine Antique Digest* 33, no. 7 (July 2005): 28A–29A. 20 bw illus.

Murphy, Martin. "The Missing Objects Project." *The Catalogue of Antiques and Fine Art* 6, no. 4 (autumn/winter 2005): 220–21. 2 color illus. (Re Cadwalader family furniture.)

Newbern, Thomas R. J., and James R. Melchor. *Classical Norfolk Furniture: 1810–1840*. Paducah, Ky.: Turner Publishing, 2004. 128 pp.; numerous color illus., bibliography, index.

Newcomber, John. "Lifestyle: The Rewards of Discipline." *The Catalogue of Antiques and Fine Art* 6, no. 1 (spring 2005): 62–73. Color illus.

Pearce, Clark. "Living with Antiques: A Federal Collection." *Antiques* 167, no. 5 (May 2005): 106–15. 14 color illus.

[Philadelphia Museum of Art]. *Florence Knoll Bassett: Defining Modern*. Philadelphia: Philadelphia Museum of Art, 2004. Unpaged; 19 color and bw illus., chronology, bibliography. (Small pamphlet by Kathryn Heisinger accompanying a temporary exhibition.)

Pilch, Tracey. "George Nakashima: Nature, Form, and Spirit." *Antiques and the Arts Weekly* (October 8, 2004): 1, 40–41. Numerous bw illus.

Chipstone Foundation Publications

www.chipstone.org

Title	*Code*	*Qty*	*Price*
American Furniture 2005	AF2005	____	$55
Back Issues Available 1994 – 2004	AFback	____	$55
American Furniture – *2 year subscription*		____	$100
American Furniture – *3 year subscription*		____	$145
Ceramics in America 2005	CA2005	____	$55
Ceramics in America 2001–2004	CAback	____	$55
Ceramics in America – *2 year subscription*		____	$100
Ceramics in America – *3 year subscription*		____	$145
If These Pots Could Talk	IFTHCL	____	$75
____________	______	____	____
Shipping		____	____

U.S. Shipping $5.00 for first book; $1.25 for each additional book.
Foreign Shipping $6.50 for first book; $2.00 for each additional book.

TOTAL ____________

Name ______________________________

Tel ______________________________

Address ______________________________

____

City State ZIP ______________________________

❏ Check payable to "UPNE"

Credit Card

❏ AMEX ❏ Discover ❏ Mastercard ❏ VISA

CC# ______________________ Expires __________

Please send to:
University Press of New England
37 Lafayette Street
Lebanon, NH 03766
University.Press@Dartmouth.edu
800-421-1561 FAX 603-643-1540 www.upne.com

Prown, Jonathan. "John Singleton Copley's Furniture and the Art of Invention." In *American Furniture 2004*, 152–204. 62 color and bw illus.

Rand, Marvin. *Greene and Greene*. Salt Lake City: Gibbs Smith, 2005. 208 pp.; illus.

Recourt, Peter. "Ephraim Willard: A New Perspective." *NAWCC Bulletin* 47, no. 1 (February 2005): 42–50. 18 color illus., bibliography.

[Reid, Brian David]. "Portfolio: Brian David Reid." *American Craft* 65, no. 3 (June–July 2005): 56. 2 color illus.

Richmond, Andrew. "Southern Sophistication on the Early Frontier: The Inlaid Furniture of Washington County, Ohio." In *American Furniture 2004*, 205–38. 39 color and bw illus.

Rieman, Timothy D., and Jean M. Burks. *The Shaker Furniture Handbook*. Atglen, Pa.: Schiffer Publishing, 2005. 128 pp.; illus.

Rini, Erik. "Edward Holmes and Simeon Haines, Cabinetmakers in Empire New York City." *Antiques* 167, no. 5 (May 2005): 124–29. 9 color and 2 bw illus.

Roberts, Ellen E. Review of Jennifer L. Howe, ed., *Cincinnati Art Carved Furniture and Interiors*. In *Studies in the Decorative Arts* 12, no. 1 (fall/winter 2004–2005): 135–39.

Sack, Albert. "Tales of Portsmouth Furniture." In *Piscataqua Decorative Arts Society: Volume 1, 2002–2003 Lecture Series*, 30–40. Portsmouth, N.H.: Piscataqua Decorative Arts Society, 2004. 16 bw illus.

Sarti, Raffaella. *Europe at Home: Family and Material Culture, 1500–1800*. New Haven: Yale University Press, 2004. 324 pp.; 12 color and 74 bw illus,. bibliography, index.

Schinto, Jeanne. "Connecticut Valley Furniture: More than 14 Years of Research Finally Bears Its Fruit." *Maine Antique Digest* 33, no. 4 (April 2005): 30B–32B. 20 bw illus.

———. "Rhode Island Clockmaking, from Claggett to Durfee." *Maine Antique Digest* 32, no. 12 (December 2004): 6D–7D. 10 bw illus.

Sessions, Ralph. *The Shipcarvers' Art: Figureheads and Cigar Store Indians in Nineteenth-Century America*. Princeton: Princeton University Press, 2005. 240 pp.; illus.

Sfirri, Mark. "Creativity in Woodturning." *Turning Points* 17, no. 2 (winter 2005): 30–33. 4 bw illus.

[Shelburne Museum]. "Quebec Country Furniture." *Antiques and the Arts Weekly* (June 3, 2005): 9. 3 bw illus.

[Simpson, Tommy]. *Milestone, 1964–2004: Forty Years Celebration Exhibition*. New York: Leo Kaplan Modern, 2004. Color illus.

Sims, Carol. "Colonial Williamsburg Acquires Baltimore Fancy Furniture." *Antiques and the Arts Weekly* (December 3, 2004): 27. 2 bw illus.

Smith, Thomas Gordon. "The Richard and Beverly Kelly Collection." In *Important New York Furniture and Decorative Arts: The Richard and Beverly Kelly Collection*. Portsmouth, N.H.: Northeast Auctions, April 3, 2005, 5–10. 1 color and 2 bw illus.

Solis-Cohen, Lita. "Chipstone Furniture Journal: A Book Review." *Maine Antique Digest* 33, no. 3 (March 2005): 47C. 1 bw illus.

———. "John Townsend at the Met." *Maine Antique Digest* 33, no. 7 (July 2005): 20A–21A. 10 bw illus.

[Southampton Historical Museum]. "Southampton Historical Museum Exhibiting Recently Found Dominy Chest-on-Chest." *Antiques and the Arts Weekly* (October 1, 2004): 80. 2 bw illus.

Sparke, Penny. *Elsie de Wolfe: The Birth of Modern Interior Decoration*. Edited by Mitchell Owens. New York: Acanthus Press, 2005. 374 pp.; numerous illus.

Spriggs, Remi. "Living with Antiques: An Americana Collection in New Jersey." *Antiques* 167, no. 4 (April 2005): 94–105. 15 color illus.

Stone, Stephanie. "Peter Follansbee: Craftsman Scholar." *Woodwork*, no. 93 (June 2005): 26–34. Color illus.

Sypher, F. J. "More on Sypher & Co., a Pioneer Antique Dealer in New York." *Furniture History* 40 (2004): 151–66. 6 bw illus.

Tannen, Rich. "Gains and Losses: Learning to Love with the Digital Workshop." In *Furniture Studio 3: Furniture Makers Exploring Digital Technologies*, edited by John Kelsey, 8–15. Asheville, N.C.: The Furniture Society, 2005. 6 color illus.

Tarule, Robert. *The Artisan of Ipswich: Craftsmanship and Continuity in Colonial New England*. Baltimore: Johns Hopkins University Press, 2004. xi + 155 pp.; 9 bw illus., 27 line drawings, index.

"Tasmania—Crossing the Divide—America." *American Craft* 65, no. 3 (June–July 2005): 52–53. Color illus.

Taylor, Fred. *How to Be a Furniture Detective*. Lenexa, Kan.: A. D. Publishing, 2004. 198 pp.; color and bw illus.

Tigerman, Bobbye. "An Idea Whose Time Has Come, Again." *Decorative Arts Trust* 14, no. 3 (fall 2004): 1–3. 4 bw illus. (Re Florence Knoll.)

Tolman, Michael. "Byrdcliffe: An American Arts and Crafts Colony." *American Craft* 65, no. 2 (April–May 2005): 40–43. 9 color and bw illus.

Trent, Robert F. "Two Important Doll-Sized Chairs Acquired by the Toy Museum." *The Luminary* 26, no. 1 (spring 2005): 3. 2 bw illus. (Re chairs from Bergen County, New Jersey, ca. 1750–1800.)

Trent, Robert F., Alan Miller, Glenn Adamson, and Harry Mack Truax II. "High Craft along the Mohawk: Early Woodwork from the Albany Area of New York." *American Furniture 2004*, 90–151. 88 color and bw illus., appendix, line drawings.

Trent, Robert F., and Harry Mack Truax II. "Vaulting Ambition: Philadelphia Gothic Revival Furniture and Other Decorative Arts,

1830–1860." In [Catalogue of] *The Philadelphia Antiques Show 2005* (Philadelphia, 2005), 90–122. 46 color illus.

Tucker, Paul. "Moorish Fretwork Furniture." *Antiques* 167, no. 5 (May 2005): 116–23. 11 color and 2 bw illus.

Walker, Stefanie, ed. *Vasemania: Neoclassical Form and Ornament in Europe; Selections from the Metropolitan Museum of Art.* New Haven: Yale University Press for the Bard Graduate Center for Studies in the Decorative Arts, Design, and Culture, New York, and the Metropolitan Museum of Art, New York, 2004. 194 pp.; numerous color illus., selected biographies, glossary, index.

Ward, Gerald W. R. "The Piscataqua on the Fenway: Portsmouth-Area Furniture in the Collection of the Museum of Fine Arts, Boston." In *Piscataqua Decorative Arts Society: Volume 1, 2002–2003 Lecture Series,* 51–56. Portsmouth, N.H.: Piscataqua Decorative Arts Society, 2004. 14 bw illus.

———, comp. "Recent Writing on American Furniture: A Bibliography." In *American Furniture 2004,* 277–84.

Weisberg, Gabriel P., Edwin Backer, and Evelyne Possémé, eds. *The Origins of L'Art Nouveau: The Bing Empire*. Ithaca, N.Y.: Cornell University Press, 2005. 304 pp.; illus.

Willoughby, Martha H. "Discoveries from the Field: Ipswich Ingenuity." *The Catalogue of Antiques and Fine Art* 6, no. 4 (autumn/winter 2005): 186–91. 4 color illus.

Wilson, Fo. "The Maker as Evidence" (book review). In *Furniture Studio 3: Furniture Makers Exploring Digital Technologies,* edited by John Kelsey, 111–14. Asheville, N.C.: The Furniture Society, 2005. Color illus.

Wilson, Kristina. *Livable Modernism: Interior Decorating and Design during the Great Depression.* New Haven: Yale University Press in association with Yale University Art Gallery, 2004. xiii + 154 pp.; numerous color and bw illus., bibliography, index.

Winchell, Terry. *Molesworth: The Pioneer of Western Design*. Salt Lake City: Gibbs Smith, 2005. 256 pp.; illus.

Wood, D. "Pause for Reflection: Looking Back at Wendy Maruyama." *Woodwork*, no. 92 (April 2005): 26–32. Color illus.

Yood, James. "The Artist Responds: Albert Paley / Art Nouveau." *American Craft* 65, no. 3 (June–July 2005): 48–51. Color illus.

Zabar, Lori. "Picturing John Townsend's Clients." *The Catalogue of Antiques and Fine Art* 6, no. 2 (summer 2005): 142–48. 10 color illus.

Zaiden, Emily. "The Arts and Crafts Movement: Design for the Modern World." *The Catalogue of Antiques and Fine Art* 6, no. 1 (spring 2005): 178–83. 9 color illus.

Zimmerman, Philip D. "The Architectural Furniture of Duncan Phyfe, 1830–1845." In *Important New York Furniture and Decorative Arts: The Richard and Beverly Kelly Collection,* 12–19. Portsmouth, N.H.: Northeast Auctions, April 3, 2005. 4 color illus., bibliography.

———. "Early American Furniture in the New Castle Historical Society in Delaware." *Antiques* 167, no. 5 (May 2005): 130–41. 14 color illus.

———. Review of Bradford L. Rauschenberg and John Bivins Jr., *The Furniture of Charleston, 1680–1820*. In *Winterthur Portfolio* 38, no. 4 (winter 2003): 257–63.

Zimmerman, Philip D., and Charles T. Butler. *American Federal Furniture and Decorative Arts from the Watson Collection*. Edited by Catherine E. Hutchins. Columbus, Ga.: Columbus Museum, 2004. 144 pp.; 75 color illus.

Index

X
Z
Y